Thoreau's Ecstatic Witness

Thoreau's
Ecstatic Witness

Alan D. Hodder

YALE UNIVERSITY PRESS/NEW HAVEN & LONDON

Designed by Mary Valencia.
Set in Adobe Garamond type by Keystone Typesetting, Inc.
Printed in the United States of America.

Library of Congress Cataloging-in-Publication Data
Hodder, Alan D.
Thoreau's ecstatic witness / Alan D. Hodder.
p. cm.
Includes bibliographical references and index.
ISBN 0-300-08959-7 (alk. paper)
1. Thoreau, Henry David, 1817–1862—Religion.
2. Religion and literature—United States—History—19th century. I. Title.
PS3057.R4 H63 2001
818'.309—dc21
2001033320

A catalogue record for this book is available from the British Library.

The paper in this book meets the guidelines for permanence and durability of the Committee on Production Guidelines for Book Longevity of the Council on Library Resources.

10 9 8 7 6 5 4 3 2 1

To Nena

The life in us is like the water in the river, it may rise this year higher than ever it was known to before and flood the uplands—even this may be the eventful year—& drown out all our muskrats There are as many strata at different levels of life as there are leaves in a book Most men probably have lived in two or three. When on the higher levels we can remember the lower levels, but when on the lower we cannot remember the higher.

Henry Thoreau, from his journal

Contents

Preface

To write about Thoreau at the beginning of the twenty-first century is a daunting enterprise to say the least. The sheer volume of critical studies, snowballing now for over a hundred years, is enough to dampen the spirits of the boldest critic. Of course, the same sort of challenges also confront the student of other canonical figures of the Romantic period, as a glance at the formidable body of scholarly studies produced over the past half century on such writers as Melville, Dickinson, and Whitman would attest. Yet Thoreau presents special challenges. More than any writer of his era, Thoreau has assumed the status of an American folk hero. If people know nothing else of nineteenth-century American literature, they are at least likely to recall something about Thoreau's sojourn at Walden Pond and the famous book he wrote about it. He is a kind of cultural icon and to that degree represents common cultural property, whether or not, or how recently, we have actually read *Walden* or "Civil Disobedience," or visited Concord and the Pond itself.

To me this fact has been especially apparent on those occasions when I have been asked by friends and acquaintances about my work on Thoreau. Instead of blank stares, my remarks often elicit a knowing response—whether of agreement and rekindled enthusiasm, or considered doubt and half-suppressed exasperation. That is to say, most people come to a book like this with some fairly definite opinions about the subject, and these opinions are apt to vary widely: a great writer, a

champion of the environment, a daring and dissident social critic, a
sneaking impostor who regularly raided his mother's cookie jar when
he got fed up with his thin fare of rice and beans at the Pond. To the
scholar anxious to extend our understanding of Thoreau in novel or
previously unsuspected directions, such popular knowledge can sometimes be rather disheartening: speaking about Thoreau to most Americans of my own generation, at least, is like speaking about a common
ancestor—it is hard sometimes to get past our closely held convictions.
Yet, by the same token, there are also advantages in working on a figure
of such sustained cultural currency, since in thinking about him, we are
inevitably thinking also to some extent about ourselves, our values, and
our culture generally, which cannot of course be a bad thing. In view of
the lasting repercussions of Thoreau's life and work in our own times, it is
hard to write about him today without implicating American culture
generally. Indeed, his writings still provide live ammunition for many of
the debates that animate American political and cultural life as we begin
the new century.

The continuing relevance of Thoreau in American life underscores
the need for unabated critical engagement with his work and his legacy,
even though so much fine scholarship and so many excellent landmark
studies have already been contributed. Particularly in the case of a writer
such as this, popular renderings may easily become skewed in their
subservience to particular social, political, or ideological agendas. We
rely on a robust and circumspect critical tradition to expose such co-
optation. At the same time, academic readings are subject to their own
agendas, as we well know. One short coming of much critical work
during the past twenty-five years, in my view, has been its debilitating
tendency toward insularity, at times even hermeticism, in its preoccupation with theory. Some critics have been overly inclined to divorce their
concerns and discourse from popular values and the life of the culture
more generally, though this has been less true perhaps in the case of Thoreau studies. When critical concerns run too much at variance with
popular understandings, they lose their traction and cultural value. In
the relatively uncultivated and frank responses of the common reader,

furthermore, we can sometimes locate kernels of truth ignored by the professional critic motivated by intellectual fashion, and his or her various critical agendas. As far as Thoreau studies are concerned, one conspicuous instance of such a disconnect between the professional critic and the popular reader has been the relative neglect in recent treatments of what we might refer to simply as Thoreau's spiritual life, despite the fact that most readers have sensed, though not perhaps always articulated, that this dimension is central to his life and work.

Like many studies of this kind, this book is a natural outgrowth of my own experience reading Thoreau and mulling over the criticism on him over the past twenty-five years. Like many Americans of the postwar generation, I first encountered Thoreau in a high school English class in which we were assigned *Walden* and "Civil Disobedience." This first encounter took place in 1968, and like many of my peers at that time, I readily identified with Thoreau's oppositionalist political stance and was, at the same time, deeply impressed by his commitment to find in nature a direct source of spiritual nourishment and renewal. In those turbulent times, it was above all the essential sanity of this voice from the American past that so impressed us: Thoreau had his crotchets, to be sure, but to many of us he represented a model of enormous credibility and appeal.

My own relationship to Thoreau became further consolidated a few years later when, as it happened, I found myself briefly ensconced in the town of Lincoln, Massachusetts, hardly a mile from Walden Pond, during a temporary hiatus in my freshman year in college. To break up my days of reading and study I commonly set off on long afternoon walks in the general direction of the Pond and Walden Woods, stopping along the way to admire the scenery. I would not have thought so at the time, but in looking back on the tranquil routine of those few weeks, I can now see that I was participating, however inadvertently, in a normative Transcendentalist exercise; what Lawrence Buell has recently referred to as the Thoreauvian pilgrimage.[1] I did not, in so many words, think of Walden Pond as a sacred site, of Thoreau as a charismatic figure, or of *Walden* as a paradigmatic text or secular scripture, but now I see this is really in a sense what they were for me. More clear was the fact that I took these rambling walks in the countryside in part to experience for myself the kind of numinous encounters with nature that I believed were at the very heart of Thoreau's own preoccupation with the natural world. These formative experiences certainly helped to inspire my subsequent interest in American Transcendentalism and to some extent even influenced the trajectory of my later education. They also explain the puzzlement I felt when, during my induction into graduate study, I realized that this felt spiritual dimension in Thoreau's writing had nothing whatever to do with the business of the professional critic—or at least so it seemed from most of the secondary books and articles we were called upon to read. I did not especially resist my acculturation in the Academy, so impressed was I by the rationale and high standards of the critical community, but I never entirely got over the impression that the general practice of many critics was to gloss over, ignore, or simply take for granted a dimension of Thoreau's life and legacy that to me seemed quite unavoidable.

The purpose of this book then is to begin to redress this critical neglect by providing a more sustained and hopefully nuanced study than has been available so far of Thoreau's religious thought and experience. I would characterize my approach to this topic as descriptive-phenomenological, so as to distinguish it from standard biography, on the one hand, and a more normative theological treatment, on the other. I also do not intend this treatment as an intellectual biography as such nor a literary-critical monograph of the usual sort, Thoreau having already been well served by distinguished examples of both of these critical modes. Instead, this book is more akin to what we might call a spiritual biography. Its concern is less with the surface details of Thoreau's life and writing than with the underlying forms of his religious and literary imagination. And while I hope this book will be of interest to other teachers and professional scholars, I have also conceived and tailored my material with interested students and general readers in mind. Having read widely in Thoreau off and on for some time, I have become convinced that his writings often reflect a distinctive pattern of experience and expression, essentially religious in nature, which, following his own usage, I have referred to as his ecstasies. My essential concern has been, as much as possible, to fathom this deeper dimension of Thoreau's life, to trace its manifestations in his thought and literary expression, and to elevate it for wider and more careful consideration.

During the long period of this book's incubation, I received inspiration and support from many sides. I would first of all like to acknowledge my general indebtedness to the editors of the Princeton edition of Thoreau's journal and his collected writings. Without their painstaking labors over many years, studies like this one would lack the necessary textual foundation. I would also like to thank the editors of the *Harvard Theological Review* for permission to quote from my earlier article " 'Ex Oriente Lux': Thoreau's Ecstasies and the Hindu Texts." In addition, I want to thank Vanessa Pintado of the Pierpont Morgan Library for her help in locating and deciphering a particularly elusive passage from Thoreau's journal.

For me the road back to Transcendentalist writing after a several-year hiatus in college led through a circuitous but in the end fortuitous study of Indian philosophy. In this sense, at least, I suppose I have to some extent followed the East-West trajectory of Thoreau's own intellectual development. For several of the insights animating my treatment of Thoreau's contemplative experience, I am much indebted to the practical teachings of the contemporary Vedic philosopher Maharishi Mahesh Yogi, and particularly to his commentary on the Bhagavad Gita, which I first encountered in college. Also, my treatment of Thoreau's Orientalism would not have been possible were it not for the masterful instruction in Sanskrit and Indian Studies that I received from Gary Tubb and the late Daniel H. H. Ingalls, with whom I first read several of the texts that were of special moment to Thoreau.

The roots of this book might well be traced, however, to a graduate seminar on American Transcendentalism that I took many years ago with Joel Porte, and I want to express, once again, my gratitude to him for his Emersonian provocations and his example as a teacher. In this context, I also want to express my longstanding thanks to Warner Berthoff, Diana L. Eck, James Engell, William A. Graham, Richard R. Niebuhr, and David M. Robinson for their mentoring and support over many years. I would also like to take this opportunity to thank my students and colleagues at Hampshire College for their support, especially Robert Meagher, whose rare sanity and unflagging sense of humor helped keep me buoyant during the years in which this book was taking shape. I also wish to thank my dean, Mary Russo, for supporting my request for the sabbatical during the fall term of 1997 that allowed me to get this project on track, and Gregory Prince for granting it. I would also like to reserve special thanks to Charles H. Taylor, without whose inspiration and support neither this book nor my work at Hampshire would have been possible in the first place.

More direct thanks are due to Kevin Van Anglen, who read an early draft of my chapter on Thoreau's Orientalism, Lawrence Buell, who kindly and scrupulously read through an earlier draft of the manuscript, and Robert D. Richardson Jr., who reviewed the manuscript in the final stages of its development. Without these expert readings and the constructive recommendations they generated, this book would be far the poorer. I wish also to thank my editors, Otto Bohlmann, Chris Erikson, and Margaret Otzel, for their thoughtful handling of the manuscript and helpful suggestions for how to improve it, as well as the other editors at Yale University Press who have helped to fashion the book into its final form. I want to express my deepest thanks, however, to my wife, Harbour Fraser Hodder, for her own searching reading of the manuscript at various stages in its evolution, her numerous insightful suggestions, and her wise counsel. It is to her that this book is dedicated.

Abbreviations

At the time the following study was composed, the critical edition of Thoreau's journal published under the auspices of Princeton University Press ran to five volumes: Journal 1: 1837–1844, ed. Elizabeth Hall Witherell et al. (1981); Journal 2: 1842–1848, ed. Robert Sattelmeyer (1984); Journal 3: 1848–1851, ed. Robert Sattelmeyer et al. (1990); Journal 4: 1851–1852, ed. Leonard N. Neufeldt and Nancy Craig Simmons (1992); Journal 5: 1852–1853, ed. Patrick F. O'Connell (1997). Except where otherwise specified, for these years I have exclusively relied on the Princeton edition. All parenthetical citations in the text of these volumes are identified by the initials "PJ," followed by the volume and page numbers.

For all journal entries subsequent to the period covered by the Princeton edition, I have consulted the 1906 edition of the journal, cited parenthetically in the text by the abbreviation "J," followed by volume and page numbers. Volume numbers refer to the independently numbered fourteen volumes of the journal rather than to the twenty-volume edition of the complete works of which it is a part. References to other works contained in the 1906 edition are indicated parenthetically by "Writings" followed by the volume number as it appears in the twenty-volume sequence and page number. Other abbreviations and fuller bibliographic information for these and other works are as follows:

CORRESPONDENCE   *The Correspondence of Henry David Thoreau.*
Ed. Walter Harding and Carl Bode. New York:
New York University Press, 1958.

CC   Henry D. Thoreau. *Cape Cod.* Ed. Joseph J.
Moldenhauer. Princeton: Princeton University
Press, 1988.

CW   *The Collected Works of Ralph Waldo Emerson.*
Ed. Alfred R. Ferguson et al. Cambridge: Harvard University Press, 1971–.

EEM   Henry D. Thoreau. *Early Essays and Miscellanies.* Ed. Joseph J. Moldenhauer and Edwin Moser, with Alexander Kern. Princeton:
Princeton University Press, 1975.

J   *The Journal of Henry David Thoreau.* Ed. Bradford Torrey and Francis H. Allen. 14 vols.
Boston: Houghton Mifflin, 1906.

JMN   *The Journals and Miscellaneous Notebooks of
Ralph Waldo Emerson.* Ed. William H. Gilman
et al. 16 vols. Cambridge: Harvard University
Press, 1960–1982.

LETTERS   *The Letters of Ralph Waldo Emerson.* Ed.
Ralph L. Rusk. 6 vols. New York: Columbia
University Press, 1939.

MW   Henry D. Thoreau. *The Maine Woods.* Ed.
Joseph J. Moldenhauer. Princeton: Princeton
University Press, 1974.

POEMS   *Collected Poems of Henry Thoreau.* Enl. ed. Ed.
Carl Bode. Baltimore: Johns Hopkins Press,
1964.

PJ   Henry D. Thoreau. *Journal.* Ed. John C. Bro-
derick et al. 5 vols. to date. Princeton: Princeton University Press, 1981–.

RP   Henry D. Thoreau. *Reform Papers.* Ed. Wendell Glick. Princeton: Princeton University
Press, 1973.

TRANSLATIONS   Henry D. Thoreau. *Translations.* Ed. K. P. Van
Anglen. Princeton: Princeton University Press,
1986.

WALDEN   Henry D. Thoreau. *Walden.* Ed. J. Lyndon
Shanley. Princeton: Princeton University Press,
1971.

WEEK   Henry D. Thoreau. *A Week on the Concord and
Merrimack Rivers.* Ed. Carl F. Hovde,
William L. Howarth, and Elizabeth Hall Witherell. Princeton: Princeton University Press,
1980.

WRITINGS   *The Writings of Henry David Thoreau.* Ed.
Bradford Torrey and Francis H. Allen. 20 vols.
Boston: Houghton Mifflin, 1906.

Introduction:
A Simple and Hidden Life

Our age has a tendency, when dealing with figures of the past, to amputate whatever we find irrelevant from what the past itself considered the body of its teaching. Certain fragments may be kept alive in the critical test tubes of the Great Tradition, while the rest is shoveled off to potter's field.

Perry Miller, "From Edwards to Emerson"

The fact is I am a mystic—a transcendentalist—& a natural philosopher to boot.

Thoreau's Journal

Over the past century and a half, Thoreau has been many things to many people. In the lengthening record of reviews and scholarly criticism, we read variously of Thoreau the eccentric hermit, the Yankee stoic, the poet-naturalist, the angry abolitionist, the philosophical anarchist and political critic, the transcendental economist, the consummate literary craftsman and philosopher of language, the proto-environmentalist and modern hero of the Wilderness Society and Sierra Club, and even Thoreau the postmodern philosopher. The stunning diversity of these portraits surely tells us something about the multifaceted career of this remarkable writer and his complexity and as a man. Yet it is hard to resist the suspicion that the extraordinary variety found in this critical portrait gallery has as much to do with the interests and attitudes of individual portraitists and the cultural contexts from which they wrote as it does with Thoreau himself. What the panoply of Thoreauvian personae suggests most of all is that, more than any writer of his day, more perhaps than any writer of the tradition, Thoreau has come to serve as a mirror of American culture, or to vary the metaphor somewhat, a kind of cultural palimpsest in which each generation of readers and critics writes over the received record without wholly effacing the images of the past. Of course all good criticism entails some degree of self-reflexivity—it would be meaningless if it did not—but the strikingly divergent portrayals we find in the critical record ought to give us some pause, even while they enlist our collective fascination. Indeed, the question still arises: why of the writers of the period was it Thoreau above all who assumed this status of cultural icon? The mere existence of such a wide array of sometimes incongruent portraits suggests that even after 150 years, there is still something essential about Thoreau's life and work that eludes us, as if we are still missing some central piece of this personality around which all such disparate images can naturally cohere.[1]

The striking variety of representations found in the critical tradition testifies to Thoreau's complexity, but the fragmentary character of this reception overall also reflects our twentieth-century legacy of academic and critical specialization. Like some comparable nineteenth-century American writers, Thoreau has become the object of such specialization. In our own day, what we see when we read Thoreau's texts depends to a considerable degree on how previous custodians of culture have conceived, classified, and transmitted them. Prompting my own treatment has been the tendency, reinforced by Thoreau's own sense of literary vocation, to construe his texts in some restrictively "literary" sense, the preserve mostly of literary scholars or historians operating within departments of English literature or American Studies. Certainly Thoreau's political writings have attracted the notice of intellectual historians and political scientists, and his natural history writings have, especially in recent years, attracted the notice of some scientists and wildlife biologists.[2] Yet this does not alter the basic fact that in recent decades the figure to which most of us have been introduced in our schools and colleges is primarily a man of letters, a "writer"—albeit a writer with scientific interests and (intermittent) political concerns. In the absence of any comparable proprietary concern from other areas of the Academy, it effectively devolved upon departments of English to foster the sort of serious academic study that Thoreau's contributions obviously deserved. But one unfortunate consequence of this departmentalization of Thoreau studies has been the inveterate tendency to overlook or dismiss the factor of religious experience in his life and writing. In contrast to Emerson and the Transcendentalist ministers, whose writings have benefited from searching analyses by both religious historians and literary scholars, Thoreau's work has been rather narrowly conceived under the secularist rubric of "American literature."

Twenty years ago most religious historians themselves would have quietly acquiesced in the literary appropriation of Thoreau, occupied as they were with questions primarily of institutional and denominational history. Until recently, the "religion" of American religious history was, for the most part, the collective religion of mainstream groups. And Thoreau, we all know, was no friend of organized religion. As an outspoken and sometimes harsh critic of institutional religious life, a religious outsider, and an inveterate iconoclast, Thoreau was of course no part of such institutional histories. But with the recent interest in American "lived religion"—the history, that is, of popular, individual, and marginalized religious forms—such relegation no longer seems warranted.[3] Thoreau was a highly accomplished and ambitious writer, of this there is no doubt, but a dispassionate reader of his journals, his letters, *Walden,* or *A Week* can hardly deny that he was an irreclaimably religious person as well.

By invoking the terms "religion" and "religious" in regard to Thoreau, I am conscious that, for some readers at least, I have already gotten us bogged down in interpretive difficulties. To those outside the various areas associated with the academic study of religion, such terms are generally construed in just those ways that, for the purposes of this study, I want especially to avoid—as denoting some form of affiliation with a particular religious denomination or group. Increasingly, these terms are often conceived rather narrowly, that is, to refer to what we may call institutional or "organized" religion, though most scholars of religion would consider such usage too restrictive, if not invidious. Students of the present generation, at least, are often perplexed by such characterizations of Thoreau: he was not religious, they will insist, though they readily concede that he was a highly "spiritual" man, meaning, I suppose, that he was undoubtedly concerned with a higher, transcendent, and in that sense spiritual life. It is as a somewhat grudging concession to the contemporary popular connotations of "spiritual" and "spirituality" that I have employed the terms in the following study. I say grudging because, while I see the need for terms such as these that center upon personal inward experience, I do not on historical grounds accept the privileging of the "spiritual" over the "religious" that this usage now often implies— the view, that is, that to be spiritual is somehow more authentic, more natural, less historically motivated than to be religious in the more conventional, collective, or institutional sense. In fact, I doubt that the easy distinction between religion and spirituality often drawn in contemporary usage is quite as demonstrable as is sometimes supposed. Even Thoreau's own iconoclastic brand of spirituality owed a good deal to the social practices, ideas, and allegiances of the motley society of friends and associates who came to be identified, at first pejoratively, as Transcendentalists.[4] Outside of this larger social and religious context, the meaning of his idiosyncratic lifestyle and distinctive literary production would be far less intelligible, even to himself.

The solution I have come to then, at least for the sake of this study, is simply to use the terms religious and spiritual in roughly synonymous ways. Thoreau was deeply religious in this view, not in an institutional, but in a primarily personal, "interior," and experiential sense. While this mode of being religious did not make much of an impression on the religious historians of a previous era, it certainly strikes a chord of recognition today. This is of course no coincidence, Thoreau having been a major source of modern American impatience with institutional religion—its ecclesiastical forms, traditions, and theology. The creeds and revelations of the past were certainly matters of perennial interest to him, but their authority paled next to the disclosures of his own private "ecstatic" experience. The reference here and in my title to the term ecstasy is entirely founded upon Thoreau's own usage in his journals and elsewhere in his writings, where it designates certain privileged experiences of unknown origin that from an early age fired his imagination and inspired some of his most distinctive prose. More to the point, these ineffable experiences must also be seen as the central facts of Thoreau's spiritual life—the fuel of his religious yearning and the foundation for his religious reflection. When he mourns the recession of boyhood euphoria in the journals of 1851, when he speculates on riverside reflections in the Concord River in *A Week*, when he writes cryptically of being a "spectator" to his own thoughts and actions in *Walden*—it is these experiences of ecstasy to which he implicitly refers. The term itself has a long and interesting pedigree in both literary and religious sources in the West, but it was conditioned for him by the writings of Wordsworth and Emerson in particular, and later, by his selective reading of certain Hindu contemplative texts. It derived, he knew, from the Greek *ek-stasis*—to stand or set apart—and this root meaning perfectly epitomized for him the strange and unsettling experiences of contemplative detachment and disjunctive perception that seem so characteristic of his mature vision. Thoreau's journal, in particular, preserves traces of these momentous experiences, whether in the form of carefully crafted epiphanies, meditative evocations, or wrenching elegiac recollections. While the spontaneity and intensity of these experiences began to taper off by the late 1840s, they made a deep and lasting impression on his religious sensibility, philosophical outlook, and literary imagination. It is clear from his representations of these episodes between 1837, when he began keeping his journal, and 1851, when he experienced their dramatic recrudescence, that the nature of these experiences tended to change somewhat with the passage of time. At whatever period though, such episodes appear to have involved exquisitely refined modes of sensory perception, particularly of hearing; a sharply altered sense of self; heightened forms of insight; and an exalted appreciation of the beauty of the natural world. It is also abundantly clear from the journalistic record that Thoreau found himself most susceptible to these moods of transport during his daily excursions among the woods and pasturelands surrounding his home. While no one can say with certainty how or why these experiences arose—perhaps not even Thoreau himself could have—it is easy enough to see that they came to function as a kind of rudder for all this subsequent religious reflection.

Given the obvious centrality of this ecstatic dimension of Thoreau's woodland experience, and its apparent religious import, it comes as something of a surprise to find how neglected it has been in most critical discussions of his work. A quick glance at the history of Thoreau's academic reputation suggests that critics of the past 120 years or so have tended to conceive of him in one of three more or less distinct ways: as primarily a nature writer, a political critic, or a literary artist.[5] In order to locate some of the apparent origins of this odd critical oversight, I would like briefly to outline these conceptions, but before I do so, it is worth pointing out by way of background that Thoreau's contemporary reviews, that is those appearing from 1840 till just a few years before his death in 1862, although somewhat mixed, generally commended his work for its originality and its compelling vision of nature.[6] Contrary to the usual view, his first book, *A Week on the Concord and Merrimack Rivers* (1849), was not on the whole badly received, though its several appreciative notices did little to rescue it from commercial oblivion. *Walden* (1854) of course fared much better. Out of some sixty-nine reviews in over thirty newspapers and magazines, nearly three-fourths were resoundingly positive. Thoreau's death in May of 1862 also received fairly wide coverage, an indication apparently of his waxing reputation in some literary circles at that time. In the three years after his death, the Boston publishing firm Ticknor and Fields seized the opportunity to issue five other Thoreau titles—*Excursions, Maine Woods, Cape Cod, Letters to Various Persons,* and *A Yankee in Canada with Anti-Slavery and Reform Papers*—in order to capitalize on his growing fame and marketability.

Despite these auspicious beginnings, Thoreau's reputation soon went into a prolonged tailspin, owing in large part to the adverse impact of a few unflattering portrayals. One of these, surprisingly enough, came from Thoreau's old mentor and friend Ralph Waldo Emerson, whose eulogy of Thoreau, delivered at the time of his memorial service and published a couple months later in the *Atlantic Monthly,* appears to have done more to dampen the reading public's esteem than to heighten it, even though sections of it were later used to market Thoreau's works. Faithful as always to the Transcendentalist ideal of uncompromising honesty between friends, Emerson praised Thoreau's gifts, while at the same time noting his obvious eccentricities. To readers expecting a more thoroughgoing apotheosis, Emerson's address seemed wan and thin spirited, as if to damn by faint praise. He eulogized his friend as a charismatic stoic but in the same breath expressed frank puzzlement at his eccentric lifestyle. Even more damaging was an acerbic review written by James Russell Lowell, the preeminent critic of his day, that appeared in 1865 in the *North American Review.* Lowell, who had experienced some testy relations with Thoreau over an editorial dispute several years before, took the opportunity to blindside the now dead writer, attacking him for a lack of originality and throwing even his mental balance into question. Though friends rallied to Thoreau's defense, it would be decades before the damage done by Lowell's salvos could be entirely repaired.

Thoreau's resuscitation from these critical setbacks may be credited to two interrelated forces of intervention—a series of increasingly effective efforts on the part of Houghton Mifflin, successor firm to Ticknor and Fields, to market Thoreau more widely as a nature writer, and the zealous advocacy of a small group of passionate admirers and friends.[7] The net result of these interventions was to filter out some of the more controversial aspects of Thoreau's life and writings, including his antinomian religious ideas and his so-called mysticism, in order to deliver a more appealing, less threatening version of Thoreau as an American nature writer. Ironically, the chief activist in this campaign was his friend and protégé Harrison Blake, a Unitarian minister turned schoolteacher from Worcester, Massachusetts, who came to look upon Thoreau as a kind of spiritual counselor. Together with several other of Thoreau's friends and admirers—including his Concord neighbors Emerson, Bronson Alcott, and the younger Franklin Sanborn—Blake spearheaded efforts to redeem

Thoreau from public scorn and elevate his position in American literary and philosophical circles. When Blake inherited Thoreau's journal manuscripts on the death of Henry's sister Sophia in 1876, he began making selections of them available for wider public consumption, publishing extracts in the *Atlantic* in 1878. Convinced of the journal's potential appeal as a form of nature writing, Blake conceived a plan modeled on some of Thoreau's own botanical notebooks in which he would group journal entries of the same date from various years in order to highlight the progression and thematic importance of the seasons. From this editorial project came the four-volume seasonal series published by Houghton Mifflin over the course of the next decade, beginning in 1881 with *Early Spring in Massachusetts.* Sales of the four books were good and Thoreau's reputation was once again on the rise. Blake thus succeeded in finding the wider readership he sought for his mentor and friend—even at the cost of underplaying the charismatic spiritual appeal that he himself so cherished—and the editors at Houghton found the niche they sought to continue profiting from Thoreau's work.[8] So successful was this effort, in fact, that by the turn of the century Thoreau was duly promoted from his status as a writer of minor importance to one of the first rank, together with Emerson, Hawthorne, and the Fireside poets, in the newly received canon of classic American writers.

The first indication of the potential upstaging of the spiritual by the political Thoreau came as early as 1876, when the *American Socialist* published extracts from a variety of his writings.[9] The burgeoning success of Blake and his editorial sponsors at domesticating Thoreau primarily as a nature writer effectively sidelined the political dimension of his writings in the United States for almost a generation, but in England the case was different. Following the publication of the first British editions of *Walden,* in 1884, and *A Week,* in 1889, Thoreau found an avid following among several influential British social progressives, including the utopian socialists Edward Carpenter and Henry S. Salt, who seized on Thoreau as a humanitarian model and social critic of great moral power.[10] After the turn of the century, the political Thoreau found a more avid readership among American readers as well. One early milestone in the propagation of Thoreau's political persona in the United States was the treatment he received in John Macy's *The Spirit of American Literature*, published in 1913.[11] Vernon Louis Parrington, in his hugely influential *Main Currents in American Thought*, published two years before the crash of 1929, lent considerable sanction to this view of Thoreau as a political activist and thinker, when he construed *Walden* primarily as a refutation of Adam Smith and "a book of social criticism."[12] The representations of Thoreau by such influential critics as Macy and Parrington prepared the way for more commitedly leftist readings of him in the 1930s and later, with the rise of the New Left, in the 1960s. Over the course of these several decades, this new image of the iconoclastic and radical Thoreau effectively competed in the United States with the older, less disruptive Victorian image of the devotee of Concord's woods and streams.[13]

The third major way that Thoreau has been appropriated historically—that is, as primarily an artist and literary craftsman—may be traced primarily to F. O. Matthiessen's monumental and highly acclaimed critical work *American Renaissance*, which first appeared in 1941. This book did more than any of its generation to consolidate and sanction the newly emergent canon of nineteenth-century American writers, by limiting its treatment entirely to the works of Emerson, Thoreau, Hawthorne, Melville, and Whitman. A socialist himself, Matthiessen was duly impressed by Thoreau's criticism of the standing social and economic order, particularly "his thoroughgoing criticism of the narrow materialism of his day," but he was equally impressed by the character of Thoreau's artistry.[14] In his treatment, Matthiessen set out to correct the earlier fixation with Thoreau as a naturalist by elucidating his literary technique, giving special attention to his theory of language, use of imagery, and experiments in organic form. Writing under the aegis of the New Criticism, with its close attention to matters of literary form and meaning, Matthiessen did much to set the parameters for the primarily literary appropriation of Thoreau's work that would dominate critical study of Thoreau for the next thirty or so years.[15]

Obviously, the three critical trends noted above reflect a host of underlying political, historical, and cultural conditions, including, for example, the early commodification of Thoreau as a nature writer, the professionalization of Thoreau studies in the early part of the century, the general secularization of the Academy and with it the artificial separation—unaccountable to the early-nineteenth-century mind—between religion and literature, the intellectual structure of the American university, changing politics in academic life over the past century, and the rise of relevant movements of social change and reform, particularly environmentalism in the late sixties. The insights provided by these interpretive approaches have been extremely important and enabling, but it is also crucial to recognize the extent to which each of these modes has, in its turn, placed fairly severe limits on what we as readers take to be the significance of Thoreau's life and writing. These are partial perspectives after all, as they must be, and they somewhat inhibit our appreciation of the wholeness of Thoreau's life even as they disclose the importance of specific aspects. The effect of imposing, however inadvertently, such critical models and stereotypes has thus been to fragment Thoreau's character and our understanding of his work. It has also effectively marginalized other crucial dimensions of his life less easy to categorize or conceptualize, in particular what I am calling here its larger religious or spiritual dimension.

To construe Thoreau's life, for example, as essentially that of an aspiring professional writer and literary artist seems at times oddly limiting and even anachronistic. Literature was Thoreau's chosen vocation, to be sure, but not in the ways or from the motives familiar to us in the twentieth century. Thoreau's mature journal, a nearly two-million-word record that critics have increasingly come to regard as his main life's work, poses the most serious problem for this sort of literary vocational reading. Though a few critics have argued that Thoreau actually intended this mammoth work for publication, the evidence for this is tenuous at best. The problem, on the other hand, with conceiving Thoreau as mainly a social agitator and critic, even as the sort of philosophical anarchist posited by Salt, is that his political commitments always seemed somewhat peripheral to the primary focus of his life. In fact, his political action generally arose in response to specific social and political crises—the war with Mexico, passage of the Fugitive Slave Act, the arrest and execution of John Brown—and were not a part of some long-range political agenda. Never a joiner, Thoreau was temperamentally suspicious of organizations, including political organizations, and gave them his support only when they were necessary for achieving the political outcomes he sought. His writings on the subject mostly take the form of occasional lectures and essays addressed to some issue or event in which he felt an urgent personal and national interest. Once the crisis passed, he was more than ready to leave politics behind in pursuit of his more secretive life in nature.

It is worth noting that these two popular conceptions of Thoreau— that of the political reformer and the man of letters—were mainly promulgated after his death, in the latter case long after, and presuppose either some significant cultural remove (as in the case of Thoreau's early English champions) or historical distance (as in the case of mid-twentieth-century American critics). What these critical orientations often share is a decided tendency to ignore or at least downplay Thoreau's religiousness. The situation is different with the conception of Thoreau the naturalist, since in its earliest versions at least, this always included a spiritual dimension. His daily excursions in the woodlots and fields around Concord were not animated by a purely scientific curiosity, Blake and his other friends knew, but were rather an essentially spiritual quest, and an awareness of this motive, however attenuated, has often hovered around subsequent appropriations of the naturalist Thoreau, even among some biocentrist ecologists of today. Yet in his efforts to achieve for his friend and teacher a more deserving status, Blake himself appears to have colluded in the general strategy of eliding from Thoreau's public image the more unorthodox or inexplicable religious features.[16] Instead, he and his publishers at Houghton Mifflin presented a somewhat sanitized, more popularly palatable rendition of Thoreau as woodsman and naturalist, minus the subversive pantheistic philosopher and religious contemplative.

It is worth pointing out that neither the identification of Thoreau as political reformer nor as literary artist finds predominant expression in the characterizations of his friends and contemporaries. More common are the images of forest recluse, religious seeker, devotee of nature, and charismatic teacher. A few excerpts from the testimony of neighbors, friends, and more or less contemporary reviewers will help to underscore this suggestive disparity. Here, first of all, are some anecdotes from Thoreau's Concord neighbors. One comes to us in the form of facetious vignette that Thoreau himself recorded in his journal of 1857 about a conversation he had had with his townsman Abel Brooks:

> About a month ago, at the post-office, Abel Brooks, who is pretty deaf, sidling up to me, observed in a loud voice which all could hear, "Let me see, your society is pretty large, ain't it?" "Oh, yes, large enough," said I, not knowing what he meant. [Brooks said:] "There's Stewart belongs to it, and Collier, he's one of them, and Emerson, and my boarder" (Pulsifer), "and Channing, I believe, I think he goes there." [Said I:] "You mean the *walkers;* don't you?" "Ye-es, I call you the Society. All go to the woods; don't you?" "Do you miss any of your wood?" I asked. "No, I hain't worried yet. I believe you're a pretty clever set, as good as the average," etc., etc.
>
> Telling Sanborn of this, he [Sanborn] said that, when he first came to town and boarded at Holbrook's, he asked H. how many religious societies there were in town. H. said that there were three,—the Unitarian, the Orthodox, and the Walden Pond Society. I asked Sanborn with which Holbrook classed himself. He said he believes that he put himself in the last. (J.9.331–32; my brackets)

That in subsequent years, Frank Sanborn, Thoreau's interlocutor in the last part of this entry, became one of the chief sponsors of the sect of idealists that later formed around Emerson and Thoreau lends further credence to this wry anecdote, which sets out what were for some the principal denominational options of midcentury Concord.

One rich source of such local legends was Edward Waldo Emerson, the writer's son, who in 1917 wrote an admiring reminiscence of Thoreau that was conceived in part to defend his old friend against aspersions on his character like those cast by Lowell in 1865. For many years Thoreau had been a surrogate parent to the Emerson children—Edward remembered him fondly as a kind of older brother figure—who dazzled them with funny stories and led them on huckleberry hunts. In his memoir, the younger Emerson seems particularly at pains to foreground what he considers to be the deeply religious character of Thoreau's life, offering as proof such anecdotal evidence as this recollection from Concord townswoman Mrs. Minot Pratt: "Henry lived in a lofty way. I loved to hear him talk, but I did not like his books so well, though I often read them and took what I liked. They do not do him justice. I liked to see Thoreau rather in his life. Yes, he was religious; he was more like the ministers and others; that is, like what they would wish and try to be. I loved him, but . . . always felt a little in awe of him."[17]

For more meticulous recollections we need to turn, however, to Thoreau's closest friends, not least Ralph Waldo Emerson himself, whose journals Edward Emerson carefully tapped for his memoir years after his father's death in 1882. Few could speak with as much assurance and insight as the older Emerson, whose friendship with Thoreau had lasted the better part of a quarter century. The eulogy, mentioned above, that he delivered on the occasion of Thoreau's funeral in 1862 offered what is perhaps his most sustained portrait of his old friend. Reading the funeral oration as it appeared in the pages of the *Atlantic* a couple of months later, Thoreau's sister Sophia professed herself "disappointed" with Emerson's representation of her brother, since the stoic figure he sought to convey there seemed so foreign to her.[18] It seems clear that Emerson's remarks reflected some of the frustrations, as well as the warmth, of what became in later years a sometimes troubled relationship.[19] As I have noted, critics have commonly viewed this oration as at best lukewarm in its praise of Thoreau, in part because it appears to have done more to slow the popular recognition of his talent than to hasten it. But viewed strictly on its own terms, Emerson's portrait is anything but disapproving and is in several respects highly revealing. In general, he heaps praise on his friend and, in the process, provides some of the most astute observations we have of Thoreau's life and character, especially his religious character. Having acknowledged Thoreau's seemingly preternatural instincts, he goes on to note an even more unusual gift:

> His robust common sense, armed with stout hands, keen perceptions, and strong will, cannot yet account for the superiority which shone in his simple and hidden life. I must add the cardinal fact, that there was an excellent wisdom in him, proper to a rare class of men, which showed him the material world as a means and symbol. This discovery, which sometimes yields to poets a certain casual and interrupted light, serving for the ornament of their writing, was in him an unsleeping insight; and whatever faults or obstructions of temperament might cloud it, he was not disobedient to the heavenly vision. In his youth, he said, one day, "The other world is all my art: my pencils will draw no other; my jack-knife will cut nothing else; I do not use it as a means."

To Emerson we also owe some of the finer touches in the emergent mythology of Thoreau as companion to the animals: "Snakes coiled round his leg," he said, "the fishes swam into his hand, and he took them out of the water; he pulled the woodchuck out of its hole by the tail, and took the foxes under his protection from the hunters." But above all, Emerson wished to make clear the extent to which Thoreau's outer life centered on a kind of spontaneous natural piety, albeit one divorced from the edicts of organized religion:

> Whilst he used in his writings a certain petulance of remark in reference to churches or churchmen, he was a person of a rare, tender, and absolute religion, a person incapable of any profanation, by act or by thought. . . . Thoreau was sincerity itself, and might fortify the convictions of prophets in the ethical laws by his holy living. It was an affirmative experience which refused to be set aside. A truth-speaker he, capable of the most deep and strict conversation; a physician to the wounds of any soul; a friend

knowing not only the secret of friendship, but almost worshipped by those few persons who resorted to him as their confessor and prophet, and knew the deep value of his mind and great heart. He thought that without religion or devotion of some kind, nothing great was ever accomplished: and he thought that the bigoted sectarian had better bear this in mind.[20]

Such characterizations as this evidently provoked little protest among Emerson's auditors in Concord's Second Church on the day of Thoreau's funeral. Only a few weeks before, Bronson Alcott, another Concord neighbor and one of Thoreau's closest friends, had eulogized Thoreau in substantially the same terms in the *Atlantic Monthly*. "I know of nothing more creditable to his greatness," Alcott wrote, "than the thoughtful regard, approaching reverence, by which he has held for many years some of the best persons of his time, living at a distance, and wont to make their annual pilgrimage, usually on foot, to the master,—a devotion very rare in these times of personal indifference, if not of confessed unbelief in persons and ideas."[21]

Another such contemporary presentation comes to us from Ellery Channing, another Concord neighbor and one of Thoreau's regular walking companions, who in 1873 produced the first book-length biography of his friend. Although this treatment consists largely of excerpts from Thoreau's own writings and reflects the efforts already underway to present him primarily as a woodsman and nature writer, Channing also underscores the religious character of his relationship to nature: "His love of wildness was real. Whatever sport it was of Nature, this child of an old civilization, this Norman boy with the blue eyes and brown hair, held the Indian's creed, and believed in the essential worth and integrity of the plant and animal. This was a religion to him; to us, mythical. He spoke from a deeper conviction than ordinary, which enforced on him that sphere and rule of life he kept. So far an anchorite, a recluse, as never to seek popular ends, he was yet gifted with the ability and courage to be a captain of men."[22]

In view of the withering attacks on organized religion to which Emerson referred in his eulogy, it is not surprising that reviewers who knew nothing of Thoreau personally were less alert to this dimension of his life. And, needless to say, some found his pantheism, his evident paganism, and especially his admiration for Asian religious ideas revolting and blasphemous alike. But such conventionally sectarian responses were far from the rule. Actually, one of the most discerning appraisals ever provided of the spiritual dimensions of Thoreau's life came from Harvard classmate John Weiss, a Unitarian clergyman, in a review published in the *Christian Examiner* in 1865. Commenting upon a meditative passage from the "Solitude" chapter of *Walden,* Weiss went so far as to construe Thoreau's love of nature in Edwardsean terms: "Here is a vein as old as the Scriptures which record the reveries of pure souls. The infinite presence cannot thus befriend the selfish and shirking temperament. So was Thoreau called and set apart for his fine observation of the natural world, and to reclaim its most neglected provinces for the indwelling love and beauty of the God who adopted him also in the wood. The calling of Jonathan Edwards was not more full of sweet and quiet rapture. How fortunate that the metaphysics of river and meadow furnished Thoreau with a body of divinity to enforce the sinlessness of Nature and refute the wrath of God!" Neither was the liberal Weiss at all distracted by Thoreau's allusions to Eastern religions: "For no writer of the present day is more religious; that is to say, no one more profoundly penetrated with the redeeming power of simple integrity, and the spiritualizing effect of a personal consciousness of God. It is in the interest of holiness that he speaks slightingly of Scripture and its holy men. 'Keep your Christ,' he says; 'but let me have my Buddha, and leave me alone with him.' He catches up this Buddha for a chance defence against the conventional Christ of Democrats, slaveholders, sharpers in trade and in society, literal theologians, and over-pious laymen."[23]

But the most fervent defense of Thoreau's religious ancestry was mounted by the Englishman A. H. Japp in response to the critical assaults by Lowell and others that had appeared in the decade after Thoreau's death. Writing under the pen name H. A. Page, Japp sought to set the record straight by situating Thoreau firmly in the tradition of Western nature mystics commencing with none other than St. Francis of Assisi: "I see a kind of real likeness between this so-called 'Stoic' of America," Japp wrote, "with his unaffected love for the slave, his wonderful sympathies and attractions for the lower creatures, his simplicities, and his liking for the labors of the hand, and that St. Francis." Japp himself had never met Thoreau, and his access to relevant sources was limited, but in his case, distance seems only to have brought the spiritual character of Thoreau's life into sharper relief: "The practical lesson of a true Transcendentalism, faithfully applied, must issue thus— and it is the same whether we see it in St. Francis, in the saintly Eckhart, in William Law, or in the naturalist Thoreau. All life is sanctified by the relation in which it is seen to the source of life—an idea which lies close to the Christian spirit." Japp concludes his frankly hagiographic treatment on a prophetic note by seeing Thoreau as one of the "prophets" of "new return" to a harmonious life in nature.[24]

Chief among the spiritual converts to whom both Emerson and Alcott alluded, however, was Harrison Blake, who, as we have seen, did so much to prop up Thoreau's faltering reputation in the 1880s. Blake had been one of the divinity school students at Harvard who sponsored Emerson's notoriously inflammatory address to the graduating class in 1838 and probably first became acquainted with Thoreau in Concord in the early forties. In 1848 Blake struck up a correspondence with Thoreau that continued throughout the next decade and resulted in one of the most frank and searching records we have of Thoreau's mature religious vision. In his first letter to Thoreau, inspired by one of Thoreau's *Dial* essays, Blake set out both the high religio-philosophical tone and the relational terms of their subsequent friendship: "If I understand rightly the significance of your life, this is it: You would sunder yourself from society, from the spell of institutions, customs, conventionalities, that you may lead a fresh, simple life with God. Instead of breathing a new life into the old forms, you would have a new life without and within. There is something sublime to me in this attitude,—far as I may be from it myself. . . . Speak to me in this hour as you are prompted. . . . I honor you because you abstain from action, and open your soul that you may *be* somewhat" (Correspondence, 213). Not in the least put off by Blake's deferential tone, Thoreau responded soon after with a fittingly elevated and teacherly letter of his own: "I am glad to hear that any words of mine, though spoken so long ago that I can hardly claim identity with their author, have reached you. It gives me pleasure, because I have therefore reason to suppose that I have uttered what concerns men, and that it is not in vain that man speaks to man" (Correspondence, 214). As the friendship deepened, the correspondence became ever more searching and substantive. Thoreau's extended responses to Blake's queries were at times magisterial, approximating in style and substance some of the more elevated passages of his published writings. Blake treasured these letters, reading them aloud among friends and associates in Worcester who would gather periodically to discuss their common interests in Thoreau and other Transcendentalist thinkers.[25]

After Thoreau's death in 1862, the kind of hagiographic treatment we detect in the letters of Blake and other disciples was kept alive in the correspondence, lectures, and writings of a tightly knit circle of friends and admirers. One leading venue for the further sanctification of Thoreau was the Concord School of Literature and Philosophy, which Alcott, Sanborn, and William T. Harris of St. Louis founded in 1879 as a kind of summer retreat center dedicated to the propagation of various brands of philosophical idealism, including Concord Transcendentalism.[26] Over the course of its nine sessions, the school attracted hundreds of students to its lectures, some from as far west as Chicago, turning the little town of Concord into a Mecca for excited would-be philosophers. While some of the town's natives poked fun at the upsurge of enthusiastic pilgrims—"The town swarms with budding philosophers and they roost on our steps like hens waiting for corn," wrote Louisa May Alcott— the wide newspaper coverage the school received suggests it was something of a cultural sensation.[27] Emerson was plainly the school's leading luminary, but Thoreau inspired great admiration as well. Blake and Sanborn, in particular, often used the school as a vehicle to champion Thoreau as a kind of New England pastoral saint. One of the best-attended presentations of the first session, repeated several times in subsequent years, was Blake's ceremonial reading from Thoreau's journals. Another popular activity sponsored by the school was the obligatory field trip—an early version of the Thoreauvian pilgrimage—to Walden Pond and the site of Thoreau's cabin, which Julia Anagnos described with mock seriousness in her 1885 memoir.[28] With the closing of the Concord School in 1887, continued propagation of Thoreau the prophet-saint was carried on, to some extent, under the auspices of the Greenacre Summer Conferences in Eliot, Maine.[29]

By the turn of the century, most of Thoreau's closest friends and the members of his inner circle were dead. Only Frank Sanborn remained to propagate the religious image of Thoreau, and his treatments were often marred by an egregious tendency toward distortion and misrepresentation. After that, Thoreau increasingly became the preserve of professional academics and critics.[30] And while an awareness of the religious Thoreau was never entirely absent from the critical literature, the topic was increasingly ignored and relegated to the sidelines of academic discourse. The characterizations of contemporaries like Ellery Channing, Bronson Alcott, and Harrison Blake—when acknowledged at all—tended to be dismissed as sentimental effusions of merely antiquarian interest.[31] Among recent scholars, Thoreau's spirituality is often simply dismissed as an artifact of his youth. According to one currently popular view, after the early 1850s or so he abandoned the religious excesses of his younger days to pursue his soberer and more scientific interest in the natural world. There will be a chance further on to consider this perspective more closely, but for now it is enough to point out how symptomatic it is of the general dismissal or soft-pedaling of Thoreau's religiousness in much of the current critical literature.[32]

The fact that neither the depiction of Thoreau as political reformer nor as literary artist particularly tallies with the more rounded spiritual image urged by his own friends and acquaintances should perhaps make us wonder. This is not to say that contemporary perspectives should necessarily be privileged over later critical ones—especially given their definite propensity (notable particularly in this case) to yield to hagiography and their own forms of understandable favoritism and myopia—but they ought to be taken into consideration. What, for our purposes, the testimony of Thoreau's contemporaries makes clear is that in his own day Thoreau was generally conceived in spiritual terms, even in some cases as a sort of charismatic, if decidedly unorthodox, religious figure.

If the nineteenth-century testimony represented above is any indication, current dismissals of the religious Thoreau may say more about contemporary academic culture than his own situation. For most readers today, he has become mainly a creature of the American literature syllabus. Conversely, he has had almost no part to play in American religious historiography, despite the emphatically religious character of so much of his life and writing. Some of the larger sociocultural reasons for this one-sided appropriation have already been touched upon, but factors peculiar to Thoreau himself are also worth nothing. It is clear, first of all, that his fascination with what were to European Americans exotic religious forms—the "pagan" religions of India, China, northern Europe, classical Greece, and indigenous America—have until recently been as much a stumbling block to historians of American religion as they apparently have been to most of their colleagues in American literature. For religious historians, such material led too far beyond the pale of their traditional Christianity-centered historical orientation, and to be frank, members of both establishments, literary and historical, found some of this non-Christian and non-Western material almost as foreign and distasteful as did a few of Thoreau's more caustic contemporary reviewers.[33] Thoreau's Romantic Orientalism was only one expression of his spiritual life, to be sure, but it is an important one and no responsible study of his religious thought can afford to ignore or trivialize it.

Another significant, and in part related, deterrent to Thoreau's reception among religious historians has been his all but total indifference to and vexed repudiation of religious doctrine and ideology. From its origins, Christianity has been a tradition much given to the promulgation of theology and creed, not least in early New England. Thoreau had little patience for the tendentious and labyrinthine theologies of the New England Protestant tradition and no good word for its sponsors. For him religion was experiential or it was nothing. When he took up a religious theme or idea, as he often would do, he did so almost always in the service of rhetoric, not systematic philosophy. To limit one's examination of Thoreau's religious life to his religious ideas is thus to overlook the heart of the matter. As we will see, at all times Thoreau's religious life essentially revolved around—was predicated upon—experiences of inspiration and euphoria in the natural world, which he customarily referred to as ecstasy. It was in recognition of the unavoidability of this fact of Thoreau's biography that in 1966 Joel Porte issued a caveat well worth pondering: "The reader of Thoreau with no sympathy for mystic states may be inclined to write off his descriptions of his ecstasies as simply hyperbole, or perhaps even affectation; but there is a good deal of evidence to show that neither explanation will suffice, that Thoreau was writing of something he knew."[34] Such experiences may be hard to talk about, and even harder to fathom, but unless we recognize their centrality in Thoreau's life, we are likely to misconceive our subject altogether.[35]

The purpose then of the following study is to provide a fuller reconstruction and analysis of Thoreau's religious thought and experience than have been available elsewhere. Naturally, this includes a thorough airing and inventory of his religious attitudes and ideas, but as I hope to demonstrate in Chapter Four, Thoreau's religious ideas cannot as a rule be properly assessed independently of the literary and rhetorical contexts in which they occurred. Analysis of Thoreau's own representations of his ecstatic experiences suggests that these passages often represent complex verbal negotiations between present feeling, memories of past experience, and other literary precedents and touchstones. Like all literary texts, these formulations are constructed from past experience and present understanding. Acknowledging the complexities involved in these acts of construction puts us on guard against naive, dogmatic, or presumptive readings of these experiences. Thoreau was not a systematic philosopher or theologian, and to treat him as such would only interfere with a genuine appreciation of the dynamic and contingent character of his religious pronouncements. Religious ideas and the propositions in which they were sometimes couched mostly served as the momentary vehicles of some larger rhetorical strategy, and thus were subject to alteration or reversal in the next breath. But there is also a deeper reason for the apparent contradictoriness and inconsistency of so many of his religious pronouncements. Thoreau was what we might now call a religious empiricist. He credited the revelations of the past, whether of the past century or the past week, only to the extent that they reflected or clarified his personal insight, experience, or intuition. In general, his own religious convictions never extended much beyond the perimeter of what he could touch or ascertain for himself, though in his case that perimeter was astonishingly wide. This recognition should give some pause to those who would seek to appropriate him, however vaguely, as "Puritan" or "Pagan" or "Hindu" or "Buddhist"; such identifications have only a provisional status at best. Thoreau showed no more respect for such sectarian distinctions than for the boundaries of the farms and woodlots he nonchalantly crossed on his daily excursions. On the other hand, he sometimes demonstrated sympathy for each of these and other traditions in surprisingly passionate, if not vehement, ways. There was no religious community whose faith claims Thoreau championed wholly and none for which he did not reserve some measure of scorn. By temperament and conviction, Thoreau was, as Emerson once said, a protestant of the most extreme type.

It is in order to make more sense of this particular brand of religiosity—personal, antiinstitutional, experiential, iconoclastic—that I have adopted, for the purposes of this study, the conception of religion and the approach to its analysis advanced a century ago by William James. In his famous treatment in *The Varieties of Religious Experience,* James provisionally characterized religion in exclusively personalistic and experiential terms as "the feelings, acts, and experiences of individual men in their solitude, so far as they apprehend themselves to stand in relation to whatever they may consider divine."[36] This definition clearly has its limitations. It certainly does not work for all persons and all forms of religious life—brashly ignoring as it does, for example, all collective religious life—but it has a special appeal for me, since it has such a direct and obvious bearing on Thoreau. Indeed, one of the distinct advantages of James's definition here is that it was elaborated with particular reference to just such mavericks of the late Protestant tradition as Thoreau himself. At one point, James even quotes a passage from the "Solitude" chapter of *Walden* to exemplify what he calls "the fundamental feature in the spiritual life," namely "the sense of Presence of a higher and friendly power."[37] Since James was among the first scholars of religion to give formal expression to a way of being religious that has become increasingly common in the United States in recent decades, his definition has the added advantage of helping us to appreciate how influential Thoreau's writings have been in shaping this modern religious sensibility. If this study of Thoreau's personalistic brand of faith helps students of certain contemporary strains of American religion understand their sources more fully, my historical objectives will have been well served.

Consistent also with James's treatment is the method adopted for this study, which I would characterize as descriptive and phenomenological in order to distinguish it from a normative theological treatment, on the one hand, and a psychologically determinative reading, on the other. Phenomenology is a term that has been pressed into service by a wide range of thinkers across several fields of the humanities and construed in a variety of more and less defined ways. For my purposes, I mean to employ the term in the several senses it has acquired in the history of religions and in literary criticism, rather than the ways identified specifically with the school associated with Edmund Husserl in the history of modern philosophy. In the field of literary studies, my usage harks back in some ways to the work of Georges Poulet and the Geneva School. Like the approach to literary analysis adopted by these so-called critics of consciousness, my concern has been to examine the entirety of Thoreau's written work as a precise verbalized embodiment of the modes of experience distinctive of its author.[38] In the field of religious studies, my usage reflects a longstanding affinity with the history of religions, particularly as it was represented in the work of the Dutch School and, more recently, Mircea Eliade. Among the several specific features associated with the religious phenomenology, several are particularly germane to the approach adopted for this study of Thoreau. First, a phenomenology of religion is less concerned with objective facts than with lived experience.

Second, it seeks to describe the forms and phenomena of experience, and wherever possible to coordinate these descriptions according to some larger classificatory scheme. Third, the phenomenologist of religion is likely to studiously avoid sectarian, reductionistic, or deterministic readings of religious experience, whether they arise from religious orthodoxy or scientific method. We may never know where Thoreau's ecstatic experiences came from, but we can certainly see how they operated within his overall religious and literary self-understanding.[39] Fourth, this is an approach that seeks as much as possible to let its subjects speak for themselves. Together with the historian's own presuppositions, questions of truth or value are, so far as possible, temporarily bracketed or withheld in the interests of getting at the nature of these experiences and their meaning for the subjects under consideration. Finally, the phenomenologist of religion readily concedes that the success of such study depends in part on an act of imaginative sympathy or intuition on the part of the investigator.[40] How much this study has been guided by these methodological strictures will quickly be seen as the following chapters unfold. Above all, it is important to emphasize that this reading has not been concerned with advancing or adjudicating any claims regarding the truth or value of Thoreau's religious experience. In keeping with the phenomenological approach, my concern has been more limited: to describe the major forms of thought and experience relevant to Thoreau's spiritual life, to show how they are mediated and represented in his writings, and to recognize their implications for an overall understanding of his life and work.

In recognition of their obvious primacy and disproportionate importance for an understanding of Thoreau's religious thought and experience, I have focused on three primary documents of his collected writings—*A Week on the Concord and Merrimack Rivers, Walden,* and the journal—though other writings have an important bearing on this subject also, as I will show. As it happens, this plan of study dovetails conveniently with the thematic and roughly chronological approach followed here: Chapters One and Two center on the early journals, Three and Four on *A Week,* Five and Six on *Walden,* and Chapter Seven on the late journals. This textual, thematic, and roughly chronological treatment seemed preferable to a more exacting biographical approach since I have become convinced that Thoreau's religious thought was not as clearly developmental as some commentators have suggested. Certainly his religious ideas and reflections show signs of seasoning, maturation, and even chastening—and this is an evolution I will attempt to demonstrate within individual chapters—but there is no real evidence of the midlife spiritual crisis and disillusionment that some critics have asserted. On the contrary, examination of relevant journal entries, early to late, suggests that Thoreau's religious thought was essentially cumulative and progressive, indicating both continuity and change, but no sudden changes of heart or drastic disavowals. In view of this more nuanced picture of Thoreau's development, I have resisted the temptation to subject the facts of his life to some Procrustean chronological scheme.

One of the most memorable features of James's treatment of religious experience in his *Varieties* was the considerable play he gave to long and fascinating citations from a wide array of sources. To some readers, all these extended citations might seem distracting or unnecessary, but closer consideration of James's procedure reveals how integral they were to his overall approach. His approach too we might fairly characterize as phenomenological, reflecting as it does James's basic commitment to holding in abeyance his own existential judgments in order to let his subjects, so far as possible, speak for themselves. In quoting Thoreau at such length in the following pages, my aim is much the same. One thing I hope the ample collection of passages reproduced below will make clear is that the life they reflect can never be adequately apprehended by literary, psychological, or philosophical categories alone.

hmm - new approach, too —
close reading +
explication of passages

One

My Life Was Ecstasy

On the night of June 12, 1851, Henry Thoreau modified his usual routine and went for a long walk to Walden Pond under the light of the advancing full moon. The next day he recorded in his journal a long account of his moonlight adventure, beginning with the following evocative entry:

Walked to Walden last night (moon not quite full) by rail-road & upland wood path, returning by Wayland Road. Last full moon the elms had not leaved out, cast no heavy shadows & their outlines were less striking & rich in the streets at night. (I noticed a night before night before last from Fair Haven how valuable was some water by moonlight like the river & Fair Haven pond though far away—reflecting the light with a faint glimmering sheen, as in the spring of the year The water shines with an inward light like a heaven on earth. The silent depth & serenity & majesty of water—strange that men should distinguish gold & diamonds—when these precious elements are so common. I saw a distant river by moon light making no noise, yet flowing as by day—still to the sea, like melted silver reflecting the moon light—far away it lay encircling the earth How far away it may look in the night and even from a low hill how miles away down in the valley! As far off as Paradise and the delectable country! There is a certain glory attends on water by night. By it the heavens are related to the earth—Undistinguishable from a sky beneath you—(PJ.3.259–60)[1]

For the next several nights, and periodically throughout the rest of that summer, Thoreau continued his moonlight excursions, setting off about dusk and returning sometimes not till daybreak. As this passage suggests, these nocturnal journeys were less motivated by the scientific interests that sometimes prompted his usual afternoon walks. In the moonlight, familiar landscapes surrounding his home assumed a mythical or dreamlike character. Time and space seemed transformed. "The light of the moon in what age of the world does that fall upon the earth?" he wondered. Countryside showered in moonlight was a world apart from that which he encountered in the glare of noonday sun. As he reflected more on his moonlight walks later that summer, it seemed to him that sun and moon represented two different states of consciousness, two different orders of reality even. At such times, he saw no "crowning advantage" in the sun's light; it did not "enlighten" the way "the silent spiritual—contemplative moonlight" did (PJ.3.272, 286). Sunlight caused his thought to "wander," whereas in moonlight he became "more collected & composed & sensible of [his] own existence" (PJ.3.354). But on June 13, the chief lesson of his prolonged exposure to moonlight the night before was to remind him of the narrow limits within which our lives are normally confined: "We do not commonly live our life out & full—we do not fill all our pores with our blood—we do not inspire & expire fully & entirely enough so that the wave the comber of each inspiration shall break upon our extremest shores—rolling till it meets the sand which bounds us—& the sound of the surf come back to us. . . . We do not live but a quarter part of our life—why do we not let on the flood—raise the gates—& set all our wheels in motion" (PJ.3.261).

In general, the summer of 1851 was a kind of watershed in Thoreau's life. He had weathered the formative years of the 1840s, including the as yet undistinguished two-year sojourn at Walden Pond, and he was entering a more settled phase of his adult life. That July he turned thirty-four and already he was feeling his age. The following fall and winter, he complained intermittently of the corrosive effects of age, a certain coarseness and laxness of discipline, a loss of elasticity, both of mind and body (PJ.4.46–47, 265–66, 383–84). His health that summer was robust, but it had not always been so, and it must have come as a rude shock earlier that spring to be fitted with false teeth, his humorous expressions of stoic nonchalance notwithstanding (PJ.3.218). During the previous decade, Thoreau's family, tightly knit as always, had been rocked first by the agonizing death of Henry's older brother, John, in 1842, and then the wasting decline of his eldest sister, Helen, who succumbed to tuberculosis in 1849. Henry himself had experienced periodic bouts of bronchitis since at least his college days; early signs, presumably, of the same disease that killed his sister and would eventually overtake him too, eleven years later in 1862. Perhaps it would have surprised him little to know that by 1851 he was already well into the autumn of his life.[2]

From the standpoint of midcareer, Thoreau must have looked back on the years since his 1837 graduation from Harvard College with a mixture of pride and frustration. Much had been accomplished, to be sure, but by most external measures, his life so far had consisted mostly of a series of experiments and false starts, with no decided success anywhere. The 1840s had been a decade of sound and fury that to some of his neighbors—and perhaps to Thoreau himself—came to signify disappointingly little. After his graduation from Harvard, he tried schoolteaching for a few years, but positions were hard to find after the financial panic of 1837, and in the end he found himself poorly suited to the work anyway. What he most wanted was to make his way as a writer. But to survive he was obliged to participate in the family pencil-making business and take odd jobs around town.

It was during his last year or so at Harvard that Thoreau became acquainted with his famous neighbor Ralph Waldo Emerson, already widely recognized as the leader of a new movement of Unitarian reformers who came to be referred to, at first pejoratively, as "Transcendentalists." Emerson quickly recognized Thoreau's originality and brilliance, and encouraged him in his literary ambitions. Their subsequent friendship came to be the most formative, if stormy, of Thoreau's adult life. In 1841 Thoreau accepted Emerson's invitation to move in with the Emerson family in the capacity of a kind of resident handyman. As was no doubt intended, this situation proved as helpful to Thoreau's professional aspirations as it did to the management of the Emerson household, since before long the two men were actively collaborating in their work on the new Transcendentalist literary magazine the *Dial.* During the years from 1840 to 1844, Thoreau's poems, essays, and translations frequently found their way into the pages of the *Dial,* notwithstanding the sometimes discouraging criticism from the magazine's first editor, Margaret Fuller. During these years, Thoreau poured most of his attention into his poetry, but despite some early successes, his poems met with a tepid reception. His talent, he soon realized, was better realized in prose.

From the perspective of American literary history, the next seven years were a time of tremendous achievement, but the significance of that achievement was not at all obvious in 1851, to Thoreau or to anyone else. In the early 1840s he had managed to break away from his exclusive dependence on the *Dial* as a literary outlet, and his travel essays and reviews began appearing more widely, in such monthlies as the *Boston Miscellany,* the *Democratic Review,* and *Graham's Magazine.* But Thoreau was looking for something he could sink his teeth into, and in the summer of 1845, he moved to the cabin he had built for himself that spring on the shores of Walden Pond, in large part so that he could devote himself without interruption to the book-length narrative he envisioned of the trip he and his brother, John, had taken on the Concord and Merrimack Rivers in 1839. He must have been pleased with the results of his work, since by the time he left Walden in 1847 he had not only completed the bulk of the manuscript for what would become his first book, *A Week on the Concord and Merrimack Rivers,* but he had also made significant headway on a projected narrative of his two-year stay at Walden. By decade's end, his now celebrated essay "Civil Disobedience" and the narrative of his 1846 trip to Maine's Mount Katahdin had also been published.

By May of 1849 then, Thoreau had reason to hope that he stood on the threshold of real literary success. Although publication of *A Week* had met with delays and difficulties, he liked his first book—he was pleased, as he noted later, with its unroofed, "hypaethral" character—and seemed to have high hopes for it (PJ.3.279). Emerson also, after hearing parts of it read aloud, thought it "a book of wonderful merit," as "spicy as flagroot, broad & deep as Menu" (Letters.3.338). Finally, on May 30, 1849, ten years after the river voyage itself, *A Week* was published in Boston, with little fanfare, by the firm of James Monroe. But despite the great sense of expectation in Concord, the book turned out to be a commercial disappointment. A few critics praised Thoreau's fresh depictions of nature, but overall the book did not do well. After such a buildup, the author must have found this reception discouraging. Privately, even Emerson began to question his buoyant former assessments of Thoreau's prospects, complaining in his journal that he "wants a little ambition in his mixture. . . . instead of being the head of American Engineers, he is captain of a huckleberry party" (JMN.11.400).[3]

In professional terms then, the previous decade had been a frustrating period of unfulfilled potential. But the disenchantment of these years extended to more personal areas as well. By the late 1840s, Thoreau's friendship with Emerson was beginning to unravel. Throughout his journals of these months, Thoreau worried repeatedly over perceived slights received at the hands of this usually unnamed "friend." His conflicted feelings about Emerson in turn helped to fuel his repeated digressions on friendship in the journals of this period.[4] Notwithstanding the brazen declarations of self-sufficiency in *Walden,* the journals portray a man who agonized deeply about the problems and possibilities of true friendship. By the end of the decade, the relationship that had seemed so full of mutual promise in the early 1840s had grown somewhat prickly, and by the early days of 1850, Thoreau was wondering whether it could be salvaged at all (PJ.3.48, 193). Thoreau's love and admiration for Emerson were too deep ever to be repudiated completely, but by 1851, he had moved out of his illustrious friend's orbit in his determination to chart his own spiritual and literary trajectory (PJ.4.137).

The disappointments of the 1840s no doubt exacted some high costs for Thoreau, but they did result in one important dividend in the form of a powerful new sense of personal autonomy and self-determination. After his famous one-night incarceration in the Concord jail in 1846 over his refusal to pay the state's poll tax, the till-then characteristically apolitical Thoreau became increasingly embroiled in issues of social conscience, particularly concerning slavery. Concord was an important way station on the Underground Railroad, and for several years Thoreau served as one of the town's leading agents, harboring runaway slaves himself, ministering to their needs, and facilitating their eventual escape to Canada. The Fugitive Slave Act, enacted in the Compromise of 1850, provoked him to high dudgeon, as it did other Northerners. In his journal entry of April 19, 1851, Thoreau lashed out at the Massachusetts authorities for their collusion the previous week in the forced return of the runaway slave Thomas Sims. Invoking the authority of Jesus—"Do you think *he* would have stayed here in *liberty* and let the black man go into slavery in his stead?"—Thoreau railed at the hypocrisy of this nominally Christian country for its countenancing of the slave trade (PJ.3.203–07). He had seized the moral high ground on the slavery issue and refused henceforth to budge.

But the summer of 1851 was a time of new beginnings. Having acquired a surveyor's compass the previous spring, Thoreau began to find more work surveying. By the beginning of 1851 the demand for his services had begun to accelerate.[5] He found these jobs more congenial than working in his father's pencil factory and certainly better for his lungs. As business picked up, he could spend more of his time outside and earn a decent income in the bargain. This work proved enabling in another respect also, for it allowed him more time to pursue his growing interest in Concord's natural history. Encouraged especially by their mother, the Thoreau siblings had grown up with a special interest in the natural world, but in recent months, Henry's interests in local flora and fauna had become much more methodical and precise. Long tracts of his journals were increasingly given over to detailed observations of local plant life, birds, animals, and other natural forms and phenomena. He began to keep lists of his observations and record facts gleaned from his readings in natural history. Already he was acquiring a reputation in Concord as an authority on the town's natural history.

The best index of the changes in Thoreau's life in the early 1850s was the journal he had begun keeping in the fall of 1837, shortly after his graduation from Harvard. Throughout most of the 1840s, Thoreau used his journal primarily as a resource for his various publishing projects. By May of 1850, however, the journal entries became conspicuously more detailed and lengthy. By the following November, Thoreau was writing in the journal almost daily, and by the beginning of the next year, his entries typically extended to many pages of his notebooks, a compositional pattern that remained unchanged for the next ten years of his life. No longer did he conceive his journals primarily as a staging area for the production of other literary works. In fact, it is clear that the journal had become important in its own right and served increasingly as the principal focus of Thoreau's literary endeavors. From this point on, his usual routine was to spend his mornings in his garret reading and writing in his journal, and his afternoons walking for several hours in the woods and fields in Concord and the surrounding towns. Field notes scribbled into a small notepad were later amplified at some length in his journals at home.

However disappointed Thoreau may have been with his personal and literary fortunes up till this point in his life, the journals of the spring and summer of 1851 give no indication of it. There is no sense of resignation in these pages and certainly nothing of defeat. On the contrary, they testify to a new vitality in his life, a resurgence of a kind of boyish exuberance, and even—to invoke a word he himself would adopt more often in the coming months—ecstasy. His contacts with nature on his daily rambles filled him with palpable delight. A lake or stream encountered on his long afternoon walks afforded a pretext to strip off his clothes and luxuriate in the cool water (PJ.3.327; PJ.4.79–80).[6] Ascetic as he was, there is something sensual and at points rapturous about the experiences reflected in these pages. "My heart leaps into my mouth at the sound of the wind in the woods," he exclaimed in his journal in

August 1851 (PJ.3.368). At the end of that summer, he noted—at first disparagingly—the erection locally of a new telegraph line. Passing by it the next week, he heard it vibrating in the wind "like a harp high overhead." The sound had an unearthly and strangely stirring resonance for him, "as the sound of a far off glorious life a supernal life which came down to us" (PJ.4.16, 28, 35). In the weeks and months to come, this "telegraph harp" would periodically send him into swoons of delight: "Why was it made that man should be thrilled to his inmost being by the vibrating of a wire?" he exclaimed in his journal. "Are not inspiration and extasy a more rapid vibration of the nerves swept by the in rushing excited spirit whether zephyral or boreal in its character" (PJ.4.238).

Bliss Irrevocably Gone

Such expressions of euphoria as we find cropping up in the journals of the early fifties cast doubt on the views of those critics who would see Thoreau pursuing a darkening way by this point in his life, dispirited and resigned after the apparent failure of his first book. Yet there is no doubt that during this period he sometimes also gave expression to an anguished sense of spiritual diminution and decline. At points, he re-called this ebbing of inspiration with deep concern—as in October of 1851, when this mood was strongly upon him: "I seem to be more constantly merged in nature—my intellectual life is more obedient to nature than formerly—but perchance less obedient to Spirit—I have less memorable seasons. I exact less of myself. I am getting used to my meanness—getting to accept my low estate—O if I could be discontented with myself! If I could feel anguish at each descent!" (PJ.4.141).

Moreover, even when Thoreau expressed rapture, especially after 1850, he rarely did so without some tinge of regret. Indeed, in the journals of this period, as in some of his most characteristic writing of the previous decade, experiences of natural euphoria are often accompanied by, and times appear to evoke, an elegiac mood of nostalgia and loss. The following passage from November of 1850 is representative: "Some distant angle in the sun where a lofty and dense white pine wood with mingled grey & green meets a hill covered with shrub oaks affects me singularly—reinspiring me with all the dreams of my youth. It is a place far away—yet actual and where we have been—I saw the sun falling on a distant white pine wood whose grey & moss covered stems were visible amid the green—in an angle where this forest abutted on a hill covered with shrub oaks—It was like looking into dream land—It is one of the avenues to my future" (PJ.3.148). Such appeals to some golden vision of the past occurred with increasing frequency throughout the 1840s, and in the heady weeks of the summer of 1851 they break out anew: "Ah that life that I have known! How hard it is to remember what is most memorable! We remember how we itched not how our hearts beat. I can sometimes recall to mind the quality the immortality of my youthful life—but in memory is the only relation to it" (PJ.3.251–52). At this time, more perhaps than ever before, the days of his youth assume an almost fabulous character, as of some remote, mythological age. That summer epitomizes this surprising, but distinctively Thoreauvian, association of loss and inspiration. To Thoreau's readers and critics, this association of exhilaration and regret, of ecstasy and mourning, is apt to seem strange, confusing, and even contradictory. Indeed, the fact that some of Thoreau's most passionate expressions of loss occurred during just this season of apparently extraordinary consolations makes no sense to us, until we realize that during this midpoint in his life, such delights ultimately impressed him as mere shadows or echoes of some pristine prior experience or, in his most hopeful moments, as promissory notes of a beatific future to come. Whatever their provenance in the present, increasingly such moments of inspiration served as agents of memory, pointers to the past. They stood as poignant reminders of how far he had receded from the spiritual heights of his youth, thus quickening and sharpening his otherwise latent awareness of loss. Moments of exquisite bliss and feelings of sorrow, so seemingly inapposite in nature, could never again be completely disjoined.

The deeper one delves into the more reflective portions of Thoreau's journals, the more one realizes how deeply suffused they are apt to be with an elegiac mood, a discovery surprising perhaps to those readers acquainted with Thoreau exclusively through *Walden* or "Civil Disobe-

dience." The plaints of 1851 only underscore a tendency already apparent in his writing for some time. In fact, feelings of loss color much of
Thoreau's most self-reflective musings, and seem indeed distinctive of his
basic sensibilities as a writer. But what is it exactly that Thoreau so longs
for, so mourns the loss of? What was the object of this distinctively
elegiac strain? And what was this youthful "immortality" to which he
referred above? These presumably are questions that are, at least to some
extent, beyond the scope of an academic treatment. But they cannot be
avoided in a study of Thoreau's spirituality, if we are to offer anything
beyond a mere accounting of his religious ideas. If a reading of Thoreau's
journals convinces us of anything, it is that his "religiousness" had less to
do with what he at any given moment believed and much more to do
with what he perceived and felt in the fluctuating ebb and flow of this
inward experience. Religion for him was an affair of the heart, an interior
matter—intuitional and sensual, rather than propositional. These experiences of inspiration and loss, as they surge into view in the summer of
1851, thus offer one promising avenue into the heart of Thoreau's spiritual life. To attempt to reconstruct such an ethereal life would be like
chasing rainbows were it not for the richness of the record Thoreau has
left us in his journal. Here we encounter a record of personal introspection and an intimacy of psychological detail perhaps unprecedented in
American religious history.

The first ostensible manifestation of Thoreau's characteristically elegiac mood occurs quite early in the literary record, in a poem entitled
"Sympathy" that he had composed and copied into his journal in June of
1839 (PJ.1.76–77). The poem takes the form of a romantic elegy written in praise of an unnamed "gentle boy." As Walter Harding tells us, the
subject of Thoreau's poem was eleven-year-old Edmund Sewall of Scitu-
ate, whom Thoreau had met earlier that month while the boy was visiting Concord with his mother. For a time Thoreau appeared to have been
enamored of young Edmund and wrote his poem as an expression of his
admiration. Critics inclined to see homoerotic tendencies in Thoreau's
personal relations might well point to this poem as an early illustration,
but no one who read the poem at the time, including Edmund's parents,

seemed to have found anything unusual there.[7] Whatever the nature of the sentiments inspiring the poem, it is clear from its style and subject matter that Thoreau was writing quite deliberately, though not perhaps wholly successfully, in a somewhat displaced tradition of English and classical elegy. Thoreau was fond of Virgil and had no doubt become acquainted with the tradition of pastoral elegy during his classical training at Concord Academy and again at Harvard College.[8] At this point in his life, he was also fresh from his recent immersion at Harvard in the study of Milton and had no doubt read "Lycidas" carefully, perhaps in preparation for one of the themes assigned by his rhetoric professor, Edward Tyrrell Channing, or while reading in one of several collections of Milton's work he consulted in the Harvard College library during his senior year and periodically thereafter.[9] Thoreau's poem, it must be granted, is conventional, even for a poetic form well known for its conventionality, and it exhibits at points some of the mannerisms of an early apprenticeship to its dictates, as for example, in its somewhat labored allusions to "Virtue's mould" or Caesar's storming of "the House of Fame." Obviously, Thoreau is writing self-consciously in the elegiac mode here, and his poem imitates some of its basic features, notably in his concern to universalize the grief of loss, as he does in the following lines, in his allusion to the music of the spheres.

> Eternity may not the chance repeat,
> But I must tread my single way alone,
> In sad remembrance that we once did meet,
> And know that bliss irrevocably gone.
> The spheres henceforth my elegy shall sing,
> For elegy has other subject none;
> Each strain of music in my ears shall ring
> Knell of departure from that other one.
>
> (PJ.1.77)

Despite the poem's artificiality, Thoreau uses the elegiac form effectively here to convey a pattern of feeling that becomes increasingly distinctive of much of his writing during the following decade.

As it happened, Thoreau's interest in Edmund Sewall proved quite ephemeral—within a few weeks, Edmund's sister Ellen had all but eclipsed her brother in Henry's affections.[10] But "Sympathy" was still significant to him for the idealized, somewhat Platonic vision of friendship that it represented. After submitting it for publication to the *Dial,* where it appeared in 1840, he used it again to introduce the long digression on friendship that he placed in the "Wednesday" chapter of *A Week.* Friendship was an important theme in the meditations of most Transcendentalists, but no one was more preoccupied with it than Thoreau. As early as 1839, he began to draft extended passages on friendship into his journal, and he continued to revise and develop them throughout the next ten years and afterward.[11] True friendship offered a glimpse of heaven, he thought, and the loss of a friend was "source enough for all the elegies that ever were written."[12] Thoreau's treatment of the theme of friendship in the published version of *A Week* makes it clear that as far as he was concerned the promise and the demands of true friendship were both impossibly high. Echoing Emerson's sober reflections on the topic, he wrote: "Friendship is evanescent in every man's experience, and remembered like heat lightning in past summers" (261).[13] In human affairs the drama of friendship upstages all others, but it "is always a tragedy" (264). Thoreau's lengthy pronouncements on the theme of friendship naturally reflect the vicissitudes of his own friendships, in particular his increasingly troubled relationship with Emerson. These actual experiences thus often undergird the Platonizing tendencies of his thoughts about friendship with an element of psychological realism. Above all, he felt that friends must be motivated by concern for one another's higher spiritual good. In practice this meant that love must be tempered always with absolute honesty, even though he recognized at the same time that the exercise of such total honesty could militate against the well-being of the friendship itself. Dishonesty in personal relations, even in the interests of social harmony, was an offense against personal autonomy and a betrayal of the high ideals of friendship. Needless to say, with so much at stake, friendship for Thoreau could be as psychologically dangerous as it was potentially liberating (Week, 272).[14]

The painful disappointments Thoreau periodically experienced in his own actual friendships certainly helped reinforce his sense of the loss of a friend as a possible source of elegy. Emerson and Edmund and Ellen Sewall were no doubt among the faces that reappeared to him in the pages of the essay on friendship that he included in the "Wednesday" chapter of *A Week*. But the chief object of Thoreau's elegiac treatment of friendship in this essay was his older brother, John, who had died suddenly of tetanus, then called lockjaw, in the winter of 1842. John was Henry's only brother and also, throughout their younger years, his closest friend, and it was with John that Henry shared his adventures in their voyage up the Concord and Merrimack Rivers in the late summer of 1839. John's death came as a severe shock to Henry: for several weeks afterward, through a kind of sympathetic psychosomatic reaction, he suffered from the same symptoms that John experienced in the last days of his life. As if John's death were not tragic enough, a few days later young Waldo, the Emersons' five-year-old son and a great favorite of Thoreau's, died quite suddenly from scarlet fever. When, after weeks of silence, Thoreau began to commit his thoughts and feelings to his journals once again, they were colored indelibly by the effects of these losses. As a poetic form, elegy thus took on new meaning for Thoreau at this time, and his elegiac moods and reflections acquired new passion and urgency. A letter of March 2 to his friend and confidante Lucy Brown—one of the first he wrote after the deaths of John and Waldo—makes it clear that Henry struggled to come to terms with the shock of this double loss by spiritualizing it: John, after all, was only "the imperfect representative" of the ideal person he wished to be, and, for his part, Waldo "died as the mist rises from the brook," like some natural deity of the ancient world (Correspondence, 62–63). Here Thoreau comes to terms with the loss of Waldo by assimilating his death to natural transformations, as they were mediated to him in the stories of antiquity. By the same token, his deep participation in the deaths of John and Waldo no doubt also helped to explain his continuing attraction to "the fables of Narcissus, of Endymion, of Memnon son of Morning, the representative of all promising youths who have died a premature death, and whose memory is melodiously prolonged to the latest morning," as he put it in *A Week,* as well as to elegiac poetry generally (58). In another letter to Lucy Brown the following January, Thoreau asks: "Do you read any noble verses now a days—or do not verses still seem noble?—For my own part they have been the only things I remembered—or that which occasioned them— when all things else were blurred and defaced. All things have put on mourning but they—for elegy itself is some victorious melody and joy escaping from the wreck" (Correspondence, 75). The point of elegy, Thoreau now realized, was to conquer death, not confirm it. It served not as an epitaph, but as a mode of assurance and an avenue of escape. In it Thoreau now found a source of consolation that would remain with him for years to come and deeply condition his religious experience. The journals too witnessed a new retrospectiveness—a kind of backward assurance derived from the epiphanies of youth: "In prosperity I remember God, . . . in adversity I remember my own elevations, and only hope to see God again" (PJ.1.368). In some sense, John's death has signaled and confirmed the death of his own former self, and Thoreau increasingly begins to look back on the days of his youth with wistful nostalgia (PJ.1.400).

As we will see in more detail later, after John's death in 1842, Henry began to conceive of the narrative of their trip on the Concord and Merrimack in 1839 as a memorial to his brother. Indeed, throughout the 1840s, *A Week* served as the principal vehicle of the elegiac strain in Thoreau's writing. Perhaps echoing lines recalled from "Lycidas," Thoreau begins his narrative by invoking his brother as muse, thus signaling the book's generic affiliation with the pastoral elegy. Throughout the narrative, John's unspoken presence serves as a constant mute reminder of the self-consciously one-sided perspective of even Henry's most compelling representations, a dramatic expression of the essentially ambivalent structure of the work as a whole. Not surprisingly, John surfaces most poignantly in the closing paragraphs of Henry's long essay on friendship. Here Henry's decade-long musings on the meaning of friendship and his grief at John's death coalesce in a climactic recognition of his friend as brother: "My Friend is not of some other race or family of men, but flesh of my flesh, bone of my bone. He is my real brother. I see his nature groping yonder so like mine. We do not live far apart. . . . Is it of no significance that we have so long partaken of the same loaf, drank at the same fountain, breathed the same air, summer and winter, felt the same heat and cold; that the same fruits have been pleased to refresh us both, and we have never had a thought of different fibre the one from the other!" (284–85). Even this revelation may still be construed in strictly Platonic terms, but for once, the identity of Thoreau's silent companion is made poignantly clear.

While Thoreau's first book served as the primary vehicle for this mood of loss during the decade of the 1840s, his second book, *Walden,* was by no means free of its somber shadings. It has always been tempting to generalize about the differences between these two books, the only two that Thoreau published in his lifetime. *A Week* was a commercial failure, *Walden* enjoyed modest success; *A Week* is somewhat loosely constructed, *Walden* exhibits a more unified artistic design; *A Week* is retrospective and elegiac, *Walden* is prophetic, triumphal. Certainly differences in perspective and tone were written into the books' respective artistic plans. Comparison, for instance, of the epigraphs that Thoreau utilizes to inaugurate each work makes such intentions clear. The narrative of *A Week* begins, as we have seen, with an epigraph invoking John's memory, while *Walden* begins with what has become one of American literature's most ostentatious disclaimers: "I do not propose to write an ode to dejection, but to brag as lustily as chanticleer in the morning, standing on his roost, if only to wake my neighbors up."

Yet a closer reading of these works suggests that such contrasts may be overdrawn. Though *Walden* was not published till 1854, five years after the publication of *A Week,* it originated, we must remember, in the same period of Thoreau's life and grew from the same imaginative soil. Indeed, at points he worked on both manuscripts during his two-year sojourn at the Pond. While it may well be true that *Walden* represents a greater artistic achievement—it has unquestionably achieved far greater fame— it recapitulates many of the themes and literary patterns introduced in *A Week,* notably Thoreau's meditations on the relation between time and eternity. Linck Johnson is probably right in suggesting that *Walden* is better viewed as a kind of sequel to *A Week* rather than as a starkly different work.[15] Thoreau's allusion to Coleridge's well-known "Ode to Dejection" in his epigraph to *Walden* is obviously meant to sharply distinguish his own project from the kind of elegiac treatment of which Coleridge's poem affords a somewhat aggravated instance. Yet, as several subsequent passages and the epigraph itself make clear, this boastful announcement is to some extent merely a ploy, a dramatic pose. The author assumes it for the sake of the rhetorical leverage it provides. In actuality, while the dominant tone of *Walden* is prophetic, melioristic, even bombastic, it is periodically offset by a somber, elegiac mood more characteristic of *A Week*. By the same token, though *A Week* tends to foreground this elegiac tone, it witnesses also to dramatic moments of joy and personal triumph. These then are not contrasting works but two sides of the same coin, alternating expressions of the same unified literary and religious sensibility.

As H. Daniel Peck has instructively shown, Thoreau's historical essay on previous inhabitants of the district around Walden Pond—the opening section of his chapter entitled "Former Inhabitants; and Winter Visitors"—provides the most extended rehearsal of this otherwise muted elegiac mood to be found anywhere in the pages of *Walden*.[16] In this section, Thoreau provides a series of portraits of former settlers of the area, from the slave Cato Ingraham to the Irishman Hugh Quoil, whose lives were, to paraphrase Thomas Hobbes, hard, squalid, and short. Thoreau introduces this narrative facetiously, and somewhat dismissively. For human companionship on his long winter nights by the side of the Pond, he was sometimes "obliged to conjure up the former occupants of these woods" (Walden, 256). Conjure, of course, is all he can do, because each of the persons whose history he now begins to unfold has long since met his or her luckless end in Thoreau's lovely woodland paradise. The only evidence left in the Walden woods of these former inhabitants are a few overgrown cellar holes and other silent ruins. Thoreau's narrative here smacks of irony. What signs remain of these previous habitations have long since been covered over by luxuriant growths of sumac and goldenrod, a fate clearly adumbrated for Thoreau's cabin as well. "Former Inhabitants" thus countenances a vision of loss and death that unsettles the Edenic world of quiet harmony that otherwise prevails throughout most of the rest of the book. This isolated look into a bleak, irrecoverable past seems to run at cross-purposes to the myth of perennial renewal that governs the rest of *Walden,* but it is certainly not inconsistent with the retrospective attitude of *A Week* or the deepening elegiac attitudes of the journals during this period.

The most characteristic, and surely the most celebrated, expression of loss in *Walden,* however, takes the form of the mysterious parable about the hound, bay horse, and turtledove that occurs in the opening pages of "Economy." This passage serves perhaps as the classic expression of the elegiac sensibility I have been documenting here: "I long ago lost a hound, a bay horse, and a turtle-dove, and am still on their trail. Many are the travellers I have spoken concerning them, describing their tracks and what calls they answered to. I have met one or two who had heard the hound, and the tramp of the horse, and even seen the dove disappear behind a cloud, and they seemed as anxious to recover them as if they had lost them themselves" (17). Standing as it does like the Sphinx on the ancient highway, this famously cryptic passage exacts an interpretive response from every passerby; indeed, the critical literature on Thoreau is legion with efforts to solve the riddle of the meaning of the hound, bay horse, and turtledove. After 150 years, one has to approach Thoreau's dark saying, therefore, with some caution and, as Walter Harding notes, a sense of humor. A review of the principal theories proposed for the solution of this puzzle indeed serves almost as an index of the general tendencies of Thoreau scholarship over the past century. Most critics have naturally assumed that the images of the hound, bay horse, and turtledove are symbolic, though what they are symbolic of remains quite up in the air. These references have been variously interpreted as symbolic of the elusive ideal of friendship; of the "spiritual reality behind nature," of "wildness," "intellectual stimulation," and "purification of spirit"; of Truth, Goodness, and Beauty, and so forth.[17] The critic Barbara Johnson shed helpful light on the question in 1987 when she suggested that Thoreau deliberately used three symbols "that clearly are symbols but that do not really symbolize anything outside themselves." Their purpose, she argues, is to "wake us up to our own losses" by evoking "the irreducibly particular yet ultimately unreadable nature of loss" itself.[18]

It turns out that Thoreau himself did not make matters any easier for his readers. When, soon after the publication of *Walden,* "Uncle Ed" Watson, one of Plymouth's local personalities, asked Thoreau what he meant by these three allusions, Thoreau merely replied, "Well, sir, I suppose we all have our losses," a response that did not particularly ingratiate him with Uncle Ed. Such anecdotes serve to reinforce our sense that these oracular interludes were quite deliberate on Thoreau's part. More enlightening perhaps is the response he included in a letter to his friend B. B. Wiley in 1857: "How shall we account for our pursuits if they are original? We get the language with which to describe our various lives out of a common mint. If others have their losses, which they are busy repairing, so have I mine, and their hound & horse may *perhaps* be the symbols of some of them. But also I have lost, or am in danger of losing, a far finer & more ethereal treasure which commonly no loss of which they are conscious will symbolize—this I answer hastily & with some hesitation, according as I now understand my own words" (Correspondence, 478). Certainly part of what Thoreau is implicitly acknowledging here is the deliberate status of these symbols as symbols and even, as Johnson rightly suggests, arbitrary or self-reflexive symbols. But Thoreau's response to Wiley does not support the view that the loss to which these symbols refer was vacuous or purely abstract, only that its nature cannot be adequately represented in words. To speak of loss without some awareness of its object makes no sense: loss by its very nature makes reference to a condition of fullness, imagined or real, even when it cannot be so specified. Indeed, the poignancy of such expressions of loss as we find in Thoreau underscores the continuing psychological awareness of that which has been lost.

To cite the passage about the hound, bay horse, and turtledove in isolation, as I have done above, minimizes the impact it has in its actual context. To be sure, it intrudes quite unexpectedly in the long chapter on "Economy" (a chapter otherwise given to what seems at first glance a fairly prosaic account of the bare facts of life at the Pond), thus calling attention to a deeper substratum in Thoreau's experience. But it is not quite accurate to say that this cryptic parable is unrelated to its immediate narrative setting. On the contrary, the paragraph on the hound, bay horse, and turtledove appears among a series of related paragraphs in a long interlude striking for its double meanings and cryptic allusions. The paragraph just preceding it, with its evocative characterization of Thoreau's efforts "to stand on the meeting of two eternities," is also of course somewhat cryptic, and it too makes explicit reference to the kind of esoteric work of which the ensuing paragraph serves as perfect illustration: "You will pardon some obscurities, for there are more secrets in my trade than in most men's, and yet not voluntarily kept, but inseparable from its very nature" (17). Indeed, the fact that such passages often take the form of apparently deliberate, disjoined nonsequiturs does not mean that we cannot sometimes glean something important about them from their immediate and wider narrative contexts. The oracular context of this famous parable provides a case in point. Perhaps we cannot know what it might mean "to stand on the meeting of two eternities, the past and future" or, in the following paragraph, "To anticipate, not the sunrise and the dawn merely, but, if possible, Nature herself!" But surely it is clear that in passages such as these Thoreau is not simply contending with "economy" as we know it. These passages circumscribe the outer borders of phenomenal experience, of "past and future," and "Nature herself," in order expressly to point beyond them. As Thoreau essentially acknowledges in his letter to Wiley, the specific symbols of the hound, bay horse, and turtledove are drawn from "a common mint." Certainly in his journal he writes as though this is the case. In 1840, for example, he uses the imagery of the lost hound in connection to the writing of "a good book." Into *A Week,* he incorporated a passage ascribed to Mencius that proves more suggestive: "If one loses a fowl or a dog, he knows well how to seek them again; if one loses the sentiments of his heart, he does not know how to seek them again. . . . The duties of practical philosophy consist only in seeking after those sentiments of the heart which we have lost; that is all" (264).[19] The associated motifs of the lost fowl and dog in the Mencius passage bear a close resemblance of course to the motifs of the *Walden* parable. Here though, they are explicitly related to the wisdom teachings of Confucianism regarding certain mysterious "lost sentiments of the heart."

This passage from Mencius is suggestive, but Thoreau's most revealing use of this loss motif occurs in the dialogue between the Hermit and the Poet at the start of his chapter "Brute Neighbors." In this whimsical vignette, the Poet arrives at the forest hermitage of the Hermit desirous of going fishing, only to find his friend immersed in a profound meditation. The Hermit, a persona of Thoreau himself, accepts his friend's invitation but puts him off for a few minutes in order to return briefly to the following meditation:

> Let me see; where was I? Methinks I was nearly in this frame of mind; the world lay about at this angle. Shall I go to heaven or a-fishing? If I should soon bring this meditation to an end, would another so sweet occasion be likely to offer? I was as near being resolved into the essence of things as ever I was in my life. I fear my thoughts will not come back to me. If it would do any good, I would whistle for them. When they makes us an offer, is it wise to say, We will think of it? My thoughts have left no track, and I cannot find the path again. What was it that I was thinking of? It was a very hazy day. I will just try these three sentences of Con-fut-see; they may fetch that state about again. I know not whether it was the dumps or a budding ecstasy. Mem. There never is but one opportunity of a kind. (Walden, 224–25)[20]

Placed side by side in this way, each of the passages cited above provides partial expression of what appears to be a shared system of imaginative associations. At the center of this shared system is the imagery of the lost hound, bird, or other animal. These are, presumably, images from the "common mint" to which Thoreau alludes in his letter to Wiley. This discrete imagery appears to be associated in Thoreau's experience somehow with Asian, specifically Confucian, texts, as is suggested by the Mencius passage and by the dialogue from "Brute Neighbors." In this latter passage, however, the images of the hound or other animals have dropped out, though they are implied by the references to whistling and the absence of tracks. Standing in their place are the lost thoughts of Thoreau's ecstatic meditation. In fact, whether explicitly, as in the case of this dialogue between the Poet and the Hermit, or implicitly, as in the case of the parable from "Economy," all of these images serve somehow to call up the loss or imminent loss of some deeply personal "sentiments of the heart" or elusive rarefied experiences of meditation.

There is no point in insisting on some particular "answer" to Thoreau's riddle about the hound, bay horse, and turtledove—for the sake of his readers, he obviously intended these images to remain merely suggestive, provocative, and open-ended. Yet, disclosure of the wider cluster of associations indicated by the three passages above suggests that, as far as Thoreau was concerned, the symbolism of loss includes, among its various personal referents, experiences of contemplative transport. In fact, from a relatively early point in time, this yearning for a kind of contemplative peace feeds directly into the larger current of elegiac sentiment that I have been tracing throughout the 1840s. Noteworthy is this expression from October of 1843, when Thoreau was only twenty-six: "Though I am old enough to have discovered that the dreams of youth are not to be realized in this state of existence yet I think it would be the next greatest happiness always to be allowed to look under the eyelids of time and contemplate the perfect steadily with the clear understanding that I do not not attain to it" (PJ.1.480).

A Witness on the Stand

As I have tried to indicate in the foregoing pages, the stream of elegiac sensibility that we find building and deepening during the 1840s has various sources, outlets, and tributaries. There was the parting from young friends such as Edmund and Ellen Sewall, growing alienation with Emerson, and of course the death of John. Yet as the years passed, these discrete losses tended to coalesce with other sources of regret or disappointment, and become merged in a deeper and more elusive sense of loss. As I suggested at the start of this chapter, however, it was only in the exhilarating summer months of 1851, in an at once painful and blissful reprise of childhood feeling, that Thoreau's by now characteristic mood of loss achieved its fullest and most vivid expression. On July 16, he recorded an entry in his journal that epitomizes better than any other the state of his soul at midlife. I cite it in full for the light it sheds not only on Thoreau's elegiac sensibility but also on the religious dimensions of his life at this time:

> Methinks my present experience is nothing my past experience is all in all. I think that no experience which I have today comes up to or is comparable with the experiences of my boyhood—And not only this is true—but as far back as I can remember I have unconsciously referred to the experience of a previous state of existence. "Our life is a forgetting," etc.
>
> Formerly methought nature developed as I developed and grew up with me. My life was extacy. In youth before I lost any of my senses—I can remember that I was all alive—and inhabited my body with inexpressible satisfaction, both its weariness & its refreshment were sweet to me. This earth was the most glorious musical instrument, and I was audience to its strains. To have such sweet impressions made on us—such extacies begotten of the breezes. I can remember how I was astonished. I said to myself—I said to others—There comes into my mind or soul an indescribable infinite all-absorbing divine heavenly pleasure, a sense of elevation & expansion—and have had nought to do with it. I perceive that I am dealt with by superior powers. This is a pleasure, a joy, an existence which I have not procured myself—I speak as a witness on the stand and tell what I have perceived The morning and the evening were sweet to me, and I lead a life aloof from society of men. I wondered if a mortal had ever known what I knew. I looked in books for some recognition of a kindred experience—but strange to say, I found none. Indeed, I was slow to discover that

other men had had this experience—for it had been possible to read books & to associate with men on other grounds.

The maker of me was improving me. When I detected this interference I was profoundly moved. For years I marched as to a music in comparison with which the military music of the streets is noise & discord. I was daily intoxicated and yet no man could call me intemperate. With all your science can you tell how it is—& whence it is, that light comes into the soul? (PJ.3.305–06)

As will become more apparent as we proceed, this passionate outpouring reads almost as a compend of the motifs most distinctive of Thoreau's religious sensibility, including especially the themes of euphoric childhood, lost innocence, rapture of the senses, music, and what he refers to as ecstasy. The pathos of the sentiments conveyed here tempts us to situate this resonantly elegiac passage alongside comparable ones considered already, in particular the dark parable of the hound, bay horse, and turtledove from *Walden*. This passage from the journal is, of course, much less cryptically couched, more openly self-revelatory, than the *Walden* parable. Yet for all its apparently unabashed sincerity and spontaneous passion, this autobiographical formulation also shows signs of a long literary probation. Thoreau's quotation of the first line of the famous fifth stanza of Wordsworth's Immortality Ode, in particular, tips us off to the passage's primary literary affiliation. Actually, Thoreau misquotes Wordsworth's line ("Our birth is but a sleep and a forgetting"), but this mistake itself suggests an easy commerce with Wordsworth's poetry based on years of familiarity. Further inspection of the journal passage of July 16 suggests that it is less original than we might have assumed. In addition to the allusion to the Immortality Ode, Laraigne Fergenson has pointed out an oblique reference to "Lines Composed a Few Miles Above Tintern Abbey" in Thoreau's phrase "my past experience was all in all."[21] In fact, the more closely we examine this journal entry, the more we realize how deeply embedded it is in the themes, ideas, and atmosphere of Wordsworth's poetical works. The Immortality Ode itself, with its famous glorification of the joys of childhood and the mysteries of preterrestrial life, serves as a virtual template of this journal passage and apparently a prime shaper of Thoreau's mature elegiac sensibility. Indeed, it is no exaggeration to say that by this point in Thoreau's life, Wordsworth had become practically second nature.[22]

Critics have for some time recognized Thoreau's general indebtedness to Wordsworth, but the exact nature and extent of this debt has been somewhat difficult to pin down.[23] There are a couple of reasons for this. First of all, Thoreau's allusions to Wordsworth tend to be indirect, echoes merely of the older poet's work. He assimilated so much of Wordsworth's thought and sensibility at such a formative period in his life that it is difficult in practice to distinguish what was borrowed from what was his own. Indeed, Thoreau's literary and religious values were imbued with characteristic tints of Wordsworth's imagination. Second, Thoreau seems to have gone out of his way to distance himself from the influence of such an overpowering literary progenitor. Indeed, as he was to do also in the case of Emerson, and to an extent Goethe, Thoreau sometimes seemed to find his own voice by repudiating or contradistinguishing himself from Wordsworth.[24]

But despite such defensive maneuvers, Thoreau drew upon Wordsworth early in his life and periodically later on. He certainly encountered him on his college reading lists, if not long before, and cites him with some frequency in the early 1840s and then again in 1851–52. *A Week* contains several references to Wordsworth and *Walden* does also. In later years, he owned two of Wordsworth's works—a copy of his *Complete Poetical Works* and, after its publication in 1850, a copy of *The Prelude*—and consulted several others elsewhere.[25] Just how much Wordsworth shaped Thoreau's literary sensibilities is better suggested, however, by some of Thoreau's essays of the early 1840s. Frederick Garber notes echoes, for example, of Wordsworth in "Natural History of Massachusetts," a nature essay Thoreau wrote for the *Dial* in 1842.[26] But "A Walk to Wachusett," a travel essay published the next year in the *Boston Miscellany,* offers even more palpable evidence. "We read Virgil and Wordsworth in our tent," Thoreau remarks in his account of this excursion, which he took with his friend Richard Fuller the previous summer.

Indeed, for the pastoral scenes sketched in this narrative, Wordsworth appears to play the part of muse and literary model both. The following passage, depicting a rural village at sunset, seems altogether steeped in Wordsworthian diction, style, and sensibility: "There was such a repose and quiet here at this hour, as if the very hillsides were enjoying the scene; and as we passed slowly along, looking back over the country we had traversed, and listening to the evening song of the robin, we could not help contrasting the equanimity of Nature with the bustle and impatience of man. His words and actions presume always a crisis near at hand, but she is forever silent and unpretending."[27] But Wordsworth's influence extended also to questions of mode and genre. While travel accounts such as Goethe's *Italienische Reise* clearly galvanized Thoreau's interest in the romantic excursion genre, Wordsworth's own travel accounts, in both prose and poetry, certainly offered memorable models as well.[28]

Even as Thoreau began to settle into his work as an essayist and travel writer in the 1840s, thus resigning himself to a vocation in prose rather than poetry, Wordsworth continued to serve as his chief model of the nature poet. In the early months of his stay at Walden, he still saw the old poet as the paragon of his own preferred style of life.[29] After that, Wordsworth drops out of sight for a time in Thoreau's journal only to reappear, as we have seen, in the summer of 1851. At this point, Thoreau appears to be reading Wordsworth once again, with renewed interest and a quickened sense of appreciation. No doubt Wordsworth's death the year before, together with the long-awaited publication of *The Prelude,* was in part responsible for this new surge of interest. Besides reacquainting himself with some of Wordsworth's poetry and prose, Thoreau also read at least two biographical works. Some of the facts encountered in these works must have seemed almost eerily familiar to him: Wordsworth's abstemiousness, his fondness as a boy for ice skating and other outdoor sports, his long walks and excursions and penchant for composing in the act of walking, his love of the countryside and resistance to entering one of the standard professions, and his loss of a beloved brother.[30] In Wordsworth's sonnet "The World Is Too Much With Us," Thoreau found justification for his own solitary tendencies and dislike of philanthropy (PJ.4.419). And in Wordsworth's observations about "relaxed attention," he even found a helpful guide for effective nature study and contemplative experience.[31] Thoreau plainly admired Wordsworth, not just because the old poet loved nature, but because he approached nature with a certain reverential but studied precision. When on August 20, 1851, Thoreau wrote, "It is the marriage of the soul with Nature that makes the intellect fruitful, that gives birth to imagination," he was invoking a Romantic trope to which Wordsworth had given authoritative expression.[32] Wordsworth's meditations on natural forms and phenomena were not driven by some protoscientific preoccupation with facts for their own sake: nature was barren, he believed, unless wedded to the human spirit. This was Thoreau's premise also, as we will see more later.

Yet even these remarkable biographical parallels and philosophical affinities do not get to the bottom of Thoreau's special sympathy for England's poet laureate, and nowhere is this better seen than in the passionate outburst cited above from July 16. Plainly Thoreau found in Wordsworth not only a literary mentor, but also someone whose religious sensibility suggestively anticipated his own. Even as early as the age of twenty-three, Thoreau began to suspect that his best experiences were already behind him. It came as a shock to realize that henceforward his life was to recede with increased rapidity from a state of wholeness to which he could never again have complete access. Adulthood, he realized, was less progression than declension, less a moving toward than a retreating from what increasingly came to seem the defining moments of his spiritual experience. Episodes of ecstatic euphoria, experienced with gratuitous oblivion and nonchalance in the days of youth, now exerted a numinous authority. Increasingly, Thoreau treasured them in memory as the central monuments of his interior and imaginative life. In the summer of 1851, the implications of this loss were once again vividly apparent, and the pain was as well. Wordsworth, he knew, had been the poet of all this: he too had glimpsed the rapturous heights of youth and keenly felt the "shades of the prison-house" of age closing in around him. In 1840, Thoreau had cited a line from Wordsworth's poem "Resolution

and Independence" that had alluded to the ecstatic early life and premature death of the poet Thomas Chatterton. Wordsworth could read the
arc of his own poetic life in these lines about Chatteron, and so, to a
degree, could Thoreau his.

Above all, then, Wordsworth was the poet of recollection for Thoreau, the poet of lost paradise and the intimations of immortality.
Throughout his long life, Wordsworth's poems continued to draw upon
memories—recollected in tranquility, as he famously phrased it—of the
luminous periods of his youth. The resulting elegiac mood colored his
most famous and representative poems.[33] Thoreau too had experienced
this paradise and known these intimations, and was equally concerned
with the challenges arising from the disparities between past inspiration
and present expression. His literary task, as he thus formulated it the
following September, could not sound more Wordsworthian: "Our extatic states which appear to yield so little fruit, have this value at least—
though in the seasons when our genius reigns we may be powerless for
expression.—Yet in calmer seasons, when our talent is active, the memory of those rarer moods comes to color our picture & is the permanent
paint pot as it were into which we dip our brush" (PJ.4.51–52). All this
helps to explain why in the bittersweet summer of 1851, Thoreau looked
once again to Wordsworth in his efforts to give adequate expression to
his mood of regretful recollection. The Immortality Ode, a poem he had
known for many years, served as the perfect literary exhibit for the
feelings he was then experiencing.[34] Indeed, the journal entry of July 16
might have been a page taken from a book of Wordsworth's own interior
life. However personal or deeply felt Thoreau's own ecstatic experiences
had been, he had to, of course, return to the literary general store for the
words and ideas to convey them. And Wordsworth was his most reliable
resource. Wordsworthian sensibility so suffuses the passage of ecstasy
from July 16 as to shape not only Thoreau's diction and style, but the
moods, emotions, and experiences to which his words give expression.
Indeed, even Thoreau's use of the term "ecstasy" itself probably owes
something to his early readings of Wordsworth. Ecstasy was a word the
poet employed to describe the epiphanies of youth, his own or those of

one of his various poetic personae. To the Boy of Winander, for example, the "ecstasies" of youth served as founts of "wisdom" when recalled in later life, just as they had for the poet himself.[35]

While the elegiac passage from July 16 explicitly witnesses to the central influence of Wordsworth, it would be surprising if the conception of ecstasy announced there did not also owe something to Emerson's own developed views on the subject. In the summer of 1841, during the two-year period when Thoreau was comfortably ensconced in the Emerson household, Emerson had gone to Waterville, Maine, to deliver an address to the undergraduate literary society of what would later become Colby College. This address, which he called "The Method of Nature," was hardly the dry academic exercise anticipated for an occasion such as this. In it, he set out to elucidate for his young listeners what he called the "law and cause of nature"—and the term he repeatedly invoked to characterize that law was "ecstasy." "Nature," he proclaimed, "can only be conceived as existing to a universal and not to a particular end, to a universe of ends, and not to one,—a work of *ecstasy,* to be represented by a circular movement, as intention might be signified by a straight line of definite length" (CW.1.124–32).

As Emerson would have it, this ecstatically circular "method of nature" was a universal law of the natural world: ubiquitous, objective, and transpersonal. But if it was the essential law of nature, this was because it was the basic law of the spiritual reality upon which nature was everywhere founded. In his address Emerson prefaced his remarks by positing that "In the divine order, intellect is primary: nature, secondary"; so it naturally followed that the laws of nature must inevitably recapitulate the laws of spirit—the laws of mind. However that may be, the spiritual and psychological provenance of Emerson's conception of ecstasy was apparent in his address: the method of nature consisted, he explained, of "unbroken obedience," it was a kind of perpetual submission to the dictates of inrushing spirit (CW.1.124). Furthermore—and this was after all the rhetorical point of his address to the young would-be writers and scholars—the ecstatic self-sacrificial mechanism of nature was also the key to success in every conceivable field of human endeavor, whether of art, poetry, morality, oratory, or religion. Connecting as it did the intensely subjective sense of ecstasy dramatized by Wordsworth to the outer field of the natural world, Emerson's vision of ecstasy must have proved particularly beguiling to Thoreau. A passage such as the following, with its suggestive illustration of ravishing audition, seems especially pertinent to Thoreau's expression of ecstatic experience in the journal entry of 1851:

> That well-known voice speaks in all languages, governs all men, and none ever caught a glimpse of its form. If the man will exactly obey it, it will adopt him, so that he shall not any longer separate it from himself in his thought, he shall seem to be it, he shall be it. If he listen with insatiable ears, richer and greater wisdom is taught him, the sound swells to a ravishing music, he is borne away as with a flood, he becomes careless of his food and of his house, he is the drinker of ideas, and leads a heavenly life. But if his eye is set on the things to be done, and not on the truth that is still taught, and for the sake of which the things are to be done, then the voice grows faint, and at last is but a humming in his ears. His health and greatness consist in his being the channel through which heaven flows to earth, in short, in the fulness in which an ecstatical state takes place in him. (CW.1.130)

Yet despite Thoreau's considerable reliance upon Wordsworth and Emerson in the passage from the summer of 1851, there is no denying its personal urgency or significance. His readings of Wordsworth, Emerson, Milton, and other writers no doubt conditioned his understanding and evaluation of his youthful experiences, as they certainly had his language and style of presentation, but there can be no question that *something* of extraordinary moment lay behind this formulation and other later life recollections. "My life was extacy," he mourned in the passage from July 16, but in what did his ecstasy consist? To put the question more pointedly, if these early life experiences were really so earthshaking and consequential to Thoreau's later religious and artistic understanding, are they not reflected somewhere in Thoreau's earliest written records? And if so, how?

I Am from the Beginning

Prior to the fall of 1837, when Thoreau began keeping his journal, we have few documentary sources that offer us much help in answering these questions. We know that Thoreau loved to spend time outside, as did other members of his family, that he found much to occupy him in the countryside surrounding Concord. We know that during the summer before enrolling at Harvard, he spent long hours lolling about on Walden Pond in a boat of his own construction that he had dubbed "The Rover."[36] But reports of this sort shed little light on the kind of experiences he later recalled with such fervor. His college themes and essays also offer little more than circumstantial support. Written occasionally, mostly on assigned topics, these essays provide a useful index of Thoreau's intellectual formation and developing style, but they are not well suited as a barometer of his spirituality, often retaining the feel merely of college exercises. One of these, however, does offer some suggestive glimpses into Thoreau's emerging religious thought and temperament. The assignment for this essay was to examine the theory of the sublime propounded in Edmund Burke's influential essay "A Philosophical Enquiry into the Origin of Our Ideas of the Sublime and the Beautiful" as it had been illustrated in Susan Ferrier's novel *The Inheritance*.[37] The topic of "sublimity" obviously found an informed and receptive audience in Thoreau, and in his treatment of it he both affirms and revises several of Burke's key propositions. This subject evidently called forth a more impassioned response than normal from the twenty-year-old Thoreau, as his fervent final paragraph suggests:

> The emotion excited by the sublime is the most unearthly and god-like we mortals experience. It depends for the peculiar strength, with which it takes hold on, and occupies, the mind, upon a principle which lies at the foundation of that worship, which we

pay to the Creator himself. And is fear the foundation of that worship? Is fear the ruling principle of our religion? Is it not rather the mother of superstition? Yes, that principle which prompts us to pay an involuntary homage to the infinite, the incomprehensible, the sublime, forms the very basis of our religion. It is a principle implanted in us by our Maker, a part of our very selves, we cannot eradicate it, we cannot resist it; fear may be overcome, death may be despised, but the infinite, the sublime, seize upon the soul and disarm it. We may overlook them, or rather fall short of them, we may pass them by, but so sure as we meet them face to face, we yield. (EEM, 98–99)

For all the feeling of these lines, the views Thoreau espouses here, as in much of his college writing, still reflect the attitudes and values of a conventional Unitarian upbringing and the content of his Harvard reading lists. Thoreau approves much of what he finds in Burke's treatise but adamantly rejects fear as a valid source of the religious life. Sounding like a good Unitarian, Thoreau dismisses fear of the divine, seeing it rather as the basis of mere superstition, and elevates direct experience instead. Yet in Thoreau's insistence on the immanence of the divine principle, we also see an early sign of his sympathy with the new views being propounded by the young Unitarian reformers known as Transcendentalists. For these young American Romantics, as for their Anglo-European mentors and models, Kant had replaced Locke as the guiding philosophical preceptor of the age. The divine must be known inwardly before it could be recognized beyond. Thoreau's views here thus represent a melange of his reading of Burkean aesthetics, Transcendentalist philosophy, the New Testament, and the teachings of Harvard's Unitarian faculty. Yet he writes about the sublime here with obvious personal conviction and dramatizes the experience of the sublime as an overpowering, ecstatic encounter. As will become increasingly clear, this emphasis on experience, rather than faith or ideas, becomes a basic ingredient of Thoreau's mature religious consciousness.

The light shed on Thoreau's inner life by such college exercises is at best indirect. A more promising gauge is provided by the journals he began keeping soon after his graduation. How best to read the published versions of Thoreau's earliest journals is somewhat complicated, however, by the fact that what survives of the journal from 1837 till 1841 takes the form of transcriptions from original documents, now lost.[38] However selective the passages of the earliest journals may have been, read sequentially they suggest a narrative, of which Thoreau, as author and transcriber, was of course the chief architect. The first headed entry, "Solitude," establishes the meditative, self-reflexive character of Thoreau's approach to his journal in these early years: "To be alone I find it necessary to escape the present—I avoid myself. How could I be alone in the Roman emperor's chamber of mirrors? I seek a garret. The spiders must not be disturbed, nor the floor swept, nor the lumber arranged" (PJ.1.5). Throughout the rest of 1837 and into the following year, entries alternate between reflections on specific themes ("Spring," "How Man Grows," "Harmony") to literary responses and citations ("Ariosto," "Goethe," "Virgil," "Zeno," "Homer") to observations involving the surrounding countryside and season ("Ducks at Goose-Pond," "Sunrise," "Ponkawtassett," "Hoar Frost").

Into these journals, Thoreau also begins to transcribe copies of his poems, some finished, some as works in progress.[39] In his eulogy of Thoreau, Emerson noted somewhat cryptically that "his biography is in his verses," an observation that only really makes sense if we understand that Emerson is refering here to a "biography" of Thoreau's solitary life in nature. In fact, the context of Emerson's remark makes it clear that the biography he alluded to is mainly Thoreau's spiritual autobiography.[40] Coming from Emerson, it is a comment worth taking note of, and one that finds abundant support if we look to the poems Thoreau copied into his journals during the first several years he kept them. Many of the poems of this period, indeed, turn on some dramatic moment of inspiration or ecstasy. This is not, to be sure, true of all of the poems from these early years, nor would it be correct to say that poems of later periods entirely neglect such themes and devices. But it is fair to say that poems drafted into the journal between 1838 and 1840 often concern themselves centrally with the poetic representation of moments of natural euphoria or spiritual transport. Such poems as "The Bluebirds," "Walden," "Cliffs," "Thaw," "The Peal of Bells," and "The Fisher's Son," all written between 1837 and 1840, witness clearly and often successfully to Thoreau's preoccupation during this period with heightened spiritual perception and consciousness.[41] One of the most suggestive of these Thoreau drafted without title into his journal in the summer of 1839:

> Nature doth have her dawn each day,
> But mine are far between;
> Content, I cry, for sooth to say,
> Mine brightest are, I ween.
>
> For when my sun doth deign to rise,
> Though it be her noontide,
> Her fairest field in shadow lies,
> Nor can my light abide.
>
> Sometimes I bask me in her day,
> Conversing with my mate;
> But if we interchange one ray,
> Forthwith her heats abate.
>
> Through his discourse I climb and see,
> As from some eastern hill,
> A brighter morrow rise to me
> Than lieth in her skill.
>
> As 'twere two summer days in one,
> Two Sundays come together,
> Our rays united make one Sun,
> With fairest summer weather.
>
> (PJ.1.80–81)

Though obviously not among the most finished of Thoreau's poems, this fragment offers a bluff narrative of his inner life figured in the more or less transparent and universal symbolism of sun and dawn. It also anticipates the figurative doubleness that, as we will see, comes to be distinctive of Thoreau's religious imagination. Drawing upon an ancient grammar of religious symbolism, he juxtaposes the sun of this world with the "sun" of his own spiritual awareness. In moments of high inspiration, however, the interior sun all but eclipses the sun of the natural world. A more successful reprise of the same symbolic pattern occurs in a poem transcribed in 1841 and later included in *A Week* under the title "The Inward Morning." The last few stanzas are representative:

> I've heard within my inmost soul
> Such cheerful morning news,
> In the horizon of my mind
> Have seen such orient hues,
>
> As in the twilight of the dawn,
> When the first birds awake,
> Are heard within some silent wood,
> Where they the small twigs break,
>
> Or in the eastern skies are seen,
> Before the sun appears,
> The harbingers of summer heats
> Which from afar he bears.
>   (Week, 294–95; PJ.1.340–41)

Poems such as these offer some suggestive exhibits of religious feeling, especially when they are viewed together, but they cannot, of course, be read as simple professions of faith or transparent records of experience. More dependable—and revealing—are several prose passages Thoreau transcribed into his journal beginning in August of 1838. Here the artistic motives have clearly been subordinated to the more dominant concern with self-expression. Thoreau announces the first of these with the blunt heading of "Consciousness": "If with closed ears and eyes I consult consciousness for a moment—immediately are all walls and barriers dissipated—earth rolls from under me, and I float, by the impetus derived from the earth and the system—a subjective—heavily laden thought, in the midst of an unknown & infinite sea, or else heave and swell like a vast ocean of thought—without rock or headland. Where are all riddles solved, all straight lines making there their two ends to meet— eternity and space gambolling familiarly through my depths. I am from the beginning—knowing no end, no aim. No sun illumines me,—for I dissolve all lesser lights in my own intenser and steadier light—I am a restful kernel in the magazine of the universe" (PJ.1.50–51). This grand afflatus must surely rank among the more dramatic epiphanies in American literature. In its magisterial evocation of a kind of thoroughgoing subjective idealism, it represents the extreme antithesis of the blissful intermingling with nature noted in 1851. It is certainly an arresting passage—even in view of the few related poetic antecedents—billowing out as it does so unexpectedly among the more mundane journal entries of the period. As it is figured in the journal, the experience begins casually enough with the kind of sensory withdrawal we might associate with some forms of meditation or contemplative prayer. Thoreau re-directs his attention away from the channels of sight and hearing to consciousness in its pure, unmediated form. With the usual avenues of experience temporarily closed off to it, consciousness slips beyond the normal confines of the personal self and undergoes a series of rapid dilations before losing all vestiges of its individuality in a cognition of absolute, unbounded being. From the standpoint of this gnosis, con-sciousness witnesses eternity and space, the entire creation, "gambolling" like fishes in its own "depths." The oceanic experience depicted here is not what theologians would describe as mystical union, since there is no deity to unite with. We might rather characterize it as a kind of soul mysticism or pure consciousness, more reminiscent of the Upanishads than theistic Christian mysticism.

In some ways, the language of this passage exhibits traces of literary influences and conventions. It bears obvious comparison, for instance, with Emerson's famous epiphany on the bare common as he described it in *Nature*. These parallels are perhaps no accident, since we know that Thoreau read Emerson's book shortly after its publication in 1836. As in Emerson's book, here the narrator suddenly finds himself afloat on and

permeable to currents of universal consciousness. Each writer, furthermore, relies on the kind of dramatic self-predications or "I am" statements reminiscent of Christ's self-revelations in the Gospel according to
John, in order firmly to authorize the cognition of expanded identity.
Finally, both epiphanies conclude on comparable notes of closure, as in
Emerson's "I am part or particle of God," and Thoreau's "I am a restful
kernel in the magazine of the universe." At such points, Thoreau clearly
resorts to inherited literary strategies, as he must, in order to convey the
experience in words.

Yet, despite the literary echoes and borrowed rhetorical devices, this
passage also exhibits a number of anomalies distinguishing it not only
from Emerson's famous "crossing" passage in *Nature* but also from other
such literary epiphanies. It is at these points of departure from previous
literary or religious formulations that this passage may provide our best
glimpses into Thoreau's experience in its less mediated form. One of the
most curious features of the experience, as it is represented here, is the
oddly matter-of-fact, even mechanical way in which it begins. For all we
know Thoreau may as well have been sitting in his family's living room as
walking in the woods. He presents us with no special circumstances, no
highly charged spiritual or natural setting, in which to consider his
illumination. Rather he begins with the oddly flat-footed conditional
clause "If with closed ears and eyes I consult consciousness for a moment." In notable contrast to the epiphanies found in such classical
religious texts as the Bible and the Bhagavad Gita, there is no religious
fanfare here, no sense of great expectation; the experience depends indeed on nothing more ambitious than a deliberate closing of the sensory
channels of eyes and ears, and an attentive consultation of consciousness.

Also noteworthy is the passage's dynamic and ambiguous character.
To represent the newly discovered sense of bodily transcendence and
heady self-extension, Thoreau first chooses the ethereal vehicle of air.
According to this initial metaphor, the liberated self is likened to a kind
of air bubble, "a heavily laden thought" floating over the rolling earth.
But before he can complete the metaphoric proposition, he shifts to a

different register, comparing himself to a "vast ocean of thought," heaving and swelling "without rock or headland." We can read this metaphoric shift as a representation of the dynamic character of the experience itself, beginning with release and detachment from the physical world but leading quickly to an identification with and immersion in transcendental being. But Thoreau's use of the disjunctive conjunction "or" may also indicate a certain, not surprising, indeterminacy—the disjunction, that is, not only between one metaphor and the next, but also the disjunction between the experience as it had been subjectively apprehended and the experience as it was later recalled and verbally reconstructed.

Immediately following the passage cited above is another entry, apparently transcribed on the same day, headed simply "Resource." It obviously extends the previous passage, and in doing so gives us an idea of the religious uses to which Thoreau was inclined to put his experience of unmediated "consciousness": "Men are constantly dinging in my ears their fair theories and plausible solutions of the universe—but ever there is no help—and I return again to my shoreless—islandless ocean, and fathom unceasingly for a bottom that will hold an anchor, that it may not drag" (PJ.1.51). Here, in the developed figuration of fathoming and anchoring, the ocean metaphor obviously assumes literary importance for its own sake, thus superseding, and perhaps to a degree obscuring, the verbal indistinctness apparent in the earlier passage. Yet this metaphor itself now serves to "anchor" this experience for Thoreau in two important respects. First of all, by characterizing it in this way, he can now situate such experiences in contradistinction to a more general set of relevant attitudes and understandings. Specifically, he now comes to conceive this experience of unboundedness as a privileged alternative to other men's "fair theories and plausible solutions." Here, in a formative period in Thoreau's life, we see the emergence of a sharp distinction between experience and theory/belief that becomes absolutely fundamental to his religious self-understanding in later years. More importantly, the oceanic language he uses to depict his experience also serves as an effective vehicle of his own religious impulses of thought and feeling. Henceforth, a fleeting and gratuitous experience of pure "consciousness," such as the passage depicts, can now assume the more consequential status of a "resource" in his own more personal lexicon of religious language and ideas.

In the journal entries recorded in subsequent weeks and months, we meet with no passages quite so ornate or imposing as this epiphany entered on August 13, but there are several that seem related. The next spring, for example, Thoreau made the following entry under the heading "Drifting": "Drifting in a sultry day on the sluggish waters of the pond, I almost cease to live—and begin to be. A boat-man stretched on the deck of his craft, and dallying with the noon, would be as apt an emblem of eternity for me, as the serpent with his tail in his mouth. I am never so prone to lose my identity. I am dissolved in the haze" (PJ.1.69–70). At first glance, this evocation seems to have little in common with the description of unboundedness from the previous summer. Here Thoreau expresses an evaporation of the sense of self, where in the earlier formulation he waxes brighter than the sun. Comparison of the two passages points up several other obvious differences. Thoreau situates the experience described here, for example, within the concrete circumstances of boating on Walden Pond, whereas the earlier epiphany is almost wholly abstract, starkly removed from the objective world. The naturalistic setting of the experience described here increases its comprehensibility, and even its appeal. Most of us can, to some extent, appreciate an experience of revery on water.

But a closer reading also reveals some strong affinities between the two passages. This experience too is no mere revery, at least as far as Thoreau conceives it. Drifting across the Pond on sluggish waters leads to the further threshold of a crossing from mere living to pure being. The invocation here of the old philosophical dichotomy between being and becoming indicates how heavily invested these experiences of natural revery had become for him by this time. The boat-man acquires the status of a personal symbol to Thoreau equivalent to the circular symbol of the serpent eating its own tail. Both are symbols of eternity and thus recall the noetic vision of pure consciousness from the previous summer in which he speaks of "all straight lines making there their two ends to meet." The boating revery results, moreover, in the kind of self-transcendence he had described in such grand terms the previous year: "I am never so prone to lose my identity." We know that Thoreau had spent many warm afternoons on the Pond since at least 1833, but from this passage we can see that such meditative drifting served an important contemplative, as well as a merely recreational, function in his life.

With the passage of time, Thoreau was increasingly inclined to represent his meditative experiences in terms of natural observations, but they continued to center on these ecstatic episodes of self-transcendence and loss of ego. The following passage from the winter of 1841 is representative of this more characteristic form of meditative self-reflection: "The eaves are running on the south side of the house—The titmouse lisps in the poplar—the bells are ringing for the church—while the sun presides over all and makes his simple warmth more obvious than all else.—What shall I do with this hour so like time and yet so fit for eternity? Where in me are these russet patches of ground—and scattered logs and chips in the yard?—I do not feel cluttered.—I have some notion what the johnswort and life-everlasting may be thinking about—when the sun shines on me as on them—and turns my prompt thought—into just such a seething shimmer—I lie out indistinct as a heath at noon-day—I am evaporating airs ascending into the sun" (PJ.1.256). In one sense, this passage represents a complete reversal from the dramatic representation of a kind of subjective idealism considered above. There, all of matter, the creation itself, is subsumed in an ocean of consciousness; here, on the contrary, subjectivity is almost entirely subsumed in matter. This effort to represent ecstasy as a progressive identification of consciousness with natural forms can be seen early on in Thoreau's poetry and increasingly in all of his writing thereafter. The following fragment, for example, from an early poem entitled "Noon," anticipates not only the passage above but also some of Walt Whitman's most characteristic verse:

—Straightway dissolved,
Like to the morning mists—or rather like the subtler mists of
    noon—
Stretched I far up the neighboring mountains' sides,
Adown the valleys—through the nether air,
Bathing with fond expansiveness of soul,
The tiniest blade as the sublimest cloud.

(PJ.1.88)

As we will see more later, the tendency illustrated here to identify the self with the world of nature comes increasingly to characterize Thoreau's journalistic meditations. Eventually, questions like the one encountered above—"Where in me are these russet patches of ground—and scattered logs and chips in the yard?"—are no longer even asked and barely implied. Yet for Thoreau such passages continue to serve implicitly as meditations on time and eternity. More importantly, notwithstanding the shift from idealism to a kind of mindful naturalism, these journal entries are still designed to provide vivid depictions of the dissolution of the boundaries of the self—"I lie out indistinct as a heath at noon-day—I am evaporating airs ascending into the sun." Apparently, as far as Thoreau was concerned, both extrication from matter and total identification with it resulted in the same coveted objective—an ecstatic loss of self.

The written record does not permit us to get to the earliest sources of Thoreau's interest in the kind of self-evaporation and egolessness he dramatizes in these passages, but he would not have had to look far for outside sanction. New England religious culture had inculcated the virtues of self-denial from its beginnings, and the religious piety preached in some of the Unitarian pulpits known to Thoreau was no exception. Henry Ware Jr., Harvard's religious chaplain, was an exemplar of this piety of asceticism and self-denial.[42] Thoreau must have assimilated such teachings in the very air he breathed. By this point in his life, he had repudiated most Christian religious teachings, but the value of selflessness for the spiritual life he evidently did not. Indeed, it is one feature of New England religious culture that he carried with him into middle age.

Intermittently in his journals he expresses longing for solitude in terms that seem reminiscent of Christian world-weariness and renunciation: "I want to go soon and live away by the pond where I shall hear only the wind whispering among the reeds—It will be success if I shall have left my self behind, But my friends ask what I will do when I get there? Will it not be employment enough to watch the progress of the seasons?" (PJ.1.347). This is a pivotal passage for this reconstruction of Thoreau's spiritual development, since it points both forward and backward. It represents, on the one hand, one of the journal's first clear adumbrations of the Walden experiment and his later studied devotions to nature. At the same time, in its concern to leave the self behind, it recalls a motive apparent in the very first journal entry he transcribed—"To be alone I find it necessary to escape the present—I avoid myself" (PJ.1.5).

However we might diagnose the preoccupation with self-denial in Thoreau's journal, these passages suggest that it was becoming a defining feature both of his temperament and his religious self-understanding. Why he retained this feature of traditional piety when he rejected so much else would seem inexplicable unless we recognize what was for him a necessary link between ecstasy and egolessness. To judge from the various passages cited above, dissolution of the boundaries of the self attracted him because it accompanied the onset of ecstasy. In these early years, in fact, the sense of egolessness was a correlate of spiritual euphoria, not some cause or antecedent condition. If he longed to leave himself behind, as he said, he did so for the bliss that such self-abandonment entailed, not because of some allegiance to a church-worn piety for its own sake. Thoreau derived positive pleasures from ascetic practices themselves, as we shall see later, but these early expressions of self-abandonment were prompted by his thirst for the ecstasy with which they had previously been associated. In the selflessness he had heard preached, he found the boundlessness for which he now yearned.

The earliest episodes of ecstatic experience arose spontaneously, it seems, in the gratuitous style characteristic of youth, but their impact and significance for him was such that the rest of his spiritual and imaginative life soon began to coordinate itself around them. Increasingly, Thoreau was drawn to solitude for the opportunity it provided for closer scrutiny of these experiences and, if possible, for their further cultivation. Intimations of the boundlessness he had glimpsed now conditioned his artistic sensibilities as well. He was quite taken, for instance, by an illuminated picture he saw in the spring of 1839 depicting "an uninterrupted horizon bounding the desert." "I would see painted a boundless expanse of desert, prairie, or sea—" he remarked, "without other object than the horizon" (PJ.1.72). But the most important consequence of these ecstatic episodes was a deepening interest in meditative experience and the kind of personal discipline and daily regimen that would best support it. Solitude for him was not an end in itself but a means to cultivate the inconstant experiences of his youth. During the day, the woods and fields offered the privacy he needed to pursue his subjective researches; at home, he could retreat to his attic garret (PJ.1.5, 121). What he sought in either case was the silence necessary for contemplative refinement: "Our limbs indeed have room enough but it is our souls that rust in a corner. Let us migrate interiorly without intermission, and pitch our tent each day nearer the western horizon—The really fertile soils and luxuriant prairies lie on this side of the Aleghanies—" (PJ.1.119–20).

Formulations such as this may be found throughout much of Thoreau's writing during the 1840s. Critics have a way of glossing over such references or reading them simply as metaphoric representations of a philosophical character. But to be fully understood they must be related to the ecstatic experience that had made such powerful claims upon him. Thoreau resorted to contemplative experience as a deliberate way of accommodating experiences and intuitions that would otherwise have remained simply ephemeral and adventitious. What is more, he conceived these experiences and their formulations as related to and governed by motives that can only be characterized in the broad sense as religious: "I shall never be poor," he wrote in 1841, "while I can command a still hour in which to take leave of my sin" (PJ.1.266). Thoreau's interest in the deliberate cultivation of meditative experience by the early 1840s indicates how significant the episodes of ecstasy had been for him, but it also suggests that they were no longer the spontaneous experiences they once had been. As late as 1837, it was enough for Thoreau merely to "consult" consciousness in order to precipitate an experience of unboundedness; by 1841 he had begun actively shaping and directing his outer life in order to better enable such experiences. Meditative silence now became the best means to enhance the condition of selflessness necessary for successful contemplation:

> When I detect a beauty in any of the recesses of nature, I am reminded by the serene and retired spirit in which it requires to be contemplated, of the inexpressible privacy of a life—How silent and unambitious it is—The beauty there is in mosses will have to be considered from the holiest—quietest nook.
>
> The gods delight in stillness, they say 'st—'st. My truest—serenest moments are too still for emotion—they have woolen feet.—In all our lives we live under the hill, and if we are not gone we live there still. (PJ.1.230)

Whatever the origins of Thoreau's early experiences of ecstasy, they are facts to be reckoned with in any complete study of Thoreau's life and writing. Giving them their due recognition is necessary if we are to avoid some of the usual misapprehensions of Thoreau's life. His detractors have sometimes accused him of misanthropy, for example, and construed his penchant for solitude as a reaction to his dislike of human society. Thoreau had his crotchets and foibles, to be sure, but this explanation for his retreat to the woods is one-sided and distorts the true picture. A fuller reading of his life shows, first of all, that he was not essentially antisocial at all; neither was he misanthropic. As we have seen earlier, he held friendship and certain friends in the utmost regard. He does at points speak dismissively of having human companions on his nature walks, but this is because they often proved distracting to his own vital concerns. Thoreau went to the woods "to transact some private business," as he famously put it in *Walden,* not to avoid company (19–20). Such "business" was private because it had to be, and unless we acknowledge its centrality in Thoreau's life, we are bound to misconceive him.

Two

A Clear and Ancient Harmony

The remarkable epiphany of consciousness Thoreau recorded in the summer of 1838 offers a dramatic touchstone of the condition of egoless self-transparency that was to become an essential feature of his subsequent spiritual aspirations and religious imagination, but it is important to recognize how uncharacteristic it is of his later religious reflections. The kind of overt transcendentalism exemplified by this charged representation of oceanic consciousness is certainly reminiscent of early Emerson and Carlyle, but it had little to do with Thoreau's own mature evocations. By the early 1840s, as we have seen, Thoreau had all but eschewed such representations of disembodied being, preferring instead to depict his episodes of inspiration consistently in the terms offered by natural forms and phenomena. Neither Emerson's ungainly hierophany of the transparent eyeball nor his own afflatus of oceanic being would ever again seem fully cogent to him. We will examine the ramifications of this shift from an early advocacy of transcendental idealism to his more characteristic transcendental naturalism more carefully when we turn to the later journals. Even as early as 1841, Thoreau could no longer fully credit a representation that conceived ecstasy occurring in some subjective hollow of the natural world. But the epiphany of 1838 is also uncharacteristic in another crucial respect. There, access to being resulted from closing off the channels of eyes and ears, in a manner reminiscent of the sensory purgation of some ascetic practices. Yet nothing could be more atypical of the vast majority of ecstatic episodes Thoreau cites in his journal. In these instances, on the contrary, heightened sensory experience itself serves as the usual gateway to moments of spiritual euphoria. Throughout most of his life, in fact, sensory experience was not the deterrent to spiritual awakening it has often been seen to be in some traditional understandings of mystical experience, but rather its principal catalyst.

A Purely Sensuous Life

Thoreau, of course, specifically acknowledges the indispensable role of the senses in his childhood moods of transport in the fervently elegiac passage discussed previously from the summer of 1851. There he speaks of the diminution of sensory awareness as one might speak of the amputation of a leg or the death of a lover: "In youth before I lost any of my senses—I can remember that I was all alive—and inhabited my body with inexpressible satisfaction, both its weariness & its refreshment were sweet to me. This earth was the most glorious musical instrument, and I was audience to its strains. To have such sweet impressions made on us— such extacies begotten of the breezes" (PJ.3.305–6). The experiences alluded to here are clearly sensory ones, at least in part. They take place within the arena of the senses and are mediated by them. To this extent, they are comprehensible to anyone who has known the fresh exhilarations of youthful life. Thoreau, however, appears to have experienced them in greater measure, or at least treasured them with more telling concern. Notwithstanding Thoreau's reputation (partly deserved) as an abstemious prude, there is hardly a greater sensualist—in the strict sense of that term—among American canonical writers. Whitman is the obvious exception, of course, but Thoreau's surprisingly warm response to his first reading of *Leaves of Grass* suggests that he found in Whitman a kindred spirit, and this shared interest in ecstatic experience is perhaps one reason for this (Correspondence, 441–42, 444–45). Indeed, there are passages in the journal when Thoreau comes across as a kind of voluptuary of nature, immersing himself for long hours, over many days, in the pleasures of his sensory contacts with the natural world. At points, even in his later journals, we find him reeling with delight for the natural world: "The strains of the aeolian harp and of the wood thrush are the truest and loftiest preachers that I know now left on this earth. I know of no missionaries to us heathen comparable to them. They, as it were, lift us up in spite of ourselves. They intoxicate, they charm us. Where was that strain mixed into which this world was dropped but as a lump of sugar to sweeten the draught? I would be drunk, drunk, drunk, dead drunk to this world with it forever. He that hath ears, let him hear. The contact of sound with a human ear whose hearing is pure and unimpaired is coincident with an ecstasy" (J.6.39). Of course, we must understand the above, admittedly hyperbolic, characterization of Thoreau's sensuality in the restricted sense in which it pertains here.[1] Thoreau was, as far as anyone has been able to discern, a lifelong celibate. There is no evidence that the sensuousness widely evident in the journal ever admitted of overt sexual expression: as far as his own attitudes toward sexual relations were concerned, he was at heart a staunch Victorian.

It is difficult to say how Thoreau's celibacy might have influenced his sensory experience, but there is certainly no reason to think of it as dulling. On the contrary, it may have served to redirect and enliven his already prodigious sensory capacities. In any case, no reader of the journal can long doubt that Thoreau was endowed with unusual sensory acuteness, particularly of sight, sound, and smell. Sometimes, indeed, he seemed to surprise himself with his extraordinary sensory prowess, as on the Sunday afternoon one July when he smelled "the clear pork frying for a farmer's supper 30 rods off," or when, on a walk in May, he became "intoxicated with the slight spicy odor of the hickory buds—& the bruised bark of the black birch" (PJ.3.327, 68). He noticed how walking at night would activate his senses of hearing and smell. Moving over the countryside in moonlight, he was guided partly by his sense of smell, and noted how "Every plant and field and forest emits its odor now, swamp-pink in the meadow and tansy in the road; and there is the peculiar dry scent of corn which has begun to show its tassels" (Excursions, 328). He especially loved Indian summer, when "all nature is a dried herb. full of yielding medicinal odors" (PJ.4.138). Such disparate experiences of heightened sensation point to an underlying condition of heightened sensory receptivity that seems to have been almost habitual for him. At times, sensation from one sensory channel would overflow into the next, producing experiences—like this one from the "Solitude" chapter of *Walden*—of exquisite synesthesia: "This is a delicious evening, when the whole body is one sense, and imbibes delight through every pore" (129).

We may read such descriptions in a merely figurative way, if we wish, but it is hard to ignore the central role played by the senses in Thoreau's writings, not only in the more innocently autobiographical passages of the journal, but also in passages conveying heavier theological and philo-sophical freight. To him the senses were as much organs of speculative wisdom as channels of perception, a fact often underscored by his fre-quent puns and wordplay. "It is not every truth that recommends itself to the common sense," he noted ruefully in "Walking," in a satiric jibe at what he sometimes considered the principal idolatry of his Yankee neighbors. In addition to the "common" senses, there were higher senses, he elsewhere speculated, "well fitted to penetrate the spaces of the real, the substantial, the eternal, as these outward are to penetrate the material universe." In this section from the final chapter of *A Week,* Thoreau proposes a distinction between common and uncommon sense that seems quite suggestive in this context:

There are perturbations in our orbits produced by the influence of outlying spheres, and no astronomer has ever yet calculated the elements of that undiscovered world which produces them. I per-ceive in the common train of my thoughts a natural and uninter-rupted sequence, each implying the next, or, if interruption occurs it is occasioned by a new object being presented to my *senses.* But a steep, and sudden, and by these means unaccountable transition, is that from a comparatively narrow and partial, what is called com-mon sense view of things, to an infinitely expanded and liberating one, from seeing things as men describe them, to seeing them as men cannot describe them. This implies a sense which is not common, but rare in the wisest man's experience; which is sensible or sentient of more than common. (386)

Evidently informing this distinction between common and uncommon sense was the influential Romantic doctrine of the creative imagination and, more specifically, the Coleridgean distinction between fancy and the imagination.[2] Emerson had conceived of the imagination as an exalted form of "vision," and Thoreau seems to have something similar in mind here.[3] Yet in important ways this formulation also echoes some of the descriptions of his own experience we have considered previously. The vertiginous transition from a "narrow and partial" defile to "an infinitely expanded and liberating" vision of things reminds us, for example, of the epiphany of 1838. More to the point, his insistence on conceiving this faculty of speculative vision as one definitively of "sense" suggests his own experientially grounded affirmation of sense experience. Indeed, it is wholly characteristic of Thoreau that such an expanded vision should have been precipitated by a catalyst he would designate only as that of sense.

Throughout this concluding section of *A Week*, the fully extended senses assume nothing less than a soteriological function; they are the "divine germs" on which our future salvation depends. For Thoreau the "way of salvation" led not through a labyrinth of gracious acts and repentant responses, but by way of a cleansed and rarefied natural sense:

We need pray for no higher heaven than the pure senses can furnish, a *purely* sensuous life. Our present senses are but the rudiments of what they are destined to become. We are comparatively deaf and dumb and blind, and without smell or taste or feeling. Every generation makes the discovery, that its divine vigor has been dissipated, and each sense and faculty misapplied and debauched. The ears were made, not for such trivial uses as men are wont to suppose, but to hear celestial sounds. The eyes were not made for such grovelling uses as they are now put to and worn out by, but to behold beauty now invisible. May we not *see* God? Are we to be put off and amused in this life, as it were with a mere

allegory? Is not Nature, rightly read, that of which she is commonly taken to be the symbol merely? (382)

The audacity of this passage is likely to be lost on us today. Not only
would such a claim, were its conditions fulfilled, place the gratified seer
beyond the realm of all but the most exalted biblical personalities, it also
smacks of an Arminianism that even the most progressive Unitarian of
Thoreau's day would have abhorred. In all such treatments, senses serve
as the conduits to nature's wider community of being. They tend both
outwardly and inwardly to a field of consciousness outside the confines
of the individual self. They liberate the seeker from solipsism and psychological isolation. In the meditation on solitude in *Walden,* for example, it is the senses that rescue the narrator from a momentary "insanity"
of separation: "There can be no very black melancholy to him who lives
in the midst of Nature and has his senses still" (131). The obvious point
here is the importance of retaining the senses in good order, but as with
similar formulations, it invites an alternative construction: one should of
course keep one's senses but one should also keep them "still." According
to this second reading, to "still" the senses—as in the case of the profi-
cient meditator perhaps—is the best way to keep them. Thoreau of
course enjoys this sort of wordplay, but as is often the case with his puns,
we find something important at stake in the implied distinction between
a merely "common" sense and this stilled sense, or what in the following
passage he designates as "sound" sense: "But there is only necessary a
moment's sanity and sound senses, to teach us that there is a nature
behind the ordinary, in which we have only some vague preëmption
right and western reserve as yet. We live on the outskirts of that region"
(Week, 383).

The Voice of the Wood

It is no accident that Thoreau resorts to an auditory pun here since, of all
the senses, hearing was for him the most expeditious messenger from
such regions beyond the ordinary: "So many autumn, ay, and winter
days, spent outside the town, trying to hear what was in the wind, to hear

and carry it express!" (Walden, 17). Coming as it does shortly after the narrator's caveat about his own "obscurities" in the early pages of *Walden,* this passage is apt to be read as a kind of fanciful conceit, but readers of the journal will recognize that it reflects an underlying biographical fact. Thoreau, it seems, was endowed with an almost preternaturally acute sense of hearing. Long passages in the journal testify to a kind of acoustic delight he experienced on his daily walks as he listened attentively to various natural sounds. A hound baying distantly in the night, the faint creaking of crickets, the trill of a tree sparrow after a shower, the distant lowing of a cow: all these sounds and many more were apt to throw him into raptures of auditory pleasure.[4] Such impressions also frequently led to some of the most revealing reflections in his journal, as in the following entry, inspired simply by "a man blowing a horn this still evening": "It is a strangely healthy sound for these disjointed times.—It is a rare soundness when cow-bells and horns are heard from over the fields— And now I see the beauty and full meaning of that word sound. Nature always possesses a certain sonorousness, as in the hum of insects—the booming of ice—the crowing of cocks in the morning and the barking of dogs in the night—which indicates her sound state. God's voice is but a clear bell sound. I drink in a wonderful health—a cordial—in sound. The effect of the slightest tinkling in the horizon measures my own soundness. I thank God for sound it always mounts, and makes me mount" (PJ.1.277). In opening up his favorite auditory pun, Thoreau makes explicit the deeper connection he senses between "sound" health and healthy "sound." His play on the adjectival and substantive meanings of the word serves to identify health with the canopy of natural sound. To be "sound" is of course to be in the enjoyment of health, of wholeness. Yet most of us experience only partial health, just as we experience only a finite range of sound. For Thoreau, by contrast, natural sounds were the harbingers of physical and psychic wholeness. They were advertisements of wider health, nature's "sound state." The sounds he heard in nature were never isolated noises but rather local perturbations of an omnipresent silent field. In the chambers of clarified sense, he claimed to hear nature's omnipresent silence amplified. Sounds alerted Thoreau to the silence underlying them. This was wholeness, he thought, this was "health": "All sound is nearly akin to Silence—it is a bubble on her surface which straightway bursts—an emblem of the strength and pro- lifickness of the undercurrent.—It is a faint utterance of Silence—and then only agreeable to our auditory nerves—when it contrasts itself with the former. In proportion as it does this—and is a heightener and inten- sifier of the Silence—it is harmony and purest melody" (PJ.1.61–62). Unless we recognize this deeper resonance of sound for Thoreau, the ubiquitous references to auditory experience in the journal may strike us as self-indulgent, an odd glut of personal gratification. It was as if all sensory experience propagated itself in some finer sense-field beyond its own. "All sights and sounds," he wrote, "are seen and heard both in time and eternity. And when the eternity of any sight or sound strikes the eye or ear—they are intoxicated with delight" (PJ.1.400).

In such reflections on Thoreau's frequent experiences of acoustic rap- ture, we see manifestations of the doubleness characteristic of Thoreau's mature ecstatic vision. Ecstasy results when a single impression overflows its own natural borders and propagates itself through a wider arena of consciousness, beyond time, beyond location. The coincidence of sound "both in time and eternity" also supplies Thoreau with broad license for his ever-active wordplay. Deciphering some of what we might term his ecstatic puns amounts to a dizzying ecstatic meditation itself, as in this passage from his late essay "Walking": "There are some intervals which border the strain of the wood-thrush, to which I would migrate,—wild lands where no settler has squatted; to which, methinks, I am already acclimated" (Writings.5.225).[6] Full appreciation of the ambiguities of this passage depends on our recognition of the competing senses available in the word "interval." In Thoreau's time, the word had both a definite spatial and temporal sense. In addition to its other meanings, interval (or intervale, as it was also spelled) was the word used in New England to designate any tract of low-lying land, especially along a river. This mean- ing serves as the vehicle of Thoreau's complex metaphor here, but in locating this "interval" next to the song of a wood-thrush, he draws on its musical meaning—one more familiar to us—as the difference in pitch between two notes. The incomprehensible identification between these two incommensurable intervals, this collision between a temporal and a spatial location, he then uses as a further metaphoric vehicle for the transcendent "place" to which he would be transported in his moments of acoustically triggered ecstasy. There will be further opportunity in a later chapter to examine some of the reasons underlying Thoreau's well-known penchant for such puns and double entendres, but this formulation serves notice of how deeply implicated they are in his religious thought more generally. Thoreau admired literary extravagance in general; as he boasts to us in *Walden,* he almost instinctively sought out verbal constructions to which his meaning could never be wholly confined (324). But an ambiguous construction, one that pointed in two directions at once, seemed especially apt for his purpose.

Thoreau's fascination with literary duplicity finds an analogue in his continual preoccupation with multifarious expressions of natural mimesis. In the structure of a leaf, the rings of a tree, or reflections on water, he everywhere saw the expressions of nature's basic law of self-duplication. But in echoes he found its purest embodiment. Drifting on the Pond, he liked to strike his paddle against his gunwales to waken the echo of the woods: "Of what significance is any sound if Nature does not echo it," he wrote in 1850. "It does not prevail. It dies away as soon as uttered. I wonder that wild men have not made more of echoes, or that we do not hear that they have made more. It would be a pleasant a soothing & cheerful mission to go about the country in search of them—articulating—speaking vocal—oracular—resounding—sonorous—hollow—prophetic places—places where in to found an oracle—sites for oracles—sacred—ears of nature—" (PJ.3.129). Proceeding from nature's unspoken depths, echoes thus had a numinous character for Thoreau. Some sounds produced echoes more effectively than others, and these, he thought, had a "double virtue" (PJ.1.320). They incited him to speculate on the deeper significance of the mimetic properties of nature.

In such meditations on the echo, Thoreau introduces a curious fiction: "The echo is, to some extent, an original sound, and therein is the magic and charm of it. It is not merely a repetition . . . but partly the voice of the wood; the same trivial words and notes sung by a wood-nymph" (Walden, 123).[7] Echoes from his flute were not so much a copy of the original melody as "an amended strain," a sound "corrected and repronounced" by nature itself (PJ.2.167). With such assertions of the "original" status of the echo, Thoreau flouts the facts of physics, of course, and he also revises the classical myth to which he often implicitly refers. As Ovid retells it, the story of Echo is actually a story of crime and punishment. To punish Echo for her complicity in Zeus's womanizing, Hera takes away her ability to speak for herself. Once a mischievous and full-bodied nymph of the forest, Echo is thus reduced in the end to a disembodied voice, the inhabitant of mountain recesses, a mere "echo" of her former self. She can repeat anything that is said to her but say nothing of her own accord. The distinguishing feature of an echo, from the standpoint of the myth then, is its self-dispossession, the *loss* of originality.

Why it is that Thoreau contradicts both ancient and modern authorities in this regard becomes more clear when we realize that in his own experience, the echo's virtue lay in its revelation of the unsounded silence behind it. Echo gives vivid expression to the background silence from which all sound arises. This is where the "originality" comes from. It goes from us human and flawed, but returns to us perfect and divine: "Though it [is] the lumberer that wakes the echoes, still they are the everlasting and natural echoes that are waked. The immense unseen background which reflects the sound is as primitive as ever" (PJ.1.445). From this standpoint, the relation between sound and echo could be dialogical, even revelatory, rather than strictly mimetic:

> I am surprised that we make no more ado about echoes—They are almost the only kindred voices that I hear. I wonder that the traveller does not oftener remark upon a remarkable echo—he who observes so many things.
>
> There needs some actual doubleness like this in Nature for if the voices which we commonly hear were all that we ever heard—What then? . . .

It was the memorable event of the day, that echo I heard—not any thing my companions said—or the travellers whom I met—or my thoughts—for they were all mere repetitions or echoes in the worst sense—of what I heard & thought before many times—but this echo was accompanied with novelty—& by its repetition of my voice it did more than double that It was a profounder socratic method of suggesting thoughts unutterable to me the speaker— There was one I heartily loved to talk with—Under such favorable auspices I could converse with myself—could reflect—the hour the atmosphere & the conformation of the ground permitted it. (PJ.5.466–67)[8]

The same sort of speculation that Thoreau used to rationalize his fascination with echoes tended also to coalesce around his enjoyment of any distant sounds. "Occasionally I hear a remote sound with so unprejudiced a sense," he wrote in his journal, "far sweet and significant—that I seem for the first time to have heard at all. It has a larger meaning and a wider undulation than I knew" (PJ.1.90). Such early reflections on the aesthetic effects of far-off sounds draw somewhat self-consciously upon the common Romantic theme of auditory distancing. Already by the late eighteenth century, Novalis had located the imaginative appropriation of distance at the heart of Romantic sensibility: "Alles wird in Entfernung Poesie: ferne Berne, ferne Menschen, ferne Begebenheit. Alles wird romantisch" [Everything in the distance will be poetry: faraway hills, faraway people, faraway events. Everything will be romantic].[9] In England the theme also found expression in the landscape poetry of the late eighteenth century. Not surprisingly, Thoreau's appropriation of the motifs associated with this convention may well have owed much to his early reading of Wordsworth, who also made much in his poetry of the "sweet" impressions of far-off sounds.[10] Yet, as in the case of his appropriation of Wordsworth's elegiac mood, so here, Thoreau alters the convention in idiosyncratic ways, even as he takes it up. "Music in proportion as it is pure is distant," he wrote in 1840. "The strains I now hear seem at an inconceivable distance, yet remotely within me. Remotes throws all sound into my inmost being and it becomes music, as the slumbrous sounds of the village, or the tinkling of the forge—from across the water or the fields. To the senses that is farthest from me which addresses the greatest depth within me" (PJ.1.199). In this recondite conversion of outermost sound to innermost reality we see once again the duplicative operation of Thoreau's religious imagination. Just as the echo elicited a meaningful discourse with silence, here he envisions an occult dialogue between outer sounds and silent depths, only now the silence is located within the auditor himself.

Celestial Airs

We do not need to wade far into the journal to recognize that Thoreau cultivated his experience of natural sound the way some of us cultivate our appreciation of music. But music too he loved, and although he had no formal musical training, he seems to have had a remarkable musical sensitivity. Even the humblest musical expressions he often found completely beguiling. A music box, received as a gift from Margaret Fuller's younger brother Richard, charmed him for many years.[11] During long evenings of study in his garret, he was often soothed by the sounds of his sister's piano from the parlor below. Sherman Paul, in particular, offers a searching assessment of Thoreau's peculiar susceptibility to music and natural sound, bringing to light the significance of these experiences for our understanding of his inner life.[12] The familiar scenes of Thoreau playing his flute on the Pond and lulling the creatures like some latter-day Orpheus are the stuff of literary myth-making, to be sure, but they have a basis in his biography: "I sit in my boat on walden—playing the flute this evening—and see the perch, which I seem to have charmed, hovering around me—and the moon travelling over the ribbed bottom— and feel that nothing but the wildest imagination can conceive of the manner of life we are living" (PJ.1.311).[13] By the time he actually took up residence at Walden in 1845, he had begun conceiving this practice explicitly in meditative terms reminiscent of the experiences of un-boundedness cited above from 1838: "When I play my flute tonight earnest as if to leap the bounds that narrow fold where human life is penned, and range the surrounding plain—I hear echo from a neighboring wood a stolen pleasure occasionally not rightfully heard—much more for other ears than ours for tis the reverse of sound. It is not our own melody that comes back to us—but an amended strain. And I would only hear myself as I would hear my echo—corrected and repronounced for me" (PJ.2.167).

We may remember that in the passage of impassioned regret for lost youth recorded in the summer of 1851, Thoreau especially mourned his loss of the early vitality of sensory experience. "This earth," he wrote, "was the most glorious musical instrument, and I was audience to its strains." He had been "daily intoxicated" and "marched as to a music in comparison with which the military music of the streets [was] noise & discord" (PJ.3.306). As with several of the other motifs in this passage, his association of his ecstatic experiences with music also owed something to the influence of Wordsworth. Indeed, the earliest recorded reference in the journal to Wordsworth's Immortality Ode makes this indebtedness clear: "There is all the romance of my youthfullest moment in music. Heaven lies about us in our infancy. There is nothing so wild and extravagant that it does not make true. It makes a dream my only real experience, and prompts faith to such elasticity, that only the incredible can satisfy it. It tells me again to trust the remotest, and finest, as the divinest instinct. All that I have imagined of heroism, it reminds and reassures me of. It is a life unlived, a life beyond life, where at length my years will pass. I look under the lids of Time" (PJ.1.242).

It should be noted here in passing that when examined in sufficient depth, key elements of Thoreau's interior life exhibit a marked tendency to cluster together around a common center of religious meaning. By a kind of associational logic or imaginative sympathy, one element in this cluster often connotes or calls up the rest. Analyzing this complex is a little like trying to disentangle a single thread from a densely woven tapestry: sooner or later, each thread intertwines with each of the others. An expository treatment such as this one is thus faced with a couple of serious challenges: it is impossible, first of all, to do justice to the human complexity of these associations, and moreover, any single approach to unraveling the complex must seem to some extent arbitrary. Analysis of Thoreau's appropriation of the themes he associated with his childhood raptures exemplifies these difficulties but also holds out promise for understanding him better when the elements of this complex can be identified. In considering Thoreau's responses to music, in particular, we find ourselves very near the heart of this complex of religious meaning.

In the passage above, for example, with the convergence of the themes of music, Wordsworthian elegy, heroism, and transcendentalist idealism, we see the emergence of several of the crucial associational links in this imaginative complex. Henceforth, experiences of music habitually assume an elegiac character, evoking a mood of regretful loss for the pristine experiences of the past. Melodies bursting forth from his freshly wound music box reminded him of a pent-up medieval fountain. "Music is strangely allied to the past—" he averred, "every era has its strain. It awakens and colors my memories" (PJ.1.469). Late in life, in the gathering overcast of middle age, Thoreau wrote as though music were the last remaining guarantor of beatitude glimpsed in youth. The following poem, entitled "Music," provides one of our most revealing portraits of the elegiac Thoreau of later years:

> Far from this atmosphere that music sounds
> Bursting some azure chink in the dull clouds
> Of sense that overarch my recent years
> And steal his freshness from the noonday sun.
> Ah, I have wandered many ways and lost
> The boyant step, the whole responsive life
> That stood with joy to hear what seemed then
> Its echo, its own harmony borne back
> Upon its ear. This tells of better space,
> Far far beyond the hills the woods the clouds
> That bound my low and plodding valley life,
> Far from my sin, remote from my distrust,
> When first my healthy morning life perchance
> Trod lightly as on clouds, and not as yet

My weary and faint hearted noon had sunk
Upon the clod while the bright day went by.
    Lately, I feared my life was empty, now
I know though a frail tenement that it still
Is worth repair, if yet its hollowness
Doth entertain so fine a guest within, and through
Its empty aisles there still doth ring
Though but the echo of so high a strain;
It shall be swept again and cleansed from sin
To be a thoroughfare for celestial airs;
Perchance the God who is proprietor
Will pity take on his poor tenant here
And countenance his efforts to improve
His property and make it worthy to revert,
At some late day Unto himself again.

(Poems, 223)

To those who would claim that Thoreau had become a disillusioned materialist in his later years, this poem must come as a sharp refutation. In sensibility and style, it is reminiscent of nothing so much as the metaphysical school exemplied by Herbert and Donne. No doubt the strikingly pervasive religious language here serves mainly the formal purposes of the poem's central conceit, but it nevertheless dramatizes what was for Thoreau the essentially religious significance of his late-life feelings of loss and their by then profound association with music. By the time he composed this poem, he seems to have been painfully sensible of the limits imposed on his former experiences by an aging physiology, but he never loses hope in the possibility of their imminent restoration.

Of the various sounds that Thoreau encountered on his daily excursions throughout the Concord countryside, nothing so fascinated him as the ethereal tones emitted by a recently installed telegraph wire linking Boston and Burlington. In late August of 1851, he came upon a party of workers erecting the fixtures for the new line, and notwithstanding the general excitement with which the invention had been greeted, his own response was dismissive: "It seems not so wonderful an invention as a common cart or a plow," he quipped (PJ.4.16, 28). Yet when he passed under the new wire on one of his walks, a few days after the line first went into operation, he was quite taken with what he experienced: "As I went under the new telegraph wire I heard it vibrating like a harp high over head.—it was as the sound of a far off glorious life a supernal life which came down to us.—and vibrated the lattice work of this life of ours" (PJ.4.35). It is clear that by the following fall, experiences evoked by this unexpected stimulus were finding a place within the larger context of his religious experience: "As I was entering the Dep Cut the wind which was conveying a message to me from heaven dropt it on the wire of the telegraph which it vibrated as it past. I instantly sat down on a stone at the foot of the telegraph pole—& attended to the communication. It merely said 'Bear in mind, Child—& never for an instant forget—that there are higher plains infinitely higher plains of life than this thou art now travelling on. Know that the goal is distant & is upward and is worthy all your life's efforts to attain to.' And then it ceased and though I sat some minutes longer I heard nothing more" (PJ.4.76).[14] In subsequent times, Thoreau typically approached the telegraph as if it were a kind of oracle in the woods. So taken was he with the unearthly music resonating from the telegraph that his journal entry of the day's observations was frequently given over to his efforts to describe and explain the feelings to which it gave rise. To him the telegraph wire was a kind of newfangled Aeolian harp brushed by the morning winds and evoking feelings of exquisite pleasure.[15] It served merely to amplify the otherwise silent, omnipresent music of the earth itself, sounds in the air he had always sensed just beyond earshot (PJ.1.365). In *Walden,* he noted how distant sound "acquires a certain vibratory hum, as if the pine needles in the horizon were the strings of a harp which it swept." This silent, subsenuous hum was the "vibration of the universal lyre," he said (123). During the elegiac summer of 1851, he was particularly sensitized to nature's music: "There is always a kind of fine Aeolian harp music to be heard in the air—I hear now as it were the mellow sound of distant horns in the hollow mansions of the upper air—a sound to make all men divinely insane that hear it—far away over head subsiding into my ear. To ears that are expanded what a harp this world is!" (PJ.3.323). The experiences of auditory rapture occasioned by the telegraph wire also served to remind him of the full-blown ecstasies of his childhood, when all experiences was apprehended as music, when "this earth was the most glorious instrument, and I was audience to its strains" (PJ.3.305–06). This "telegraph harp," as he often referred to it, thus put him in touch once again with a reality that had begun to elude him in his later life.

The language of these musings on natural music makes clear how much these passages owed to Thoreau's understanding and elaboration of the classical notion of the music of the spheres, to which he makes frequent reference even in his earliest journals.[16] In *A Week*, Thoreau cited Jamblichus's description of Pythagoras, who "employing a certain ineffable divinity, . . . extended his ears and fixed his intellect in the sublime symphonies of the world, he alone hearing and understanding, as it appears, the universal harmony and consonance of the spheres, and the stars that are moved through them, and which produce a fuller and more intense melody than anything effected by mortal sounds" (176). Thoreau had obviously found much to ponder in Jamblichus's account of Pythagoras's life and in the annotations that Thomas Taylor, its English editor, included in his translation.[17] Pythagoras abstained from meat and wine, preached a stern regimen of bodily asceticism, and counseled his disciples to seek out solitude so as to better support their philosophical meditations—all teachings that Thoreau would obviously have taken very much to heart. Pythagoras also taught an esoteric doctrine of preexistence and rebirth that had important repercussions even in some later European attitudes. Wordsworth's reflections on preexistence in the Immortality Ode presuppose something of the teachings of the Pythagoreans and Neoplatonists, as did Thoreau's own response to Wordsworth in the elegiac formulation of 1851.[18] Even more momentous for Thoreau, perhaps, was his discovery of the indispensable role played by music in Pythagorean philosophy. According to an ancient commentary cited by Taylor, most Pythagoreans deduced the existence of the harmonies of the spheres on the analogy of ratios believed to exist between their astronomical intervals.[19] Tradition maintained, however, that Pythagoras heard them directly himself and, inspired by their ineffable beauty, fashioned a curriculum for his academy in which music, together with mathematics, played a central role. Central to his teaching was the belief that music could be used directly to purify the soul of the aspiring philosopher. Accordingly, music was played in the Pythagorean Academy both before bed and upon rising, to better cultivate mind and body.

Thoreau must have found the Pythagorean curriculum quite intriguing, since he had certainly experienced the transformative potential of music. Although he enjoyed singing and dancing as forms of amusement, music had a deeper interest for him. It was, he thought, a kind of "natural language," through which all people of a certain level of refinement might someday communicate (PJ.1.165). Even in its recreational forms, it could lift us up; in its finer forms, it revealed to us our higher destinies. But in Thoreau's experience, sphere music need not remain the province of a few rarefied souls from antiquity; it depended on nothing more rare than properly clarified sense. Furthermore, sphere music was audible in the silence he sensed all about him in nature. What he read of sphere music in books, he experienced for himself, he thought, in the silence of the outdoors. Experiencing this omnipresent silence, indeed, represented the only real form of communion: "Silence is the communing of a conscious soul with itself.—If the soul attend for a moment to its own infinity, then and there is silence. She is audible to all men—at all times—in all places—and if we will we may always hearken to her admonitions" (PJ.1.60–61). To Thoreau's way of thinking, sound and silence were alternate sides of a single coin. The music of nature was audible and inaudible both. What arose from silence passed through sound before subsiding into silence again: "All sounds are her servants and purveyors—proclaiming not only that their mistress is, but is a rare mistress, and earnestly to be sought after. Behind the most distinct and significant, hovers always a more significant silence which floats it. The thunder is only our signal gun, that we may know what communion awaits us—Not its dull sound, but the infinite expansion of our being which ensues we praise—and unanimously name sublime" (PJ.1.61). To hear the music of the spheres, Thoreau believed, was merely a matter of attending the silence in which we always exist.

Besides Pythagoras, Thoreau's reflections on the character of music were also indebted to his reading of George Herbert, the Cambridge Platonist Ralph Cudworth, and in particular Sir Thomas Browne, all of whom helped elaborate on the metaphysics of celestial sound. Thoreau was so taken with one passage in particular from Browne's *Religio Medici* that he transcribed it into his journal at some length: "There is something in [music] of divinity more than the ear discovers: it is an hieroglyphical and shadowed lesson of the whole world, and creatures of God,—such a melody to the ear, as the whole world, well understood, would afford the understanding. In brief, it is a sensible fit of that harmony which intellectually sounds in the ears of God. [It unties the ligaments of my frame, takes me to pieces, dilates me out of myself, and by degrees methinks resolves me into heaven.]" (PJ.1.446–47).[20] Browne's formulation was especially compelling for Thoreau because it corroborated his own experience. He knew firsthand the exhilarations of which Browne wrote, and the sense of release. In his experience also, music had the power to take down the walls of the self. At one point in his journal, Thoreau asks himself how this could be—"Why was it made that man should be thrilled to his inmost being by the vibration of a wire?" The answer is simply that man and wire are similarly strung: "Are not inspiration and extasy a more rapid vibration of the nerves swept by the in rushing excited spirit" (PJ.4.238). Thoreau alludes to the ancient doctrines of sphere music in *Walden* when he speaks of the "undulation of celestial music" to which he wakes in the morning (89). In the same way that the earth serves as a harp for the celestial musician, so the human body, properly tuned, serves as a harp in moments of ecstasy: "In enthusiasm," he noted, "we undulate to the divine spiritus—as the lake to the wind" (PJ.1.206). Thus when, during his first summer at Walden, he seeks to entertain a "speaking silence" in order that his "ears might distinguish the significant sounds," he had the tradition of sphere music still clearly in mind (PJ.2.174). For Thoreau then, as for Wordsworth,

Browne, Plato, and Pythagoras, the sounds of nature were resonant with the cognitions of higher life. For him, as for them, music ultimately served what can only be called a religious use as a catalyst for ecstasy and a bridge to the supernatural. "The prophane never hear music—" he had written in 1840, "the holy ever hear it. It is God's voice—the divine breath audible. Where it is heard there is a sabbath. It is omnipotent—all things obey it as they obey virtue. It is the herald of virtue" (PJ.1.144). Indeed, to Thoreau all of nature's sounds were quickly assimilated to music, and music to ecstasy, from the creaking of a cricket to the singing of a telegraph wire: "He that hath ears," he parodied, "let him hear" (PJ.3.323). Even as late as 1857, music was still capable of pitching him into a fit of euphoria:

> What an elixir is this sound! I, who but lately came and went and lived under *a dish cover,* live now under the heavens. It releases me; it bursts my bonds. . . .
>
> We hear the kindred vibrations, music! and we put out our dormant feelers into the limits of the universe. We attain to a wisdom that passeth understanding. The stable continents undulate. The hard and fixed becomes fluid. . . . When I *hear* music I fear no danger, I am invulnerable, I see no foe. I am related to the earliest times and to the latest. (J.9.217–18)

A Drummer in the Night

Given the important role of sound and music in Thoreau's inner life, we may better understand the justification for his placement of his "Sounds" chapter before the one entitled "Solitude" in the composition of *Walden.* "Solitude," as we will see further on, provides the staging for one of the most suggestive representations of ecstasy in all of his writings; it is thus consistent with Thoreau's experience that "Sounds" would serve as its necessary precursor. But Thoreau's first book, *A Week on the Concord and Merrimack Rivers,* also affords ample opportunity for the literary representation of ecstatic experience and never more memorably than in the famous vignette of the night drummer at the conclusion of the

"Monday" section. This episode, which ostensibly occurred one evening during the brothers' 1839 voyage, appears to have an important place, not only in the book later written about the adventure, but also in Thoreau's personal spiritual history. As the two brothers lie awake on the bank of the river, the faint sound of "some tyro beating a drum" is enough to float them on a mood of rising euphoria:

> No doubt he was an insignificant drummer enough, but his music afforded us a prime leisure hour, and we felt that we were in season wholly. These simple sounds related us to the stars. Aye, there was a logic in them so convincing that the combined sense of mankind could never make me doubt their conclusions. I stop my habitual thinking, as if the plow had suddenly run deeper in its furrow through the crust of the world. How can I go on, who have just stepped over such a bottomless skylight in the bog of my life. Suddenly old Time winked at me,—Ah you know me, you rogue,—and news had come that IT was well. . . . I see, smell, taste, hear, feel, that everlasting Something to which we are allied, at once our maker, or abode, our destiny, our very Selves; the one historic truth, the most remarkable fact which can become the distinct and uninvited subject of our thought, the actual glory of the universe; the only fact which a human being cannot avoid recognizing, or in some way forget or dispense with. . . . I have seen how the foundations of the world are laid, and I have not the least doubt that it will stand a good while. (173–74)

The drummer, we soon find, is drumming "for a country muster," but he unwittingly also marches the narrator out into a state of transport. Thoreau draws here again, of course, on the mystique conventionally associated with distant sound, but he does so in an entirely personal manner. In one form or another, the drum motif and the military music that accompanies it may be found in much of Thoreau's writing and were inseparable from the imaginative complex that we have just been exploring. This motif makes its most celebrated appearance, of course, in one of the most quoted lines in American literature: "If a man does not keep pace with his companions, perhaps it is because he hears a different drummer. Let him step to the music which he hears, however measured or far away" (Walden, 326). These famous lines acquire a fuller resonance when we see their relation to the night drummer of A Week and Thoreau's sustained meditations on the relation between music and ecstasy throughout his journals.[21] When, as we saw earlier, Thoreau looks back mournfully at the raptures of his youth, he notes that "For years I marched as to a music in comparison with which the military music of the streets is noise and discord" (PJ.3.305–06).

In his elaboration of the night-drummer passage cited above, Thoreau goes on to explore the deeper relation between music and heroism: "As polishing expresses the vein in marble and grain in wood, so music brings out what of heroic lurks any where. The hero is the sole patron of music. That harmony which exists naturally between the hero's moods and the universe the soldier would fain imitate with drum and trumpet. When we are in health all sounds fife and drum for us; we hear the notes of music in the air, or catch its echoes dying away when we awake at dawn" (Week, 175). Music always brought out heroic virtue, Thoreau thought, and heroism was always played out against a background of music. Though somewhat unexpected, coming as it does on the heels of the narrator's transcendent cognition of the metaphysical structure of the world, this section of martial imagery epitomizes another of the central tendencies of Thoreau's religious imagination. Throughout his writings, especially the journal, themes of war and heroism have a marked presence.[22] In December of 1839 Thoreau entered a long passage in his journal on the theme of "Bravery," which, together with some reflections on the same theme drafted the next summer, he eventually drew upon both for the essay entitled "The Service" that he submitted unsuccessfully for publication in the Dial in 1840 and the passage from A Week cited above.[23] In his journal he noted that "Though music agitates only a few waves of air, yet it affords an ample plain for the hero's imagination to maneuvre on" (PJ.1.480). In light of this fascination with such imagery of war and heroism, it comes as no surprise that Thoreau's favorite books— the Iliad, the Bhagavad Gita, Ossian—are basically stories of war.

What all this talk of war and heroism has to do with music and ecstasy remains unclear, however, until we realize that Thoreau conceived of the warrior's life essentially in moral and religious terms, and the religious life, conversely, in heroic and military terms. Moral virtue was something to be aspired to, fought for. "Virtue is the deed of the bravest," he wrote in 1842. "It is that art which demands the greatest confidence and fearlessness. Only some hardy soul ventures upon it—it deals in what it has no experience in. The virtuous soul possess a fortitude and hardihood which not the grenadier nor pioneer can match" (PJ.1.354). Courage and strength were as much the virtues of the religious ascetic as the military conqueror. While Thoreau never specifically invokes the Pauline idea of the soldier of Christ, he often comes close. His own spiritual life, especially the spiritual heights of his youth, he consistently depicts in martial terms: "I wish I could be as still as God is. I can recall to my mind the stillest summer hour—in which the grasshopper sings over the mulleins—and there is a valor in that time the memory of which is armor that can laugh at any blow of fortunes" (PJ.1.349). In Thoreau's imaginative life generally, the hero marching to battle serves as the type of the saint who overcomes the weaknesses of the flesh and thus conquers the world. The following journal passage from the summer of 1840 offers an early expression of the personal religious rationale driving the imaginative convergence of these themes:

> War is the sympathy of concussion—We would fain rub one against another—its rub may be friction merely but it would rather be titillation. We discover in the quietest scenes how faithfully war has copied the moods of peace. Men do not peep into heaven but they see embattled hosts there. Miltons' heaven was a camp. When the sun bursts through the morning fog I seem to hear the din of war louder than when his Chariot thundered on the plains of Troy. Every man is a warrior when he aspires. He marches on his post. The soldier is the practical idealist—he has no sympathy with matter, he revels in the annihilation of it. So do we all at times. When a freshet destroys the works of man—or a fire consumes

them—or a Lisbon earthquake shakes them down—our sympathy with persons is swallowed up in a wider sympathy with the universe. A crash is apt to grate agreeably on our ears. (PJ.1.124)

This idiosyncratic passage exemplifies a certain bloody-mindedness not uncharacteristic of Thoreau's existential meditations. Its severe countenancing of violence and death in some ways anticipates the dispassionate voyeurism of his later encounter with the beached corpses in *Cape Cod* (3–14). The odd admission that "friction" may at last prove "titillation" points to a fact about Thoreau's own ascetic experience that I will return to at a later point: for him, apparently, as for the soldier or seeker of valor, pain and pleasure, war and peace were reversible oppositions. But the main reason for citing this passage here is that it dramatizes better than most what was for Thoreau the crucial link in this evolving imaginative association between soldier and saint. Like "the practical idealist," the soldier "has no sympathy with matter, he revels in the annihilation of it." Indeed, for both soldier and idealist the destruction of matter represents more a triumph than a defeat. The concussions of the drum may well result in localized death, but they also presage a "wider sympathy with the universe."

Taken in the context of the passages cited previously, Thoreau's meditation here on the "sympathy of concussion" reflects a kind of psychological or spiritual apocalypticism endemic to his religious thought. He had no use, of course, for millenarians and other biblical literalists, but the Book of Revelation still retained a certain imaginative appeal, as it had for many Romantics before him.[24] In *Nature,* Emerson had spoken of "the apocalypse of the mind" and drawn heavily on the tropes and themes provided in the Bible's climactic last book.[25] Carlyle had also relied upon apocalyptic figuration in his dramatization of the revelations of his protagonist Teufelsdröckh in *Sartor Resartus.*[26] If anything, apocalyptic themes and figuration are more displaced from biblical models in Thoreau's treatment, but they are recognizable nevertheless in his representations of his earliest ecstatic experiences. In such Romantic representations, the whole drama of the biblical apocalypse is interiorized. The momentous events of end-time take place not in the heavens above but within the arena of the individual soul or psyche. The long-awaited destruction of the world, the divine marriage, and the creation of the new heaven and earth so vividly depicted in Revelations 19–21 are now conceived as symbolic representations of climactic stages in the soul's journey to the Absolute or the psyche's opening to higher consciousness. To such Romantics, the cataclysmic events presented in the Book of Revelation could not be taken literally, but they did represent certain crucial truths about the interior spiritual and imaginative life.

Especially compelling was St. John's vision of the creation of the new heaven and earth out of the ashes of a smoldering world. Construed in this inward sense, the destruction of the sinful world was the Bible's way of dramatizing the religious truth that spiritual birth necessitated the destruction of the former self, a truth fully consistent after all with the ethical and spiritual teachings of Jesus. While Thoreau had pretty much jettisoned the entire biblical paraphernalia of Final Judgment, divine marriage, and eschatological destiny, at least as descriptions of historical reality, he still had strong personal reasons for subscribing to the notion of an inward apocalypse. His own youthful experiences of ecstatic release testified to the truth that destruction of the old self was necessary to make way for the new. When, in the entry on "Consciousness" from the summer of 1838, he described the dissipation of the "walls and barriers" of the self as the first stage of his revelation of oceanic being, he was no doubt aware of the figurative precedents established by the apocalyptic visions of St. John. When he approvingly copied down Thomas Browne's remarks on the liberating power of music, these biblical models were also before him. Thoreau credited these representations because he knew from his own experience that unless the personal ego was dissolved or transcended, no access to the higher world of the spirit was possible. In the idiosyncratic constellation of themes and images that we have seen informing his religious imagination, the warrior served as the principal agent or symbol of this interior apocalypse. He was the one above all who shook the foundations of the old world in order to give rise to the new, and music was everywhere his accompaniment and, indeed, his principal means: "Wherever he goes, music precedes and prepares the way for him. His life is a holiday and the contagion of his example unhinges the universe. The world puts by work and comes out to stare. He is the one only man. He recognizes no time honored casts and conventions—no fixtures but transfixtures—no governments at length settled on a permanent basis. One tap of the drum sets the political and moral harmonies all ajar. His ethics may well bear comparison with the priest's. He may rally, charge, retreat in an orderly manner—but never flee nor flinch" (PJ.1.94). In view of this densely conceived imaginative association of music, heroism, and ecstatic experience, it is not surprising that the ecstasy by the riverbank in *A Week* was brought on by the faintly audible beating of a distant drum. This faint sound marshalled all the powers of nature in breaking down the walls of the sleeper's self and opening him up to the timeless reality beyond. Yet, as we have seen, many sounds in nature could perform this service for Thoreau. Matters of indifference to some, the wind in the trees or the vibrations of a telegraph wire might at any moment whirl him into a higher orbit. When the long-awaited annihilation of self began, ecstatic release was imminent.

In view of the general complexity and inaccessibility of the experiential dimensions of Thoreau's religious life, it seems safest to adhere as closely as possible to the biographical and historical evidence available to us in our efforts to construe them. When literary historians and biographers have attempted to say something more substantive about these experiences, the results have sometimes proved most worthwhile. After forty years, Sherman Paul's explication of some of the spiritual foundations of Thoreau's creative life remains in many ways unrivaled.[27] Other critics have contributed to a more historically contextualized understanding of Thoreau's religious thought in more modest ways. For example, the historical instincts that led Mason Lowance to consider Thoreau's ecstatic recollection of 1851 in relation to Jonathan Edwards's youthful conversion experiences and Emerson's romantic organicism are entirely vindicated by the insights they yielded. Thoreau's youthful raptures and the corresponding awakening of his senses certainly do appear to have some precedent in the conversion experiences described in

Edwards's *Personal Narrative* and what he characterizes there as a "new sense of things."[28] Actually, the representations Thoreau provides in his early journals of these episodes of spiritual euphoria bear a kind of distant family resemblance to the conversion experiences encountered in the journals of New England's young people, especially those of his Unitarian contemporaries. The heavily Christological import of Jones Very's notorious mystical euphoria contrast sharply, of course, with Thoreau's representations, but both emphasize self-abandonment and new birth in ways illustrative of the continuing hold of New Testament piety and interiorized apocalypticism, even in the most liberal circles of the Unitarian Church.[29]

A closer analogue to the 1838 epiphany, for example, may be found in Margaret Fuller's account of a conversion-like religious euphoria that she experienced at the age of twenty-one as she walked in the fields of Groton shortly after attending church on Thanksgiving Day: "I saw there was no self; that selfishness was all folly, and the result of circumstance; that it was only because I thought self real that I suffered; that I had only to live in the idea of the ALL, and all was mine. This truth came to me and I received it unhesitatingly; so that I was for that hour taken up into God. In that true ray most of the relations of earth seemed mere films, phenomena."[30] Recorded in 1840, nine years after the event itself, this account bears some of the earmarks of her own by-then-waxing Transcendentalism, and is indeed reminiscent in certain respects of Emerson's epiphany on the bare common in *Nature,* but its circumstances and style also hark back to the kind of experiences Edwards recounted in the *Personal Narrative.* In contrast to Edwards and Very, and even to Fuller and Emerson, Thoreau seems intent on purging from his own representations any trace whatsoever of the old theological language, but his accounts of ecstasy still bear some traces of biblical tradition. That Thoreau both recognized some relation between his youthful experiences and those witnessed in the religious history of his region, and sought to distinguish himself from them, is suggested by this revealing confession in a letter of 1853 written in response to a query from his friend Harrison Blake: "I have had but one *spiritual* birth (excuse the word,) and now whether it rains or snows, whether I laugh or cry, fall farther below or approach nearer to my standard, whether Pierce or Scott is elected,—not a new scintillation of light flashes on me, but ever and anon, though with longer intervals, the same surprising & everlasting new light dawns to me, with only such variations as in the coming of the natural day, with which indeed, it is often coincident" (Correspondence, 296–97). Here Thoreau characteristically sets his experience in an entirely naturalistic context of discourse, yet nevertheless acknowledges its theological affiliations. Notwithstanding Thoreau's spirited antinomianism and his own idiosyncratic brand of Transcendentalism, we cannot forget that his work grew out of a common set of assumptions, attitudes, and practices shared by other members of the Transcendentalist community. From the perspective of historical distance, this community appears less inchoate and loosely knit than it perhaps seemed to its participants at the time. Religious writers, like all other writers, exemplify their traditions, at least as much as they deviate from them, and even this fierce individualist was no exception in this regard.

As representations of early ecstatic experience, the passages considered in the last two chapters represent a blend of influence and originality. As we have just seen, these early epiphanies have something in common, not surprisingly, with the kind of post-Christian Romantic epiphanies found in the writings of Emerson, Fuller, and Carlyle. But Thoreau's ecstatic formulations also depart from these obvious models and precedents in revealing ways. The epiphany of the night drummer exemplifies these variations from New England and other literary precedents. There is, first of all, no trace of traditional Christian elements in this formulation, and little of theistic worship generally. The substance of the narrator's revelation on the riverbank is an immanent and transcendent "IT," not a personal deity as such. In depicting his experience, Thoreau thoroughly purges it of the last traces of biblical mythology: this divine reality is neither he nor she, above nor beyond, past nor future, but is now timelessly here. Even more unusual is the mediating role performed by the senses. Not only is sensory experience affirmed, here the senses serve as the veritable channels of divine inspiration: "I see, smell, taste, hear, feel, that everlasting Something to which we are allied, at once our maker, our abode, our destiny, our very Selves; the one historic truth, the most remarkable fact which can become the distinct and uninvited subject of our thought, the actual glory of the universe; the only fact which a human being cannot avoid recognizing, or in some way forget or dispense with" (Week, 173–74). However ineffably transcendent this divine reality may be, Thoreau encounters it habitually through the mundane human agency of the five senses. This fact suggests something about the theology implied by such an experience: in identifying the divine reality as "the actual glory of the universe," *A Week*'s narrator confirms the pantheistic tendencies he so cavalierly avows earlier in the book. We encounter the absolute, in this view, not in some exalted spiritual afflatus, but in and through the very skin of the world. Finally, the catalyst for this climactic experience comes not from pulpit, prayer, or holy writ, but rather from the faint music of a distant drummer.

These motifs distinguish Thoreau's epiphany from comparable ones of Emerson or Fuller, and remind us once again of the important place of Wordsworth in Thoreau's spiritual self-formation. Emphasis on heightened sensory acuity as a vehicle of ecstasy, meditations on distant sights and sounds, even the tendencies to pantheism—these features of the night-drummer passage characterize Wordsworth's early epiphanies also. Indeed, Thoreau's representation of his ecstasy on the banks of the Merrimack probably owes more to "Tintern Abbey" and the Immortality Ode than it does to *Nature* or the New England conversion paradigms. In the mournful recollection of his youth's ecstasies from the summer of 1851, with which we began this exploration of Thoreau's ecstatic experiences, Wordsworth obviously played an indispensable role. Above all, Wordsworth was to Thoreau the poet of fond memory and remembrance of things past. The elder poet looked to the ecstasies of youth as the creative source of his artistic achievements; many of his most memorable poems present a meditative reconstitution of past in present, or as he famously put it in the preface to *Lyrical Ballads,* of "emotion recollected in tranquility."[31] Wordsworth's genius lay in his ability to fashion poetic forms from fugitive past experience, to create artistic objects out of a lost and irrecoverable time. In this way, his art often served as memorials—locations of and for memory—of moments of insight and bliss no longer accessible in any other way.[32] The retrieval of a lost past through memory gave rise to a compensatory unity in the present. Indeed, this simultaneous awareness of past and present, of the poet now and then, epitomizes Wordsworth's poetic consciousness and sensibility.

Thoreau also needed the consolation afforded by this reconstituted vision of past in present—especially in later years as the fullness of his earlier inspirations began to wane. Even the epiphany of the night drummer, after all, was recreated from the distance of years. Given the example of Wordsworth, it should not surprise us that Thoreau looked to one of his own poems as a vehicle for the expression of inspiration witnessed in the night-drummer epiphany. As we have seen, poems had been his favorite way of enshrining the memories of youthful ecstasy, and the lines he cites in *A Week* seemed to convey special import for him. Here in full are the stanzas from the poem upon which Thoreau drew to highlight the meaning of the night-drummer passage:

> But now there comes unsought, unseen,
> Some clear, divine electuary,
> And I who had but sensual been,
> Grow sensible, and as God is, am wary.
>
> I hearing get who had but ears,
> And sight, who had but eyes before,
> I moments live who lived but years,
> And truth discern who knew but learning's lore.
>
> I hear beyond the range of sound,
> I see beyond the range of sight,
> New earths and skies and seas around,
> And in my day the sun doth pale his light.

A clear and ancient harmony
Pierces my soul through all its din,
As through its utmost melody,—
Farther behind than they—farther within.

More swift its bolt than lightning is,
Its voice than thunder is more loud,
It doth expand my privacies
To all, and leave me single in the crowd.

It speaks with such authority,
With so serene and lofty tone,
That idle Time runs gadding by,
And leaves me with Eternity alone.

Then chiefly is my natal hour,
And only then my prime of life,
Of manhood's strength it is the flower,
'Tis peace's end and war's beginning strife.

(Poems, 230–31)

In his eulogy to Thoreau, Emerson, we remember, had noted the special spiritual significance of his verses, and nowhere does this appear more true than in this poem, unblushingly titled "Inspiration." These lines help to essentialize the spiritual biography we have attempted to reconstruct at length in the last two chapters. In the epiphany of the night drummer, Thoreau rearranges and selectively intersperses these lines within the prose presentation. Constituted in this way both of prose and poetry, this passage from the last few pages of "Monday" represents one of Thoreau's most sustained efforts to verbalize his ecstatic experience. He draws also of course on years of reading, but the resulting presentation is wholly his own. The passage on the night drummer employs paradoxes and rhetorical reversals in ways distinctive of Thoreau's treatment of his ecstatic experience in *Walden* and his later essays. "How can I go on," he writes, "who have just stepped over such a bottomless skylight in the bog of my life." The disorienting nonsequitur of the "bottomless skylight" exemplifies Thoreau's mature strategies for the representation of strangely altered consciousness. To the dual experience of past in present exemplified in Wordsworth, Thoreau adds his own characteristic "double consciousness" in which above and below, localized and un-localized, temporal moment and unbounded witness, severally coexist.[33] The music of the spheres, the "clear and ancient harmony" of the poem, becomes audible in the distant beat of the drum in the recollection from the brothers' original voyage. The effect of this music, he writes, is to "expand my privacies/To all, and leave me single in the crowd." In this suggestive formulation, the merging of above and below crystallized in the paradoxical image of the bottomless skylight finds an analogue in the competing expansions and contractions of the ecstatic mind. In this climax of the narrator's flowering ecstasy, expanded privacy encompasses physical distinctness without swallowing it. The ecstatic seer takes on the generalized anonymity of the crowd while remaining localized as one among many. As in the epiphany from the summer of 1838, the private self here stretches to unfamiliar dimensions beyond its localized physical expression. As we will see later, this "ecstasy," this disorienting experience of the self outside its normal moorings, appears to offer broad experien-tial sanction for Thoreau's oddly disjunctive imagination and his most distinctive rhetorical strategies.

Three

To Redeem This Wasted Time

During the 1840s, Thoreau's main showcase for the experiences and evolving imaginative formation of music, heroism, and ecstasy was his first book, *A Week on the Concord and Merrimack Rivers,* published in 1849. This book took the form of a reflective travel narrative about a boat trip he had taken with his brother, John, in 1839, and it epitomizes his considered efforts to resolve the claims made upon him in early middle life by his youthful fits of euphoria and his foreboding sense of spiritual recession. The book's competing dialectical themes of Indian versus white man, East versus West, contemplation versus action, timeless present versus historical past—all these Thoreau marshals to some degree in the service of his underlying struggle to reconcile the transcendental and temporal conditions of his own experience. To characterize *A Week* as a book of youthful "ecstasy," as Sherman Paul was inclined to do, proves helpful, therefore, if only because it makes explicit acknowledgment of the experiential sources of his literary inspiration.[1] The book's literary structure itself reflects these ecstatic sources: Thoreau deliberately punctuates his account of the brothers' voyage upriver with a series of meditative moments that contribute an inward vertical dimension to the prevailing outward movement of the narrative. The integrated movement of meditation and action results in a kind of religious double vision on the part of the book's narrator. In general, the inward dimension occasioned by the narrator's meditative moments lends a sense of greater

depth and resonance to his account of outward adventure, but the reflex-
ivity thus enjoined can also at times prove quite destabilizing to its
ostensible significance. There are always two ways of looking at a thing,
the narrator seems to suggest, and this story of mock heroism is no
exception. Thematically, of course, this dual vision finds ample expression in the list of paired ideas noted above, but it originates at the level of
narrative in the strategically developed device of the two brothers—one
voiced, the other silently looking on. Critics have for some time acknowledged the ambiguous design of *A Week* in regard to its action and
themes. Less acknowledged is the extent to which its author deliberately
manipulates the literary modes and genres informing his narrative in
order to drive the meaning and structure of the work as a whole. Since
the ambiguous thematic and formal structure of *A Week*—its "complex
weave"—has such a close bearing on Thoreau's developing religious
thought and experience, it deserves more sustained attention than his
other works.[2]

Some Pure Mythology Today

The boat trip itself began modestly enough on the afternoon of Saturday,
August 31, 1839, when the two brothers wheeled their fifteen-foot dory,
the *Musketaquid* (Grass-Ground River) to the bank of the neighboring
Concord River and set off for what would amount to a two-week vaca-
tion from their schoolteaching duties at Concord Academy. Henry and
John had conceived the voyage earlier that spring as a break between the
summer and fall sessions of their school. Upon shoving off, the brothers
rowed their boat in a northeasterly direction down the Concord River till
they reached its confluence with the Merrimack just north of the town of
Billerica. Upon entering the Merrimack, the brothers turned their boat
upstream in a northerly direction toward the river's source in the lake and
mountain country of New Hampshire. Crossing over the state line, they
rowed against the current past the towns of Tyngsborough, Hudson,
Bedford, and Manchester, before temporarily stowing their boat and
abandoning the river phase of their journey at Hooksett. From Hooksett they traveled by stage to Plymouth, from which point they began a

four-day excursion into the White Mountains that culminated in their hike to the summit of Mount Washington on Tuesday, September 10. Two days later, the brothers returned to Hooksett, where they retrieved their boat and began their return voyage, sailing now quickly with the wind and current down the Merrimack and back up the Concord. On Friday night of the second week, they made it home.

Evidently, Thoreau did not harbor any grand literary designs for this journey at the time of the voyage itself. Nothing of the trip appears in his journal of 1839, but he did keep a log of the trip's itinerary that, together with a few narrative and descriptive passages, he copied into his journal the following summer. "Our boat was built like a fisherman's dory," he wrote at that time, "with thole pins for four oars. Below it was green with a border of blue—as if out of courtesy the green sea and the blue heavens. It was well calculated for service—but of consequence difficult to be dragged over shoal places or carried round falls—" (PJ.1.125).[3] The surprising brevity of these entries suggests that Thoreau had little inkling in 1840 of the ambitious literary edifice to which they would eventually give rise. Sometime after John's death in January of 1842, however, the trip up the Merrimack to the White Mountains took on new meaning for Henry, as he began to conceive it as the basis for a travel narrative that would in some sense also serve as a memorial to his brother.[4] Over the next few years, Thoreau began collecting material for this envisioned narrative in a notebook he referred to as the "Long Book," which he took with him when he moved to Walden Pond in the summer of 1845. It was there, during his first year at the Pond, that he completed the first draft of *A Week*.[5] When Thoreau submitted a lengthier second draft for publication two years later, his manuscript was rejected, but this initial rejection served only as an impetus for yet further refinement and revision. Finally, in 1849, after a ten-year gestation, the Boston firm of James Munroe published Thoreau's manuscript at the author's own expense.[6]

The literary form Thoreau selected to convey his account of the brothers' voyage upriver was what has been termed the romantic excursion narrative, a type of travel writing long familiar to him and one to which he repeatedly turned throughout his literary career. Before launching forth on his ambitious plans for *A Week* in 1844, Thoreau had already produced two shorter excursion narratives, "A Walk to Wachusett" and "A Winter Walk," in which he began to explore the imaginative potential of the excursion genre. Actually, all of Thoreau's most characteristic finished work falls loosely within this generic category, from his book-length treatments—*A Week, Walden, Maine Woods,* and *Cape Cod*—to many of his shorter essays. Throughout his life, in fact, Thoreau read voraciously in travel literature of all kinds, and despite his vaunted parochialism, he traveled a good deal outside of his native town. John Christie has identified at least 172 separate travel accounts that Thoreau read over the course of his life, not including the many briefer accounts that were legion in the periodicals of his day.[7] While at Harvard, he had become acquainted with Henry Brackenridge's *Journal of a Voyage up the River Missouri,* Thomas L. McKenney's *Sketches of a Tour to the Lakes,* and Ross Cox's *Adventures on the Columbia River,* all accounts that of course anticipate Thoreau's own narrative in obvious ways.[8] In the winter months after his graduation from college in 1837, he made use of his new conversancy in German in his efforts to work his way through Goethe's *Italienische Reise,* a retrospective account of the poet's journey through Italy at the age of thirty-seven.[9] Thoreau admired Goethe's treatment above all for the way it combined objective detachment with romantic feeling and reflection, and he soon came to look upon Goethe as a model for his own approach to travel writing.[10] Among literary mentors, Wordsworth too helped shape Thoreau's approach to his work. Sometime after its publication in 1839, he read Wordsworth's extended essay on the English lakes region, *A Guide Through the District of the Lakes in the North of England.* Here, in the "Topographical Description" appendix, Thoreau encountered an important precedent for the practice of interspersing poetry and descriptive prose that would distinguish his own treatment in *A Week.*[11] Indeed, for literary models Thoreau did not have far to look: the American writers Poe, Melville, Irving, Longfellow, and Cooper had all written in the travel mode, and his friend Emerson would later do so as well.[12] In 1844, Margaret Fuller had published a travel sketch, *Summer on the Lakes,* that perfectly epitomized the reflective and digressive style of the romantic excursion genre. To Transcendentalists such as Fuller and Thoreau, one major appeal of the excursion genre was the open inclusiveness of its form. In practice it came to serve as a kind of literary anthology: not only did it provide ample accommodation for the kind of romantic reflections and feeling distinctive of the genre, but it could also serve the purposes of natural history, social criticism, religious discourse, and even poetry—a feature that Thoreau was quick to exploit in *A Week*.

Yet even such a catholic designation as this does not take full stock of the generic complexity of this book. The romantic excursion provided a suitable form in which to convey the story of the voyage, but the impetus for the project, as we have seen, appears to have come from the premature death of John in 1842. In his reconstruction of the development of *A Week*, Linck Johnson shows how this elegiac concern shaped Thoreau's designs for the book even in its earliest stages. Like other Transcendentalists, Thoreau had a special interest in the topic of friendship, as we have seen, and had drafted several extended entries on the subject into his journal of 1839. After John's death, however, these reflections acquired even greater resonance for him, and he decided early on to include a substantial excursus on friendship in the body of *A Week*, with implicit reference to John. Also prominent in Thoreau's earliest conceptions of the book were the narrator's meditations on the autumnal landscape in the "Friday" section and his slightly ominous forecasting of fall.[13] The narrator's proleptic awareness of his companion's imminent death transforms the figure of John from a passive character in the narrative to a kind of ubiquitous, even numinous presence in the narrator's awareness, a fact announced by Thoreau's invocation of John as his "Muse" in the opening epigraph of the book. Indeed, this awareness of the imminent presence of death fundamentally alters the meaning and status of the journey for him and for us. In what seemed at first blush a kind of mock-heroic travel narrative, we now also recognize elements of pastoral elegy in the tradition of Milton's "Lycidas." As he continued to revise over the next seven years, Thoreau worked to shape his manuscript better to convey this elegiac motive, incorporating themes and motifs from the tradition of the classical elegy.[14] In keeping with this tradition, he takes pains to universalize the grief felt at the death—here incipient—of the pastoral hero. John's death casts a pall over all of nature's processes, thus lending a fateful and tragic cast to the narrative's basically epic and comic pattern. We encounter this tragic mood early on in the story in the narrator's rueful digression on the fate of the shad and other fishes since the damming of New England's inland waterways.[15] From this point in the narrative onward, we can no longer appreciate the redemptive possibilities of this voyage without also recognizing its tragic implications.

Recognition of the elegiac function of Thoreau's narrative helps explain its surprisingly marked retrospective orientation. More than any of Thoreau's other major works, *A Week* is quintessentially a book about time, about memory, and about the possibility of redeeming the past in the present.[16] As the brothers row upstream into the north country of New Hampshire, they simultaneously drift back in time through earlier historical times and epochs. Thoreau conceived the book as a memorial to his dead brother, but he utilizes this memorial as a medium for a wider meditation on the meaning and origins of time in general. What began as an excursion through space, a story perhaps of boyish hijinks and high adventure, soon becomes an excursion into the recesses of the past. At points, the trip seems to serve almost entirely as a vehicle for the narrator's investigations of history—personal, local, regional, literary, and even natural history. People and places encountered along the river's shore interest Thoreau more often as memorials of some momentous event in the colonial past than as landmarks or milestones of contemporary New England life. In this way, the voyage out entails a voyage back, a quest for adventure becomes a quest for origins. The *Musketaquid* thus moves along two trajectories at once, across space and back through time. By highlighting the implied temporal trajectory of his narrative, Thoreau considerably raises the stakes of this holiday trip upcountry, as he recasts the literal voyage, at least to some extent, as a conceit for his inward, transcendental journey.

This preoccupation with origins signals the role of yet a third narrative genre in the imaginative design of the book. As the travelers move back in time, their journey also assumes obvious mythic proportions. In the course of his temporal speculations, the narrator does not confine his remarks to history alone, but frequently ranges beyond historical time into a timeless and universal mythical past. Myth, of course, plays a central role in Thoreau's religious thought, as we will see. In *Walden* he extolls the "heroic books," the scriptures, and the classics of the various nations as the best of books, and here they constitute important sources of instruction as well (Walden, 100–10). "Mythology is only the most ancient history and biography," he avers—where the historian leaves off, the mythologist begins (Week, 60).

As far as the overall construction of *A Week* is concerned, however, Thoreau relies upon myth more as an enabling vehicle in the elaboration of his narrative than simply as a topic of learned consideration. Like other classic American writers of the Romantic period, he too was an aspiring mythmaker and often looked to myths of the ancient world for precedent and support in his desire to create an American mythology unique to the contemporary people and circumstances of life on the North American continent.[17] "The poet is he who can write some pure mythology today without the aid of posterity," he tells us in *A Week,* and before long, we suspect that in such formulations he merely points to the arc of his own ambition (60). Indeed, shortly after embarking on their trip down the Concord, the brothers pass an old fisherman "with a long birch pole" who stands silently at the outskirts of the town as a kind of monument to some bygone past. Human life must strike this old fisherman as a river, the narrator speculates, and so it was for the narrator himself (24). "I had often stood on the banks of the Concord," Thoreau confides in his preliminary meditations on the river, "watching the lapse of the current, an emblem of all progress, following the same law with the system, with time, and all that is made; the weeds at the bottom gently bending down the stream, shaken by the watery wind, still planted where their seeds had sunk, but ere long to die and go down likewise; the shining pebbles, not yet anxious to better their condition, the chips and weeds, and occasional logs and stems of trees, that floated past, fulfilling their fate, were objects of singular interest to me, and at last I resolved to launch myself on its bosom, and float whither it would bear me" (12–13). Thoreau feels well justified in associating this "muddy and much abused Concord river" with the august rivers of world fame (12). It is a type of these great rivers, just as these rivers are a type of the river of life itself. As the brothers drift downstream, the current of the river becomes assimilated to the current of their dreams, and they float "from past to future as silently as one awakes to fresh morning or evening thoughts" (20). Yet as the brothers enter the channel of the Merrimack the next day, they turn their craft deliberately against the river's natural current, in keeping with their plan to follow the river back to its mountainous source. From this point on, the symbolism Thoreau attaches to this upriver voyage helps sustain the elegiac motive of the narrative and promote his deepening interest in the past. Now the brothers row heroically against the stream of time, against the normal currents of history, intent on tracing the river of life to its source by reaching the headwaters of time itself. Defying the otherwise irreversible fate of all earth's creatures, they seem bound to transcend time, history, and their human condition altogether.[18] To reach such a destination represents as much a spiritual as a physical triumph, and on returning back downriver, they convey the benefits of their redemptive power and knowledge with them for the benefit of a fallen world. This, at least, is as the myth would have it.

As in all of his finished works, Thoreau seems at pains in *A Week* to bury the mythological designs of the voyage deep below the surface details of his narrative. He alerts us to the existence and operation of such mythological structures with an occasional hint or allusion, preferring as usual to steer close to the actual realities of time and place to which he feels most committed. Here he allows the innocent facts of the brothers' basic itinerary to do most of the work for him. Their announced plan to travel up the Merrimack to its source in the White Mountains, and ultimately to Mount Washington, the loftiest summit of all, lifts the mythical potential of the narrative clearly into view, if only because such a journey falls so neatly into the age-old pattern of the mythical quest. We do not need to have read much in myth to glimpse the sacred geography standing vaguely behind the actual physical topography of the brothers' voyage to the great New England mountain. Thoreau had already exploited the imaginative and mythical potential of the mountain ascent in "A Walk to Wachusett," a shorter travel piece written in 1843, and would do so again a few years later in his account of the vertiginous ascent of Mt. Katahdin in 1846.[19] These precedents were no doubt in his mind as he worked to elaborate and refine his treatment of his climb of Mount Greylock in the "Tuesday" chapter and his cryptic handling of the brothers' ascent to Agiococook (Mount Washington) in "Thursday." In mythical terms, this voyage up the Merrimack, contrary to its natural course, amounts to following the river of life back to its source on the sacred mountain, the *axis mundi,* at the center of the world. The voyage thus recapitulates the mythical hero's sacred quest, or, at a cosmogonic level, what Mircea Eliade refers to as the myth of the eternal return.[20] Whether construed at a heroic or cosmogonic level, this is essentially a myth of redemption and rebirth. Penetration to the center of the world, the source of time, leads to a restoration of the health and vitality of the physical and social world. Thoreau carefully plays down the mythical character of the voyage to the White Mountains, but the basic itinerary of the journey clearly evokes the archetype of the mythical quest to the center of the world, as he well knew. By no means extraneous to the narrative itself, this myth of rebirth actually informs and fuses the genres of the romantic excursion and pastoral elegy on which Thoreau also heavily depends. Consistent with his synthetic generic design, the transhistoric character of myth helps to universalize the dramatic action of the romantic excursion and eternalize the elegiac quest for lost origins.

The New Adam's Rise

Following R. W. B. Lewis, we might best identify the American Romantic adaptation of this generic rebirth myth as the myth of the American Adam.[21] In this more colloquial version of the myth, the North American wilderness offers the ideal setting for a re-creation of the biblical account given in Genesis 2–3, only in this case, the hero of the story redeems humanity's fallen state and recovers its long-lost innocence. To traditional Christians such readings were at best premature, since for them any true restoration of the conditions of Paradise had to await the Second Coming of Christ at the end of the world, and at worst blasphemous, since they were often posited independently of the saving action of Christ. But this did not stop the Romantic writers of Emerson's generation. Emerson himself had sketched the requirements and conditions for the American recovery of lost paradise in *Nature,* and Whitman boldly enacted the myth in the extended body of his poetic work in *Leaves of Grass.* Thoreau epitomized the characteristic Romantic rereading of the Fall story in quoting the playful revision of the first lesson from the old New England Primer:

> In Adam's fall
> We sinned all.
> In the new Adam's rise
> We shall all reach the skies.
> (PJ.3.187)[22]

In contrast to the biblical myth, whose focus finally is upon Adam's expulsion from Paradise, these Romantic versions envisage a paradise regained in the auspicious environment of North America, in effect reversing the direction of biblical history and turning back the clock of biblical time. In *A Week,* Thoreau instigates his own overhaul of the old Judeo-Christian story, but the revision of the Fall myth he inaugurates here is both more complex and ambiguous than anything we find in either Emerson or Whitman. Thoreau's scathing critique of Christian values and institutions in the "Sunday" section of *A Week* makes it clear that he was not above radical surgery when it came to the Christian tradition, but he never rejected the biblical version of the Fall story out of hand, especially given its obvious relevance for himself, John, and their journey together in 1839. On the contrary, he presents this Romantic rebirth myth almost exclusively in the traditional terms afforded by the Christian story of the Fall. The uneasy juxtaposition of these two myths sets up a dissonance in the narrative that Thoreau appears eager to exploit throughout.

While the overt action of the narrative of *A Week* conforms quite comfortably to the pattern of the triumphal heroic quest as we have seen, Thoreau periodically undercuts expectations raised by this traditional story with countervailing, and sometimes quite ominous, references to the Fall. These references he places cryptically throughout the narrative as if to warn his readers that all is not as it would seem on this late summer pilgrimage of youth. Hardly has the story begun before we are treated to the first of these somewhat disquieting caveats in the form of a set of puns carefully deposited in the reflective passage on the Concord River cited above. "I had often stood on the banks of the Concord," the narrator tells us in the prefatory chapter, "watching the lapse of the current, an emblem of all progress, following the same law with the system, with time, and all that is made." Consistent with the old metaphor of the river of time, Thoreau makes it clear that this "current," like the current of life itself, flows progressively toward the ocean of being; it is, he carefully adds, "an emblem of all progress." But his choice of the word "lapse" to denote this movement oddly undercuts and confuses this apparently intended meaning. "Lapse" is one of Thoreau's favorite words in *A Week,* presumably because it serves as such an effectively subversive pun. Lapse can mean to flow, as in the lapse of a current, but for most readers in his day and our own, it has the more common meanings of oversight, error, or backsliding. In a theological context, of course, it has the graver connotation of humankind's most disastrous "lapse," the disobedience in the Garden of Adam and Eve. The word then squints both ways, we might say, forward and backward both. The designation "current," moreover, hardly helps to clarify the ambiguity. In context, it appears to denote the movement of the river, but elsewhere Thoreau uses it in the temporal sense of that which is "current" or contemporary. What can he mean then to speak of "the lapse of the current" as "an emblem of all progress"? At the very least, we are no longer completely confident that this river moves inexorably in such a promising direction.[23]

The ambiguity lightly countenanced here becomes more unsettling as the narrative proceeds. At strategic intervals along the shore, Thoreau plants more clues as if to confirm our growing misgivings about the nature or consequences of the brothers' confident quest. The otherwise buoyant narrative cataloguing the species of fish populating the Concord in "Saturday" suddenly admits of a tragic note, when the narrator comes to the sad history of the shad and other migratory fish. For salmon, alewives, and shad, as for the Indians and white fishermen who depended upon them, the erection of a dam at Billerica was not the boon it was to upriver farmers, but an unmitigated disaster. By Thoreau's time these migratory fish had long been denied their upriver spawning grounds and were thereby reduced almost to extinction. "Shad are still taken in the basin of Concord River at Lowell," Thoreau writes, "where they are said to be a month earlier than the Merrimack shad, on account of the warmth of the water. Still patiently, almost pathetically, with instinct not to be discouraged, not to be *reasoned* with, revisiting their old haunts, as if their stern fates would relent, and still met by the Corporation with its dam. Poor shad! where is thy redress?" (36–37). In subsequent pages, the Billerica dam comes to serve as a kind of emblem of the violence perpetrated by Europeans against the harmonious aboriginal order. Everywhere along the riverbank, the brothers witness the signs and consequences of this decisive and, for some, deadly act. White fishermen too of course suffered the effects of the Billerica dam and looked back on the days when shad swam freely upriver as an age of plenty. The narrator can even recall an old Concord fisherman in whom the effects of this tragic alteration were readily apparent: "I can faintly remember to have seen this same fisher in my earliest youth, still as near the river as he could get, with uncertain undulatory step, after so many things had gone down stream, swinging a scythe in the meadow, his bottle like a serpent hid in the grass; himself as yet not cut down by the Great Mower" (35).

Allusions and vignettes such as these reinforce the reader's growing apprehension that the stream of progress upon which the two brothers are conveyed may also turn out to be a river of death and decay. By far the most frequent expressions of this subversively postlapsarian view of time are the various allusions to apples and apple trees, and, through them, the biblical scenes of the Garden of Eden, that Thoreau deliberately strews along the way. Not surprisingly, it is once again at Billerica that we encounter the first reference to the apple tree motif: "Some spring the white man came, built him a house, and made a clearing here, letting in the sun, dried up a farm, piled up the old gray stones in fences, cut down the pines around his dwelling, planted orchard seeds brought from the old country, and persuaded the civil apple tree to blossom next to the wild pine and the juniper, shedding its perfume in the wilderness" (52). Here, as throughout the narrative, the apple tree serves as a kind of insignia of European civilization, just as the native pine and juniper represent the aboriginal way of life: "Every one finds by his own experience, as well as in history, that the era in which men cultivate the apple, and the amenities of the garden, is essentially different from that of the hunter and forest life, and neither can displace the other without loss" (54). Subsequently, the apple tree assumes a conspicuous position in several crucial passages depicting early collisions between Indian and white cultures. The most significant of these, Thoreau's recounting of the Hannah Dustan story in the "Thursday" section, bluntly foregrounds this motif by describing in stark detail the actions of marauding Indians as they dashed out her infant's brains against an apple tree.

In this re-creation, the apple tree represents the main site of conflict between indigenous and white cultures. Elsewhere it also becomes a point of contestation between European culture, especially Christian religious culture, and Thoreau himself. Henry and John take pleasure biting into a good crisp apple in much the same way they take pleasure in violating the Christian Sabbath. As they pause to consider the unblemished glories of a Sabbath noon, they luxuriate guiltlessly in the shade offered by a nearby apple tree (89). In such scenes, the apple obviously wields more than mere political and economic significance; it also symbolizes a vision of time and experience that the narrator of *A Week* audaciously rejects. The overall action of the narrative suggests that the brothers spurn the distinctively Christian meanings associated with the apple in their ambition to achieve their own spiritual redemption independent of the dictates of Christian myth. Yet it is curious that Thoreau in effect reinstates the Christian myth of the Fall at the same time as he appears to be rejecting the Christian doctrines attached to it. The whole movement of the voyage he characterizes with motifs and images borrowed from the Christian Fall story. For example, the crusty farmer or "melon man" dwelling between the river and Uncannunuc Mountain, whom the brothers encounter as they approach their final destination, calls up vague associations with his Adamic predecessor. He superintends his own "melon" patch (a word derived from the Greek word for "apple") under different conditions but with the same solicitude paid by Adam to the fruits of his own garden.[24]

A microcosm of the overall movement of the voyage to the headwaters of the Merrimack and back may be found in the digressive set piece Thoreau includes in the final pages of "Tuesday," as Lawrence Buell has suggestively shown.[25] After passing a set of rapids known as Moore's Falls, the brothers briefly abandon their boat to explore the unknown shore.

> At length the unwearied, never sinking shore, still holding on without break, with its cool copses and serene pasture grounds, tempted us to disembark; and we adventurously landed on this remote coast, to survey it, probably without the knowledge of any human inhabitant to this day. But we still remember the gnarled and hospitable oaks which grew even there for our entertainment, and were no strangers to us, the lonely horse in his pasture, and the patient cows, whose path to the river, so judiciously chosen to overcome the difficulties of the way, we followed, and disturbed their ruminations in the shade; and, above all, the cool free aspect of the wild apple trees, generously proffering their fruit to us, though still green and crude, the hard, round, glossy fruit, which, if not ripe, still was not poison, but New English too, brought hither its ancestors by ours once. These gentler trees imparted a half-civilized and twilight aspect of the otherwise barbarian land. Still further on we scrambled up the rocky channel of a brook, which had long served nature for a sluice there, leaping like it from rock to rock through tangled woods, at the bottom of a ravine, which grew darker and darker, and more and more hoarse the murmurs of the stream, until we reached the ruins of a mill, where

now the ivy grew, and the trout glanced through the crumbling flume; and there we imagined what had been the dreams and speculations of some early settler. But the waning day compelled us to embark once more, and redeem this wasted time with long and vigorous sweeps over the rippling stream. (232–33)

Here Thoreau might as well be taking a page from a New England sketchbook, so great is his fidelity to the details of this landscape, but the "cool copses," "serene pasture grounds," and "hospitable oaks" that grow there for the brothers' "entertainment" lend it an uncharacteristically inviting, even paradisal air. The apple trees and signs of "some early settler," in particular, once again call up vague associations with Edenic myth, but the relations between this upland New England scene and the Garden of Eden are attenuated and carefully problematized. Here the two brothers do not encounter Paradise directly, of course, but only some surviving remnant: the old farm is all run out, the pastures are overgrown, and the ancient mill has been reduced to ruins. It is a scene, moreover, that we, like them, now encounter only through the mists of memory and the brothers' own doubtful "dreams and speculations." Furthermore, these are not, after all, cultivated apples they discover, but wild ones, "crude" descendants of the more delicate English stock of the original settler. At the same time, no archangel with flaming sword bars access to this New World garden, and no prohibitions fence off the fruits growing here. As in the larger narrative pattern of the book, the brothers come to this lowly paradise at will and go from it refreshed and revitalized. These are points Thoreau wishes to make in this apparent digression, however oblique its relation to Adamic myth and the rest of his narrative. This kind of revisionism is possible, in fact, only to the extent that the lineaments of the Fall myth remain at least partially visible. When, late in the afternoon, the brothers cast off once again from this isolated shore, they feel pressed to make up for lost time. As if to affirm the spiritual possibilities envisioned for the voyage overall, Thoreau deliberately invokes some old theological usage in characterizing the brothers' concern at this point to "redeem this wasted time."

This inset story thus epitomizes the larger narrative both in its essential up and back structure and in its coupling of the Romantic version of the myth of paradise regained with the biblical myth of paradise lost. From the standpoint of tradition, of course, these stories represent historically sequential, not commensurate, narratives, as Milton's own literary re-creations demonstrate. In *A Week,* however, Thoreau seems intent on superimposing one myth upon the other within the parameters of a single narrative, effectively annulling all chronological distance. This mythic dovetailing amounts to a kind of generic experiment on Thoreau's part that has important implications for our reading of his text and our understanding of his religious thought. The effort to wed the biblical myth of the Fall to the Romantic myth of rebirth may strike us as promising at first, but it cannot long postpone our realization that such a union can never last. These two myths draw upon the same narrative structures and materials, but represent two fundamentally different views of time, history, and the human condition. With its triumphant personal and collective vision of the new American Paradise, the Romantic myth stands in an at best uneasy relationship with the tragic vision of the biblical Fall story. Yet Thoreau puts the dissonance thus engendered to careful use in accentuating his creation's formal ambiguity.

The unstable juxtaposition of these two myths provides a generic basis for the kind of religious or existential double vision to which *A Week* everywhere bears witness. It is tempting simply to read Thoreau's first book, once we recognize its basic narrative structure, as a kind of nineteenth-century quest narrative, in which our heroes penetrate to the transcendental source of time, then return to the light of common day redeemed and revivified. But this, as we have seen, is not how Thoreau manipulates the underlying mythic structures. Nowhere does the narrative witness to any absolute conquest of time or history, even in its most inspired moments; instead Thoreau seems committed to dramatizing the tension and interpenetration in human experience between time and eternity, fall and redemption, history and myth. The best symbol for this thematic co-presence of time and timelessness is, of course, the river itself. In "the lapse of the current," a contemplative onlooker such as

Thoreau perceives both the value of change and nonchange, what is perpetually "current" and what "lapses" into past or futurity (12–13). Elsewhere he exemplifies the paradox of temporal co-presence more matter-of-factly: "All streams are but tributary to the ocean, which itself does not stream, and the shores are unchanged but in longer periods than man can measure. Go where we will, we discover infinite change in particulars only, not in generals" (124).

The principal distinction of *A Week* lies, in fact, in its fundamental ambivalence, an ambivalence that manifests itself everywhere thematically and imagistically, as well as structurally. The truth about what we encounter along the banks of the river also depends upon the perspective from which it is viewed. We are required to come to terms with this fact as early as the opening paragraph of the book, when Thoreau asks us to consider the river on which the brothers set off under two separate designations—the Musketaquid, or "Grass-Ground River," as the Indians would have it, and the "Concord River," as the Europeans referred to it. The narrator prefers the Indian over the European designation, especially since the subsequent history of Concord so often belied its idyllic name, but his main concern is to indicate the sharply divergent understandings to which the respective names give expression. There is much at stake in a name, after all—at least these names. The Indian and the English words represent two totally different perspectives on the same elemental reality. Thoreau introduces this terminological distinction in the relaxed and casual manner characteristic of the travel genre, but he makes it quite deliberately in order to inaugurate the series of Indian versus European encounters and interpretive standoffs that comes to shape much of his subsequent narrative. Periodically thereafter, he makes it clear that what we see in this New England voyage in and through time depends upon whether we view it from a red or white perspective. In fact, Thoreau predicates his handling of much of the narrative on this ambipolar perspective, from parts of his diatribe in the "Sunday" section to his accounts of the Lovewell fight and Hannah Dustan incident later on. The validity of the Fall myth itself depends of course upon whether we see it through Indian or European eyes.

The book's characteristic double perspective also finds marked thematic expression in the opposition between East and West, upon which Thoreau bases much of his continued discussion of religion and ethics in the "Monday" section. So crucial is an understanding of Thoreau's Orientalism to his religious thought that it will receive a chapter of its own further on. Here it is enough simply to point out that this dichotomy provides another principal vehicle in the articulation of the book's determinedly disjunctive view of reality. In a distinction common to other early nineteenth-century Orientalist treatments, Thoreau conceives the East as a land of contemplation and the West as a land of action. The distinction between action and contemplation lines up in turn with the book's more basic thematic oppositions between time and timelessness, history and transcendence, suffering and redemption. Thoreau illustrates the sometimes rivaling claims of action and contemplation in his depiction of the daily routine of the brothers in their voyage upriver. The narrator characterizes the progress of each day naturally enough in terms of the usual diurnal cycles of rest and activity, sleep and waking. In addition, each day is broken up by a period of "nooning" when the two brothers temporarily beach their boat, have lunch, and enjoy some meditative midday repose. "There are moments when all anxiety and stated toil are becalmed in the infinite leisure and repose of nature," the narrator writes. "All laborers must have their nooning, and at this season of the day, we are all, more or less, Asiatics, and give over all work and reform. While lying thus on our oars by the side of the stream, in the heat of the day, our boat held by an osier put through the staple in its prow, and slicing the melons, which are a fruit of the east, our thoughts reverted to Arabia, Persia, and Hindostan, the lands of contemplation" (125–26). Appropriately for the imaginative schema of this book, such a period of rest also provides the narrative context for Thoreau's appreciative disquisition on contemplation and India's "noontide philosophy" in "Monday" (147).[26]

Nowhere is the doubling propensity characteristic of *A Week* more clearly foregrounded, however, than in the basic relationship between the two brothers. At points Thoreau utilizes this relationship to help

convey and concretize the philosophical themes of action and contemplation upon which he elsewhere reflects: as one brother rows, the
other looks on; as one sleeps, the other meditates.[27] Of course, this
feature of the narrative's basic plot merely reflects the actual facts of the
voyage itself, but Thoreau obviously develops his characterization of the
relationship in ways consistent with the elegiac and imaginative designs
of the book. Throughout the narrative, the silent, almost ghostlike figure
of John functions as a kind of doppelgänger in respect to the bolder
figure cut by Henry himself. Never in *A Week* does John assume a
completely concrete or conspicuous character in his own right—never is
he specifically described or heard from—but his unspoken presence lends
a depth to the narrative it would not have otherwise. We know what the
narrator thinks and perceives, and sometimes what the brothers experienced or thought together, but John himself remains something of a
cipher. His own particular views or individuality go perpetually unreported. There is some reason to think, as Linck Johnson has argued, that
this bloodlessness results in part from Henry's efforts in the years following John's tragic death to idealize his brother, consistent with the conventions of elegy, along the lines described in his essay on friendship.[28] But
idealizing John in this way also helps to convey dramatically the kind of
divided vision to which the book repeatedly gives expression.

The clearest expression of this dividedness in respect to the motif of
the two brothers occurs in the ominously prophetic final paragraph of
"Sunday." "One sailor," the narrator notes portentously, "was visited in
his dreams this night by the Evil Destinies, and all those powers that are
hostile to human life, which constrain and oppress the minds of men,
and make their path seem difficult and narrow, and beset with dangers,
so that the most innocent and worthy enterprises appear insolent and a
tempting of fate, and the gods go not with us. But the other happily
passed a serene and even ambrosial or immortal night, and his sleep was
dreamless, or only the atmosphere of pleasant dreams remained, a happy
natural sleep until the morning; and his cheerful spirit soothed and
reassured his brother, for whenever they meet, the Good Genius is sure
to prevail" (116). The source of this evil prophecy was of course the fact

of John's death three years later. Nowhere in the narrative does Thoreau explicitly acknowledge his brother's death, but it obviously shaped his conception of the text in essential ways. Here in the prophecy of death's imminence, we realize that despite their outward solidarity, on some level the two brothers have already begun to part ways, one ruled over by the "Evil Destinies," the other by the "Good Genius." As Henry wanders into fields of light, John pursues a dark and unfortunate way, thus epitomizing the disjunctively comic/tragic vision informing the work as a whole. But the fact of death alone does not convey the full significance of John's role in the narrative. Throughout, John plays the part of a kind of privileged spectator, remaining on the fringes of the action of the voyage even as he participates centrally in it. The figure of John moves about in the background, presumed but never fully manifested, as a kind of sign of or gesture to some larger reality to which we have no direct access in the narrative itself. Indeed, to some extent, Thoreau treats John as a silent double of himself, a witness to all his experience who yet remains somehow unclaimed and unspoken for within the boundaries of the constructed narrative. This imagined relationship between the two brothers—one active, the other silent and uninvolved—adumbrates the representation of ecstatic self-spectatorship in *Walden* to which we will return in Chapter Five. Here it dramatizes a sense of self-transcendence characteristic of Thoreau's disjunctive imagination and mature ecstatic vision. One important effect of John's understated presence is to destabilize the narrator's own matter-of-fact representations. Conspicuous by virtue of his mute alterity, John in effect relativizes the authorial voice and heightens the text's potential for ambivalence, irony, and paradox.

Crucial to the view of *A Week* as a record of personal inspiration and a narrative of spiritual quest has been the recognition that Thoreau deliberately structures his account in terms of a series of alternations between action and contemplation, narration and reflection. We may even read the book as a loosely arranged but progressive series of epiphanous moments, as long as we recognize that Thoreau places these epiphanies in careful tension with countervailing historical pressures.[29] The auroral reflections entertained on Sunday morning, the grand afflatus brought on by the night drummer at the end of "Monday" discussed in the last chapter, and the retrospective account of the ascent of Mount Saddleback at the beginning of "Tuesday" all exemplify Thoreau's careful preoccupation with and orchestration of spiritual inspirations in the body of *A Week*. These moments of inspiration deliberately interrupt the temporal action of the story as if to mitigate the pressures of history and perhaps foreshadow some climactic triumph over time itself. Yet, as morning passes inexorably to noon, and day to evening, even these moments of vision must inevitably yield their consolations to the disappointments and limitations of private experience. Perhaps the clearest expression of such promising but ultimately vitiated vision is provided in Thoreau's recollection of his climb to the top of Mount Greylock ("Saddleback") in the Berkshire hills. While he grounds his descriptions carefully, as usual, in the details of the actual experience, he graces his account with obvious religious overtones. Having arrived at the summit of Greylock just before sunset, Thoreau spends the night huddled against the wall of the Williams College observatory. At dawn, he climbs the observatory tower to be met with a vision of unspeakable grandeur. Stretched out before him in all directions is an undulating sea of clouds irradiated by the rising sun: "As the light in the east steadily increased, it revealed to me more clearly the new world into which I had risen in the night, the new terra-firma perchance of my future life. . . . It was such a country as we might see in dreams, with all the delights of paradise." Yet, notwithstanding "the gorgeous tapestry" at his feet, in the end, Thoreau concludes this elevated digression by mourning the existence of "some unworthiness" or "stain" in his own character that separates him from the irresistible perfection of his natural surroundings (188–90). We realize, moreover, that the enchantment we witness in this account owes as much to the filtering influence of memory as it does to the actual experience itself.

In view of the mythic pattern of the quest upon which the narrative of *A Week* essentially depends, we would expect the climactic episode in this string of epiphanies to be reserved for the brothers' eventual ascent of Mount Washington. This was, after all, the true peak experience, as it were, of the brothers' actual journey and as such, it invites some sort of comprehensive treatment. Yet, oddly enough, Thoreau says almost nothing about it. What he offers instead is an elliptical interlude of three short paragraphs in which he provides little more than a summary of the final journey up the Pemigewasset, past its fountainhead in the Amonoo-suck, and eventually to the summit of the mountain he refers to here only by its Indian name, Agiocochook. It is almost as if this passage were designed as a surrogate for some fuller treatment Thoreau never wrote or chose to omit. Indeed, he appears to go out of his way to undercut the very climax that the quest myth entitles us to anticipate. Critics have remarked of course on this anomaly in the narrative and sought to explain it in various ways.[30] One clue for understanding this cryptic interlude may be suggested by Thoreau's dependence on native terms in his description of this final ascent. In deference to the Indian traditions associated with these wild places, he resorts almost entirely here to the Algonquin names—Pemigewasset, Amonoosuck, Agiocochook. Here again we seem to find ourselves on contested mythical terrain. The mountaintop may represent the natural goal of the heroic quest in some European narratives, but Native Americans considered such places the sanctuary of gods, basically off-limits to human beings and dangerous in the extreme. This native conception of the sacred mountain impressed itself upon Thoreau during his harrowing ascent of Mount Katahdin on his trip to Maine in the late summer of 1846. There was nothing heavenly about the blasted summit of Katahdin or the treacherous ascent to it. The natural world Thoreau encountered there was "vast," "titanic," utterly inhospitable to human life (MW, 64–65). Only in the myths of ancient Greece or the beliefs of native North Americans could he find a suitable response to his vertiginous experience of this bleak and inhospitable landscape. These were the precincts of the Algonquin god Pomola, who "is always angry with those who climb to the summit of Ktaadn" (65). Thoreau had recorded his notes on the 1839 trip to Mount Washington long before this first trip to Maine, but these experiences on Katahdin were no doubt in his thoughts as he worked to revise the manuscript of A Week in the months before its publication.[31]

Like Katahdin, Agiocochook proves a less auspicious place than we might have expected. The brothers come to this "Unappropriated Land" across "stumpy, rocky, forested and bepastured country" and trees "prostrate" over what remains of the Amonoosuck. We hear nothing in this passage of sublime aerial views or mountain vistas. On the contrary, the narrator seems eager to gloss over the four days in the mountains in as few words as possible. The one observation he does see fit to record—the vignette of the self-conscious soldier boy "in full regimentals" retreating ignominiously down the mountainside—seems especially out of place, until we realize how emblematic it is of the conception of mountaintop experience that Thoreau seems concerned to sketch for us here. "Poor man!" the narrator exclaims, "He actually shivered like a reed in his thin military pants, and by the time we had got up with him, all the sternness that becomes the soldier had forsaken his face, and he skulked past as if he were driving his father's sheep under a sword-proof helmet" (313). As we have seen previously, Thoreau elsewhere extolls military bearing and the heroic character, but such mortal heroism obviously makes a ludicrous impression against the backdrop of the mountain's raw preternatural power. No doubt the narrator recognizes something of his own condition also in the pathetic picture of this "poor man." It is one thing, this cryptic, understated treatment seems to say, to mythologize about transcendental experience, it is quite another to experience or describe it. The peak experience, it turns out, not only heaps scorn upon our human frailty, it also refuses the ambitions of our words. Indeed, hardly are we aware of having reached the goal of the voyage before the narrator plunges us into his discursive account of the return.

Elisha's Apple Tree

The degree to which Thoreau seeks to revise and compromise the heroic mythology of rebirth on which the narrative partly relies only becomes fully apparent during the precipitous return voyage back down the Merrimack. From the standpoint of the hero myth, the voyage of return must be conceived as an act of renewal and redemption, but Thoreau makes sure to characterize their return as one also of decline and Fall. He signals the reassertion of the tragic mythology of the Fall in the quotation from George Herbert that he invokes to inaugurate this final leg of the journey. The fragment epitomizes the ambivalent mood of joy and foreboding that especially dominates the brothers' reentry into the normal stream of time and civilization.

> Sweet days, so cool, so calm, so bright,
> The bridal of the earth and sky,
> Sweet dews shall weep thy fall to-night,
>   For thou must die.
>   (314)

On returning to Hooksett to retrieve their boat, the brothers revisit the garden of "the melon man," where they procure a watermelon, now fittingly ripe, to tide them over on their return journey. As they embark once more, the river rushes them quickly downstream past the landmarks encountered so painstakingly in their laborious passage upriver the week before.

In his treatment of the last two days of *A Week*, Thoreau whiles away his time reflecting on the topics of Goethe, poetry, Ossian, and Chaucer, among others, but the most memorable digression in this final stage of the journey is the one involving Hannah Dustan, colonial heroine of the town of Haverhill. As their boat sweeps downriver, past the scene of one of colonial America's most notoriously bloody episodes, Thoreau recounts the grisly story of Dustan's capture by warring Indians on a raw March morning in 1697, the savage murder of her infant, and the even more savage revenge she later wreaks on her captors as she tomahawks them to death in their sleep and makes off with their scalps. In retelling this horrific tale, Thoreau twice makes reference to the apple tree against which the Indians were said to have smashed the skull of the screaming infant and concludes his account with the cryptic remark: "and there have been many who in later times have lived to say that they had eaten of the fruit of that apple-tree" (324). In his commentary on the Hannah Dustan story, Thoreau connects this latter-day mother of Haverhill to a long line of matriarchs stretching back sixty generations to "Eve the mother of mankind" herself. Like this most illustrious ancestor, Hannah, it appears, has left her descendants with a contested and deeply troubled legacy. We are not sure whether to revere or revile her. Was she a hero or a criminal herself? Is her story one of sin or redemption? Whatever the answer, it is clear that Thoreau conceives of this incident as a fateful moment in the early history of relations between the Indians and white men. Noting the precedent afforded by Milton, he presents the story of Hannah Dustan as a kind of American original sin and the account as a kind of New World *Paradise Lost.* As their boat glides quickly past the scene of her infamous deed, Thoreau imagines the brothers following in the wake of Dustan, her nurse, and a young English boy as they made their harrowing escape by canoe downriver toward the safety of the English settlements, ten Indian scalps—early trophies of the genocide already underway—still bleeding at their feet.

Before dawn the next morning, the brothers' last on the river, they detect a slight change in the night air. Overnight, almost imperceptibly, the season had turned. "We had gone to bed in summer," writes Thoreau, "and we awoke in autumn; for summer passes into autumn in some unimaginable point of time, like the turning of a leaf" (334). As they set off once more, they note everywhere the early signs of seasonal change: "We soon passed the mouth of the Souhegan and the village of Merrimack, and as the mist gradually rolled away, and we were relieved from the trouble of watching for rocks, we saw by the flitting clouds, by the first russet tinge on the hills, by the rushing river, the cottages on shore, and the shore itself, so cooly fresh and shining with dew, and later in the day, by the hue of the grape vine, the goldfinch on the willow, the flickers flying in flocks, and when we passed near enough to the shore, as we fancied, by the faces of men, that the Fall had commenced" (335). Although the autumn equinox was still almost a week away, Thoreau highlights the first signs of fall so as to provide an appropriate natural setting for the heightening elegiac mood of the book's closing pages. Still flushed with enthusiasm from the adventure they have just completed, the brothers return to a different world than the one they had left two weeks previously. Never in the whole experience of the voyage have we been so struck by the sense of dissonance between inner and outer experiences of reality. The anticipated sense of triumph is here undercut by the palpable sense of impending death. These symptoms of transformation lend greater credence to the religious and existential implications of the Fall myth on which Thoreau has often relied and to which he sometimes alludes in the construction of his narrative. Yet, even in the face of the mounting evidence of life's downturn, *A Week* retains its heroic and basically hopeful outlook. The apothegm that he tucks unobtrusively into the "Friday" section might almost serve as the motto of the book: "There is something even in the lapse of time by which time recovers itself" (351).

In the "Friday" chapter, Thoreau returns to the apple tree motif twice more in order to dramatize for the last time the divided religious vision informing the book as a whole. The first reference occurs in the curious account of the freshet of 1785, when, according to one authority, the river had risen twenty-one feet above the usual high-water mark. By Thoreau's time, the reports of such an unprecedented and nearly inconceivable spring flood had been subject to much doubt, and few were left who really believed the story. Yet, according to tradition, one old inhabitant of the town had marked the height of the flood by driving a nail into an apple tree behind his house. This old tree was named "Elisha's apple tree," in honor of an Indian friendly to the white settlers who had been killed by other Indians very near the spot. When in the year 1818, an engineer for a projected railroad made inquiries as to the seasonal habits of the river, he was conducted to the old apple tree by the current owner of the property. Although the nail marking the height of the freshet of 1785 was by then no longer visible, the owner directed the engineer to reach inside the hollow of the tree in order to feel the point of the nail that was still sticking through the other side. In this vignette, the apple tree continues to serve Thoreau as a site of contestation between two cultures, two myths, and two worlds of meaning. As an Indian friendly to whites, Elisha seems well suited to serve as the emblem of this particular apple tree's mixed symbolic legacy. Indeed, his status is reminiscent of the wild apple trees themselves, successor trees to those planted by the first European settlers. Like these now wild trees, he too was a kind of hybrid between the worlds of old Europe and native North America. It is interesting to note that Thoreau felt a special kinship with the wild apple tree, as he notes in his journal of 1851: "But our wild apple is wild perchance like myself who belong not to the aboriginal race here—but have strayed into the woods from the cultivated stock—where the birds where winged thoughts or agents have planted or are planting me" (PJ.3.232).

In terms of its religious significance, at least, Elisha's apple tree certainly reflects such a divided legacy. On the one hand, like the prohibited apple tree of biblical tradition, this tree functions as a kind of reminder or memorial to later generations. On the other hand, this tree is not associated with Adam and his legacy, but with Elisha and his. Like the summit of Agiocochook that Thoreau hesitates to describe, we must conceive this apple tree in New World, not Old World terms. The event to which Elisha's apple tree bears witness was not some "original sin" as Europeans conceived of it, but a now all but unimaginable season of nature's power and plenty. Unburdened—as Thoreau also was—by any ideologies of the Fall, any sense of fundamental divorce between man and nature, Native Americans were free to construe an episode of natural fullness as a measure of human possibility as well. We might even say that Elisha's tree is less a tree of fall than a tree of spring and—to shift once again to a biblical register—Easter. It offers a constant record, not of lapse but of highest possibility. In his treatment of the railroad engineer's skeptical inquest, Thoreau even hints at such Christological overtones: "When he came to this house he was conducted to the apple-tree, and as the nail was not then visible, the lady of the house placed her hand on the trunk where she said that she remembered the nail to have been from her childhood. In the meanwhile the old man put his arm inside the tree, which was hollow, and felt the point of the nail sticking through, and it was exactly opposite to her hand" (356). This vignette provides a curious reenactment of the story of the Doubting Thomas who refused to believe in the resurrected Lord until he touched with his own hands the wounds left by the nails of crucifixion.[32] But where the Doubting Thomas touches and believes, the doubting engineer touches yet still rejects. Viewed in this context, Thoreau's concluding reflection seems more pointed: "But as no one else remembered the river to have risen so high as this, the engineer disregarded this statement, and I learn that there has since been a freshet which rose within nine inches of the rails at Biscuit Brook, and such a freshet as that of 1785 would have covered the railroad two feet deep" (356).

Thoreau's handling of the story of Elisha's apple tree and the great freshet of 1785 prompts us to envision a sort of coalescence between the tree of Adam's temptation and Fall, and the "tree" of Christ's crucifixion and resurrection. Thoreau is not the first in Western tradition to imagine a connection between these two fateful trees—analogies between Adam and Christ were part of the familiar stock of biblical typology—but it is convenient for him to do so here. Elisha's apple tree retains some of the tragic associations it has in the biblical tradition yet assumes new meaning in its association with the unprecedented freshet of 1785. Through it, Thoreau intensifies the tensions and ambiguities he has so carefully built into the narrative till this point. How we read the figure of the apple tree—as a forbidding reminder of a terrible Fall or as a testament of prior and perhaps prospective fullness—depends, the story seems to say, in the end on who we are. From his standpoint, Thoreau habitually sees it both ways and takes pains to design the narrative of his voyage to convey this disjunctive vision. In the end though, as far as the freshet of 1785 is concerned, he seems inclined to credit the traditional evidence. He has seen his own freshets after all—natural and personal—and though they never perhaps rose quite so high, they tend to confirm the mark recorded on Elisha's apple tree.

The motif of the apple tree occurs once more in *A Week,* this time in the last paragraph of the narrative, in the context of Thoreau's description of the brothers' eagerly awaited homecoming late Friday night: "We had made about fifty miles this day with sail and oar, and now, far in the evening, our boat was grating against the bulrushes of its native port, and its keel recognized the Concord mud, where some semblance of its outline was still preserved in the flattened flags which had scarce yet erected themselves since our departure; and we leaped gladly on shore, drawing it up, and fastening it to the wild apple-tree, whose stem still bore the mark which its chain had worn in the chafing of the spring freshets" (393). Still preserving the marks of a previous spring's high water, just as Elisha's apple tree had done, this apple tree of Concord seems to point to a legacy of resurrection rather than of death—but only subsequent experience would tell for sure. Like so much else in this book, the concluding vignette reflects the curious double consciousness that was fast becoming the hallmark both of Thoreau's literary imagination and spiritual vision.

Four

Born to Be a Pantheist

The voyage upriver to the White Mountains and back provided Thoreau with the basic structure around which to weave *A Week*'s complex and curiously invested narrative. The familiar form of the romantic excursion narrative suited his designs particularly well, since it offered him the kind of inclusive structure he needed to accommodate his other literary and philosophical objectives: he exploits its encyclopedic possibilities in order to incorporate poems, historical accounts, scientific observations, and other miscellaneous material. But if *A Week* provides the best formal reenactment of Thoreau's early religious experience, it also offers the fullest expression we have of his considered religious views. The chapters entitled "Sunday" and "Monday," in particular, provide one of our most sustained expressions of Transcendentalist religious ideology. Representations of Thoreau's religious thought may also be found elsewhere in his writings: *Walden, Cape Cod,* and the journal, as well as the occasional essays—"Life Without Principle" and "Walking," for instance—but nowhere does he treat these topics as exhaustively as he does in *A Week*. It is entirely characteristic of Thoreau's religious thinking that in this case the treatment occurs in the context of a narrative about his own experience. This format offers literary confirmation of a fact crucial to our understanding of Thoreau's religious thought: that his religious ideas are only really explicable in reference to the momentous experiences of euphoria that were the real ballast of his spiritual life.

It is in recognition of the experiential cast of Thoreau's religious thought that the following inventory of his religious ideas adheres to the general contours of his own treatment of religion in "Sunday." Key to appreciating the views expressed here, however, is a recognition of the degree to which they are embedded in a narrative about his previous experience and predicated on the rhetoric of what becomes, in effect, his own (albeit revisionist) Sunday sermon. In other words, it is misleading to consider the views expressed here independently of their rhetorical context and their relation to Thoreau's prior experience. Thoreau rejected metaphysics and systematic theology as so much hubris, and saw little value in religious propositions for their own sake. His own "theology," if we can use this term for such a subversive religious thinker, was rhetorically invested, pointedly critical, deliberately unsystematic, and experientially fueled. It offered a vision of the world beholden to no tribunal but nature and his own experience. It was, in effect, a kind of negative theology, or what, in keeping with its experiential character, we might call a theology of ecstatic experience.

From the time of its first appearance, the acerbic digressions of "Sunday" have at times presented a stumbling block to the book's full appreciation. Horace Greeley scolded Thoreau for his "misplaced Pantheistic attack on the Christian Faith," and James Russell Lowell likened his digressions on exotic religious thinkers to "snags" that an oarsman might come upon on an otherwise placid river journey.[1] Thoreau's practice of interpolating long digressions about religion into the body of a travel narrative has been defended, when it has been defended at all, mostly on literary grounds, as somehow consistent with the literary plan or genre within which he was working. Less recognized is the fact that this format also has an important religious or theological rationale. It is no accident, indeed, that Thoreau's most developed discussion of religion takes the form of a *critique* of existing institutions, and does so within the context of a narrative exploring the adequacy and meaning of the Christian mythology of the Fall. "Sunday" offered the perfect opportunity, after all, to reflect critically on the implications of the doctrine of the Fall and the religion he considered its chief proponent, if not perpetrator.

Thoreau signals his preoccupation with the Fall in "Sunday," and the book as a whole, in the opening paragraph of the chapter. Here he anticipates his subsequent challenge to Christianity by pointing to a suggestive disparity between the auroral natural day that greets the brothers as they awake and the religious mindset of the tradition that holds it apart as sacred. "It was a quiet Sunday morning," the narrator writes, "with more of the auroral rosy and white than of the yellow light in it, as if it dated from earlier than the fall of man, and still preserved a heathenish integrity" (43). As the boat gets underway, *A Week*'s narrator finds the lush and luxuriant vegetation bordering the river more reminiscent of "Persian gardens" and "the artificial lakes of the east" than a conventional New England landscape (45). In this exotic natural setting, we seem for the moment transported to some Oriental or even prelapsarian garden. Thoreau indicates the paradisal character of this "natural Sabbath" in his meditations on the river's fathomless transparency and the spontaneous echoes from adjacent cliffs and woods (46). In this auroral place, the usual walls of experience seem to fall away, and the brothers witness "manifold visions in the direction of every object, and even the most opaque reflect the heavens from their surface" (48). In the crystalline responsiveness of atmosphere and water, these two men in a skiff appear to float among the trees' endless reflections, problematizing our usual distinctions between reality and reflection, the real and the unreal, the upper and the lower worlds (48–49). Here, in a section of river presided over only by the sun, the brothers encounter a natural world still unstained by human contact and the old agonies and dread of Western experience. The atmosphere is one of perfect serenity.

Into this pristine and primeval natural setting, the history of the old town of Billerica, to which the narrator then turns, signals the entrance of a rude and destructive intruder. As we have seen, Thoreau's remarks on Billerica initiate the long and painful story of European seizure of Indian lands and the eventual destruction of the native way of life to which he returns periodically throughout the narrative. In stark contrast to the perennial freshness and youth of the river paradise, this Billerica is an "old gray town," already in its "dotage." In some sense, Billerica typifies age itself, unrelieved by new life: "I have never heard that it was young," the narrator remarks mockingly (50). It is an emblem of physical and spiritual decay, a place of run-down farms and worn-out buildings, where even nature seems to have lost its vitality. To places such as Billerica, Europeans came to build their houses, clear their lands, and plant their orchards over the bones of dead Indians (53). Until this point in their voyage, the brothers have enjoyed a side of nature hardly touched by the presence of the adjoining towns, but here, just above Billerica Falls, a canal built to circumvent the rapids interrupts the natural course of the river and mars the beauty of its natural scenery. The arrival at Billerica thus represents a turning point in the actual voyage itself, but it also provides the pretext for Thoreau's Sunday morning tirades against the Christian religion. Before Billerica, the stately, slow-moving Concord floated the brothers silently along through a virtual paradise of luxuriant greenery, but here at Billerica Falls, they "heard this staid and primitive river rushing to her fall," as if to provide an appropriate natural analogue for the religious views and values Thoreau would now begin to excoriate.

Pagoda Worship

Serving as the point of departure for this long excursus on Christianity is Thoreau's caustic treatment of the institution of the Christian Sabbath. As their boat passes beneath the last bridge over the canal, the brothers endure some hard looks and "heathenish comparisons" from a small company of sanctimonious churchgoers looking down on them from above. But the miscreants exult in their infidelity, parrying official criticism with their own mock professions of pagan faith. This "sunday" was the day set aside for the sun, after all, and basking in its rays, they were among its "truest observers." Aligning himself with the pagan rather than the Christian calendar, Thoreau recalls a line from Hesiod recounting the birth of the "golden-rayed Apollo," ancient Greek god of the sun. Indeed, as far as the voyagers are concerned, much Christian observance of the Sabbath amounts to a desecration. "There are few things more disheartening and disgusting," he asserts, "than when you are walking the streets of a strange village on the Sabbath, to hear a preacher shouting like a boatswain in a gale of wind, and thus harshly profaning the quiet atmosphere of the day. You fancy him to have taken off his coat, as when men are about to do hot and dirty work" (76).

Thoreau's comments on the Sabbath suggest that what really got under his skin was less the practice itself than the censoriousness and rigidity with which it was observed. It was nothing more than a superstition, he thought, raised to the level of unassailable dogma and then used as a blunt instrument to keep people in line. Late the previous summer, "the sound of the sabbath bell" one morning evoked irritation, as well as pleasure: "One is sick at heart of this pagoda worship—" Thoreau remarked, "it is like the beating of gongs in a Hindoo subterranean temple" (PJ.1.51). It was this exclusivist conformity and manifest intolerance for other ways of worship that most galled him about the Christian churches of his day. He encountered enough intolerance in his own native region to suspect that what passed under the name of religion was generally little more than provincial sectarianism or bigoted ethnocentrism. In subsequent years, this suspicion hardened into conviction as he read more widely in travel accounts involving other cultures:

> I am astonished to find how much travellers both in the east and west permit themselves to be imposed on by a name—That the traveller in the east for instance presumes so great a difference between one Asiatic and another because one bears the title of a christian & the other not— . . . As if a Christian's dog were something better than a Mahometan's.—I perceive no triumphant superiority in the so called Christian over the so-called Mahometan. That nation is not Christian where the principles of humanity do not prevail, but the prejudices of race. I expect the Christian not to be superstitious—but to be distinguished by the clearness of his knowledge—the strength of his faith, the breadth of his humanity. A man of another race, an African for instance, comes to America

to travel through it, & he meets with treatment exactly similar to that which the American meets with among the Turks—& Arabs— & Tartars— The traveller in both cases finds the religion to be a mere superstition & frenzy—or rabidness. (PJ.4.98–99)

So far as he was concerned, religious sectarianism was an offense against the spirit of religion and an embarrassment to the teachings of Christ. "The Gods are of no sect," he quipped in 1841, "they side with no man." Nothing in the natural world, furthermore, confirmed the sort of exclusivist sectarianism he found in the Christian pulpits; outdoors he only saw evidence of "the grand catholicism of nature, and the unbribable charity of the gods" (PJ.1.301).

Thoreau's handling of religion in *A Week* suggests that he was apt to share with William Blake the radical view that the institutions of religion operated everywhere in complicity against the very sources of their own inspiration. He admired Christ but inveighed against Christians. An institution conceived originally as a vehicle of transcendence soon deteriorated into a mere caretaker of history, a familiar irony dramatized here by the questing brothers' encounters with expressions of official Christendom on Sunday morning. Further along, Thoreau acknowledges Chateaubriand's observation that love of religion increases with age, only to add ruefully that it signals at the same time "the gradual decay of youthful hope and faith" (133). Unfortunately, religion had become an agent of death and decay, rather than youthfulness, inspiration, and rebirth. "We check & repress the divinity that stirs within us," he wrote caustically in 1851, "to fall down & worship the divinity that is dead without us. . . . If it were not for death & funerals I think the institution of the Church would not stand longer" (PJ.4.188–89). Religious institutions spring up, he thought, where religious inspiration dies down. In "Life Without Principle," he put it more picturesquely: "In short, as a snow-drift is formed where there is a lull in the wind, so, one would say, where there is a lull of truth, an institution springs up. But the truth blows right on over it, nevertheless, and at length blows it down" (RP, 177).

The clergy, more than any other group, bore primary responsibility for this unnatural senescence of religion. Thoreau grew up in a Unitarian parish and numbered many Unitarian clergymen among his friends, but he could not forgive them their failure to take proper cognizance of life's greatest and most innocent favors. In his notoriously incendiary address to Harvard's Divinity School in 1838, Emerson had dismissed the ministry as antiquated, but Thoreau went even further, venting with drenching sarcasm his indignation for the philistinism and moral bankruptcy of the New England clergy: "The church! it is eminently the timid institution, and the heads and pillars of it are constitutionally and by principle the greatest cowards in the community" (J.11.325). Spiritual myopia was bad enough, but moral hypocrisy he found intolerable. When Thoreau formally resigned from the church in which he had been raised in 1840, he did so as an expression of nonsupport and noncompliance, but as the years went by, his disapproval of his own and other New England churches became ever more strident (RP, 79). Particularly reprehensible to him was some churches' early opposition to the abolitionist movement. Thoreau spoke out in support of abolitionism early on and became one of its strongest and most effective local spokesmen. In view of Christian ethical teachings, the churches' opposition to abolitionism struck him as the most repugnant form of moral hypocrisy.[2]

Since indignation over the Church's moral obtuseness often skewed later representations, his treatments of religion before the passage of the Fugitive Slave Act in 1850 sometimes strike us as more temperate and perhaps more representative of his general attitudes. This entry from 1841, for instance, provides a particularly helpful indication:

> When I have access to a man's barrel of sermons, which were written from week to week, as his life lapsed—though I now know him to live cheerfully and bravely enough—still I cannot conceive what interval there was for laughter and smiles in the midst of so much sadness. Almost in proportion to the sincerity and earnestness of the life—will be—the sadness of the record. When I reflect that twice a week for so many years he pondered and preached

such a sermon—I think he must have been a splenetic and melancholy man, and wonder if his food digested well. It seems as if the fruit of virtue was never a careless happiness—

A great cheerfulness have all great wits possessed—almost a prophane levity—to such as understood them not—but their religion had the broader basis in proportion as it was less prominent. The religion I love is very laic. The clergy are as diseased, and as much possessed with a devil as the reformers—They make their topic as offensive as the politician—for our religion is as unpublic and incommunicable as our poetical vein—and to be approached with as much love and tenderness. (PJ.1.289)

Comments such as this place Thoreau on the most extreme fringe of the radical Reformation. The almost constitutional antipathy to priests and the priesthood evinced here he held in common with other dissenting groups, such as Quakers, who also stood within a broad tradition of radical protestantism. As this journal entry demonstrates, he never repudiated religion itself, nor even Christian values as such, but only their corporate, ecclesiastical, and political forms. In general, Thoreau refused to conceive of religion in institutional terms; on the contrary, it was for him strictly a private concern—"as unpublic and incommunicable as our poetical vein." And he was profoundly uncomfortable with ostentatious and self-congratulatory professions of faith. Bristling at the gaudy display of the words "Glory to God in the highest" on a neighbor's house, he remarked that "A simple and genuine sentiment of reverence would not emblazon these words as on a signboard in the streets. . . . What is religion? That which is never spoken" (J.11.112–13). Playing on the word's etymology sometimes helped him essentialize the issue, as he does here in *A Week:* "In most men's religion, the ligature, which should be its umbilical cord connecting them with divinity, is rather like that thread which the accomplices of Cylon held in their hands when they went abroad from the temple of Minerva, the other end being attached to the statue of the goddess" (78). In this sense, "religion," a word probably derived from the Latin *re-ligio* (to tie or bind back) constitutes that "ligature" or tie that binds us back to our divine source. As happens, however, in such cases as Cylon's accomplices, the cord may sometimes break, leaving the worshipper lost and disoriented, or more often, the cord may simply become a restraint—a chain rather than a spiritual umbilical cord (64).

Hieroglyphs to the Unborn

It is characteristic of Thoreau's religious outlook, and indeed of Transcendentalism generally, that virtually the only collective expression of tradition for which he held any real regard was religious scripture and myth. As we have seen, myth and the manipulations of myth form the backbone of his narrative in *A Week*. It is a topic, moreover, to which he returns frequently, not only here, but in many of his other writings as well. As far as he was concerned, myth served as a kind of narrative template or archetype for religion. In key respects, the defense he offers of myth in *A Week* harks back to Aristotle's vindication of poetry in *Poetics*. Like poetry, myth offered a higher and more universal expression of truth than history: "To some extent, mythology is only the most ancient history and biography. So far from being false or fabulous in the common sense, it contains only enduring and essential truth, the I and you, the here and there, the now and then, being omitted" (60).[3] It must be recognized, however, that the sort of truth to which myth gives expression bears little relation to the propositional truths of philosophy, the empirical truths of science, or even the dogmatic truths of religion. Rather, myth stands on a metaphysical border between a sort of ideal Platonic form and its concrete ideational or physical expression, forever exceeding the sum of its discrete interpretations:

> The hidden significance of these fables which is sometimes thought to have been detected, the ethics running parallel to the poetry and history, are not so remarkable as the readiness with which they may be made to express a variety of truths. As if they were the skeletons of still older and more universal truths than any whose flesh and blood they are for the time made to wear. It is like striving to make

the sun, or the wind, or the sea, symbols to signify exclusively the particular thoughts of our day. But what signifies it? In the mythus a superhuman intelligence uses the unconscious thoughts and dreams of men as its hieroglyphics to address men unborn. In the history of the human mind, these glowing and ruddy fables precede the noon-day thoughts of men, as Aurora the sun's rays. The matutine intellect of the poet, keeping in advance of the glare of philosophy, always dwells in this auroral atmosphere. (61)

This particular formulation distinctly anticipates some later nineteenth-century German myth theories, as well as the analytic psychology of Carl Jung, in its association of myth with dreams and "unconscious thoughts," but the privileged position accorded the poet marks it as a quintessentially Romantic construct.[4] Like other Romantics, Thoreau conceived ancient mythmakers as the true paragons of poetry (60). Indeed, like other American writers of the period, he envisioned a new Western mythology for a continent and civilization yet bereft of its own: "The West is preparing to add its fables to those of the East. The valleys of the Ganges, the Nile, and the Rhine, having yielded their crop, it remains to be seen what the valleys of the Amazon, the Plate, the Orinoco, the St. Lawrence, and the Mississippi will produce. Perchance, when, in the course of ages, American liberty has become a fiction of the past,—as it is to some extent a fiction of the present,—the poets of the world will be inspired by American mythology" (Writings.5.233).[5]

Thoreau's confident association of myth with the inspired poet reflects the crucial role played in Romantic thought by the idea of the creative imagination. Conceived as an integrative faculty, synthesizing and fusing the creative and speculative powers of human reason, the creative imagination provided Romantic thinkers with a firm basis upon which to reconcile otherwise conflicting antinomies of culture—of reason and feeling, science and religion, philosophy and art.[6] The poet was often conceived to have a special place in such philosophies of culture as the architect and re-creator of tradition. No less for Thoreau and his Transcendentalist friends than for Herder, Schelling, Coleridge, Shelley, and Carlyle did the inspired poet stand at the foundations of human culture—literary culture certainly, but religious and political culture as well. Romantic theories of religion consequently tend to focus on the origin and inspiration of religion rather than on problems associated with its institutionalization. It was the religious founders—Jesus, Moses, Muhammad, Buddha, Confucius, Zarathustra—who drew the attention of Romantic thinkers, not their subsequent rationalizers and custodians. These figures were admired more for their creative and visionary gifts than for their theological, philosophical, or ecclesiastical innovations. Transcendentalists such as Emerson and Thoreau, in particular, conceived such figures as inspired poets in their own right, each witness to his own distinctive revelation of universal truths that, nevertheless, ultimately transcended and overpowered the individual contributions of each. Indeed, sanctioning the religious outlook of most Romantics, and justifying their characteristic antisectarianism, was a religious universalism that reached beyond the boundaries of Christianity and the Western world altogether. Thoreau provided a succinct expression of this sort of Romantic universalism in his reflections in *Walden* on Christian conversion experience: "The solitary hired man on a farm in the outskirts of Concord, who has had his second birth and peculiar religious experience, and is driven as he believes into silent gravity and exclusiveness by his faith, may think it is not true; but Zoroaster, thousands of years ago, travelled the same road and had the same experience; but he, being wise, knew it to be universal, and treated his neighbors accordingly, and is even said to have invented and established worship among men" (108).

Such heady expressions of religious perennialism as we find among American Transcendentalists presupposed two academic initiatives that were of enormous consequence to the formation of Thoreau's religious judgments. The first of these, the so-called Higher Criticism, was the new school of biblical criticism originating in Germany in the last decades of the eighteenth century.[7] Adapting the historical methods first devised for the analysis of classical literature to the narratives of the Old and New Testaments, these biblical scholars began to question the old interpretive assumptions of literalness, historical veracity, authorial unity, and narrative consistency upon which traditional beliefs in biblical sacredness had rested. Considering biblical narratives from a purely literary point of view relative to other ancient texts, these critics noted suggestive parallels. In particular, they pointed to apparent biblical analogues for stories from other ancient literatures, some only recently discovered, that had always been characterized as myths. More and more they began to suspect that biblical narratives themselves consisted of a complex assortment of myth, legend, and folktales, as well as ancestral history. Suddenly, and shockingly, even some of the revered stories of Jesus were now seen as having precedents in other ancient mythological stories. This recognition led to efforts to separate and disentangle the mythical from the historical threads of various biblical books, on the belief that the true historical record had been somehow corrupted by dubious mythical elements. By the 1830s, the Higher Criticism was making important inroads among theologians and biblical scholars in New England, and Thoreau appears to have kept himself abreast of its findings.[8] These new critical perspectives find an echo, for example, in the following journal entry from the spring of 1849: "The fragments of fables handed down to us from the remotest antiquity in the mythologies and traditions of all nations would seem to indicate that the life of Christ his divine preeminence & his miracles are not without a precedent in the history of mankind.— . . . All the gods that are worshipped have been men—but of the true God of whom none have conceived—all men combined would hardly furnish the germ" (PJ.3.16–17). For Thoreau, the critical findings of the Higher Criticism effectively confirmed the patent falsity of traditional Christian claims of biblical exclusivity and privilege. However, in contrast to those who viewed myth as an offense against reason—and this included both the new biblical critics and their faithful detractors—Thoreau, like other Romantics, held ancient myths in the warmest regard.

Even more consequential for Thoreau, however, were the momentous findings of a previous generation of European scholars whose rediscovery of the languages, literatures, and cultures of India and the Far East led to a dizzying extension of European knowledge of the non-Western world and eventually to the movement one commentator dubbed the Oriental Renaissance.[9] The English colonial presence in India, in particular, precipitated a flood of previously unknown information on Asian cultures in the form of translations and scholarly monographs that revolutionized Europe's understanding of itself. As the older commerce in tea and spices was increasingly supplemented by a new commerce of ideas and textual artifacts, European poets, intellectuals, and scholars found it increasingly hard to deny their own provincialism. Early Orientalists were particularly impressed by the wealth of Hindu, Chinese, and later, Buddhist myth and sacred traditions. The irrefutable richness and sheer diversity of these traditions forced such Westerners to rethink the privileged position formerly accorded the literary traditions of the Bible and classical Greece. The stories of the Old Testament, and even the narratives of Jesus, began to look suspiciously like imaginative variants of the myths and sacred stories familiar from classical antiquity and other parts of the world. Thoreau's characteristic willingness to consider myths from disparate cultures in relation to one another clearly reflects the preoccupations and methods of the new Orientalist scholarship and comparative mythology.[10] We will turn to some of the more personal religious ramifications of Thoreau's avid interest in non-Western religious traditions in the next chapter. Here it is enough to point out that his acquaintance with this new Orientalist scholarship fueled considerably his own religious universalism and his impatience with religious sectarianism of any sort.

Thoreau's internalization of the assumptions and methods of Indo-European comparative mythology helps to account for some of the more whimsical and, to its first readers, sacrilegious passages in the "Sunday" section of *A Week*. In his tongue-in-cheek juxtaposition of the Greek Jove and Judeo-Christian Jehovah, for instance, the biblical deity suffers sadly by comparison: "He is not so much of a gentleman, not so gracious and catholic, he does not exert so intimate and genial an influence on nature, as many a god of the Greeks" (65). Thoreau prefers the polytheistic arrangement instead, as encouraging more delegation of power. But of all the Greek gods, it is not surprising that Thoreau feels the most kinship with Pan, the ubiquitous god of nature: "In my Pantheon, Pan still reigns

in his pristine glory, with his ruddy face, his flowing beard, and his
shaggy body, his pipe and his crook, his nymph Echo, and his chosen
daughter Iambe; for the great God Pan is not dead, as was rumored. No
god ever dies. Perhaps of all the gods of New England and of ancient
Greece, I am most constant at his shrine" (65). There is of course a grain
of truth in this farfetched ascription of faith: who better than the sylvan
Pan should have pride of place in a Thoreauvian pantheon? Of course,
the purpose of this passage is not really to offer a profession of faith but to
illustrate and dramatize the subversive claim that *all* theological representations arise as human self-projections and serve the interests of particular groups: "It seems to me that the god that is commonly worshipped in civilized countries is not at all divine, though he bears a divine
name, but is the overwhelming authority and respectability of mankind
combined. Men reverence one another, not yet God" (65). Here again
we find Thoreau clearly anticipating similar theoretical developments, in
this case the kind of projectionist theories of religion advanced first by
his German contemporary Ludwig Feuerbach, and later the French so-
ciologist Émile Durkheim.[11] For him, as for them, the gods constitute a
kind of human self-projection, and this is as true of the labyrinthine
theological systems of Thomas Aquinas as it is of the primitive mythologies of South Sea Islanders. Yet in Thoreau's case, this critical perspective on theology does not necessarily entail a rejection of the supernatural; it is merely an expression of the priority assigned in his and
Romantic theory generally to the creative imagination. Actually, Thoreau approved of the creative and transcendental impetus that drove
theological reflection of all sorts, and even appears to welcome the fruits
of the theological imagination, as he does those of the literary imagination, so long as these theological expressions do not calcify into the
inhibiting forms of religious dogma: "I find I can tolerate all—atomists—
pneumatologists—atheists, and theists—Plato—Aristotle—Leucippus—
Democritus—and Pythagoras—It is the attitude of these men, more than
any communication, which charms me. It is so rare to find a man
musing" (PJ.1.140). His interesting remark further along in "Sunday"—
"What man believes, God believes"—is apparently not intended either

to deny the supernatural or reduce it to human fantasy, but to elevate the dignity of human consciousness by accentuating its autonomy and freedom (66).

This intellectual background helps to explain some of Thoreau's subsequent comments about Christianity in the "Sunday" chapter of *A Week,* but as far as Thoreau's earliest readers were concerned, it would never have excused his impious attacks on the Christian faith. As his disquisition on religion gathers momentum, it quickly becomes apparent that Thoreau's main objective is to subject Christianity to a trenchant and thoroughgoing critique: "One memorable addition to the old mythology is due to this era,—the Christian fable. With what pains, and tears, and blood, these centuries have woven this and added it to the mythology of mankind. The new Prometheus. With what miraculous consent, and patience, and persistency, has this mythus been stamped upon the memory of the race? It would seem as if it were in the progress of our mythology to dethrone Jehovah, and crown Christ in his stead" (66–67). The ostensible triumphalism of this passage hardly conceals what believers could only construe as a damning concession. To recast the Christian story in terms familiar from pagan mythology amounted to a blasphemous repudiation of the basic terms of the Christian faith— "the new Prometheus," indeed. It was one thing to question the traditional privileging of Christianity in the dry and sober conventions of a theological tract, but the cheekiness of Thoreau's tone especially raised some hackles: "I trust that some may be as near and dear to Buddha, or Christ, or Swedenborg, who are without the pale of their churches. It is necessary not to be Christian, to appreciate the beauty and significance of the life of Christ. I know that some will have hard thoughts of me, when they hear their Christ named beside my Buddha, yet I am sure that I am willing they should love their Christ more than my Buddha, for the love is the main thing, and I like him too" (67).

Yet, if we set aside for a moment the polemical nature of this treatment, it is possible to see that as far as he himself was concerned, Thoreau's embrace of Romantic thought and the latest findings of comparative mythology actually opened the way for a more meaningful appropriation of the Christian faith. Here in *A Week,* Thoreau claims to have come to a true appreciation of the value of the New Testament only lately, "having been slightly prejudiced against it in my very early days by the church and the Sabbath school . . . It would be a poor story to be prejudiced against the Life of Christ," he notes, "because the book has been edited by Christians. In fact, I love this book rarely, though it is a sort of castle in the air to me, which I am permitted to dream" (71). For him, the validity of the New Testament is enhanced, not compromised, by the existence of other sacred scriptures. Like other Transcendentalists, he conceived it as one important link in a ring of inspired texts encircling the world, and looked forward to a day when all these books could be brought together in the form of one definitive "Bible or book of books" (PJ.2.260). "The reading which I love best is the scriptures of the several nations," he writes here, "though it happens that I am better acquainted with those of the Hindoos, the Chinese, and the Persians, than of the Hebrews, which I have come to last. Give me one of these Bibles, and you have silenced me for a while" (71–72). Romantics reveled in the existence of other newly discovered sacred writings as proof of their own religious perennialism, however much the mere presence of these writings could be seen to vitiate the exclusivist claims of any given tradition. Ironically, it was precisely against the backdrop of world scriptures that Christ's own teaching seemed so earthshaking:

> It is remarkable, that notwithstanding the universal favor with which the New Testament is outwardly received, and even the bigotry with which it is defended, there is no hospitality shown to, there is no appreciation of, the order of truth with which it deals. I know of no book that has so few readers. There is none so truly strange, and heretical, and unpopular. To Christians, no less than Greeks and Jews, it is foolishness and a stumbling block. There are, indeed, several things in it which no man should read aloud more than once.—"Seek first the kingdom of heaven."—"Lay not up for yourselves treasures on earth."—"If thou wilt be perfect, go and sell that thou hast, and give to the poor, and thou shalt have treasure in

heaven."—"For what is a man profited, if he shall gain the whole world, and lose his own soul? . . . " Think of repeating these things to a New England audience! thirdly, fourthly, fifteenthly, till there are three barrels of sermons! Who, without cant, can read them aloud? Who, without cant, can hear them, and not go out of the meeting-house? They never *were* read, they never *were* heard. Let but one of these sentences be rightly read from any pulpit in the land, and there would not be left one stone of that meeting-house upon another. (72–73)

At moments such as this, we see how strong were the claims made upon Thoreau by Christian moral and spiritual teachings, notwithstanding his sometimes flippant unorthodoxy. For reasons I will touch on in the next chapter, he held certain Asian religious teachings in especially high regard but was nevertheless disappointed by their apparent lack of moral courage. In the midst of his extended discussion of the Bhagavad Gita in the "Monday" chapter, he practices a little comparative religion, in the older evaluative sense of that term, by contrasting Christianity and the New Testament with Hinduism and the Bhagavad Gita. Although Hinduism comes off pretty well in this profile, what commentators sometimes fail to point out is that Christianity on the whole does even better. Compared with the religion of the Hindus, "Christianity . . . is humane, practical, and, in a large sense, radical. So many years and ages of the gods those eastern sages sat contemplating Brahm, uttering in silence the mystic 'Om,' being absorbed into the essence of the Supreme Spirit, never going out of themselves, but subsiding further and deeper within; so infinitely wise, yet infinitely stagnant; until, at last, in that same Asia, but in the western part of it, appeared a youth, wholly unforetold by them,—not being absorbed into Brahm, but bringing Brahm down to earth and to mankind; in whom Brahm had awaked from his long sleep, and exerted himself, and the day began,—a new avatar" (136). As far as the Gita is concerned, it turns out to be "not practical in the sense in which the New Testament is. It is not always sound sense in practice. The Brahman never proposes courageously to assault evil, but patiently to starve it out. His active faculties are paralyzed by the idea of cast, of impassable limits, of destiny and the tyranny of time. Kreeshna's argument, it must be allowed, is defective" (140). As was true for many later Americans, the Hindu caste system, the institution upon which the ancient Hindu lawbooks are after all predicated, is the one thing about India that Thoreau really cannot swallow: "Thank God, no Hindoo tyranny prevailed at the framing of the world, but we are freemen in the universe, and not sentenced to any cast" (148).[12] In this way, once again, the de-privileging of Jesus leads to a reappreciation of his distinctive contribution.

Consistent with the radical views of such Transcendentalist Unitarians as Emerson, Thoreau elevates Jesus only to the degree that he expresses and embodies certain universal spiritual and ethical truths, not as an object of worship in and of himself. As Emerson had done in the Divinity School Address, Thoreau rejected what he conceived to be the excessive preoccupation with the historical person of Jesus. The farmers of Concord were as ripe for revelation, he thought, as any first-century resident of Palestine: "The gods are partial to no era, but steadily shines their light in the heavens, while the eye of the beholder is turned to stone. There was but the sun and the eye from the first. The ages have not added a new ray to the one, nor altered a fibre of the other" (157). In the final analysis, the figure of Jesus served Thoreau as guarantor and symbol for a mode of spiritual awakening possible to anyone, at any time, anywhere. This conviction of the immanence and, indeed, imminence of transcendental revelation can also be seen in his intricate play on the traditional associations of the sun and morning star with the person of Christ in the famous peroration of *Walden:* "I do not say that John or Jonathan will realize all this; but such is the character of that morrow which mere lapse of time can never make to dawn. The light which puts out our eyes is darkness to us. Only that day dawns to which we are awake. There is more day to dawn. The sun is but a morning star" (333).[13]

One of the most surprising and, at first, perplexing features of "Sunday," and Thoreau's religious thought generally, is his scathing treatment of conventional morality. Notwithstanding his evident admiration for Jesus and the lofty teachings of the Sermon on the Mount, he repeatedly heaps scorn on the pious forms of do-goodism that had become a habitual trait of New England religious life. There was something quite suspect, he thought, even pathological, in this exaggerated concern with other people's difficulties: "Men have a singular desire to be good without being good for any thing," he notes sarcastically in *A Week*, "because, perchance, they think vaguely that so it will be good for them in the end. The sort of morality which the priests inculcate is a very subtle policy, far finer than the politicians, and the world is very successfully ruled by them as the police-men. It is not worth the while to let our imperfections disturb us always. The conscience really does not, and ought not to, monopolize the whole of our lives, any more than the heart or the head. It is as liable to disease as any other part" (74). Philanthropy, in particular, often moved him to expressions of biting sarcasm. In the sanctimonious exercise of public virtue everywhere around him, he often discerned a certain moral duplicity. Blame for the Billerica Dam with its consequent destruction of the courageous shad population, which, as we have seen, assumes such an important symbolic place in the narrative, he lays at the feet of a human self-centeredness that he wittily, but pointedly, refers to as "phil-*anthropy*." "Away with the superficial and selfish phil-*anthropy* of men,—who knows what admirable virtue of fishes may be below low-water mark" (37).

At first blush, Thoreau's antiphilanthropic invective may strike us as mean-spirited and uncharitable in the extreme. In his essay "Self-Reliance," Emerson had also somewhat inexplicably lashed out against philanthropic excesses, but Thoreau helps to show us why. To the world, philanthropy may well pass as a form of disinterested benevolence, but as the etymology of the term suggests, it is often motivated largely by self-love and human self-interest. In the public expressions of benevolence practiced by the churches, Thoreau saw a charity drained of its spontaneous goodness and converted to the interests of the religious and social status quo. What in Jesus had been a spontaneous expression of love was now reduced to routinized expressions of individual and social coercion. Thoreau's remarks on charity may sometimes strike us as crotchety, but it is hard to deny the brutal truth of his psychological insights.

> In our holiest moment our devil with a leer stands close at hand. He is a very busy devil.—It gains vice some respect I must confess thus to be reminded how indefatigable it is—It has at least the merit of industriousness—When I go forth with zeal to some good work—my devil is sure to get his robe tucked up the first—and arrives there as soon as I—with a look of sincere earnestness—which puts to shame my best intent. He is as forward as I to a good work—and as disinterested. He has a winning way of recommending himself by making himself useful—how readily he comes into my best project—and does his work with a quiet and steady cheerfulness which even virtue may take pattern from. . . . Just as active as I become to virtue just so active is my remaining vice—Every time we teach our virtue a new nobleness we teach our vice a new cunning. When we sharpen the blade it will stab better as well as whittle—The scythe that cuts will cut our legs. We are double-edged blades—and every time we whet our virtue the return stroke straps our vice. (PJ.1.259–60)[14]

Elsewhere in Thoreau's writing this sort of ruthlessly dispassionate inventory of human motives leads to his most disconcertingly stark visions of the human heart. Peering through a knothole into a locked and darkened refuge for shipwrecked sailors on Cape Cod, the narrator sees nothing but bare walls and an empty fireplace, "the wreck of all cosmical beauty" and no "humane house" after all (CC, 60). As in other forms of religious behavior, Thoreau recognized in the panderings of philanthropy the predictable and deceitful operations of the personal ego, and a religion grounded in philanthropy could merely represent a kind of collectivized egotism (PJ.4.418–19). The religion he sought would release him from the confines of the ego, not bring about its steady perpetuation: "I never met a man who cast a free and healthy glance over life—but the best live in a sort of sabbath light—a Jewish gloom. The best thought is not only without sombreness—but even without morality. The universe lies outspread in floods of white light to it. The moral aspect of nature is a disease caught of man—a jaundice imported into her—To the innocent there are no cherubims nor angels. Occasionally we rise above the necessity of virtue into an unchangeable morning light—in which we have not to choose in a dilemma between right and wrong—but simply to live right on and breathe the circumambient air" (PJ.1.315).

The Alphabet of Heaven

If philanthropy passed as a counterfeit of virtue, theology was little more than an impertinence. Thoreau appears to have had even less regard for the theologians and the "Doctors of Divinity" than he did for the clergy: he would rather listen to the "chickadee-dees" than the "D.D.s." any day, he said (RP, 167). It required an unusual form of hubris for any human being to expatiate on the nature of God or the metaphysical structure of the universe. Some of his most savage satire in the "Sunday" section of *A Week* is reserved for his treatment of Christian theology:

> Most people with whom I talk, men and women even of some originality and genius, have their scheme of the universe all cut and dried,—very *dry,* I assure you, to hear, dry enough to burn, dry-rotted and powder-post, methinks,—which they set up between you and them in the shortest intercourse; an ancient and rotting frame with all its boards blown off. They do not walk without their bed. Some to me seemingly very unimportant and unsubstantial things and relations, are for them everlastingly settled,—as Father, Son, and Holy Ghost, and the like. These are like the everlasting hills to them. But in all my wanderings, I never came across the least vestige of authority for these things. They have not left so distinct a trace as the delicate flower of a remote geological period on the coal in my grate. The wisest man preaches no doctrines; he has no scheme; he sees no rafter, not even a cobweb, against the heavens. It is clear sky. (69–70)

As we have seen, Thoreau did not object to the activity of such metaphysical speculation in itself, only the uses to which it was later put. Seizing upon one such theological scheme, no matter how time-honored, had a way of closing off all the others. Whatever security such theological systems offered was more than negated by the resulting loss of mental freedom. Intellectual systems that began as inspired conjectures about the unknown quickly turned into a mental cul-de-sac. To such incursions on his own freedom, Thoreau of course was as sensitive as an eyeball: "We may believe it, but never do we live a quite free life, such as Adam's, but are enveloped in an invisible network of speculations—Our progress is only from one such speculation to another, and only at rare intervals do we perceive that it is no progress.—Could we for a moment drop this by-play—and simply wonder—without reference or inference!" (PJ.1.58). The animus against Christianity evident in the pages of "Sunday" appears to be partly attributable, indeed, to his impatience with Christian theologizing. He seems to write in the belief that Christians were somehow more preoccupied with this mode of religious expression than the rationalizers of other traditions, a forgivable bias coming from someone reared in a region of the country notorious for its convoluted theological systems. Such attempts to corral divine power within the humanly conceived axioms of a theological tract struck him as more pagan than the pagans themselves. One of the reasons he so admired what he read of Hindu theological reflections was that they seemed more fully cognizant of their own limited and provisional status. The fanciful cosmogonic regress that he discovered in his reading of the "Laws of Manu" appealed to him, for instance, because it seemed explicitly to acknowledge the ineffability of any imputedly first cause: "The very indistinctness of its theogony—implies a sublime truth. It does not allow the reader to rest in any supreme first cause—but directly hints of a supremer still which created the last.—The creator is still behind the increate.—The divinity is so fleeting that its attributes are never expressed" (PJ.1.325). In his journal Thoreau repeatedly held up the extravagant mythological systems of the Druids, the Greeks, and the

Hindus as a corrective to the arcane and humorless theological reasonings of the Christians. Yet he acknowledged such dogmatic tendencies in all traditions and characteristically deplored them: "Every author—be he ancient lawgiver or modern philosopher—writes in the faith that his book is to be the final resting place of the sojourning soul and sets up his fixtures therein as for a more than oriental permanence, but it is only a caravansery—which we soon leave without ceremony" (PJ.1.428).

A word like "fixture" neatly encapsulates the basic reason for Thoreau's disdain of theological systems: in their misguided efforts to fix and contain spiritual reality in words, they fall inevitably short of the mark. The reality of the divine life is not a fixture but a flow, forever outpacing and superseding human efforts to arrest and define it: "The universe will not wait to be explained. Whoever seriously attempts a theory of it is already behind his age. His yea has reserved no nay for the morrow. The wisest solution is no better than dissolution" (PJ.1.122). Such objections to what he conceived to be the excesses and hubris of theological speculation stemmed from an abiding conviction in divine incommensurability that was in turn related to Thoreau's felt sense of the gross disparity between discursive formulations and experiential awareness. "The destiny of the soul can never be studied by the reason—" he wrote in 1842, "for its modes are not extatic" (PJ.1.401). In the often revealing correspondence he carried out with his friend and protégé Harrison Blake, he sometimes exhibited the personal, experiential, and passional basis of his repeated debunking of theological language: "Let God alone if need be. Methinks, if I loved him more, I should keep him,—I should keep myself rather,—at a more respectful distance. It is not when I am going to meet him, but when I am just turning away and leaving him alone, that I discover that God is. I say, God. I am not sure that that is the name. You will know whom I mean" (Correspondence, 257). Here and in other such references, Thoreau seems to be groping for a "theology" adequate to his ecstatic experiences, one that would transcend the more pedestrian operations of mere reason.

Embedded within Thoreau's assaults on theology and theologians is an implied critique of theological language itself. More than other religious thinkers of his day, Thoreau was quick to perceive the complex normative burden of theological doctrine and formula. Far from being the transparent representations of revelation and experience they were often taken to be, these theological formulations were seen to operate everywhere in the service of authority and tradition. Always sensitive to the incursions of authority, Thoreau recognized such mystification when he encountered it and fiercely exposed it at every turn.

> If I ever see more clearly at one time than at another, the medium through which I see is clearer. To see from earth to heaven, and see there standing, still a fixture, that old Jewish scheme! What right have you to hold up this obstacle to my understanding you, to your understanding me? You did not invent it; it was imposed on you. Examine your authority. Even Christ, we fear, had his scheme, his conformity to tradition, which slightly vitiates his teaching. He had not swallowed all formulas. He preached some mere doctrines. As for me, Abraham, Isaac, and Jacob, are now only the subtilest imaginable essences, which would not stain the morning sky. Your scheme must be the frame-work of the universe; all other schemes will soon be ruins. The perfect God in his revelations of himself has never got to the length of one such proposition as you, his prophets, state. Have you learned the alphabet of heaven, and can count three? Do you know the number of God's family? Can you put mysteries into words? Do you presume to fable of the ineffable? Pray, what geographer are you, that speak of heaven's topography? Whose friend are you that speak of God's personality? Do you, Miles Howard, think that he has made you his confidant? Tell me of the height of the mountains of the moon, or of the diameter of space, and I may believe you, but of the secret history of the Almighty, and I shall pronounce thee mad. Yet we have a sort of family history of our God,—so have the Tahitians of theirs,—and some old poet's grand imagination is imposed on us as adamantine everlasting truth, and God's own word! Pythagoras says, truly

enough, "A true assertion respecting God, is an assertion of God";
but we may well doubt if there is any example of this in literature.
(Week, 70–71)[15]

In this withering tirade, we witness the heights Thoreau's religious indignation could sometimes reach. It infuriated him to see doctrines and
formulas originating purely in sectarian mythology passed off as the
purest religious tender. His criticism here in his reference to Pythagoras
of the formulaic or propositional character of these religious expressions
suggests that his dissatisfaction with Christian theology arose as much
from its conventionally propositional form as its theological substance. A
venturesome and bold writer in his own right, Thoreau was certainly not
guilty of underestimating the expressive potential of the written word,
but he was quite convinced that nothing divine could come from academic syllogisms. If human beings wanted representational models for
their theological expressions, they had best look for them, he thought, in
the innocent and ubiquitous expressions of the natural world.

Inspiring special incredulity were the various dogmatic assertions of
divine personality so central to the Christian faith. It is certainly possible
to cite passages in Thoreau's writings where he invokes terms such as
"God" or "Nature" in what can only be construed as a personalistic
sense. In the weeks following John's death in January of 1842, for example, Henry's journal gives vent to several expressions of piety that obviously owe much to more conventional patterns of Christian worship:
"If nature is our mother is not God much more? God should come into
our thought with no more parade than the zephyr into our ears—only
strangers approach him with ceremony. How rarely in our English
tongue do we find expressed any affection for God. No sentiment is so
rare as love of God—universal love. . . . I feel as if I could at any time
resign my life and the responsibility of living into Gods hands—and
become an innocent free from care as a plant or stone" (PJ.1.370–71).
Yet formulations such as this need to be weighed in relation to the sort of
vehement attacks on personifications of the divine we find here in "Sunday." Examination of the full range of Thoreau's religious reflections

might well lead us to the disapproving conclusion that he was anything but consistent in his theological views, but this would perhaps not surprise us coming from a Transcendentalist. Indeed, it is hard to resist the observation that, like the Bible, his writings support several quite different theological perspectives. But, as with scriptural interpretation, such passages must be considered in the psychological and rhetorical contexts in which they appear. In the months following John's death, Thoreau's religious emotion seemed to move as easily in traditional channels of faith as it did at other times in more naturalistic terms. Furthermore, we must keep in mind the range of expressive functions such reflections might perform: as with any religious thinker, what Thoreau imagines in moments of high religious feeling, grief, or euphoria may actually have little to do with what he thinks in a mood of speculation or critique. Such caveats notwithstanding, the general tendency of his more formal religious pronouncements is to cast suspicion on the kind of theological personalism traditionally represented in Christian theology. Chastened as he clearly was by his wide reading in comparative mythology, Thoreau found nothing particularly distinctive or indeed compelling about traditional Christian conceptions of Jesus. Doctrines of the Trinity, the Incarnation, or the Sonship of Christ impressed him as memorable expressions of the Western poetic and theological imagination, not as existential truths. They were not different in kind, after all, from the elaborate personifications of the supernatural he found in the Greek or Hindu mythologies. To appreciate such beliefs as expressions of the religious imagination was one thing; to insist on them as if they were scientific fact and "adamantine everlasting truth" was quite another: "It is remarkable, that almost all speakers and writers feel it to be incumbent on them, sooner or later, to prove or to acknowledge the personality of God. Some Earl of Bridgewater, thinking it better late than never, has provided for it in his will. It is a sad mistake. In reading a work on agriculture, we have to skip the author's moral reflections, and the words 'Providence' and 'He' scattered along the page, to come at the profitable level of what he has to say" (77–78).

Allowing for a perhaps wider range of rhetorical representations,

Thoreau's formal religious views were probably not materially different from Emerson's. They both expressed considered doubt about traditional Christian views of the personality of God, and in both cases, this skepticism about personalistic theology led at times to expressions of sympathy for what might best be termed negative theology—a theology, that is, proceeding by a series of negative predicates and grounded in a thoroughgoing conviction of the absolute ineffability of the Godhead.[16] In the journal passage from 1849 cited earlier, Thoreau appears to embrace a Euhemerist theory of mythological origins in considering the life of Christ, together with the foundational stories of other traditions: "All the gods that are worshipped have been men—but of the true God of whom none have conceived—all men combined would hardly furnish the germ" (PJ.3.17). The insistence driving this remark on the utter inconceivability of God is consistent with his criticisms of Christian theology in "Sunday." In poking fun later on at the notion of "a Society for the diffusion of Useful Knowledge," Thoreau remarks, "Methinks there is equal need of a society for the diffusion of useful Ignorance—for what is most of our boasted so called knowledge but a conceit that we know something which robs us of the advantages of our actual ignorance—" (PJ.3.184). This passage may well be chalked up to Thoreau's characteristic contrariness, but his advocacy here of a kind of studied unknowing in relation to the things of this world assumes a prominent place in his later devotions to nature, as we will see later on. Its relevance is even more direct of course to the things of the other world.

Perhaps the most revealing and, to Thoreau, pernicious manifestation of Christian preoccupation with theological forms was the tradition's penchant for and elaboration of doctrinal creeds. In the creedal statement, Christian teaching showed its true parochial and exclusivist colors. It was obvious to Thoreau that the purpose of creeds was less to teach than to foster conformity, and for him such declarations of particularism were clearly anathema. In his remarks on creeds and the grounds of credence here in *A Week,* Thoreau introduces a distinction between faith and belief apparently lost on most Christian theologians of his day. Faith, in this view, is composed of far finer stuff than the tendentious formations of creed: "A man's real faith is never contained in his creed," he writes, "nor is his creed an article of his faith. The last is never adopted. This it is that permits him to smile ever, and to live even as bravely as he does. And yet he clings anxiously to his creed, as to a straw, thinking that that does him good service because his sheet anchor does not drag" (78).[17]

Thoreau's remarks on faith here in "Sunday" and elsewhere in his writings deserve some close consideration. Clearly, he rejects the notion that faith can be conceived as a set of beliefs or creedal statements propositionally framed and programmatically inculcated. Characteristically, faith warps closer to the pole of experience in Thoreau's religious thought than to communal belief. He conceives it as a mode of knowledge, but knowledge unmediated by tradition or inherited views. Indeed, faith arises naturally from a kind of subtle contact with transcendent life that precedes or transcends the workings of verbal intelligence. In one of the meditative interludes of the voyage, Thoreau offers fuller expression of the deeper groundings of faith:

> As we sat on the bank eating our supper, the clear light of the western sky fell on the eastern trees and was reflected in the water, and we enjoyed so serene an evening as left nothing to describe. For the most part we think that there are few degrees of sublimity, and that the highest is but little higher than that which we now behold; but we are always deceived. Sublimer visions appear, and the former pale and fade away. We are grateful when we are reminded by interior evidence of the permanence of universal laws; for our faith is but faintly remembered, indeed, is not a remembered assurance, but a use and enjoyment of knowledge. It is when we do not have to believe, but come into actual contact with Truth, and are related to her in the most direct and intimate way. Waves of serener life pass over us from time to time, like flakes of sunlight over the fields in cloudy weather. (291–92)

The kind of knowledge Thoreau alludes to here obviously stands in distinct contrast to the discursive knowledge of theology and the propositional knowledge of the traditional creeds. The fruits of such knowledge evidently cannot serve as the subject of memory or reflection because it transcends the activity of speech; it is "interior," rather than objective, closer to feeling than cognition. That he should represent this sort of affective knowledge as a form of "contact" is entirely characteristic of Thoreau, since it was often mediated for him, as we have seen previously, by a peculiarly heightened form of sensory experience. In comparison with the inherited assurances of the Christian and other traditional faiths, this experiential faith or affective knowledge seemed completely abstract, but for him its authority was sufficient to deprivilege some of their most time-honored claims. However abstract, this ecstatic knowledge provided the footing upon which Thoreau erected his entire critique of theology and organized religion in *A Week*. Perhaps the following passage from "Walking" provides the best illustration, however, of his conception of and commitment to an ecstatic faith:

> My desire for knowledge is intermittent; but my desire to bathe my head in atmospheres unknown to my feet is perennial and constant. The highest that we can attain to is not Knowledge, but Sympathy with Intelligence. I do not know that this higher knowledge amounts to anything more definite than a novel and grand surprise on a sudden revelation of the insufficiency of all that we called Knowledge before,—a discovery that there are more things in heaven and earth than are dreamed of in our philosophy. It is the lighting up of the mist by the sun. Man cannot Know in any higher sense than this, any more than he can look serenely and with impunity in the face of the sun: " 'Ὡς τὶ νοῶν, οὐ κεῖνον νοήσεις,—', 'You will not perceive that, as perceiving a particular thing,' say the Chaldean Oracles. (Writings.5.240)[18]

World Within a World

More even than *Walden, A Week* thus opens a window onto the religious thought of Henry Thoreau. Yet, in this his first book, it is sometimes hard to make out his actual religious attitudes amid the rhetorical thrusts and flourish of his invective. Thoreau's vehemence in "Sunday" should not be construed as a rejection of religiousness itself, however, only some of its institutional expressions. Indeed, it is Thoreau's own cherished religious inspiration that fuels his indignation. He launches his salvos, after all, with the passion of an engaged, if alienated, critic, not some dispassionate outsider. Yet in our efforts to identify his own beliefs, we are often reduced to reading between the lines of his criticism. It is like reimagining a photograph with only the negative in hand. The religious character of this narrative is further blurred by the unusual nature of Thoreau's religious sensibility, in particular his all but total rejection of organized religion, his dismissal of theological presentations, and his embrace of an ecstatic religion of nature for which there had been no real precedent till that time in American religious history. His decision, furthermore, to stage his religious insights, as well as the "Sunday" critique, in the dramatic form offered by a narrative of action, discovery, and even disappointment certainly does not help matters much. Yet it is easy to understand the pertinence of this choice for the religious profile we have seen emerging in these pages.

Reading the "Sunday" chapter against the backdrop of the journal helps to put Thoreau's criticisms of religion in a better perspective. The profile we find here is of a man animated by religious passion throughout his life, and subject, especially in his younger years, to moods of heightened religious euphoria. It did not seem to matter that he found in nature, rather than traditional conceptions of deity, the principal object and arena of his devotion; it was devotion all the same. There was no point in becoming too attached to particular divine names and faces, since what really mattered was the elusive reality moving within and behind them, and the devotion paid to it. Clearly Thoreau recognized this transference of religious attention to nature at an early point in his life. In a journal entry from October of 1842, he writes: "I feel that I draw nearest to understanding the great secret of my life in my closest intercourse with nature. There is a reality and health in (present) nature; which is not to be found in any religion—and cannot be contemplated in antiquity—I suppose that what in other men is religion is in me love of nature" (PJ.2.55). Thoreau's later journal, to which we will return in the final chapter, provides us with by far the most revealing forum for understanding the nature of this mature religious attention to nature. It is enough now simply to emphasize that this devotion to nature represents the central fact to be reckoned with in any adequate appraisal of his religious thought.

The obvious centrality of nature in Thoreau's religious thought and experience has no doubt proved the main obstacle to a just appreciation of his religious life. Americans at the start of the twenty-first century are better able than those of earlier times to grant some credence to this religious premise, since "nature religion" has come to be widely recognized at least as an intelligible form of American religiosity (in part through Thoreau's own influence), however suspect it remains in the eyes of much mainstream culture.[19] We cannot forget that suspicion about nature and natural religion still ran quite deep in the post-Puritan culture of Thoreau's midcentury New England—as it still does in much American Christianity—notwithstanding the elevation of nature in eighteenth-century Enlightenment thought. Before the Romantic movement, there was no real precedent for this kind of religious devotion to nature, in and for itself, in the Euro-American religious tradition. However unheralded Thoreau has been as a religious thinker till now, he can certainly be seen as a foundational figure in this as in other areas of American culture. Of course, Thoreau was not the first white American to harbor special religious feeling for the natural world. Jonathan Edwards's meditations on the forms of the natural world offer a memorable touchstone of an American religious sensibility that became increasingly common throughout the eighteenth century. But the main difference between Thoreau's approach to nature and the religious uses to which nature was put by earlier American writers, including to some extent Emerson himself, was that where previous religious writers tended to conceive of nature in the terms provided by Christian scriptural culture and tradition, Thoreau on the contrary conceived of human religious forms in the terms provided by the natural world: "I believe in the forest, and in the meadow, and in the night in which the corn grows," he wrote humorously in "Walking," in a pointed revision of the old Trinitarian creeds (Writings.5.225). It strikes us as entirely characteristic of Thoreau, furthermore, that when he visited the great Church of Notre Dame during his visit to Montreal in 1850, he expressed his sense of religious awe only by recourse to analogies from the natural world: "The Catholic are the only churches which I have seen worth remembering, which are not almost wholly profane. . . . But I was impressed by the quiet, religious atmosphere of the place. It was a great cave in the midst of a city; and what were the altars and the tinsel but the sparkling stalactites" (Writings.5.12–13).

In repeating, as one must, the worn-out characterization of Thoreau as a lover of nature, we expose ourselves, however, to the dangers of routine and premature conceptualization. What, after all, does it mean to speak of Thoreau as a "worshipper of nature"? The connotations such conceptions call up for us are by now so hackneyed as to preclude much real insight. The real problem seems to lie in our confident presumption as readers and admirers of Thoreau that we know what he meant by his frequent use of the term "nature." Yet, on closer examination, such assumptions prove completely unwarranted. Nowhere in his writing does Thoreau offer a definitive or systematic definition of this inchoate term. "Nature" serves him as a convenient point of departure or designation, but what it consists of can hardly be specified beyond a few rote and superficial references to meadows, rocks, and streams. It might well be argued, in fact, that the meaning of nature was precisely the question that fired Thoreau's life and works. What we uncritically assume an understanding of was exactly the mystery that preoccupied him throughout his life and inspired his best work. It is as if we fancy ourselves at the end of an inquiry that he was always just beginning anew.

Nothing underscores this problem better than the recognition that soon dawns on any reader who ventures beyond the familiar terrain of *Walden:* Thoreau, we soon discover, appears to conceive of "nature" quite differently at different times and places. The moods it inspires and the reflections it provokes also vary markedly. The beneficent pastoral landscape of Walden Pond has little to do with the blasted, life-threatening wilderness atop Mount Katahdin. In *Walden,* the Pond itself—pure, tranquil, endlessly reflective—serves as the perfect embodiment of nature. Thoreau ponders the translucent waters as a medium of revelation. In its seasonal transformations, the Pond mirrors the elemental rhythms of the natural world. In pondering the breaking up of the ice in spring, he even conceives of Walden in Christological terms. "Walden was dead and is alive again," he writes, intoning the story of the Prodigal Son, with its traditional typological reference to the person of Christ himself.[20] Yet, this receptive, self-effacing, Christlike divinity of Walden Pond seems utterly foreign to the sacred precincts of Pomola, the Native American deity haunting the summit of Mount Katahdin. Impatient of human frailty, the divinity Thoreau encounters in the primeval forests of Maine or on the wind-ravaged outer banks of Cape Cod is characterized by raw power, not beneficent love. He revered this wildness also—however inimical it might one day prove to his own human welfare—and admired the Indians, who eschewed all religious sentimentality in their sober estimations of divine power (55–56). Both of these visions of nature, the pastoral and the wild, make their claims upon Thoreau's religious sensibility, as do others besides.

Neither do the journals speak in unison about the religious meaning of nature, though the inconsistencies themselves sometimes prove instructive. At points, Thoreau appears to conceive himself all but completely assimilated to the organic life of nature. On December 2 of 1840, he enters this note in his journal: "I should wither and dry up if it were not for lakes and rivers. I am conscious that my body derives its juices from their waters, as much as the muskrat or the herbage on their brink" (PJ.1.199). The following January, he remarks on an opposing impression while wandering through some snow-covered woods: "You glance up these paths, closely imbowerd by bent trees, as through the side aisles of a cathedral, and expect to hear a quire chanting from their depths. You are never so far in them, as they are far before you. Their secret is where you are not, and where your feet can never carry you" (PJ.1.239). Here it is nature's absolute inaccessibility that most impresses him. Intimate to the organic processes of his own body, nature could at the same time seem utterly foreign. At once immanent and transcendent, the secret of nature's life refused to be grasped in human categories, and eluded even her most ardent devotee.

Even in later years, when Thoreau became increasingly preoccupied with observing and documenting the visible minutiae of natural forms, he was always acutely aware that life itself, whatever it was, could never be pigeonholed in scientific terms. It was neither wholly concrete nor wholly abstract, but an ever-moving wheel of transformation.

> This stream of events which we consent to call actual & that other mightier stream which alone carries us with it—what makes the difference— On the one our bodies float—& we have sympathy with it through them—on the other our spirits.
>
> We are ever dying to one world & being born into another— and probably no man knows whether he is dead in the sence in which he affirms that phenomenon of another—or not. Our thoughts are the epochs of our life—all else is but as a journal of the winds that blew while we were here. (PJ.3.95; Correspondence, 265)

Recognition of the central position of nature in Thoreau's spiritual life provides a reliable basis for any fuller inventory of the character of his religious thought, however much nature itself turns out to be peculiarly resistant to his or our definition. It is indeed remarkable the extent to which Thoreau takes his cues about religion from his attentive study of nature's processual structure. And the first qualification incumbent upon the sincere devotee of nature was, apparently, that of solitude. As we have seen, this was among the chief attributes of Thoreau to which nineteenth-century popularizers drew attention. Indeed, the image of the forest hermit has always added considerably to his general mystique. But his friends and family always bridled at the imputation that he was antisocial or misanthropic. In fact, as far as we know, Thoreau enjoyed friends and family as much as anyone. Whatever spiritual nourishment he derived from his daily excursions in the countryside depended on a quiet and collected attention to nature's forms and phenomena. He was not opposed to socializing for its own sake; it was only that it often tended to detract from the single-mindedness necessary for full devotion. In a letter to Blake from 1856, he provided one of the clearest statements we have of the relationship between society and solitude in the religious experience he sought:

> As for the dispute about solitude & society any comparison is impertinent. It is an idling down on the plain at the base of a mountain instead of climbing steadily to its top. Of course you will be glad of all the society you can get to go up with. Will you go to glory with me? is the burden of the song. I love society so much that I swallowed it all at a gulp—i.e. all that came in my way. It is not that we love to be alone, but that we love to soar, and when we do soar, the company grows thinner & thinner till there is none at all. It is either the Tribune on the plain, a sermon on the mount, or a very private *extacy* still higher up. We are not the less to aim at the summits, though the multitude does not ascend them. Use all the society that will abet you. But perhaps I do not enter into the spirit of your talk. (Correspondence, 424)

Other features of Thoreau's religious thought found even more direct sanction in nature's perceived attributes. Chief among these were change and metamorphosis: nothing in nature ever remained the same; all was governed by an absolute imperative of growth. To Thoreau and Emerson both, life's secret seemed to lie in its endless, dizzying metamorphosis. Nature's resiliency, its absolute propensity to recover and re-create itself in a continual process of death and rebirth—this is what drew their interest, more than the particular findings of natural history. But Thoreau went further than Emerson or any other Transcendentalist did in his efforts to peruse and document the seasonal cycles of natural change. After 1850 his journal was dedicated in large part to his observation and scrupulous documentation of detailed manifestations of seasonal change in the surrounding countryside of Concord. It followed from Thoreau's attention to natural change that a religion of nature, if true to its inspiration, must shape itself according to similar dictates. These are in part the grounds, of course, for Thoreau's impatient dismissal of creeds, systematic theology, and religious institutions generally. All these religious forms had a way of ossifying around a few insights, thus becoming inert and unresponsive to ongoing inspiration and change. The kind of stasis preserved by such forms Thoreau deemed contrary to natural growth.

Like other features of Thoreau's thought that we have already considered, this emphasis upon the process of thought and experience, rather than some fixed expression of truth, may strike us as remarkably modern in its anticipation of dominant tendencies in process theology and pragmatist philosophy.[21] Truth for him was not a result finally achieved, but a process of continuous opening and illumination. He was quite convinced at least that the fixed formulations of religion contained very little truth in this sense. Truth was not a property inhering in a proposition but a state of awakened consciousness. "We Yankees are not so far from right," he wrote in 1840, "who answer one question by asking another. Yes and No are lies—a true answer will not aim to establish anything, but rather to set all well afloat. All answers are in the future and day answereth to day—do we think we can anticipate them?" (PJ.1.139).

Yet his preoccupation with natural change also shaped his religious thought in more concrete ways. In natural evolution, he found evidence of an invisible, underlying pattern of spiritual transformation. As we have seen, he looked with special favor upon the Pythagorean and Wordsworthian doctrines of rebirth and transmigration. The Brahmanical literature only seemed to confirm these claims. In early life, he was inclined to construe such intimations of future life along naturalistic lines: "To-day I feel the migratory instinct strong in me, and all my members and humors anticipate the breaking up of winter. If I yielded to this impulse it would surely guide me to summer haunts. This ill defined restlessness and fluttering on the perch, do no doubt prophecy the final migration of souls out of nature to a serener summer, in long harrows and waving lines through the spring weather, over what fair uplands and fertile pastures winging their way at evening—and seeking a resting place with loud cackling and uproar!" (PJ.1.231). More often, he considered specific manifestations of natural change as the types or harbingers of spiritual transmigration. While visiting a menagerie in Boston in 1851, he was "struck by the gem-like changeable greenish reflections from the eyes of the grizzley bear," and thought they suggested the unavoidable idea of transmigration (PJ.3.277).

This emphasis on the continuous metamorphosis of nature also helps to explain other characteristic features of his religious thought. Like other Romantics, for example, he elevated the imagination to the level of a religious, as much as an artistic, ideal. Imagination he saw as nature's own creative power as it expressed itself in and through the minds of men and women. Because the imagination could so easily overpower and remake the shadow world of outward facts and actual events, it occupied a more privileged ontological position (Correspondence, 265). To some extent, this affirmation of natural and intellectual dynamism also makes sense of his curiously dismissive attitudes toward the negative conditions of sin, suffering, and despair. Like Emerson, Thoreau appears to have conceived of these states as strictly privative, that is, as a privation merely of some larger and more substantial good. He certainly recognized the darker sides of human life, and knew real suffering at first hand, but he could simply find no warrant for sadness and resignation in the perennial flux and resurgence of the natural world. "The doctrines of despair, of spiritual or political tyranny or servitude, were never taught by such as shared the serenity of nature," he wrote in the "Natural History of Massachusetts": "The spruce, the hemlock, and the pine will not countenance despair" (Writings.5.105). In his journal he remarked, "Surely joy is the condition of life. Think of the young fry that leap in ponds—the myriads of insects ushered into being of a summer's evening—the incessant note of the hyla with which the woods ring in spring. the *non chalance* of the butterfly carrying accident and change painted in a thousand hues upon his wings—or the brook-minnow stemming stoutly the current, the lustre of whose scales worn bright by the attrition is reflected upon the bank" (PJ.1.167).

Thoreau's distinctive view of truth as a function of experience, rather than a property of the world's or mind's relation to it, led him to place special importance on perspective. As a young man, he liked to meditate on the view of the world available to him from what he called his "perspective window" in the attic of the family house (PJ.1.73). At times, he would also mimic a technique learned from writers on the picturesque by viewing the landscape through the bottom of a tumbler, in order to bring the world into a neater focus, noting, "our eyes too are convex lenses" (PJ.1.129–30). Confirmed Transcendentalist that he was, he naturally emphasized individual consciousness as the originating center of the outer world:

> Let us wander where we will the universe is built round about us, and we are central still. By reason of this if we look into the heavens they are concave—and if we were to look into a gulf as bottomless it would be concave also—The sky is curved downward to the earth in the horizon—because I stand on the plain.
>
> I draw down its skirts. The stars so low there seem loth to go away from me—but by a curcuitous path to be remembering and returning to me. (PJ.1.323)

Yet while the hegemony of consciousness inevitably conferred special authority on the observer, the limitations of vision necessarily relativized his or her perspective. This lesson, in particular, Thoreau took very much to heart. "The universe is wider than our views of it," he wrote memorably in *Walden* (320). Not only beauty, but reality itself depended on the eye of the beholder. This recognition of the dependence of knowledge on perspective and one's state of mind would seem to impose a sobering limit on human knowledge, but to him it served as fodder for the imagination. What new worlds opened, he sometimes wondered, through newly baptized ears and eyes?

In our efforts to characterize Thoreau's religious life, we readers should heed his lessons on the shaping value of perspective. Critics have found various portrayals tempting: Thoreau as post-Puritan stoic, as lapsed Christian pietist, as pantheist, as closet Buddhist or Hindu anchorite. Each of these portrayals sheds light on distinctive features of his religious thought and piety, but each tends to overdetermine the evidence. In fact, Thoreau was fundamentally an eclectic religious thinker, who eschewed all sectarian labels. He appropriated what he liked or found meaningful from his readings and simply abandoned the rest. The following entry, drafted into his journal in 1850, comes as close to a Thoreauvian profession of faith as anything does: "I do not prefer one religion or philosophy to another—I have no sympathy with the bigotry & ignorance which make transient & partial & puerile distinctions between one man's faith or form of faith & anothers—as christian & heathen—I pray to be delivered from narrowness partiality exaggeration—bigotry. To the philosopher all sects all nations are alike. I like Brahma—Hare Buddha—the Great spirit as well as God" (PJ.3.62).

Yet if we stand back from the religious profile sketched in the preceding pages, we can find support in certain broader characterizations. Thoreau was above all a religious empiricist. Here I do not, of course, mean empiricist in the Lockean philosophical sense, because Thoreau was no more a follower of Locke than were his Transcendentalist peers. Contrary to Locke, he believed in innate knowledge and the originating power of human consciousness. When he spoke of experience, he emphatically included feeling and intuition, along with sensation and intellect. But despite this qualification, he was an empiricist still, in the sense of that term later elaborated by William James, in his unwavering trust in and reliance upon experience.[22] No authority in heaven or on earth could ever contravene the evidence supplied by his own direct experience. "Whatever of past or present wisdom has published itself to the world," he wrote as a young man, "is palpable falsehood till it come and utter itself by my side" (PJ.1.49).

Notwithstanding the disappointments and sobering reappraisals of the 1840s, Thoreau never abandoned this basic article of his faith. It accounts for much that is distinctive about his religious temperament and values, and at the same time, helps explain his discomfiture with organized religion. He could take nothing at second hand, especially in so vital an area as the human soul. Faith he deemed vital, as we have seen, but faith for him was a kind of "infinite expectation of the dawn," as he put it famously in *Walden,* uncontaminated by the parochial adherences of religious belief (90). In *Walden,* indeed, he affirms the primacy of experience as forthrightly as he ever did:

> I went to the woods because I wished to live deliberately, to front only the essential facts of life, and see if I could not learn what it had to teach, and not, when I came to die, discover that I had not lived. I did not wish to live what was not life, living is so dear; nor did I wish to practise resignation, unless it was quite necessary. I wanted to live deep and suck out all the marrow of life, to live so sturdily and Spartanlike as to put to rout all that was not life, to cut a broad swath and shave close, to drive life into a corner, and reduce it to its lowest terms, and, if it proved to be mean, why then to get the whole and genuine meanness of it, and publish its meanness to the world; or if it were sublime, to know it by experience, and be able to give a true account of it in my next excursion. For most men, it appears to me, are in a strange uncertainty about it, whether it is of the devil or of God, and have *somewhat hastily* concluded that it is the chief end of man here to "glorify God and enjoy him forever." (91)

Yet it is important to see that such Thoreauvian disclaimers were never made in a spirit of atheism or resignation, but in just deference to his ever-active thirsting for direct experience. This was the problem with Christianity, after all: the hallowed place of religious inspiration had been given over to the lesser divinity of hope: "Every where 'good men' sound a retreat, and the word has gone forth to fall back on innocence. Fall forward rather on to whatever there is there. Christianity only hopes. It has hung its harp on the willows, and cannot sing a song in a strange land. It has dreamed a sad dream, and does not yet welcome the morning with joy" (Week, 77; PJ.1.167). Those interested in Thoreau's scientific researches will find nothing new or surprising in such assertions of his empiricism. Yet readers admiring of his scientific prowess may well find themselves bewildered by the apparently incongruous juxtapositions in his journal of dry-eyed scientific notes and fervent mystical expostulations. But there is no need to see a contradiction here between Thoreau's science and his religion, as long as we recognize both as distinct expressions of his fundamental commitment to knowledge gained through direct experience. To objections that his religious, or for that matter, his scientific insights sometimes seem to extend well beyond what we would normally consider the evidence of the senses, Thoreau would respond that all depends on the purity of the senses. His religious insights, as we saw earlier, were as much dependent on the activity of an aroused and informed sense experience as were his scientific findings. In matters of faith, Thoreau's empiricism was a religious empiricism, grounded finally in heightened sense experience and life-transforming ecstasy.

This unwavering commitment to experience naturally gave Thoreau's religious life an inward and contemplative turn. "Heaven is the inmost place," he wrote in 1841: "The Good have not to travel far" (PJ.1.349). As we will see in the next chapter, he had to look outside the traditions of the Western world to find resources adequate to support this inward quest, but from his earliest years, he was disposed to believe that the search for God must begin within the human mind and heart. Like other Romantics, Thoreau sought transcendent truth in the common precincts of the everyday and thought no century of religious history more divinely favored than his own: "I am not taken up, like moses, upon a mountain to learn the law," he wrote in 1840, "but lifted up in my seat here, in the warm sunshine and genial light" (PJ.1.147). He demeaned the privileged revelations of antiquity in deference to the gospels of the present time: "The wood thrush is more modern than Plato and Aristotle. They are a dogma, but he preaches the doctrine of this hour" (PJ.1.159). But for all his devotion to the plant and animal life around him, he recognized that the depths of his own consciousness offered the most direct access to the divine life: "The divinity in man is the vestal fire of the temple, which is never permitted to go out, but burns as steadily, and with as pure a flame, on the obscure provincial altar, as in Numa's temple at Rome" (PJ.1.164).

In keeping with the widely held Romantic and mystical conviction that the Kingdom of Heaven lay within, Thoreau characteristically interiorized the substance of biblical and other religious revelations. The human mind he conceived as the true sanctuary of God and the site of the final revelation: "The unconsciousness of man—is the consciousness of God—the end of the world" (PJ.1.109). Thoreau's core belief in the immanence of the divine in human being inspired at once his loftiest assessments of human life and his most scathing assaults on its shortcomings. In sanguine moods, it was natural for him to affirm the characteristic Transcendentalist faith in the infinitude of the individual person: "Man the crowning fact—the god we know. While the earth supports so rare an inhabitant there is somewhat to cheer us. Who shall say that there is not god, if there is a *just* man" (PJ.3.229). While society and social intercourse often obscured the better, deeper reaches of human nature, he persistently sought them out in all his social relations. If his contempt for human frailty sometimes got the better of him, this was because the stakes were so high: "I would not forget that I deal with infinite and divine qualities in my fellow. All men indeed are divine in their core of light but that is indistinct and distant to me, like the stars of the least magnitude—or the galaxy itself—but my kindred planets show their round disks and even their attendant moons to my eye" (PJ.2.175).

From an early point in his life, Thoreau made it his chief concern to investigate the depths of his own nature. The Sunday after Christmas in 1841, he provided an early statement of the centrality of this inward quest in his developing spiritual life: "He is the rich man who in summer and winter for ever—could find delight in the contemplation of his own soul. I could look as unweariedly up to that cope—as into the heavens of a summer day—or a winter night. When I hear this bell ring—I am carried back to years and sabbaths when I was newer and more innocent I fear than now—and it seems to me as if there were a world within a world. Sin I am sure is not in overt acts or indeed in acts of any kind, but is in proportion to the time which has come behind us and displaced eternity. That degree to which our elements are mixed with the elements of the world—The whole duty of life is contained in this question How to respire and aspire both at once" (PJ.1.348). In the note of regret found in this entry, we see yet another early expression of the elegiac mood that came to be so characteristic of Thoreau's mature spirituality. No doubt such early expressions of interest in contemplation were directly inspired by the ecstasies experienced earlier in life. Thoreau never forgot these experiences, even as they became less vivid and more infrequent with the passage of time. Indeed, they formed the cornerstones of his spiritual life, and as we have just seen, deeply shaped all his religious values and ideas. His recollections of these ecstatic moods and moments of insight fueled his impatience with the indirect and to him unsatisfying provisions of tradition. In childhood these experiences had come upon him with force and spontaneity; later on, their strength and frequency abated. Yet they did not die out entirely, and Thoreau found with experience that they were susceptible to some cultivation. To this end, he dedicated much of his subsequent spiritual life. While recognizing the need of mental and physical conditioning for the cultivation of contemplative experience, he found little to edify him in the Harvard curriculum. The Eastern texts he came across in Emerson's library, however, gave him more to go on, as we shall now see.

Five

The Artist of Kouroo

From the standpoint of marketing and sales, *A Week* turned out to be something of a fiasco, a fact hardly mitigated by Thoreau's famously stoic, as well as humorous, avowals of failure. When, four years after its first appearance, he finally acquiesced to his publisher's petitions that he accept the 706 unsold copies piled in the warehouse, he noted wryly in his journal, "I have now a library of nearly nine hundred volumes, over seven hundred of which I wrote myself" (J.5.459). In addition to the commercial disappointment, Thoreau must have found the book's critical reception somewhat disheartening also. Though reviewers generally commended the book's author for his rare glimpses of nature, some notices were also at times carping and critical. Various factors might be cited for this guarded reception—the book's "pantheism," its lack of ostensible structure and mixing of genres, the digressive and ruminating character of its argument—but surely another was its insistent, perhaps zealous, and sometimes saucy Orientalism. Even critics otherwise sympathetically disposed to Transcendentalist eccentricity were clearly put off by Thoreau's seeming sacrilege. To James Russell Lowell, Thoreau's approving recitals of Eastern lore seemed like so many unnecessary digressions: "What . . . have Concord and Merrimack to do with Boodh?" he sneered.[1]

For critics such as Lowell, Thoreau's wild juxtapositions of incongruous cultural forms were as much an assault on aesthetic judgment as on religious fidelity. But for other early reviewers, Thoreau's offense was primarily theological. In promoting the Buddha to the same rank as Christ, in elevating the scriptures of the East alongside those of the West, he was plainly striking a raw nerve. It was not the case of course that liberally educated readers of 1849 were unprepared for objections, in the abstract, to the ascendency of the Christian faith; what they found hard to take, though, was this brazen assault on Christian supremacy by way of a series of irreverent comparisons with various, to them, preposterous Hindu, Buddhist, and Chinese religious forms. As always, Thoreau was stubbornly unrepentant in the publication of his pagan infidelities. When Greeley later complained of the stumbling blocks created by his "defiant Pantheism," Thoreau retorted simply that unfortunate as that might be, it could not be helped, since he "was born to be a pantheist" (Correspondence, 293–94).[2]

As one of the first American writers to transgress these sometimes unspoken cultural and aesthetic boundaries, Thoreau was clearly cognizant of the risks involved. In contrast to other early students of Asian traditions, he mixes images of Orient and Occident with a kind of cavalier abandon, even bravado, as if to invite critical and commercial rejection. But why such flirting with commercial disaster? Why the invitation to literary oblivion? As it turns out, such questions lead us directly into the heart of Thoreau's spiritual and imaginative universe.

Ex Oriente Lux

Although Transcendentalist Orientalism exhibited several features distinctive of the Transcendentalist movement generally—its broad eclecticism, personal reflexiveness, and perennialist vision of truth—even in its most ebullient phase, this formative period of later American fascination with "the East" was never more than a provincial manifestation of a much larger European cultural phenomenon inseparable from Romanticism itself.[3] With the circumnavigation of Africa by European trading ships in the late fifteenth century and the gradual breakup of the Ottoman Empire, Europe slowly began to emerge from centuries of relative isolation. Not surprisingly, the first European reports about the peoples and cultures of South and East Asia tended to come primarily from traders and the missionaries who soon followed in their wake. These first contacts paved the way, however, for more serious religious, cultural, and scholarly exchanges, which in turn resulted in the careful cultivation by other European missionaries and scholars of various non-Western languages, literatures, and religious and philosophical texts and traditions. Apart from a few sensationalistic medieval accounts, the first serious scholarly treatments of Chinese traditions came from the Jesuit missionaries who maintained an active presence in China throughout the seventeenth and eighteenth centuries. It was principally their work that helped inspire the vogue for Confucianism among French Enlightenment thinkers—Confucius was one of Benjamin Franklin's favorite sources as well—and provided the foundation for the development in the early nineteenth century of academic sinology in France and, somewhat later, the rest of Europe.[4] Modern European scholarly interest in India may be dated to 1784, with the founding of the Asiatic Society of Bengal, a scholarly initiative underwritten in its early years by the British East India Company. Established to promote the study of Indian civilization, the society would make a lasting contribution to the study of India in the West, in its sponsorship of numerous important translation projects and a wide range of articles on Indian cultures and traditions.[5] By the early nineteenth century, these scholarly initiatives had helped to galvanize a more widespread interest in Asian culture and tradition among educated Europeans that was later dubbed the Oriental Renaissance, by way of analogy to the great rebirth of interest in Europe's own classical culture during the fourteenth and fifteenth centuries.[6]

Following the precedent set by Britain's first Orientalists, American Transcendentalists looked to the classical texts of Hinduism as the chief exhibit of Eastern wisdom.[7] This was in part a natural consequence of the disproportionate attention that had been paid till then to Hindu India by English-speaking scholars under the aegis of the British colonial government. By virtue of the concerted labors of British colonial agents, works of and about Hindu culture enjoyed a significantly wider publication and distribution in Britain and the United States throughout the first half of the nineteenth century than works involving other non-Muslim Asian cultures. Until the turn into the nineteenth century, Chinese philosophies and religion were mostly the preserve of French scholars. Even so, by the first decades of the nineteenth century, works of and about Chinese tradition, in particular the Neo-Confucian canon, were also making their way to American shores in the form of French and English translations, and they too found a ready audience among the Transcendentalists by the 1830s and '40s. For its part, Buddhism was poorly represented in the work of the first generation of European Orientalists, a fact that helps explain the Transcendentalists' tendency to conflate Hindu and Buddhist ideas in their earliest references to them.[8] In fact, except for the French Orientalist scholar Eugène Burnouf—a portion of whose early work Emerson and Thoreau included in translation in the January 1844 issue of the *Dial*—most Western readers had little real understanding of Buddhism until well after 1850, when the first European translations of the Pali and Mahāyāna canons and books about Buddhism started to become available in the West.[9] Thus while the Transcendentalists did not by any means limit their Eastern readings to Hindu texts—Chinese and Persian texts in particular were especially important—Hindu literature nevertheless often exemplified for them the contemplative values and the tradition of philosophical idealism that they most prized.

The image of India and the Orient we see refracted in the letters and journals of Concord's Transcendentalists in the mid-1840s exhibits many of the features we have come to associate with European Orientalism generally.[10] There is nothing surprising in this, since Emerson and his friends read the same books and relied on the same travel accounts as the Orientalists of England, Germany, and France. In actuality, for the most part, Transcendentalist Orientalism essentially represents a somewhat provincial and belated recrudescence of Orientalist discourse generally. On the one hand, the Americans fully subscribed to Orientalist caricatures, for example, of Indian "superstition," idolatry, caste tyranny, and sloth. Earlier in his life, Emerson had scoffed at India's "immense 'goddery,' " while Thoreau was always ready to repudiate as "Hindoo tyranny" what he conceived to be India's conservatism and preoccupation with caste.[11] On the other hand, for these Transcendentalists, as for the German Romantics, French eclectics, and some British Indologists, India was also the "cradle of humanity" and a living relic of the Golden Age; she epitomized a benign and venerable conservatism reflecting the timelessness of human experience; her ancient scriptures—the Vedas, laws of Manu, and Purāṇas—exemplified better than any other literature their own favorite doctrines of literary organicism and Romantic primitivism; her philosophers served as the virtual paragons of an uncompromising philosophical idealism; and her religion represented a pure type of contemplation and mysticism.[12] None of this was original to the Orientalists of Concord; indeed, most such formulations are immediately recognizable as reworked Orientalist stereotypes.

As the catalyzing figure in this story, Emerson invariably receives more sustained treatment in studies of early American Orientalism than does his sometime protégé Thoreau. This is understandable, but from both a literary and a religious standpoint, Thoreau's case is far more interesting. Whereas Emerson's allusions to Eastern lore seem everywhere decorously constrained, if not domesticated, within his characteristically urbane cosmopolitanism, Thoreau fashions them as links in his overall imaginative vision. This is a fact that even casual readers of Thoreau's published works would have trouble denying. In contrast to the protracted period of preparation and incubation that preceded Emerson's mature reception of Eastern literature, Thoreau's engagement with South Asian literature began quite suddenly with his reading of Emerson's copy of William Jones's translation of *The Laws of Manu* in 1840, and his response quickly became almost unreservedly enthusiastic.[13] To judge from college reading lists, he read little from or about Asian traditions during his studies at Harvard College, though he was no doubt familiar with some basic facts and the usual stereotypes.[14] His sporadic first references to India in his journals are, if anything, conventionally derogatory: the earliest journals are punctuated with hackneyed references to the Indian juggernaut, Asian "serenity" and "indolence," and conventionally romantic images of "domes and minarets"—the familiar stock of eighteenth-century Oriental tales. Other early passages make it clear that Thoreau's attitudes had also been shaped by the usual polarities of the standard Orientalist grammar: "I cannot attach much importance to historical epochs—or geographical boundaries—when I have my Orient and Occident in one revolution of my body" (PJ.1.172).[15] This last entry was made on August 14, 1840, and until this point in time, his depictions of Asian civilization consisted invariably of a kind of familiar Orientalist pastiche. Three days later, however, on August 17, he provided his cautious first assessment of Jones's translation of *Manu*, a book Emerson had recently borrowed from the Boston Atheneum and lent him to peruse: "Tried by a New England eye, or the mere practical wisdom of modern times—they are simply the oracles of a race already in its dotage, but held up to the sky, which is the only impartial and incorruptible ideal, they are of a piece with its depth and serenity" (PJ.1.173–74, 178).

Thoreau's reading that August marked the beginning of a devotion to Asian, especially Hindu, classics that continued for the next fifteen years. The next spring, he was immersed in *Manu* once again, and now his tone of qualified admiration was replaced by flushed enthusiasm:

That title—The Laws of Menu—with the Gloss of Culucca—comes to me with such a volume of sound as if it had swept unobstructed over the plains of Hindostan, and when my eye rests on yonder birches—or the sun in the water—or the shadows of the trees—it seems to signify the laws of them all.

They are the laws of you and me—a fragrance wafted down from those old times—and no more to be refuted than the wind.

When my imagination travels eastward and backward to those remote years of the gods—I seem to draw near to the habitation of the morning—and the dawn at length has a place. I remember the book as an hour before sunrise.

We are height and depth both—a calm sea—at the foot of a promontory—Do we not overlook our own depths? (PJ.1.311–12)

During the next few years, Thoreau continued his reading of Hindu, Confucian, and Sufi texts, supplementing Emerson's collection with texts drawn from the Harvard College library. While collaborating with Emerson on the proposed "Ethnical Scriptures" column of the *Dial* in 1843, he became better acquainted with several texts representing the Confucian tradition. For his extracts of "The Sayings of Confucius," which appeared in the April 1843 issue, he drew upon the first volume of Joshua Marshman's translation of the works of Confucius as well as an anonymous collection of fragments.[16] Throughout the next ten years, Thoreau continued to draw extensively on the Confucian material for exempla and anecdotes in the composition of his lectures and essays. *Walden* alone contains at least fifteen references to Chinese texts. For almost all of these later citations, however, Thoreau's source was Pauthier's 1841 French translation of the Neo-Confucian *Four Books,* published under the title *Confucius and Mencius.* At some point during the 1840s, Thoreau prepared an English translation of generous selections of Pauthier's work, upon which he subsequently drew for his Confucian citations. The lion's share of these citations came from Pauthier's rendering of the *Analects* (*Lun-yü*) and the *Mencius* (*Meng-tzu*). Needless to say, Thoreau found much to admire in these materials. The paragraphs from the *Four Books* singled out for translation suggest that he was especially taken with the Confucian ideal of the superior man, the uncompromising nature of Confucian morality, and the Confucian values of good governance. However, several of these extracts, especially those taken from the *Chung-yung* (The Doctrine of the Mean), have a decidedly un-Confucian otherworldly and contemplative character, reflecting perhaps Taoist and Buddhist influences on the Neo-Confucian materials. For example, one extract from the *Analects* that Thoreau copies out at some length narrates the story of the Neo-Confucian disciple Tian, who finds life's greatest virtue in retiring to nature to "bathe in the waters of the Y"—a vocation that must surely have endeared him to his Yankee cousin.[17]

Thoreau's knowledge of Persian and Sufi literature rested largely on his appreciative reading of Sa'di's *Gulistan* (The Rose Garden), which he encountered in Emerson's library probably as early as the summer of 1840.[18] A classic of Persian literature, *The Gulistan* served both writers as a window onto the rich tradition of worldly wisdom, love mysticism, and poetic symbolism distinctive of Persian Sufism. For his part, Emerson raised Sa'di to the status of a kind of poetic icon, in recognition of his graceful treatment of the themes of love, friendship, and contemplative tranquility. Thoreau was similarly impressed, citing passages from the *Gulistan* at least six times in *A Week*. His references to Sa'di, Hafiz, and other Muslim writings suggest that he was inspired, here again, above all by their representations of religious contemplation, renunciation, and nonattachment. From Sa'di, for instance, he obtained the portrait of the "azad" or religious independent, which served as a sort of sanction and point of arrival for the "Economy" chapter of *Walden* (79).[19]

Notwithstanding the obvious importance of the Confucian and Sufi materials, as far as Thoreau's religious reflections and his representation of these in his writings were concerned, here again Hinduism took center stage. Large sections of the "Sunday" and "Monday" chapters of *A Week* are taken up by extended citations, with commentary, of various Eastern texts, especially *The Laws of Manu* and Charles Wilkins's translation of the Bhagavad Gita, which did not arrive in Concord until 1845, when Emerson borrowed a copy from his friend James Elliot Cabot and, shortly thereafter, purchased a copy of his own.[20] Thoreau, whose reactions were conditioned by his appreciative reading of *The Laws of Manu* in 1840, apparently took his turn with the Gita while still ensconced at Walden Pond. Beginning in June of 1846, he began copying out long extracts from Emerson's copy, together with approving running commentary. Many of these entries he soon transferred to the "Monday" section of *A Week*, but *Walden* also proved a decided beneficiary, as Thoreau wished to make clear in its pages: "In the morning I bathe my intellect in the stupendous and cosmogonal philosophy of the Bhagvat Geeta, since whose composition years of the gods have elapsed, and in comparison with which our modern world and its literature seem puny and trivial" (298).[21] Though clearly more nimble in its weaving of Hindu materials than *A Week*, *Walden* repeatedly offers a showcase for Thoreau's Oriental research and affiliations, and does so at several critical junctures, from the prolonged and unflattering comparison of the daily life of Concord townspeople with the penance "of Brahmins sitting exposed to four fires" at the start of "Economy," to the suggestive depiction of the author sitting yogi-like in his doorway "from sunrise till noon, rapt in revery," to the Hindu-inspired fable of the artist of Kouroo at the book's conclusion (4, 111, 326).

By the beginning of the next decade, Thoreau was familiar with several other classical Hindu texts, including Wilson's translation of the *Viṣṇu Purāṇa,* William Ward's translations of excerpts from the six systems of Indian philosophy, Rammohan Roy's translations of selected Upanishads, and Colebrooke's translations of the *Sāṃkhya-kārikā.*[22] Besides English translations, Thoreau also looked into French translations, especially Langlois's translation of the *Harivaṃśa,* an appendix to the voluminous Indian epic the *Mahābhārata.* For reasons we can only guess, Thoreau himself prepared a partial translation of one episode from Langlois's translation, which he entitled "The Transmigration of the Seven Brahmans."[23] References in the published writings suggest that of all these texts, *Manu,* the Bhagavad Gita, and the *Sāṃkhya-kārikā* were the most influential.[24] After 1850, references in the journals to Asian religions become less frequent. Thoreau's journals and letters witness a renewed burst of enthusiasm in 1855, however, with the arrival in Concord of a trunkload of forty-four mostly Hindu books from Thoreau's English friend Thomas Cholmondeley, though this was an event more important for the further transmission of Oriental ideas than for their formative impact on Emerson and Thoreau themselves. Thoreau nonetheless dubbed it a "princely gift," thanked his benefactor profusely, and proceeded to build a driftwood case especially to house them (Correspondence, 387–88, 397–98).[25]

Like his Transcendentalist friends, Thoreau was an eclectic reader, and this fact holds as much for his Asian readings as for his other interests. To some extent, this impression necessarily results from the limited nature of his sources. From the contemporary standpoint, or even from the standpoint of an Indologist of fifty years ago, Emerson and Thoreau's early collection of Hindu sources must seem idiosyncratic—the Bhagavad Gita, of course, but why *The Laws of Manu* or the *Sāṃkhya-kārikā?* It is clear that Transcendentalist impressions of Hindu literature and culture were dictated in part by the academic and aesthetic inclinations of Britain's first generation of Sanskritists, and in part by the political and economic exigencies of the first British translation projects. *The Laws of Manu* is a telling case in point. First published in 1794 as *Institutes of Hindu Law, Manu* was one of the earliest translations to be prepared by William Jones under the auspices of the Asiatic Society of Bengal. A distinguished jurist, as well as prodigious philologist, Jones assumed responsibility for this project in keeping with recently formulated colonial policy stipulating that British magistrates must govern India in accordance with native custom and law. As the most ancient compendium extant, *Manu* was naturally first in line for translation. Jones undertook this translation project, in other words, out of professional need and in order to further the political objectives of the colonial administration. The circumstances of this text's publication thus exemplify the collusion between academic knowledge and colonial politics characteristic of much Orientalist discourse. Today *The Laws of Manu* might seem an unlikely choice as an introduction to Indian studies; for Thoreau it was nearest to hand.[26] Thus, at one level, Thoreau's Orientalism, especially in its earliest phases, cannot be separated from the Orientalist schematization, homogenization, and projection to which he was heir. Despite the vast differences among the cultures of South, East, and Western Asia, for him, as for many Orientalists of his day, India came to epitomize the Orient generally.

Faced with his depiction of himself in *Walden* as a kind of Hindu anchorite, his interest in meditative experience, and his discontent with the attenuated spirituality of the Unitarian community, critics have generally acknowledged the ubiquity of Thoreau's South Asian references, but views of how best to construe the impact of his Hindu studies on his intellectual life and literary productions have been decidedly at variance. On the one hand are those critics, such as Arthur Christy, who have maintained that Thoreau did in some sense practice yoga and did think of himself essentially as a yogi.[27] The other school of interpretation—the debunkers of Thoreau's yogic claims—tends to find this view naive and reductive, seeking rather to construe such assertions as affectation and rhetorical shape-shifting. To such critics, Thoreau's Oriental interests were merely a passing fad, having little real bearing on his mature work.[28] In the context of this study, I would like to suggest that in *Walden* and elsewhere, yoga operates as a kind of spiritual model and imaginative construct, zealously distilled from his Eastern reading and thoughtfully elaborated, for the calculated purpose of representing to himself and his would-be readers authentic experiences of ecstasy with which, as we have seen, he had long been familiar. In this view, Thoreau's "yoga," like his preoccupation with Asian thought generally, was neither adventitious nor ancillary, but crucial to his rhetorical constructions in *A Week* and *Walden,* and to the personal reflections they were conceived to represent.

A Passage of the Vedas

One of the anomalous facts of Thoreau's life experience often duly noted by his biographers but resistant to interpretation was his preoccupation with natural sound. Meditations on natural sounds assume a prominent place in his published writings, but not until we begin leafing through the journals do we realize what a crucial role they played in Thoreau's interior imaginative life. In his meditations sounds in nature were quickly assimilated to music, and music to ecstasy. As we have seen, this acoustic rapture serves as a leitmotif in Thoreau's journals and often provides the starting point or key ingredient to some of his most searching reflections.[29] In several of his earliest journal entries, music also comes to be curiously associated with heroism, poetry, and war. The music that such heroes hear, however, is not the boisterous din of fife and drum, but the subtler, barely audible, endlessly varied music of the natural world itself—what Thoreau often likened to the music of the spheres. By his twenty-first year, this imaginative complex had become a distinctive and generative component of Thoreau's imaginative vision. By this time it is already clear that his theory of sound had begun to serve the kind of literary rationale—a defense of literature as the propagation and publication of silence—that it did in the closing pages of *A Week.* The only thing lacking from this personal artistic vision was some sort of literary sanction, and this is where the Eastern books came in. In August of 1838, in his first explicit reference to Asian texts, he associates ancient literature with music. But with his reading of *Manu* two years later, he makes the connection more specifically to the Vedas: "A strain of music reminds me of a passage of the Vedas" (PJ.1.52; 173). While working on his manuscript for *A Week*, Thoreau amplified this somewhat cryptic entry in the context of his commentary on the epiphany brought on by the night drummer that I noted previously. The reference to Homer immediately following this epiphany from "Monday" reminds us that the main influence on Thoreau's articulation of the drummer of the night is the Platonic and medieval tradition of the music of the spheres, but with his invocation of the Vedas, he indicates a second: "A strain of music reminds me of a passage of the Vedas, and I associate with it the idea of infinite remoteness, as well as of beauty and serenity, for to the senses that is furthest from us which addresses the greatest depth within us. It teaches us again and again to trust the remotest and finest as the divinest instinct, and makes a dream our only real experience" (Week, 174–75).

Though unrelated to the classical tradition of sphere music, the Hindu conception of the origin and ontology of the Vedas provided another informative precedent for Thoreau's apprehension of celestial sounds and an important exhibit of his early philosophy of language. At this point in time, Thoreau did not have access to translations of any Vedic hymns themselves—*Manu* is traditionally categorized as a legal text (*dharma-śāstra*), not part of Vedic revelation (*śruti*) per se. Nevertheless, *Manu* does provide a definitive statement of how Indian tradition conceived and understood "the Veda." Here Thoreau read that Veda was the attribution given to a compendium of sacred traditions believed to be uncreated, preexistent, and universal. He discovered that the Veda was considered the archetype of the created world, and that Hindus conceived of the creation and destruction of the world as the alternation between waking and deep sleep.[30] He found that the Veda was understood to be not only the charter of all human laws and traditions, but also the matrix of nature itself. Transcendental in nature, it yet manifested itself in the form of speech.[31] Elsewhere in the Vedic literature, Veda is even personified as *Vāk,* or procreative "speech." Silent in its depths but manifest in sound, the Veda thus provided an exact analogue for Thoreau's developing philosophy of natural sound. When Thoreau wrote, therefore, that a strain of music reminded him of a passage of the Vedas, he might have meant not only that it reminded him of some passages from *Manu,* but also that a strain of music was analogous to, could be construed as, a passage of the Vedas. Like the Vedic hymns he was reading about, the sounds of nature arose, at first inaudibly, out of the wellspring of cosmic silence. In the months after his first reading of *Manu,* Thoreau elaborated on this important new association between Veda and music: "Music is the Crystalization of Sound. There is something in the effect of a harmonious voice upon the disposition of its neighborhood analogous to the law of crystals—it centralizes itself—and sounds like the published law of things. If the law of the universe were to be audibly promulgated no mortal lawgiver would suspect it—for it would be a finer melody than his ears ever attended to. It would be sphere music" (PJ.1.249). In this reflection, Thoreau makes it clear that he does not accept Vedic self-representations literally—*Manu,* too, stood in need of revision—but what he conceived as the ancient Vedic philosophy of sound supplied the perfect touchstone for his own developing Transcendentalist theory of literature and a suggestive imaginative rationale for his experiences of acoustic delight. This identification of a Vedic analogue for his own private reflections on the relationship between sound and silence is the product of Thoreau's unique imaginative synthesis, but it also reflects a level of conversancy with *Manu*'s text not shared by Emerson or Alcott.

This sort of close scrutiny of *The Laws of Manu* also encouraged him to treat the Vedic literature as one of his earliest exemplars of literary organicism and a kind of Romantic primitivism. "In Literature it is only the wild that attracts us," he wrote in "Walking," and though he goes on in this late essay to despair of locating in any single tradition a purely naturalistic literature, his longstanding ideal of literary organicism appears to have owed some of its earliest formulations to *Manu* (Writings.5.231).

I know of no book which has come down to us with grander pretensions than this, and it is so impersonal and sincere that it is never offensive nor ridiculous. . . . It seems to have been uttered from some eastern summit, with a sober morning prescience in the dawn of time, and you cannot read a sentence without being elevated as upon the tableland of the Ghauts. It has such a rhythm as the winds of the desert, such a tide as the Ganges, and is as superior to criticism as the Himmaleh mountains. Its tone is of such unrelaxed fibre, that even at this late day, unworn by time, it wears the English and the Sanscrit dress indifferently, and its fixed sentences keep up their distant fires still like the stars, by whose dissipated rays this lower world is illumined. (Week 148–49)

This sort of preoccupation with literary organicism was by no means peculiar to Thoreau—it is an important part of his Romantic inheritance—but he had better reasons than other writers of the period for considering Indian literature in this way. In the creation story that opens Manu's account, the lawgiver makes it clear that the three primordial Vedas—*Rig, Yajur,* and *Sāma*—were derived from a natural source— "milked out," as the lawgiver puts it, "from fire, from air, and from the sun." In *A Week,* Thoreau quotes this verse with particular approval, adding, "Nor will we disturb the antiquity of this Scripture. . . . One might as well investigate the chronology of light and heat" (Week, 153).[32] In this fanciful appropriation of *Manu,* Thoreau exemplifies the literary ideal to which he professed himself devoted. His appropriation, though it requires an at least imaginative acquiescence to the Hindu tradition's naturalization and therefore privileging of its sacred canon, in effect sanctions his own programs of literary organicism.

While *Manu* was crucial to the development of Thoreau's reflections on natural sound and literary wildness, it left its deepest impression on his attitudes toward the body and his ideas about personal asceticism. The best-known digest of Thoreauvian asceticism, the "Higher Laws" chapter of *Walden,* details his thoughts on the topics of vegetarianism, chastity, and human nature generally. It is fair to say that among critics, at least, "Higher Laws" has not been the most popular of *Walden*'s chapters, presumably because of its imputed preachiness and apparently overt moralizing. Here, it is thought, we encounter Thoreau at his most conventional. He begins the chapter, for example, by drawing a sharp distinction between the "higher" and lower reaches of human nature, a distinction most of his readers would no doubt recognize as traditionally Pauline. And the rest of the chapter may strike us as a mixture of Victorian prudishness and Grahamite eccentricity.[33] "Higher Laws," we conclude, is Thoreau's concession to the reform-minded values of his times.

Most puzzling is the fact that Thoreau's flight to the Spirit in "Higher Laws" seems so much a variance with the downward or physicalist tendency evinced by the rest of the book. This is the same writer, after all, who ended his earlier chapter on the heavenly reflections of Concord's ponds with the memorably satiric quip "Talk of heaven! Ye disgrace the earth," and who throughout *Walden* and his other writings seems so committed to opposing and counteracting the idealistic vaporizing of some Transcendentalist rhetoric (Walden, 200). The truth about "Higher Laws," however, is that it is neither a conventional temperance tract nor a paean to Thoreauvian primitivism, but an odd combination of both. It begins with Thoreau's mock confession of his craving for raw woodchuck, but quickly centers on the existential contradiction upon which the rest of the chapter, if not the entire book, is predicated: "I found in myself, and still find, an instinct toward a higher, or, as it is named, spiritual life, as do most men, and another toward a primitive rank and savage one, and I reverence them both. I love the wild not less than the good" (210). The problem reserved for the rest of the chapter is how the two are to be reconciled. References elsewhere in Thoreau's writing suggest that his attitude toward the body were intractably ambivalent. On the one hand, he could write: "I must confess there is nothing so strange to me as my own body—I love any other piece of nature, almost, better," a sentiment that achieves haunting metaphysical elaboration in the account of Thoreau's vertiginous ascent of Mount Katahdin (PJ.1.365; MW, 71). On the other hand, he could conceive the body as a kind of temple of the spirit (PJ.1.139; Walden, 221). There was nothing apparently disingenuous about such pious affirmations, despite their biblical overtones; they clearly followed from his personal experience. In contrast to Emerson, who, as we saw, found his ecstasy on a bare common through the disembodied medium of a transparent eyeball, Thoreau's revelations regularly occurred in the woods through the medium of his physical senses, hearing above all. For him, at least, "higher" life depended on his physical health and the soundness of sense. The following journal passage, entered at age twenty, became a cornerstone of the mature Thoreauvian faith: "I never feel that I am inspired unless my body is also, . . . The body is the first proselyte the Soul makes. Our life is but the Soul made known by its fruits—the body. The whole duty of man may be expressed in one line—Make to yourself a perfect body" (PJ.1.137–38).

This waggish reversal of the old catechism states this aspect of Thoreau's faith as well as anything could, but how and whether he could reconcile this affirmative sense of the value of the body in the construction of higher life with his felt sense of disgust for his own body remains a question for most readers.[34] Whatever the answer, a close consideration of his notes from *The Laws of Manu* suggests that here, once again, teachings from the Hindu tradition suggested some perspectives to which he felt quite drawn. Thoreau found it particularly refreshing that Manu dwells as much upon the gross physical functions of human life—"how to eat, drink, cohabit, void excrement and urine"—as he does upon final beatitude, "however offensive it may be to modern taste" (Walden, 221). Such comprehensiveness Thoreau admires for its own sake, especially since it is so conspicuously absent from official expositions of New England faith, but he also recognizes that Manu's careful strictures on physical self-culture reflect a fuller and more adequate assessment of the crucial role played by the body in the religious life itself.

As his reading of Indian religious literature opened out to encompass other texts in the next several years, he must have seen that while superficially similar, the traditions of Indian and Western asceticism were built upon entirely different foundations. To be sure, India was the home of some of the world's most outlandish forms of physical austerity, as he wittily illustrates in the opening pages of "Economy" (Walden, 4). At the same time, however, the traditions of yoga taught that spiritual growth depended upon the sedulous cultivation of the body through such practices as regular fasting, physical conditioning, and breath control. In some of these classical texts, at least, perfection of the body—not its mortification—was the central goal of religious asceticism, a fact Thoreau obviously understood, though it was nowhere a part of the standard Orientalist lexicon. But Thoreau's insight into Hindu thought went deeper. Citing an aphorism in "Higher Laws" from Roy's Vedic commentary, Thoreau goes on to maintain: "Yet the spirit can for the time pervade and control every member and function of the body, and transmute what in form is the grossest sensuality into purity and devotion. The generative energy, which when we are loose, dissipates and makes us unclean, when we are continent invigorates and inspires us" (Walden, 219). Here the transmutation of "generative energy," not its repression, comes to be seen as a driving force in the religious life. This idea, regularly illustrated in Hindu stories about saints and asceticism, apparently struck a chord of recognition. In this view, asceticism and sensuality were not so much opposing impulses as different expressions of the same generative energy. The ascetic life was attended by its own set of pleasures, a fact affirmed by Manu and verified for Thoreau by his own experience. Here again is Thoreau responding to his recent readings of Manu:

> The very austerity of these Hindoos is tempting to the devotional as a more refined and nobler luxury. They seem to have indulged themselves with a certain moderation and temperance in the severities which their code requires, as divine exercises not to be excessively used as yet.
>
> One may discover the root of a Hindoo religion in his own

private history.—when in the silent intervals of the day or the night he does sometimes inflict on himself like austerities with a stern satisfaction. (PJ.1.327)

More than Atlantic Depth

Although Thoreau's most characteristic expressions of euphoria in nature are commonly inaugurated for him by some form of acoustic excitement, sometimes sight supplants hearing as the principal medium of higher consciousness. These representations take various forms, but they generally proceed from meditations on the reflecting surfaces of neighborhood lakes and streams, Walden Pond above all. Thoreau's authorization for these formulations of ecstatic vision also appears to come principally from India.

Early journal entries already betray a fascination with the reflecting properties of water, whether of rivers and woodland lakes, sheets of ice, or snow in the moonlight. As in the case of the natural echoes with which he was equally fascinated, Thoreau found special virtue in the mimetic character of these reflections. He digresses for pages in his journals on the reproduction, in the river beneath, of trees along the river bank; of cloud formations across the pond; or the moon in a lake's inlet. One of the earliest of these treatments provided the source for one of the boatman's reflections on the Concord River: "I stood by the river today considering the forms of the elms reflected in the water. For every oak and birch too, growing on the hill top, as well as for elms and willows, there is a graceful etherial tree making down from the roots—as it were the original idea of the tree, and sometimes nature in high tides brings her mirror to its foot and makes it visible—Anxious nature sometimes reflects from pools and puddles the objects which our grovelling senses may fail to see relieved against the sky, with the pure ether for background" (PJ.1.127–28).[35] Here we see exemplified one of Thoreau's distinctive patterns of reflection and a prime instance of the operation of his characteristically disjunctive vision. He does not record anything not actually seen in the reflective surface of the river, but his commentary indicates that this phenomenon was as suggestive to him for its philosophical implications as for its perceptual properties. Nature, he supposed, provides such reflections so that we can see what, with our "grovelling senses," we may have missed before. Nature accomplishes this disclosure, interestingly enough, not by a change of substance, but by switching the "background." What makes this new perception especially suggestive is that, in contrast to the first appearance against the invisible ether, in the reflection we recognize the background also—in the transparent but visible substance of the water. In such reflective scenes, "background" merges with foreground in the makeup of the overall vision.

What an echo from the cliffs or reflections in water have in common of course is duplication and self-reproduction, and—whether of sight or sound—this was a feature of nature's functioning that Thoreau found endlessly suggestive, even consoling. Throughout nature could be seen a pattern of correspondence—of statement and response; of substance and shadow—numberless instances of the duality that nature loved (PJ.3.190; J.3.51). To Thoreau in his own reflections, these expressions of nature also had a kind of soteriological value: "There needs some actual doubleness like this in nature, for if the voices which we commonly hear were all that we ever heard, what then?" (J.4.493). Whether empirical or figurative, this doubleness runs all through Thoreau's writing—it is indeed a distinctive feature of his outlook, as we have seen.

His first book provided Thoreau with a forum for a fuller articulation of such reflections:

> It required some rudeness to disturb with our boat the mirror-like surface of the water, in which every twig and blade of grass was faithfully reflected; too faithfully indeed for art to imitate, for only nature may exaggerate herself. The shallowest still water is unfathomable. Wherever the trees and skies are reflected there is more than Atlantic depth, and no danger of fancy running aground. We noticed that it required a separate intention of the eye, a more free and abstracted vision, to see the reflected trees and the sky, than to see the river bottom merely; and so are there manifold visions in the direction of every object, and even the

most opaque reflect the heavens from their surface. Some men have their eyes naturally intended to the one, and some to the other object. (Week, 48)

Here the river explicitly assumes the role of a kind of philosopher's looking glass only hinted at in the more naturalistic entries of the journal. It serves as a vehicle of meditation whose revelations depend as much upon the philosopher's proficiency ("a separate intention of the eye") as on some objective reality imputed to the river itself. The odd primacy of the reflected images comes to be correlated with a whimsical doctrine of election in which "a more free and abstracted vision" is elevated over naked eyesight in order to recognize "the Atlantic depth" and "manifold visions" inherent in the simple object. The cognition that results from such gifted perception turns the ordinary upside-down and leads to the kind of paradox of which Thoreau is so fond: "The shallowest still water is unfathomable."

More philosophically invested still is the famous meditation on time that initiates the peroration of "Where I Lived, and What I Lived For" in *Walden:* "Time is but the stream I go a-fishing in. I drink at it; but while I drink I see the sandy bottom and detect how shallow it is. Its thin current slides away, but eternity remains. I would drink deeper; fish in the sky, whose bottom is pebbly with stars. I cannot count one. I know not the first letter of the alphabet. I have always been regretting that I was not as wise as the day I was born" (98). The vehicle of this meditation on time, and of the familiar metaphor with which it opens—the "stream" or river of time—calls up once again this distinctively Thoreauvian preoccupation with the curiously dichotomous character of watery reflections. Here the narrator downplays the significance of the metaphoric vehicle itself— "Time is *but* the stream I go a-fishing in"—in his concern to downplay the ontological reality of time, but by the same token relies upon the actual reflective properties of the transparent stream to draw his readers' attention to its deeper transcendental meaning. What prompts the revelation of "eternity" on which the meditation turns, in actuality, is the real or imagined physical reflection of stars in water. It is this suggestive intermingling of stars among the pebbles of the stream that leads to the strange conceit of "fish in the sky," and even, perhaps, of fishing in the sky, depending on whether we read "fish" as a noun or verb. The mounting ambiguities are of course very much to the point of this increasingly vertiginous passage. The conflation of sky and water, stars and fish, above and below upsets the narrator's ordinary conceptions of space, and reduces him to a condition of ecstatic innocence reminiscent of precognitive infancy. So complete is his absorption in this glimpse of eternity beyond the stream of time that for the moment even the operations of counting and spelling seem beyond his comprehension. And here again, we note a Wordsworthian echo in the note of "regret" that he was not as "wise" as the day he was born.

As this memorable passage suggests, of all Thoreau's midcareer writings, *Walden* may well serve as the best showcase for his metaphysical meditations on the reflective properties of neighborhood lakes and streams. From the book's earliest inception, the Pond had come to serve as the principal pretext for his reflections on the self. As the book evolved through its various revisions, the revelatory character of the Pond came increasingly to the foreground, most notably in the chapter "The Ponds," which serves as the centerpiece of the book as a whole. The bulk of this chapter was written after the beginning of 1852, coincident with and immediately subsequent to a two- or three-year period in which the journals manifest a continual fascination with the reflective characteristics of water.[36] "We see things in the reflection," he avers in his journal in 1852, "which we do not see in the substance" (PJ.5.332). On a day of Indian summer, such as *Walden*'s narrator describes in "The Ponds," Walden's reflective properties are brought to near perfection. At times like this, the Pond comes to be recognized as a virtual embodiment of the world around it—the tree-lined banks, the drifting clouds, the sky itself. Reflections on the glassy water are so vivid as to prompt a perceptual shift, which in turn results in some speculative reorientation. In such reorientation, polarities and distinctions undergirding waking experience are suddenly reversed: outside is inside, upper is lower, sky settles onto water.

The controlling metaphor for all of these reflections, whether of a theological or contemplative sort, is the mirror. In "The Ponds" Thoreau compares Walden to "a perfect forest mirror," a mirror eternally fresh and preternaturally sensitive to the forms of the air (188). In such representations, the mirror serves as the perfect description of what could actually be seen, but in elaborating on its reflections as he does, Thoreau draws upon a tradition of figuration of great antiquity and almost worldwide extent. In the West, it appears to have its deepest roots in Plato and the Platonizing philosophers of later tradition.[37] Among Christian writers, Paul's metaphor for revelation (1 Cor. 13) was of course germinal. In a slight adjustment of this use, later writers, including some Puritan preachers, construed the mirror more specifically as a metaphor for Scripture itself.[38] In all of these applications, the mirror served as a guarantee of fidelity. For Transcendentalists and Swedenborgians nature supplanted scripture as the medium of divine revelation: for them nature as a whole, or one of her parts, was the veritable mirror of the divine.[39]

Thoreau's use of the metaphor is obviously indebted to this Transcendentalist reading, but he presses it harder than Emerson or any of his contemporaries did. As he seeks an interior reference for the reflections of Walden, he reconstrues the mirror as a metaphor for the contemplative mind. In doing so, he places himself in the company of contemplatives and mystics across several traditions of the world, from Kabbalah to Zen, for whom the mirror or mirrorlike devices served to initiate a process of self-displacement and auto-reflection calculated to induce, or at least to represent, a kind of mystical ecstasy. In his canonical narration of the Buddha's enlightenment, for example, the Indian writer Aśvaghoṣa notes of the enlightened Sage that "the world appeared to him as though reflected in a spotless mirror."[40] Similarly, adepts of Zen typically speak of "the mirror mind" of Zen practice.[41]

Thoreau could not have been influenced by most of these representations, of course, but he was probably aware of some of the Platonic and Hindu antecedents. Of these, the latter were surely most suggestive. In Emerson's copy of the Gita, for example, he came across a simile in which the world of ignorance was compared to a mirror coated with rust.[42] In

Ward's excerpts from several of the six systems of Indian philosophy, he found Spirit or the mind of the yogin variously compared to a mirror. In one formulation that must have especially struck a chord, a text of the Sāṃkhya system compared the world to a magic show or a reflection on water. And in a passage from the *Yoga-sūtra,* the classical textbook of the philosophy of yoga, Thoreau read how the yogin, "having brought his mind to a fixed state . . . becomes absorbed in the Being contemplated, in the same manner as the crystal receives the image of whatever is reflected upon it."[43]

These texts repeatedly take up metaphors of reflection in their treatment of yogic meditation or *samādhi* in much the same way as Thoreau does in his own meditations on Walden. Like these contemplative mirrors, of which it can be an example, the Pond in its purity initiates a process of self-displacement and a reversal of perceptual frames. Commonly it appears simply transparent. However, to the practiced eye of a devoted speculator, it bodies forth not only the surrounding hills and trees, but the onlooker himself. For the moment, so long as the waters remain calm, we become spectactors of ourselves, privileged to stand as if outside looking on, seeing subject as if it were object. To most passersby this phenomenon was perhaps unremarkable; to Thoreau it appears to have been deeply suggestive.

Scattered as they are throughout his writings, these episodes of seeing himself in the surface of the Pond appear to have served as a natural type for Thoreau's own reflections on ecstatic vision. A vivid manifestation of nature's self-duplication and reflexiveness, they provide concrete sanction for the various operations of Thoreau's own disjunctive imagination. As we saw in *A Week,* this doubling activity is evident in the doppelgänger theme dramatized by the two brothers, one of whom rows while the other looks on, one of whom meditates while the other sleeps. In *Walden* the doppelgänger theme is not as conspicuous as it is in *A Week,* nor as dramatically sustained, but it resurfaces in overt form in the complementary relationship between Thoreau and his brutish alter-ego Alec Therien, the Canadian woodchopper. Its most consequential manifestation, however, is not between brothers or friends, but between the poet and himself, and it finds its most vivid portrayal not in company, but in a famous passage from "Solitude," which, for the sake of fuller explication, I present in full:

> With thinking we may be beside ourselves in a sane sense. By a conscious effort of the mind we can stand aloof from actions and their consequences; and all things, good and bad, go by us like a torrent. We are not wholly involved in Nature. I may be either the drift-wood in the stream, or Indra in the sky looking down on it. I *may* be affected by a theatrical exhibition; on the other hand, I *may not* be affected by an actual event which appears to concern me much more. I only know myself as a human entity; the scene, so to speak, of thoughts and affections; and am sensible of a certain doubleness by which I can stand as remote from myself as from another. However intense my experience, I am conscious of the presence and criticism of a part of me, which, as it were, is not a part of me, but spectator, sharing no experience, but taking note of it; and that is no more I than it is you. When the play, it may be the tragedy, of life is over, the spectator goes his way. It was a kind of fiction, a work of the imagination only, so far as he was concerned. This doubleness may easily make us poor neighbors and friends sometimes. (134–35)

Although this passage is removed from the kind of explicit reflection that I have been examining, and psychologized to an unprecedented degree, the reference here to the ambiguity between "the drift-wood in the stream, or Indra in the sky" suggests its reflective affiliations: it results from a more developed meditation on the visual reflections of the stream. In contrast to the more committedly naturalistic observations, this one makes clear its subjective point of reference right from the start. As with many of Thoreau's most serious reflections, he begins here with a play on words: in its common figurative sense, to be "beside oneself" may be taken as an expression of discomfiture or pathology. Provision of the immediate qualification "in a sane sense," however, calls attention to the figuration, inviting us to consider what literalizing the metaphor might mean, and signaling that the figurative connotations are intended merely as a sort of rhetorical subterfuge. As a result, we are more likely to be cognizant with him of the etymological play underlying this formulation, his implied equation of the English phrase with the Greek *ek-stasis*.

In a journal entry that appears to have provided one of the sources of this passage, Thoreau describes the perception of surfaces with the word "salutary" and then goes on to introduce the same phrase noted above: "The perception of surfaces will always have the effect of miracle to a sane sense" (PJ.5.309). In writing of the "playful wisdom" of Viṣṇu Śarma, author of the *Hitopadeśa*, a Hindu collection of fables, he admires "the pledge of sanity . . . that it sometimes reflect upon itself" (PJ.2.40; Week, 147). "Sanity" Thoreau conceived as a mark of natural health and related it to the fullness of sense, the "sound senses" of a fully awakened human being. From these references, the burden of "sane sense" is clearer: it serves as a tag phrase evoking and in part describing Thoreau's own peculiar conception of what he refers to elsewhere as ecstasy.

The association of this phrase with Viṣṇu Śarma is somewhat ephemeral, but it signals the Hindu matrix out of which this reflection comes. A more obvious indication is the reference to Indra, the Vedic sky god, which appears oddly out of place and perhaps uninstructive to most readers of *Walden,* until we recognize how deeply indebted this passage is to Eastern, and especially Hindu, sources. Indra is a familiar figure in Hindu literature, even though his former status as king of the gods later came to be superseded by other deities. In the Gita, Thoreau would have found him described as "the prince of celestial beings."[44] In one possible source of this reference in *Walden,* Thoreau cites Indra as a kind of paragon of the celestial regions, who nonetheless must necessarily have a dwelling on earth (PJ.3.227). In the philosophical literature, Indra comes to be invoked conventionally for mainly illustrative purposes, in much the same spirit as Thoreau invokes him in "Solitude."[45] In Roy's abridgment of the Vedānta system, Thoreau found a defense of the early Vedic claim of Indra as supreme on the grounds that anyone, "in consequence of being united with divine reflection, may speak as assuming to be the Supreme Being."[46] In this later instance, the exponent of Vedānta specifically links the mythological deity Indra to the practice of yoga and the quest for final emancipation, in a way that was perhaps suggestive for Thoreau.[47]

"I Would Fain Practise the Yoga Faithfully"

With the possible exception of the apparently anomalous allusion to Indra, the most obvious references in the "Solitude" passage are to figures drawn from the theater. In his ecstatic condition, the narrator describes himself as the mere "scene" of his "thoughts and affections." He is conscious of a "certain doubleness" in which a part of him stands aloof from himself as a critic and "spectator," observing but "sharing no experience": "When the play, it may be the tragedy, of life is over, the spectator goes his way. It was a kind of fiction, a work of the imagination only, so far as he was concerned." This theater imagery was integral to the original passage in its journal form also and points to an important source of Thoreau's figuration, here and elsewhere, that has been little discussed. Throughout his writings, and dating from an early time, Thoreau often recurred to the imagery and concepts of the theater.[48] Why this should be so in a writer temperamentally suspicious of such imputedly ephemeral amusements as society and the theater is unclear, until we see that in doing so he was tapping into a mode of figuration of quite ancient vintage and direct pertinence. This was the *topos,* its roots once again in Plato, that came to be elaborated in the medieval notion of *theatrum mundi,* the theater of the world. For Christians, Augustine had provided one of its most authoritative early formulations: the world is a theater of which the spectator is God.[49] Though Christian relations with the playhouse were always uneasy at best, this conception of theater as world appeared to have some biblical sanction. It was even attractive to Puritans, who were compelled to insist on a depreciation of man and the world as vanity, on the one hand, and on God's absolute sovereignty on the other.[50]

Though no Puritan, Thoreau was also drawn to this ancient conception of God as a kind of transcendental spectator of the world. As with all such theological and cosmological figures, no sooner does he appropriate it, however, than he seeks to interiorize and remodel it for his own purposes: "I had this advantage, at least, in my mode of life, over those who were obliged to look abroad for amusement, to society and the theatre, that my life itself was become my amusement and never ceased to be novel. It was a drama of many scenes and without an end" (Walden, 112). In this scene, like the one in "Solitude," Thoreau has psychologized the topos of theatrum mundi and arrogated absolute spectatorship to himself. This is, of course, precisely the kind of move that the Puritans sought to avoid, and there is no precedent for it in previous Western use of the figure, so far as I know. Thoreau did find precedent for it elsewhere, however, most dramatically in the Hindu tradition, where a similar world-as-stage conception occurs. And, in contrast to the Christian usage, Indian poets and philosophers had little hesitation about adopting the cosmological idea in an interior sense, especially in the traditions of yoga.[51]

One illustration of this may be found in the following extract from *A Week:* "A Hindoo sage said, 'As a dancer having exhibited herself to the spectator, desists from the dance, so does Nature desist, having manifested herself to soul—. Nothing, in my opinion, is more gentle than Nature; once aware of having been seen, she does not again expose herself to the gaze of the soul' " (382–83). This passage consists of a conflation of two sūtras from the *Sāṃkhya-kārikā,* which Thoreau had been poring over in 1851, the year before he drafted the first version of the "Solitude" passage into his journal. In his journal of May 6 of 1851, he appended two other verses from the *Kārikā* to an extended passage from the *Harivaṃśa* on the topic of yoga and the nature of the yogin (PJ.3.215–16).[52] Although the reference above is to a dance performance, the metaphor has obvious analogous metaphysical associations with the theatrum mundi topos. Typically, Indian philosophers depict the world as a kind of dance or play, of which the transcendent soul is the silent witness and impersonal spectator. It is evident from Thoreau's treatment of the theater imagery in "Solitude" and elsewhere that its primary significance for him lay in the idea of the self as "spectator."

While the passage from "Solitude" has been thoroughly naturalized, the reference to Indra betrays its Hindu affiliations. Thoreau worked up this passage from journal entries made in August 1852, not long after the period when he was reading the *Sāṃkhya-kārikā* and Roy's translations of the Upanishads. In the *Sāṃkhya-kārikā*, in particular, he found a thoroughly elaborated philosophical basis for the odd experience of doubleness he describes in "Solitude." The Sāṃkhya philosophy, of which the *Sāṃkhya-kārikā* provides an authoritative expression, sets out a cosmological system based upon the foundational dualism of spirit (*puruṣa*), on the one hand, and nature or matter (*prakṛti*) on the other. Life and evolution result, it is thought, from the mingling and confusion of these two principles, while liberation (*mokṣa*) results from fully and finally distinguishing between them. In the Sāṃkhya and Yoga systems of Indian philosophy, the ideas of "spectator" (*draṣṭṛ*) or "witness" (*sakṣin*) thus have a technical significance: they describe the eternal status of the soul (*puruṣa*) as separate from nature (*prakṛti*) and the phenomenal levels of life. While the soul appears at times to be entangled in nature, its essential character is pure, eternal, and unchanging. Liberation results when this reality—the absolute and eternal separation of *puruṣa* and *prakṛti*—is perfectly and finally recognized. Once this recognition occurs, the soul is never again deceived by the dramatic actions of nature. Sūtra 19 of the *Kārikā*, which Colebrooke translated in what has now become a more or less conventional rendering, epitomizes the character of the silent witness: "And from that contrast . . . it follows, that soul is witness, solitary, bystander, spectator, and passive."[53] In a similar vein, Ward's collection of passages from the *Yoga-sūtra* includes a reference to Spirit as "a mere spectator of the universe."[54] In this sort of cosmological application of the Sāṃkhya system, the *puruṣa* stands as the immensity of being outside the limited domain of the world. When the author of "Solitude" speaks of "a certain doubleness by which I can stand as remote from myself as from another," these precedents were still fresh in his mind.

Thoreau was obviously quite taken with this experiential and contemplative aspect of Indic tradition. In a famous letter to his friend Harrison Blake, he copied out a couple of passages from the *Harivaṃśa* to which he gives an explicitly autobiographical reference:

"Free in this world, as the birds in the air, disengaged from every kind of chains, those who have practised the *yoga* gather in Brahma the certain fruit of their works."

Depend upon it that rude and careless as I am, I would fain practise the *yoga* faithfully.

"The yogin, absorbed in contemplation, contributes in his degree to creation: he breathes a divine perfume, he hears wonderful things. Divine forms traverse him without tearing him, and united to the nature which is proper to him, he goes, he acts, as animating original matter."

To some extent, and at rare intervals, even I am a yogin. (Correspondence, 251; PJ.3.215–16)

The self-attributions contained here have been overinterpreted by some commentators, but they do suggest that at some level Thoreau had taken the literature on yoga very much to heart. In introducing the Gita extracts that he includes in the "Monday" section of *A Week,* he quotes Warren Hastings's prefatory note to Wilkins's translation at some length.

To those who have never been accustomed to the separation of the mind from the notices of the senses, it may not be easy to conceive by what means such a power is to be attained; since even the most studious men of our hemisphere will find it difficult so to restrain their attention, but that it will wander to some object of present sense or recollection. . . . But if we are told that there have been men who were successively, for ages past, in the daily habit of abstracted contemplation, begun in the earliest period of youth, and continued in many to the maturity of age, each adding some portion of knowledge to the store accumulated by his predecessors; it is not assuming too much to conclude, that as the mind ever gathers strength, like the body, by exercise, so in such an exercise it may in each have acquired the faculty to which they aspired, and that their collective studies may have led them to the discovery of new tracks and combinations of sentiment, totally different from the doctrines with which the learned of other nations are acquainted; doctrines, which however speculative and subtle, still, as they possess the advantage of being derived from a source so free from every adventitious mixture, may be equally founded in truth with the most simple of our own. (138).

Thoreau was not, of course, in a position to practice yoga in any literal sense, because the texts to which he had access do not explain the details of such practices. In implicit recognition of this fact, he appears to appropriate the term yoga, and other references to Indian philosophy, in a somewhat figurative sense to represent his own contemplative experiences generally. In response to an invitation by the young Isaac Hecker to accompany him on a kind of pilgrimage to Europe in 1844, Thoreau regretfully declined, while conceding: "But the fact is, I cannot so decidedly postpone exploring the *Farther Indies,* which are to be reached you know by other routs and other methods of travel. I mean that I constantly return from every external enterprise with disgust to fresh faith in a kind of Brahminical Artesian, Inner Temple, life. All my experience, as yours probably, proves only this reality" (Correspondence, 156). But notwithstanding his oblique appropriation of the philosophy and practice of yoga, the divine hearing that he mentions in the letter to Blake, and the repeated references to the separation between self and activity that occur in the Gita and the *Kārikā,* seem nonetheless to have found fertile ground in Thoreau's personal experience. Common to all of his re-creations of ecstatic vision is some representation of self-displacement, of the self standing outside its habitual station. Reflections of the self on water provided a concrete image of such *ek-stasis,* which is why it typically served as the rhetorical starting point or literary staging for the speculations to follow.

The Fairest of All the Creations of Brahma

One final illustration of Thoreau's appropriation of Hindu materials will serve to epitomize the deeper personal significance of this literature for him and his literary handling of it. Nowhere does *Walden* sustain the kind of extended interrogation of Hindu literature that we find in the

"Monday" section of *A Week*, where Thoreau transcribes a string of his favorite passages appended with his own running commentary. What we find in *Walden*, rather, is that such references have undergone a thorough imaginative assimilation in the service of his overarching artistic designs. Such references are not less momentous, however, and they often appear at crucial junctures in the book's unfolding development. Two such cases—the story of the king's son in "Where I Lived and What I Lived For" and the cryptic story of the artist of Kouroo in the penultimate sequence of the concluding chapter—take the form of teaching parables that effectively frame the narrative of Thoreau's sojourn at the Pond. Like the Yankee yarn about the mysterious bug hatched from a farmer's table after sixty winters, both of these parables are stories of transformation, but Thoreau makes it clear that unlike the New England story, he derives these stories from his Hindu sources. The former, the import of which is more or less self-explanatory, he copied from his reading of the *Sāṃkhya-kārikā* (Walden, 96).[55] The source of the Kouroo story, however, is a good deal more elusive.[56] For the sake of easy reference, I reproduce this vignette in its entirety:

> There was an artist in the city of Kouroo who was disposed to strive after perfection. One day it came into his mind to make a staff. Having considered that in an imperfect work time is an ingredient, but into a perfect work time does not enter, he said to himself, It shall be perfect in all respects, though I should do nothing else in my life. He proceeded instantly to the forest for wood, being resolved that it should not be made of unsuitable material; and as he searched for and rejected stick after stick, his friends gradually deserted him, for they grew old in their works and died, but he grew not older by a moment. His singleness of purpose and resolution, and his elevated piety, endowed him, without his knowledge, with perennial youth. As he made no compromise with Time, Time kept out of his way, and only sighed at a distance because he could not overcome him. Before he had found a stock in all respects suitable the city of Kouroo was a hoary

ruin, and he sat on one of its mounds to peel the stick. Before he had given it the proper shape the dynasty of the Candahars was at an end, and with the point of the stick he wrote the name of the last of that race in the sand, and then resumed his work. By the time he had smoothed and polished the staff Kalpa was no longer the pole-star; and ere he had put on the ferrule and the head adorned with precious stones, Brahma had awoke and slumbered many times. But why do I stay to mention these things? When the finishing stroke was put to his work, it suddenly expanded before the eyes of the astonished artist into the fairest of all the creations of Brahma. He had made a new system in making a staff, a world with full and fair proportions; in which, though the old cities and dynasties had passed away, fairer and more glorious ones had taken their places. And now he saw by the heap of shavings at his feet, that, for him and his work, the former lapse of time had been an illusion, and that no more time had elapsed than is required for a single scintillation from the brain of Brahma to fall on and inflame the tinder of a mortal brain. The material was pure, and his art was pure; how could the result be other than wonderful? (326–27)

Those interested in Thoreau's Asian readings have long cited this story as an apparent instance of his at least oblique indebtedness to Hindu sources. To be sure, the designation "Kouroo" is Sanskritic; the allusion to "Brahma" and "kalpa" obviously situates the story in a Hindu context; and the reference to "Candahars" is a South Asian designation. Nevertheless, the story of Kouroo's artist—of the artist's carefully conceived and endlessly persevering efforts to make the perfect staff and the astonishing transformation that results when after many eons it is finally completed—appears nowhere in the Vedic or any other literature, as far as I can discover. More likely, it represents a sort of mélange of Asian sources—Hindu, Confucian, Taoist: Thoreau peoples his imaginative setting with Hindu names and places, conjures up his plot out of related fables of transformation, but fashions his moral to convey a personal artistic vision. Like much of *Walden* generally, it is a meditation on time, self-determination, transcendence, and artistic creation. The artist of Kouroo is, of course, in some sense a representation of Thoreau himself, the artist of *Walden*. Both have undertaken a work of modest means, pursued it with unwavering devotion, and reserved for it only the most lofty ambition. Kouroo is mainly, perhaps, a parable about artistic work, about the importance of devotion, perseverence, and self-sacrifice. At no point does the artist pause to consider the results of his labors or their exorbitant personal costs. The real significance of the artist's work lies in the fact that it was *disinterested*—caring nothing for consequences, for costs, for self. The work is significant for its own sake and the discipline it requires and occasions.

Lyndon Shanley's reconstruction of the evolution of *Walden* indicates that Thoreau composed the story of the artist of Kouroo, along with much of the rest of "Conclusion," during the sixth and final recensions of his manuscript, that is, sometime between 1853 and 1854.[57] During this same period, Thoreau wrote several of his more teacherly letters to his friend Harrison Blake. In one of these, dated December 1853, he digresses at length on the special transformative powers of devotion to work. One section of this letter bears a striking resemblance to the ostensible moral of the Kouroo story; indeed, it provides the best key I know of for its explication: "How admirably the artist is made to accomplish his self-culture by devotion to his art! The wood-sawyer through his effort to do his work well, becomes not merely a better wood-sawyer, but measurably a better *man*. Few are the men that can work on their navels,— only some Brahmins that I have heard of" (Correspondence, 311). The sarcastic repudiation of Brahmanical navel-gazing, seemingly gratuitous in context, represents a kind of authorial subterfuge: this facetious dismissal deflects a level of indebtedness that Thoreau seems unwilling here fully to concede. When the same advice is dressed up in parabolic form in *Walden,* however, its Hindu origin is implicitly acknowledged.

On the face of it, there is nothing particularly noteworthy in the advice Thoreau tenders here to his friend Blake: it sounds Thoreauvian enough, if not typically Yankee. But what is the point of placing this same lesson in the Hindu framework in *Walden?* Actually, Thoreau's use of the identificatory tag "Kouroo" helps tip us off to the story's philo-sophical affiliations. The name Kouroo (or "kuru," as it would be trans-literated today) occurs frequently in the Bhagavad Gita, a text Thoreau knew well, and in the *Mahābhārata,* the great epic of India, of which the Gita is a brief episode. In these works it designates a remote ancestor of the story's heroes and the familial dynasty of which he was thought to be the progenitor. The Gita consists essentially of a dramatic dialogue be-tween Arjuna, the chief warrior of his day, and his charioteer and guru, Krishna, considered by tradition to be an avatar or earthly incarnation of the great god Vishnu. The dialogue of Krishna and Arjuna takes place moments before the onset of a catastrophic fratricidal war between the two sides of India's great dynastic family in the no man's land between the two opposing forces. The field upon which their armies meet to join battle is designated significantly as "the field of the Kurus." Realizing that the impending battle spells certain destruction for his entire family, Arjuna resolves not to fight and appeals to Krishna for counsel. It quickly becomes apparent, however, that Arjuna's painful dilemma serves merely as a pretext for the fuller revelation of Krishna's wisdom. The ensuing teachings constitute the bulk of the Gita's narrative, and over the cen-turies they have attracted a large body of commentary. Yet, like other wisdom literature, the teachings of the Gita have been interpreted in various sectarian, often inconsistent, ways, in part because they seem so broadly eclectic and perhaps contradictory. Some commentators inter-pret Krishna as counseling primarily devotion to God (*bhakti*) as the best path to emancipation, others philosophical discernment (*jñāna*), and still others practical service (*karman*).[58] Thoreau offers his own fairly lengthy commentary on the Gita, both in his journals and in *A Week,* and it is interesting to see where his commentary stands relative to this broader tradition.

In late June of 1846, after he had had some time to digest his reading of Emerson's Gita, Thoreau began to devote many pages of his journal to his transcription of and commentary on Gita verses. Reviewing these against Wilkins's translation, one is at first struck not so much by what he selects for comment as by how much he altogether ignores. Nowhere in these records does Thoreau acknowledge the central devotional or theological messages of the Gita, or the famous theophany of Krishna that for many readers has been seen as the dramatic center of the work. The first verse Thoreau selects for citation in his journals, Bhagavad Gita 3: 7, indicates the general concern and tenor of most of his readings: "The man is praised, who, having subdued all his passions, performeth with his active faculties all the functions of life, unconcerned about the event" (PJ.2.253–54). As the subsequent entries confirm, Thoreau focuses in his readings of the Gita almost exclusively upon those passages concerned with the analysis of right action (*karman*), particularly as they relate to the Gita's influential doctrine of disinterested action or *karma yoga*. These are the verses that he selects for inclusion in "Monday" also: "Let the motive be in the deed and not in the event," the Gita declares. "Be not one whose motive for action is the hope of reward" (Week, 139).[59] In this last verse, a translation of Bhagavad Gita 2: 47, Wilkins translates the Sanskrit *phalam,* or "fruit" (as in the fruit of an action), as "event," but the sense is clear enough in context.

Thus essentialized is the Gita's teaching of disinterested action— action, that is, in which the actor focuses entirely on the work at hand with no consideration for its worldly results or rewards.[60] This is, to be sure, one of the central tenets of the Bhagavad Gita. For Thoreau, however, it was apparently the only one of real significance. Not only was it the focus of his explicit Gita citations and commentaries, it was also the focus of his more oblique Hindu-inspired narratives, the story of the artist of Kouroo above all. Reexamination of this otherwise cryptic story in the light of these apparently related passages from his letters and journals indicates that the story's doctrinal pith, as it were, is Thoreau's personal appropriation of the Indian teachings about disinterested action. The account of Kouroo's artist, then, is not simply a story about the value of discipline and hard work; rather, it represents Thoreau's personal appropriation and understanding of the Gita's teachings about the value of disinterested action as a path *(mārga)* to self-transformation. While the story of the artist of Kouroo may be seen as yet another expression of Thoreau's tendency to construct a kind of personal mythology out of his readings, it rests upon a specific philosophical conviction for which the Gita verses catalogued in "Monday" and the journals supply the necessary context.

Yet the story we encounter in *Walden*'s final pages is obviously less concerned with subtle points of philosophy or religious psychology than with artistic expression. The story may also be interpreted as an allegory of the creation of *Walden* itself, one which showcases Thoreau's own artistic credo. And here we begin to see more of Thoreau's personal appropriation at work. As early as 1842 he had written: "The artist must work with indifferency—too great interest vitiates his work" (PJ.1.391). Another note recorded fresh from a recent immersion in *Manu* similarly prefigures the story he composed ten years later: "A perfectly healthy sentence is extremely rare. Sometimes I read one which was written while the world went round, while grass grew and water ran" (PJ.1.219). And in *A Week,* he provided the clearest adumbration yet of the vignette in *Walden:* "The true poem is not that which the public read. There is always a poem not printed on paper, coincident with the production of this, stereotyped in the poet's life. It is *what he has become through his work.* Not how is the idea expressed in stone, or on canvass or paper, is the question, but how far it has obtained form and expression in the life of the artist" (343). Devotion, discipline, and the pursuit of perfection are certainly some of the central values that Thoreau's parable of Kouroo's artist was intended to highlight, but the real key to the story is the impact of the artist's persevering devotion to his craft on the artist himself. Artistic creation, or so the parable seems to say, is not an end in itself, but a discipline, a religious pursuit, whose value in the end accrues to the artist, not the finished piece for its own sake.

At this point, the Gita's ideal of disinterested action and Thoreau's own ideals of artistic vocation can be seen to converge. This application of the religious ideals of the Gita to artistic pursuits is a defensible elaboration of the Gita's doctrines, but it is somewhat idiosyncratic and surely Thoreauvian and Romantic in its emphasis on yoga as a model for artistic work. The story of the artist of Kouroo represents an image of India molded according to the pressures of Thoreau's own religious and

artistic vision. The Kouroo story is thus less biography than it is autobiography, in a Thoreauvian mode.

Just as from a literary standpoint *Walden* often succeeds where Thoreau's more ungainly first book does not, so the story of the artist of
Kouroo succeeds in a way that the catalogue of Gita verses does not. But
recognition of its link to the Gita draws our attention to the fact that the
story is less fanciful, more philosophically invested, than we normally
take it to be. It also prompts us to take another look at the Gita's doctrine
of disinterested action in relation to Thoreau's work and to consider
what, after all, it meant for him. A closer look at these verses and the
story they later inspired indicates that they all turn on a single paradox—
the Gita's apparently esoteric identification of action and nonaction.
Several of the Gita's most notorious instances of this paradox Thoreau
includes in his catalogue in "Monday": "He who may behold, as it were,
inaction in action, and action in inaction, is wise amongst mankind. He
is a perfect performer of all duty"; and, "Wise men call him a Pandeet,
whose every undertaking is free from the idea of desire, and whose
actions are consumed by the fire of wisdom. He abandoneth the desire of
a reward of his actions; he is always contented and independent; and
although he may be engaged in a work, he, as it were, doeth nothing"
(Week, 139).

Kouroo's artist labors through countless eons of time only to find in
the moment of his awakening that all was a necessary illusion. Like the
wise pandit, he also acts, as he later comes to find, without really having
acted. Paradoxes like this were part of Thoreau's literary stock in trade. In
Walden and elsewhere, he periodically resorts to puns, reversals, and
paradoxes—literary shock tactics, as it were—in his efforts to wake his
readers up to the deeper meanings of their own lives. Related antinomies—as between progress and rest, heroism and renunciation, sound
and silence—run throughout his writings. But why he should lean so
heavily upon this particular paradox between action and inaction at such
a strategic point in *Walden* seems puzzling until we recognize how deeply
founded it was in Thoreau's own life experience. It is but one more
manifestation of the curiously bifurcated vision or double conscious-

ness—as between understanding and reason, time and eternity, appearance and reality—that we have already seen dramatized in the chapter on "Solitude" and elsewhere in his work.[61]

"In My Brain Is the Sanscrit"

Such introductions of selected elements from the Hindu texts begin to reveal to us the nature of Thoreau's Oriental appropriations. When, in the epiphany of the night drummer from "Monday" considered previously, he remarks that "a strain of music reminds me of a passage of the Vedas," it is clear that the reference to the Vedas comes into play only by a process of association. Thoreau associates "Vedas" with "a strain of music," first of all, and also somehow with the strange experience called up by the distant drum. The ecstasy comes first, then its successive elaborations. It is true that in the journals, the Asian materials are sometimes the object of sustained and primary attention, but even there, in the careful transcription of passages from the Eastern texts, it is clear that they are marshalled in the service of some ulterior personal quest.

Thoreau's approach then to his reading of Asian texts, as for his reading in general, might best be described as a kind of intellectual bricolage. This is not to suggest that he was naive or uncritical. Despite the limited range and value of his sources, he had as good a grasp of these materials as any American of his generation. An attentive reader, he was perfectly conscious of when he was yanking ideas out of context and refitting them for new uses. To questions of whether in this creative reconstruction he was really getting it right, he would have responded that all historical interpretation necessarily involved some element of personal construction, and appropriately so, since in the final analysis, the subject of history and the purpose of its study are nothing other than a revelation of the self: "Critical acumen," he wrote, "is exerted in vain to uncover the past; the *past* cannot be *presented;* we cannot know what we are not. But one veil hangs over past, present, and future, and it is the province of the historian to find out, not what was, but what is" (Week, 155).[62]

Nothing better illustrates the distinctive character of Thoreau's mature thinking about India than the Orientalist set piece with which he concludes his chapter "The Pond in Winter" in *Walden*. At its climax is the magniloquent eulogy noted before of the Bhagavad Gita, but it begins with an extended and detailed account of Walden's seasonal participation in the American ice-cutting industry. During the winter of 1846–47, his second in residence at the Pond, Thoreau observed carefully as a company of some one hundred Irishmen and their Yankee overseers came to Walden for the purpose of harvesting its ice. Cut into large blocks, hauled onto shore, and eventually loaded onto waiting wagons, the ice was then conveyed by train to the Charlestown docks, from whence it was shipped to the tropics.[63] Having described the business of cutting ice in some detail, Thoreau then appends the following whimsical but revealing final paragraph:

> Thus it appears that the sweltering inhabitants of Charleston and New Orleans, of Madras and Bombay and Calcutta, drink at my well. In the morning I bathe my intellect in the stupendous and cosmogonal philosophy of the Bhagvat Geeta, since whose composition years of the gods have elapsed, and in comparison with which our modern world and its literature seem puny and trivial; and I doubt if that philosophy is not to be referred to a previous state of existence, so remote is its sublimity from our conceptions. I lay down the book and go to my well for water, and lo! there I meet the servant of the Brahmin, priest of Brahma and Vishnu and Indra, who still sits in his temple on the Ganges reading the Vedas, or dwells at the root of a tree with his crust and water jug. I meet his servant come to draw water for his master, and our buckets as it were grate together in the same well. The pure Walden water is mingled with the sacred water of the Ganges. With favoring winds it is wafted past the site of the fabulous islands of Atlantis and the Hesperides, makes the periplus of Hanno, and, floating by Ternate and Tidore and the mouth of the Persian Gulf, melts in the tropic gales of the Indian seas, and is landed in ports of which Alexander only heard the names. (297–98)

Thoreau's contextualization of this passage indicates that he is fully cognizant of the commercial system that in some sense both underwrote and enabled his reading of the Bhagavad Gita. The East Indian consumption of Walden ice was not intended for Indians themselves, a fact convenient enough to ignore from far-off Concord. Moreover, as the ice trade taking place under his very nose makes clear, Americans also profited from the British colonial presence in India. By situating his own reading of the Bhagavad Gita in the Concord-to-India ice trade in this way, Thoreau calls attention to the economic exigencies underlying Orientalist discourse, but any conclusions he might draw here about the ostensible complicity between knowledge and power he blithely abandons in the interests of illustrating another, for him, more important set of lessons. In his juxtaposition of the well of Walden with the well of the Gita, in which he bathes his intellect, Thoreau insists that the traffic between India and Concord is circular and reciprocal, not one-way or univocal. It is not so much, or necessarily, reciprocal at the level of material commodities, but it is and must be emphatically reciprocal at the level of knowledge and experience. Thoreau and the Brahmin's servant draw from the same transcendental well, and as they do so, distinctions of time and place evaporate.

The formulation from *A Week* noted above—"we cannot know what we are not"—is thus key to understanding Thoreau's epistemology and his philosophy of history. It also has obvious bearing on his spiritual life and his appropriation of Asian literature. If his appropriation seems unduly self-reflexive or opportunistic, this is because, in his view, it could be no other way. What we see or understand from our reading depends on who we are. Debunkers of the significance of Thoreau's reading of Asian texts, or those who are inclined to depreciate its influence, have been quick to cite the following fragment from the journals of 1851 in their support: "Like some other preachers—I have added my texts—(derived) from the Chineses & Hindoo scriptures—long after my discourse was written" (PJ.3.216). Such debunkers tend to construe this as an admission that these readings were really in some sense simply derivative or a mere embellishment. In context, however, this fragment is not exactly the disclaimer it is sometimes taken to be. At one level Thoreau is saying something about the compositional order, an editorial comment actually, of two particular "discourses," namely *Walden* and *A Week*.[64] On another level, he appears to be waxing philosophical and saying something in the same spirit as the comments on history cited above. Given his views on knowledge, he could hardly do other than insist on the priority of his own "discourse," whether chronologically or, better, existentially. In any case, this fragment is certainly not to be construed as a repudiation of the importance to him of these scriptures. This is especially clear when we see that it is sandwiched within a profuse and enthusiastic set of citations and commentary from the *Harivaṃśa* and *Sāṃkhya-kārikā*. If these texts were in reality so expendable, we would be hard put to explain their domination of this entry and of so much of the writing generally. Thoreau had reservations about this literature and was formally disinclined to indicate a dependence upon it, but he invoked it repeatedly and with abandon. Even after the long and surprisingly equivocal exploration of the Asian texts in the "Monday" section described above, he concludes on a note ringing with promise and admiration: "*Ex oriente lux* may still be the motto of scholars, for the Western world has not yet derived from the East all the light which it is destined to receive thence" (Week, 143). If the author of these lines had so many reservations or qualifications, why then was he at the same time so devoted to it?

The answer to this question, I believe, and an explanation of Thoreau's intractable ambivalence in regard to the question of influence, has to do with his fascination with what he was able to glean from these texts about Eastern contemplative practices and specifically yoga, as Christy sensed. From the time of his earliest references to India in particular, it is clear that Thoreau subscribed to the Orientalist notion of the East as the "land of contemplation" (PJ.1.386). Already this particular cultural evaluation was coming to be governed by a Kiplingesque opposition—India was the land of contemplation and mysticism, Europe was the land of reason and activity. India, thought Thoreau, would provide a much needed corrective and balance to Palestine.[65] In an imaginative, though somewhat idiosyncratic, elaboration of the Orientalist polarities of East and West, Thoreau envisaged a progressive movement from East to West, as characteristic of human life as of the life of nations.[66] In contrast to the evolutionists of a later period, however, his assessment of this trajectory was not necessarily sanguine. This was, again imaginatively, simply the curve of human destiny; it followed the arc of the sun from sunrise to sunset, and never more clearly so than for those Americans dwelling in the westernmost outposts of human civilization. Yet much might be lost in this "progress," and we have seen how caustic Thoreau was apt to be in his treatment of some of the West's most touted advances. Particularly victimized by this movement from East to West were the contemplative values still treasured in the East. As I noted in the previous chapter, Thoreau was quite drawn to the idea, if not the practice, of contemplation. In one respect, at least, the Hindu tradition towers above all others, and this is in its treatment of contemplation: "Western philosophers have not conceived of the significance of Contemplation in their sense" (Week, 137).

Such references to Eastern contemplative and ascetic practices suggest that Thoreau's admiration for them was completely genuine. Yet despite this admiration, he never entirely abandoned his reservations about Eastern cultures generally nor compromised his autonomy as a Westerner and American. As far as he was concerned, the sun still traveled from east to west, and so did he. Actually, this astronomical metaphor helped him to sanction his own ambivalence by conceiving his East-West arc as a circle. "There is an orientalism in the most restless pioneer," he thought, "and the farthest west is but the farthest east" (Week, 150). Formulations such as this suggest the extent to which Thoreau was inclined at this point in his life to supplement his horizontal with a verticle imaginative axis when it came to thinking about what "the East" meant to him. The "India" of his imagination turned out to be neither a place nor a time, but a state of consciousness. He conceived of India, and all epochs of human history, as if it could be recovered by traversing the levels of his own mind: "Farthest India is nearer to me than Concord & Lexington" (PJ.1.494). Experiences of Orient and Occident were all encompassed, he noted, "in one revolution of my body" (PJ.1.172). This propensity to see the whole of human history epitomized in the experience of each individual naturally grew out of Transcendentalist thought, yet in this instance Thoreau's appropriation seems a little defensive, even edgy. In wanting to appropriate the contemplative knowledge and experience of the Eastern seers, he at the same time refuses to concede to them any ultimate authority in this area: "In the New England noon tide I have discovered more materials of oriental history than the Sanscrit contains or Sir W. Jones has unlocked. I see why it is necessary there should be such history at all.—Was not Asia mapped in my brain before it was in any geography? In my brain is the sanscrit which contains the history of primitive times. The Vedas and Angas are not so ancient as my serenest contemplations" (PJ.1.387).

However one construes this somewhat strained sense of spiritual dominion, whether as a function of philosophy or Yankee independence, Thoreau seems unwilling to retreat from his claim. Contemplation is as much his field of expertise as it is the Brahmin's, or should be. He cannot deny or ignore the Hindu representations because his own life confirms them. By the same token, the fact that he participates in contemplation in some sense already precludes the transfer of complete authority to the Hindu texts. What then was the exact role of the Asian literature in Thoreau's spiritual life? If, as it appears, Thoreau heard some echoes of his own early ecstasies in the Eastern texts, then it seems that their main value was a confirmation, elaboration, and principal expression of his own experiences. Technically, Thoreau may well have "added" these texts long after his discourse was written, but they were the only texts he could have added, since apparently they were the only ones conversant with what he was writing about.

On May 6, 1851, Thoreau entered a long summary into his journal of the method, psychology, and metaphysics of the classical system of yoga, as it had been described for him in the *Harivaṃśa,* including an analysis of "Poroucha" (*puruṣa*), the transpersonal Self of the Sāṃkhya-yoga system of philosophy, and how at the moment of liberation, the self came to recognize itself as totally separate from the mind, senses, and body. Concluding this discussion, he remarks, "They are not ordinary practices which can bring light into the soul" (PJ.3.216). July 16, two months later, was the date on which Thoreau recorded the long elegy to the ecstasies of his boyhood with which I began this study. Suggestively, it concludes its reminiscences of the bliss of childhood with the same formulation: "With all your science can you tell how it is—& whence it is, that light comes into the soul?" (PJ.3.306). While science apparently could not answer this question to anyone's satisfaction, perhaps the Hindu tradition could.

Six

To Speak
Somewhere Without Bounds

I ts calculated obscurity notwithstanding, the story of the artist of
Kouroo provides us with some important clues for understanding
Walden as a whole. Reading the Kouroo story as a parable of spiritual
awakening helps us first of all to clarify the nature of Thoreau's curious
mode of self-representation in this his masterwork. Newcomers to *Walden* often find it tempting to read this famous book as the "simple and
sincere account of his own life," which the author himself appears to
recommend in his opening paragraphs. It takes some further reading and
study to realize that such an implied autobiographical claim cannot be
taken completely at face value. For all its reliance upon Thoreau's actual
experience at the Pond, *Walden* is after all a highly crafted narrative, one
painstakingly revised and polished over the nine-year period from 1845
till 1854, and clearly responsive to other tribunals than the simple empirical fact.[1] As teachers of *Walden* are often compelled to point out, the
character of the book's first-person narrator is, in part at least, a construct
of the author's imagination and ulterior rhetorical designs. Thoreau depicts the persona of *Walden* as a sort of representative Yankee—wily,
resourceful, at times self-effacing—who affirms our better selves even as
he punctures our illusions and ridicules our pretensions and hypocrisy.[2]

So also for the narrative as a whole. Despite its various fastidious
compilations of facts, figures, and measurements, *Walden* is not so much
a straightforward autobiography—a simple narrative of Thoreau's outer

life at the Pond—as it is an account of his inward and imaginative explorations, a fact even his most discerning readers sometimes lose sight of. The ostentatious display of fidelity to the facts of house and garden that we find for example in the "Economy" chapter serves in the final analysis mainly to guarantee the truth of the author's inner experience. This is the real burden of the story. Thus while Thoreau seems fully inclined to exercise his poetic license in reshaping the outer facts and form of his narrative—as in his decision (freely acknowledged) to condense the actual experience of two years and two months into the seasonal cycle of one year—he refuses to compromise the essential truths of his experience. This is presumably the lesson of the Kouroo vignette. There is, it seems to insist, a deep and unavoidable relationship between the artist and his creation. To this extent, *Walden* too may be construed as a telling account of Thoreau's life; indeed, if we take the moral of the Kouroo story to heart, it *must* be so construed. Thoreau's insistence on the vital link between his life and his literary creations was a cornerstone of his mature artistic vocation, and qualified in this way, it points the way to a productively autobiographical reading.

As *Walden*'s quintessential illustration of the ideal relationship between art and lived experience, the Kouroo story thus serves to crystallize Thoreau's personal artistic vision. It also provides broad sanction for the kind of biographical approach taken in this study to Thoreau's published writing as a whole. "It is not in man to determine what his style shall be," he wrote in his glowing assessment of the literary style of Carlyle. "He might as well determine what his thoughts shall be."[3] Art, he liked to think, grew as naturally from a person's character as an acorn from an oak tree. Such claims are familiar in Romantic theory, of course, and this conviction is part of what critics mean when they discuss this dimension of Thoreau's artistic philosophy under the rubric of literary organicism. It is true that the aptness of comparisons between natural processes and human creativity, especially in a case as apposite as that of Thoreau, sometimes leads us to forget that it rests ultimately on a metaphor. Writers do not of course really behave like oak trees or pine forests, however consoling it might be to think so, and such analogies usually end up just where they begin. In practice, at least in the case of Thoreau, organicism serves as a metaphor to characterize the intimate relationship that may and ought to pertain between an author's spiritual, psychological, and aesthetic experience and his or her literary expression. In this qualified sense, it is certainly easy to see that Thoreau pursued the implications of the organic analogy farther and more rigorously than most writers of his day. Conceiving organicism primarily as a metaphor for the relationship between art and artist is important because it invites us to go beyond the usual slogans and declarations of advocacy to which criticism of Thoreau's "organicism" is sometimes limited. His theoretical interest in organicism is well known, of course, as are some of its most obvious literary dividends, but the repercussions of his commitment to organic self-expression extend well beyond merely formal considerations and literary allegiances. In *Walden*, style answers to authorial consciousness to a surprisingly consistent and revealing extent, in spite of the book's various and complex rhetorical motives. Patterns of self-reflection and ecstatic experience I discussed previously in relation to Thoreau's earlier writing surface repeatedly here at the level of literary style and rhetorical practice. To pursue these correspondences with all the attention sanctioned by Thoreau's own avowed commitments leads to a fuller reading of his ecstatic witness and a richer appreciation of its most famous literary result.

Duly impressed with Thoreau's painstaking study of natural forms and its apparent impact on *Walden*'s "organic style" and structure, F. O. Matthiessen was the first modern critic to give extended consideration to this dimension of his literary theory and practice. The slow and cumulative growth of the *Walden* manuscript, he suggested, appeared to reflect the natural processes Thoreau observed all around him.[4] Like the nineteenth-century sculptor Horatio Greenough, who championed a sort of artistic functionalism, Thoreau committed himself to the idea that form should follow function, not the reverse, thus rejecting older neoclassical conventions that subordinated artistic inspiration to the predeterminations of form. "Let the ornaments take care of themselves," he argued in his own ruminations on architectural style in the "Economy" section of *Walden:* "What of architectural beauty I now see, I know has gradually grown from within outward, out of the necessities and character of the indweller, who is the only builder,—out of some unconscious truthfulness, and nobleness, without ever a thought for the appearance; and whatever additional beauty of this kind is destined to be produced will be preceded by a like unconscious beauty of life" (47). The full implications of this artistic credo only become apparent when we recognize that this section on house building in *Walden* stages an elaborate homology in which the building of a house comes to represent the development of the self and even the creation of the cosmos.[5] As is so common in Thoreau's work, the implied relation between microcosm and macrocosm rests however on a somewhat surreptitious pun on "indweller," a common nineteenth-century rendering of the Sanskrit terms *śarīrin* or *antaryāmin* roughly equivalent to our term "soul."[6] The "house" thus constitutes a natural outgrowth of its inhabitant in the same way the body expresses the soul and the material creation unfolds from absolute being. Indeed, the relation of house to indweller is so intimate, one may as well read the house as a virtual representation of the "indweller." As far as *Walden* is concerned, then, Thoreau's professed organicism must be understood to include an interior spiritual dimension as well. It is not enough to say that form follows function, since in an inspired text, form naturally and spontaneously reflects the consciousness of its author, a belief that has important implications for our reading of *Walden* in particular.

The Art of Writing

Despite the Romantic appeal that literary organicism held for Thoreau, the practical question of how one moved from organic theory to expository practice could nowhere be answered by the theory alone. It was one thing to invoke analogies between the wilds of nature and the written word, and quite another to fashion the words, sentences, and paragraphs that would produce the impact upon his readers that he desired. No simple formulas existed for the execution of such organic ideals in specific expository formations. But he did receive some helpful guidance during his four years at Harvard from his writing teacher, Edward Tyrrel Channing, the college's Boylston Professor of Rhetoric and Oratory from 1819 to 1851.[7] An accomplished scholar and exacting teacher, Channing served as an influential tutor not only to Emerson and Thoreau but a host of other preeminent scholars and writers as well. Before Channing's arrival on the Harvard faculty, the teaching of rhetoric there had been dominated by the neoclassical rhetorical precepts inculcated in Hugh Blair's text *Lectures in Rhetoric and Belles Lettres* (1783). John Quincy Adams, Channing's predecessor in the Boylston chair, leaned heavily on Blair and contributed his own manual, *Lectures on Rhetoric and Oratory* (1810), which was also steeped in neoclassical precepts. A popular teaching text of the period, Blair's *Lectures* upheld the Ciceronian elevation of matters of style and emphasized the elaboration of stylistic ornament for its own sake. During Channing's early years at Harvard, however, new rhetorical models and values were beginning to challenge and in some institutions would soon supplant the older neoclassical strictures. In 1832, two years before Thoreau's arrival in Cambridge, Channing responded to these changing values by dropping from his curriculum Blair's text and substituting Richard Whately's more up-to-date *Elements of Rhetoric* (1828). Having absorbed many of the values expounded in George Campbell's *Philosophy of Rhetoric* (1776), Whately rejected many of the older rigidly neoclassical conventions and expounded in their place a rhetoric emphasizing literary arrangement, "perspicuity" of style, and audience psychology.[8] Whately, a onetime colleague of John Henry Newman at Oxford and later Anglican archbishop of Dublin, designed his text in considerable part as a resource for Christian apologists in their debates with perceived enemies of the faith. Whately's concern with polemic and related rhetorical strategies would turn out to have significant applications for Thoreau's writing.

While implementing the teachings of Whately and Campbell on argument and style, Channing added some emphases of his own. In responding to his students' biweekly themes, he particularly stressed naturalness and vividness in word choice, rejected stylistic superfluity, and discouraged as artificial the use of the inflatable periodic sentence once popular in public orations. Channing was also concerned to dispense with distinctions between oratory and written discourse by promoting the application of rhetorical conventions and analysis to all forms of literary argumentation. Literary texts, he taught, should be governed by the same canons of rhetorical effectiveness once considered the province only of oratory.[9] In doing so, Channing was reflecting the natural intermingling of written discourse and oratory common in nineteenth-century American literary culture.

When the young Thoreau matriculated at Harvard in the fall of 1834, this then was the system of rhetoric he encountered. Channing served as Thoreau's main writing preceptor during all four of his years in Cambridge, relying upon the texts of Campbell and Whately all the while. And though Thoreau had little good to say about his Harvard experience later on, he did receive some valuable early lessons about effective writing from Channing. Although the distinctively gnarled and gritty style of his mature writings is a far cry from the decorous style approved in the Harvard classroom, his expository practice appears to owe a significant debt to his mentor's strictures about diction and style, and his remarks about composition echo at several points the teachings he received in the Harvard classroom. His dependence, for example, on analogy, the identification of inconsistencies, and forms of indirect persuasion in *Walden* finds clear authorization in Whately's text. So too does his practice of favoring terse aphoristic sentences, rhetorical questions, and complex cumulative sentences in the composition of his characteristically long paragraphs. Throughout his life, Thoreau periodically commented on the art of composition in his journals and letters.[10] Consistently he praised the compact, well-hewn sentence characteristic of aphorisms and proverbs, and eschewed the overextended and prosaic sentence structure characteristic of some contemporary writers. "Their sentences are not concentrated and nutty," he observed in 1851, "Sentences which suggest far more than they say, which have an atmosphere about them—which do not merely report an old but make a new impression—Sentences which suggest as many things and are as durable as a Roman Acqueduct To frame these that is the *art* of writing. Sentences which are expensive towards which so many volumes—so much life went—which lie like boulders on the page—up & down or across. Not mere repetition but creation. Which a man might sell his grounds & castle to build" (PJ.4.8).

Thoreau's preference for lively words, words drawn from colloquial speech and nature, and his rejection of abstract, florid, or unduly Latinate diction was also consistent with Channing's teachings and the new rhetoric of Whately and Campbell. Moreover, all of these literary values accorded well with the rising tide of Romantic theory and practice to which he was exposed through such literary models as Goethe, Carlyle, and Emerson. Above all, Thoreau followed his teachers in cultivating a forceful, lively, and natural prose style. Effective prose must be polished but it should also stay close to the springs of action and thought. It must retain an organic connection to the experience and consciousness of its author. "Who cares what a man's style is," he exclaims in his essay on Carlyle, "so it is intelligible—as intelligible as his thought. Literally and really, the style is no more than the *stylus,* the pen he writes with—and it is not worth scraping and polishing, and gilding, unless it will write his thoughts the better for it. It is something for use, and not to look at" (EEM, 232). Notwithstanding his careful application as a literary craftsman, Thoreau's commitment to spontaneity remained for him a kind of literary article of faith, evident in his remarks about effective writing early and late. "We should not endeavor cooly to analyze our thoughts," he wrote, hardly a year out of college, "but keeping the pen even and parallel with the current, make an accurate transcript of them—Impulse is after all the best linguist" (PJ.1.35).

A Word Wiser than Any Man

The most graphic expression of Thoreau's investment in literary organicism, however, was his well-attested preoccupation with language, etymology, and historical linguistics. As his friend and sometime walking companion Ellery Channing once remarked, there is a rather marked "philological side" to much of Thoreau's reading and writing.[11] A competent classicist when he arrived at Harvard, Thoreau achieved considerable proficiency in Greek and Latin by the time he graduated in 1837, and was conversant with several other European languages as well, including French, German, Italian, and Spanish. Later in life, inspired by his travels among the Penobscot Indians of Maine's north woods, he added the study of various Algonquin tongues. Among the books in his study could be counted some seventeen dictionaries. The mid-nineteenth century was a time of heightened philological interest in America, and Thoreau followed these developments carefully. Like other writers of his generation, he was particularly fascinated with the developing science of language, in particular the linguistic study of individual words, their etymological roots, and relations to one another. Actually, Thoreau's interest in rifling words for their concealed etymological values appears to have owed something to the rhetorical training he received at the hands of Channing, who had emphasized the importance of such knowledge for persuasive written expression. An effective writer, Channing insisted, must habituate himself to the "analysis of terms, and follow them down their history from their primitive use through the changes they have experienced and the various purposes to which they have been applied."[12] Thoreau not only heeded Channing's advice, he capitalized on it in unprecedented ways; indeed, it became a fundamental tenet of the literary program he pursued throughout his life. Perhaps the most graphic expression of Thoreau's interest in etymology and the organic metaphor occurs in his essay "Walking": "Where is the literature which gives expression to Nature? He would be a poet who could impress the winds and streams into his service, to speak for him; who nailed words to their primitive senses, as farmers drive down stakes in the spring, which the frost has heaved; who derived his words as often as he used them,— transplanted them to his page with earth adhering to their roots; whose words were so true and fresh and natural that they would appear to expand like the buds at the approach of spring, though they lay half-smothered between two musty leaves in a library,—ay, to bloom and bear fruit there, after their kind, annually, for the faithful reader, in sympathy with surrounding Nature" (Writings.5.232). It is tempting to construe the language of this passage as essentially metaphorical, but conceived in relation to Thoreau's own work, it clearly is not. The activity to which he alludes—of reconnecting words to their primitive senses—accurately represents a significant part of the actual literary practice that gave rise to *Walden* and other writings.

Yet Thoreau was also interested in the science of language for its own sake—for the philosophical and theological insights to which it could give rise—and not simply as an aid to strong prose. The results of recent Western philological study had featured centrally in some of the key philosophical works of the Enlightenment period, works Thoreau had encountered in college and in later years. John Locke, whose philosophical perspectives still exerted enormous sway in the Unitarian culture of Harvard College, devoted a substantial section of his *Essay Concerning Human Understanding* (1690) to the nature of words and verbal meaning. David Hume built upon Locke's linguistic analyses, though to diametrically opposed ends, in his elaboration of an epistemological skepticism. The philosophers of the Scottish or so-called Common Sense school, Thomas Reid, Dugald Stewart, and George Campbell, also sought to rework Locke's ideas but in ways more in keeping with Locke's own stated objectives. Reid, whose volume *Essays on the Intellectual Powers of Man* (1785) remained a staple of Harvard's philosophy curriculum throughout the early nineteenth century, predicated much of his epistemological discussion on an analysis of the explication of words that was in part indebted to Locke, as did Dugald Stewart in his equally influential three-volume work *Elements of the Philosophy of the Human Mind* (1792–1827).[13]

The philosophical contributions of French Enlightenment thinkers also frequently focused squarely on the topic of language. Here too Locke often provided the point of departure, but unlike their British and Scottish colleagues, several of these French thinkers developed some of the recent work in historical and comparative philology in much more radical and, to Thoreau and other Romantics, beguiling directions. Throughout the latter part of the eighteenth century, interest in the origin of language and the relationship between contemporary languages had been gathering steam. The dawning recognition that most European languages ultimately derived from a common source led some of the philosophes and their Romantic successors and contemporaries to speculate often about the origins of all language. By the last two decades of the eighteenth century, the search for a common Indo-European language became a significant feature of the *Weltanschauung* of the Romantic period, and several of these French intellectuals contributed importantly to its conceptualization. Charles de Brosses, whose theories had been summarized in Hugh Blair's *Lectures on Rhetoric and Belles Lettres,* elaborated an organic theory of language that posited an aboriginal phonetic relationship between words and the things to which they referred. De Brosses believed that all modern languages stemmed from a common primitive language whose words had been formed organically in accordance with the structure of the human vocal organs and the form of the sensory objects to which the words were conceived to refer. Study of etymological roots and relationships, he asserted, could reveal the isomorphic relationship that naturally existed between words and things. De Brosses's linguistic speculations found significant support in the work of his colleague Antoine Court de Gebelin, who also found in etymology the key to understanding the origins of and relationships between contemporary European cultures.

The work of French Enlightenment thinkers was not as accessible in New England as the work of their British colleagues, but Thoreau did manage to consult some of it during his years of study at Harvard. Records from his senior year suggest that he consulted Court de Gebelin's etymological dictionary for some parodic etymologizing of his own.[14] And while Blair's text had been superseded in the Harvard curriculum by Whately and Campbell, it was still well known in New England schools and colleges, and Thoreau later kept a copy of a recent edition in his study.[15] In the last two decades of the eighteenth century, the discovery of Sanskrit gave greater impetus to historical linguistics and helped to usher in a new wave of interest in language study, coincident with the Romantic movement.[16] In the early nineteenth century, American writers and thinkers too became absorbed in the study of language and heavily invested in its implications.[17]

If anything, after his graduation from college in 1837, Thoreau's interest in language theory began to intensify. "A Word is wiser than any man," he wrote in the summer of 1840, "—than any series of words. In its present received sense it may be false, but in its inner sense by descent and analogy it approves itself. Language is the most perfect work of art in the world. The chisel of a thousand years retouches it" (PJ.1.160). Also crucial to his maturer conceptualization of the intrinsic power of words was apparently the pioneering work of Hungarian-born pedagogue and theorist Charles Kraitsir, who, like de Brosses and other earlier Romantic thinkers, advanced a theory of natural language based on what he perceived to be universal organic laws of language formation. Kraitsir, whose theories were championed by Thoreau's fellow Transcendentalist, Elizabeth Peabody, arrived in Boston in 1844, where he began expounding on his innovative ideas about foreign language instruction in a series of lectures, the substance of which he later published in book form.[18] Thoreau consulted Kraitsir's writings and, while revising the manuscript of *Walden* several years later, also examined the theories of Richard Trench, whose recent work *On the Study of Words* (1851) spoke directly to Thoreau's etymological interests. During the same period, he also consulted a work by the Swedenborgian thinker J. J. G. Wilkinson: "Wilkinson's book to some extent realizes what I have dreamed of a reeturn to the primitive analogical & derivative senses of words—His ability to trace analogies often leads him to a truer word than more remarkable writers have found.—As when in his chapter on the human skin he describes the papillary cutis as 'an encampment of small conical tents coextensive with the surface of the body'—The faith he puts in old & current expressions as having sprung from an instinct wiser than science—& safely to be trusted if they can be interpreted" (PJ.4.46).[19] Further animating Thoreau's philological speculations throughout the period of the composition of *Walden* were his conversations with the Penobscot Indian guide Joe Polis during his several trips to Maine's north woods.[20]

Though conversant with the Swedenborgian and correspondential language theories espoused by Sampson Reed, Guillaume Oegger, and Emerson in his early writings, Thoreau soon came to pursue a more idiosyncratic and radical line of inquiry under the influence of writers such as de Brosses, Court de Gebelin, Wilkinson, Kraitsir, and Trench and through his own study of Native American words. In the view that he came to elaborate, language was neither arbitrary in its connection between signifier and signified, as Locke and the Scottish philosophers had insisted, nor symbolically correspondential in the sense depicted in Emerson's *Nature*. Rather, as Michael West and Philip Gura have demonstrated, Thoreau came to believe that in their origins, the sounds of which words were composed stemmed organically from the natural objects to which they referred. Surely the most dramatic, if somewhat macabre, expression of this sustained preoccupation with the organic basis of language is Thoreau's curious treatment in the "Spring" chapter of *Walden* of the relationship between words and the foliage-like designs etched by a spring thaw into a railroad embankment abutting Walden Pond (304–09). What begins as a straightforward set of natural observations soon turns into a kind of cosmological meditation on the mechanics of creation itself. In gazing at the vaguely reminiscent patterns on the sand, *Walden's* narrator unexpectedly finds himself transported "nearer the vitals of the globe," as if in the presence of the "Artist" of the world, who in publishing his creations abroad employs a system of natural shapes and sounds on which the author of *Walden* himself also depends in his more limited inscriptions. Like other philologists of his day, Thoreau believed in the existence of an original ur-language, only in his view this was not a human language but the language of nature itself: "In all the dissertations—on language—men forget the language that is— that is really universal—the inexpressible meaning that is in all things & every where with which the morning & evening teem. As if language were especially of the tongue. Of course with a more copious hearing or understanding—of what is published the present *languages* will be forgotten" (PJ.2.178). Such speculations about natural language were often the site of creative interference with his readings of Asian texts, as I noted earlier. When in his excursions Thoreau encountered forms in nature that struck him as the expressions of a kind of archaic primeval tongue, as he did in his reflections on the embankment in thaw, he characteristically imagined them as expressions of a natural hieroglyphic or as Chinese or Sanskrit characters: "The cracks in the ice showing a white cleavage—what is their law? somewhat like foliage but too rectangular—like the characters of some oriental language. I feel as if I could get grammar & dictionary and go into it" (PJ.4.238–39).

Thoreau's speculations on natural language demonstrate how thoroughly he believed the principle of organicism could characterize the relationship between language and nature, but he was just as deeply convinced that it should and must govern the relationship between the artist and his or her creation. What the ancient tongues and the representations in the ice or the thawing embankment held in common of course was that to most of us both remain mysterious and hard to read. But nature demanded more of her readers than merely the study of old roots. With prolonged application, Celtic and Sanskrit would one day yield up their secrets. To read and understand the language of nature it was not enough to ransack old dictionaries or chase down far-flung etymologies. For this, there was also what we might call a spiritual prerequisite: "He is richest who has most use for nature as raw material of tropes and symbols with which to describe his life. If these gates of golden willows affect me, they correspond to the beauty and promise of some experience on which I am entering. If I am overflowing with life, am rich in experience for which I lack expression, then nature will be my language full of poetry,— all nature will *fable,* and every natural phenomenon be a myth. The man of science, who is not seeking for expression but for a fact to be expressed merely, studies nature as a dead language. I pray for such inward experience as will make nature significant" (J.5.135).

Scientific knowledge was necessary but not sufficient for this kind of deeper apprehension of nature, as Thoreau had discovered in his own daily excursions. To read nature fully, it was also essential to approach nature's forms and phenomena in an appropriately clarified and reverential spirit. Nature spoke only to those who were awakened to the media and modes of her self-disclosures. As I discussed previously, Thoreau believed that active cultivation of the senses was a requirement for this most esoteric branch of language study. This was the practical implication, after all, of his frequent meditations on the music of the spheres. Ancient harmonies there may be, but they sound themselves only in the ears of the disciplined auditor. "The morning wind forever blows," he writes in *Walden,* "the poem of creation is uninterrupted; but few are the ears that hear it. Olympus is but the outside of the earth every where" (85). Above all, the contemplative of nature must be alive to the omnipresent silence underlying all of nature's forms and phenomena, since in contrast to human languages, for all but the most subtle of ears, nature's speech was typically unvoiced, even unsounded. Here also Asian conceptions of language—the eloquent silence of Confucius or the transcendental hymns of the Vedas—proved instructive. Silence for Thoreau was the source of speech, of thought, of time and creation, in much the same way as it was depicted in these traditions. Silence was also, he thought, the medium of contemplation—"the communing of a conscious soul with itself" (PJ.1.60). As for the philosophers of the East, such contemplative stillness provided the basis of self-reflection and the arena for an intelligible study of nature. It was only in such a spirit of quiet recollection, attentive receptivity, and silence in action that a meaningful study of nature could take place.

The practical outcome of Thoreau's speculations about language, both the contemplative and philological sort, was to consolidate his ambition to serve as a faithful transcriber of nature, at a perhaps unprecedented level of precision. His earliest model for this was Goethe, whose genius for giving "an exact description of objects" especially impressed him. In one of his earliest journal entries, he praises Goethe for the fidelity of his descriptions: "He is generally satisfied with giving an exact description of objects as they appear to him, and his genius is exhibited in the points he seizes upon and illustrates. His description of Venice and her environs as seen from the Marcusthurm, is that of an unconcerned spectator, whose object is faithfully to describe what he sees, and that too, for the most part, in the order in which he saw it. It is this trait which is chiefly to be prized in the book—even the reflections of the author do not interfere with his descriptions" (PJ.1.16).[21] Thoreau's characterization of Goethe's relationship to his subject as one of an "unconcerned spectator" suggestively prefigures *Walden*'s dramatization of the ecstatic witness and theater of the world topos in the passage from "Solitude" considered in the last chapter. There Thoreau builds into his notion of spectator elements drawn from his readings of Indian philosophy. In this early reference, the term is obviously concerned more narrowly with literary activity, yet its relevance to the later, more esoteric usage is striking nevertheless. Goethe's model suggests that to achieve full command of his or her materials the artist, like the religious philosopher, must take up the detached position of contemplative witness and onlooker.

This advocacy of fact over fiction, characteristic of Thoreau's writing early and late, appears to have had an important bearing on his poetics also. Ideally conceived, poetry, like literary nonfiction, clearly served a mimetic function; it was not so much a making as a remaking, one governed by a high degree of fidelity. "The poet," he wrote in 1853, "must bring to Nature the smooth mirror in which she is to be reflected" (J.5.183). His use of the mirror image here obviously echoes his fascination with the reflections of Walden and other natural mirrors. In bringing his "smooth mirror" to the feet of Nature, the poet merely seeks to emulate the mimetic mode of nature's own self-representation. Thoreau's frequent glossological imitations and etymological unpacking thus in some sense strive simply to reproduce nature's own expressions as they were reflected in his imagination through the language afforded by nature itself. The poet, in other words, is not someone who fabricates new forms but, on the example of nature, simply and devotedly reflects, represents, and recapitulates the ones that already exist. In this sense, the poet stands in the same relation to nature as the surface of the pond to the tree-lined shores. By invoking this analogy for artistic inspiration, Thoreau draws knowingly of course upon a poetic conceit of quite ancient classical vintage, yet for him it functions as more than mere literary artifice or convention. According to this conception, poetry results when the poet steps out of the way, as it were, and simply exhibits the reality that is. "The peculiarity of a work of genius," Thoreau wrote in 1852 in praising Shakespeare, "is the absence of the speaker from his speech—He is but the medium. You behold a perfect work, but you do not behold the worker. I read its page but it is as free from any man that can be—remembered as an impassable desert" (PJ.4.294). As I will show in the final chapter, during the last decade of his life, the chief vehicle for his elaborations and applications of this impersonal theory of literary creation was his mature journal, but earlier writings, like the following journal passage from 1841, provide obvious precedents: "Good poetry seems so simple and natural a thing that when we meet it we wonder that all men are not always poets. Poetry is nothing but healthy speech. Though the speech of the poet goes to the heart of things—yet he is that one especially who speaks civilly to nature as a second person—and in some sense is the patron of the world. Though more than any he stands in the midst of nature—yet more than any he can stand aloof from her. The best lines perhaps only suggest to me that that man simply saw or heard or felt, what seems the commonest fact in my experience" (PJ.1.338). Here Thoreau elevates Goethe's virtue of writing as an unconcerned spectator to the status of a universal poetic ideal. In both passages, the efficacy of the writer rests on a sort of paradoxical status involving both an absorption in and aloofness from the natural world. Again we are reminded of the ecstatic witness in Thoreau's treatment of "Solitude." Like the Hindu sages about whom Thoreau was beginning to read, the poet was in his view a contemplative and quietist: "The poet is partaker of a repose which is akin to the central law of the universe—No excitement is the mode in which he acts—He is perfectly poised, and rests as it were on the axis of the universe. He cannot but be wise and holy and brave" (PJ.1.437).

It was characteristic of Romantic thought to shift emphasis from the work of art to the artist, the poem to the poet: Emerson lionized his "representative men," Carlyle his heroes, Thoreau his John Brown. Emerson's dictum that "Art is the path of the creator to his work" epitomizes the view, echoed widely throughout his writing, that the culmination of artistic work is the maturation of character.[22] And this is the view of course that Thoreau's parable of the artist of Kouroo also means to convey. The point of this story is to prompt us to read *Walden* as an extended narrative of Thoreau's own inward exploration, a record of his self-transformation. The artist's creative activity turns out in the end to be centripetal, spiralling inward onto the artist himself. As if to prefigure the parable, Thoreau had earlier observed, "He is the true artist whose life is his material—every stroke of the chisel must enter his own flesh and bone, and not grate dully on marble" (PJ.1.139). Yet if *Walden* can be read from outside in—as the path of the artist to his real work of self-transformation—so it can also be read from inside out as a set of verbal configurations responding minutely to its author's central governing vision. This, at least, is the guarantee offered by Thoreau's unique devotion to his brand of literary organicism. In considering his preoccupation with the relationship between the artist and his or her art in this way, we begin to appreciate the fuller resonance of his treatment in the early pages of *Walden* of the relationship between a house and its "indweller." The passage puts us effectively on notice that, in this book at least, the character and action of the indweller may be found at every level of the work's architecture.

Not Till We Are Lost

Thoreau owes his reputation as a master of English style in large part to the resourcefulness and versatility of his writing. Though his subjects may sometimes be mundane, his treatment of them draws upon a wide range of figurative, rhetorical, and generic resources. In all this, his voice remains unfailingly clear and audible, though its tone is as shifting and mercurial as the breeze. Especially characteristic of this voice is its ubiquitous humor, whether manifested in the continual fusillade of puns and double entendres, the withering satire, the droll vignettes, or the occasional bitter gibe. Humor accompanies, and often helps to convey, Thoreau's most sober reflections, to such an extent that the lines between the serious and the ridiculous, comic and tragic, sacred and profane, simply begin to evaporate. This seems quite calculated and entirely consistent with his objective to revolutionize our routinized lives. In December of 1840, for example, he ponders the surreptitious appearance of otter tracks in the snow next to his house, as if they were the signature of some

alien preternatural being, and concludes his observation with the following facetious admission: "It is my own fault that he must thus skulk
across my premises by night.—Now I yearn toward him—and heaven to
me consists in a complete communion with the otter nature" (PJ.1.200).
The tone here is mock religious, the note of high seriousness undercut by
the exaggerated drama of the missed encounter. Yet the drollery cannot
at the same time cancel the meaningfulness of the theological reversal, so
characteristic of Thoreau, introduced, albeit leavened, by the otter/other
pun. Here, as in some other instances, it is hard to decide whether humor
is the means and testimony the end, or the other way around. The
essential feature of such puns and other wordplay is the unexpected
juxtaposition of two otherwise incongruous referents or axes of meaning.
The calculated introduction of a second disparate but competing sense
of a word wrests the reader's attention away from the more obvious
meaning and results momentarily in a sense of release, illumination, and
elation that we commonly experience as amusement. Thoreau understood better than most religious writers that even in its most mundane
expressions, humor was cognitively related to deeper forms of spiritual
and psychological insight. It was an "indispensable pledge of sanity," he
thought, and a crucial ingredient in "transcendental philosophy" in particular, which "needs the leaven of humor to render it light and digest-
ible" (EEM, 235). As such early procedural remarks suggest, Thoreau's
utilization of humor in *Walden* and other mature writings was highly
deliberate, part and parcel of even his most religiously invested reflections: "Humor is not so distinct a quality as for the purposes of criticism,
it is commonly regarded, but allied to every, even the divinest faculty"
(EEM, 237). Playing constantly between two disparate levels of meaning
helped to free his readers from their fatal penchant for single vision and
habitual experience. In *Walden* the Thoreauvian pun reproduces in min-
iature the sort of disjunctive vision that informs several of the book's
most famously provocative passages.[23]

Given Thoreau's interest in historical linguistics, it is not surprising
that he was particularly drawn to what we might call the etymological
pun. Examples of this may be found all through his writings, not least in

Walden itself, in his play on words such as "philanthropy," "religion," "agriculture," or, in the book's closing pages, "extravagant." His treatment of this last term seems particularly pointed, occurring as it does just before the artist of Kouroo vignette in the apparently more confessional and self-reflexive final pages of "Conclusion." The paragraph in question begins with the following combative apologia for *Walden*'s at times vertiginously obscure style:

> It is a ridiculous demand which England and America make, that you shall speak so that they can understand you. Neither men nor toad-stools grow so. As if that were important, and there were not enough to understand you without them. As if Nature could support but one order of understandings, could not sustain birds as well as quadrupeds, flying as well as creeping things, and *hush* and *who,* which Bright can understand, were the best English. As if there were safety in stupidity alone. I fear chiefly lest my expression may not be *extra-vagant* enough, may not wander far enough beyond the narrow limits of my daily experience, so as to be adequate to the truth of which I have been convinced. *Extra vagance!* It depends on how you are yarded. (324)

In this first section of the paragraph, Thoreau defends his literary practice in *Walden* by shrewdly turning the anticipated censure of "extravagance" back on his would-be accusers. The sword, it seems, cuts both ways. To counter the blow of extravagance, which in its conventional meaning has come to take on the predominantly negative connotation of that which is excessive or unreasonable, Thoreau parries with its older, more positive, and in his view, more accurate etymological sense of straying beyond limits or boundaries. In this instance of Thoreauvian wordplay, he wastes no time with coy implications, waiting for his reader to "get" the pun, but drives his point home more expeditiously by immediately providing his own gloss on the term extravagance. In this way, he converts an imputed weakness to a strength, and his success in doing so depends of course on his knowledge and resourceful use of etymology. But this play on the word extravagance as a wandering out

and beyond does not end here, since after the ensuing comparison between the migrating buffalo and the extravagant cow, he continues his
meditations on the word in a way that reverberates with his own deeper
preoccupations in *Walden:*

> I desire to speak somewhere *without* bounds; like a man in a
> waking moment, to men in their waking moments; for I am con-
> vinced that I cannot exaggerate enough to lay the foundation of a
> true expression. Who that has heard a strain of music feared then
> lest he should speak extravagantly any more forever? In view of the
> future or possible, we should live quite laxly and undefined in
> front, our outlines dim and misty on that side; as our shadows
> reveal an insensible perspiration toward the sun. The volatile truth
> of our words should continually betray the inadequacy of the re-
> sidual statement. Their truth is instantly *translated;* its literal
> monument alone remains. The words which express our faith and
> piety are not definite; yet they are significant and fragrant like
> frankincense to superior natures. (324–25)

As this etymological meditation unfolds, we can see how much of Thoreau's underlying vision he is apt to concentrate in a single pregnant
word. The religious language of this passage and, in particular, the revealing reference to "a strain of music" reflects its affiliations with the
complex of associations discussed in Chapter Two as central to Thoreau's
spiritual and imaginative life. But the prescription for good living that he
offers here—of living "quite laxly and undefined" on the side with which
we confront "the future or possible"—at once reminds us of the bifurcated structure of the ecstatic witness of "Solitude" in its juxtaposition of
bounded and unbounded experience and points forward to the ideal of
disinterested action exemplified by the artist of Kouroo. All of this,
moreover, is contained in the word extravagant itself, which, like the
states of ecstatic experience it is in part conceived to suggest, epitomizes
the quintessentially Transcendentalist idea of stepping outside the en-
closed sphere of boundaries.[24]
   Close inspection of *Walden's* style turns up other manifestations of

this disjunctiveness. For my purposes it will be enough merely to identify several such constructions that are similarly distinctive of his style and typical of his representation of ecstatic vision. The first of these, what we might characterize as the enigma or enigmatic construction, exemplifies Thoreau's preoccupation with the literary representation of obscurity or indeterminacy. One memorable instance of this type of formulation occurs in Thoreau's numinous encounter with Walden Pond itself in the quasi-theophany from "The Ponds": "It struck me again tonight, as if I had not seen it almost daily for more than twenty years,—Why, here is Walden, the same woodland lake that I discovered so many years ago; where a forest was cut down last winter another is springing up by its shore as lustily as ever; the same thought is welling up to its surface that was then; it is the same liquid joy and happiness to itself and its Maker, ay, and it *may* be to me. It is the work of a brave man surely, in whom there was no guile! He rounded this water with his hand, deepened and clarified it in his thought, and in his will bequeathed it to Concord. I see by its face that it is visited by the same reflection; and I can almost say, Walden, is it you?" (193). At first, this brightly lyrical passage presents no real difficulties to the understanding, even when it introduces, somewhat whimsically it appears, a distinct theological dimension with its reference to the Pond's creator. But the final sentence turns us completely around. Until this point, the passage has been reflective in a temporal and theological sense only, recalling the Pond's pastoral history and offering serene assertions of its divine origins. It reminds us once again of the importance of memory and the elegiac strain in Thoreau's most poignant reflections. But the high-stakes and apparently indeterminate question posed in the last sentence suddenly arrests that temporal reflection and shifts abruptly to the present tense: "I see by its face that it is visited by the same reflection; and I can almost say, Walden, is it you?" What is the "reflection" to which he alludes here? Apparently not the historical or even the theological reflection, since this is not a reflection pondered but a reflection seen directly on the surface of the Pond itself. The ambiguity of the final sentence depends heavily, of course, on Thoreau's usual play on the word reflection. The merely thoughtful reflections of the Pond's history and origins at this point culminate in a visual apprehension of the mysterious nature of the Pond itself. But what is the burden of this immediate face-to-face encounter? What is the meaning of the pronoun "it"? To whom does "you" refer? And what are we to make of the narrator's hesitation to invoke the apparently weighty question "I can *almost* say, Walden, is it you?" (my emphasis). The question that the narrator considers, but refrains from asking, appears to dramatize a scene of divine recognition reminiscent of Christ's postresurrection appearances. But in this case of almost-recognition, the revelatory question is raised but never really posed. The narrator stands on the brink of a revelation but proceeds no further than the anticipation of a question. The reflection that he sees and the formulation in which he represents it thus remain fundamentally indeterminate. To some extent, such ambiguity results from the uncertain character of the reflection itself—it is both the guarantor and the spoiler of certainty. We feel something great is announced in the narrator's question but never achieve any clarity about what that is. Thoreau leaves the question and the scene itself enigmatic.

Thoreau's phrasing here owes something to the famous passage from Paul: "But now we see as through a glass darkly but then face to face" (1 Cor. 13 King James Version). The Greek term that has been translated in the King James Version as "darkly" ("dimly" in the New Revised Standard Edition) is *aenigmata,* a word that originally referred to a "riddle" or dark saying, and later came to mean any indirect or reflected image. Whether construed as a speech act or a visual perception, the aenigmata served consequently as a vehicle of only partial disclosure. Interestingly, and not surprisingly given his etymological inclinations, Thoreau makes the same connection: the character of the water's reflected image suggested to him a model for one of his favorite rhetorical forms—the enigma.

Whatever the connection between Thoreau's watery reflections and his dark obliquities, it is clear from an early point in time that he was fascinated by the character of enigmatic writing. Like Emerson, he found the legend of the Sphinx highly suggestive and devoted several pages of his journal to a detailed exegesis of Emerson's poem of that name

(PJ.1.279–86). *Walden* in particular is well known for its representations of enigma in strategic places, not least in the caveat about necessary "obscurities" that introduces the dark parable of the hound, the bay horse, and the turtledove that I discussed earlier. Obscurity results, the narrator suggests there, from an effort "to improve the nick of time" and "stand on the meeting of two eternities" (17). The character of the relationship between these "two eternities," past and future, thus appears to have some bearing on the formulation that results.

Emerson, Sophocles, and St. Paul no doubt all encouraged Thoreau's propensity for enigmatic sayings, but his reading of Manu also seems to have served as an important catalyst. The sentences of this ancient scripture came as close as any could, he thought, to the open, unpretentious, and sibylline expressions of nature. They were so original, so unprepossessing, as to seem at times almost beyond determinative meaning. In a long and appreciative digression on the *Laws of Manu* in *A Week*, Thoreau considered Manu's formulations to be commensurate with the "depth and serenity" of the sky. "Give me a sentence which no intelligence can understand," he exclaims in veneration of the dignified obscurity of these ancient formulations.[25] If an assertion was to do justice to nature, it had to partake of its obscurity, as the Vedas appear to have done. As his treatment of Manu proceeds, he once again elaborates on the organic relationship he sees between the words of these ancient traditions and the natural forms in the New England landscape: "The fair water lies there in the sun thus revealed, so much the prouder and fairer because its beauty needed not to be seen. It seems yet lonely, sufficient to itself, and superior to observation.—So are these old sentences like serene lakes in the south-west, at length revealed to us, which have so long been reflecting our own sky in their bosom" (Week, 151). In this simile, Thoreau makes explicit the imaginative connection between his reflections on water and the enigmatic formulations of his rhetoric. "I do not suppose that I have attained to obscurity," he wrote in the final pages of *Walden,* "but I should be proud if no more fatal fault were found with my pages on this score than was found with the Walden ice" (325). Both representations had a way of announcing some higher reality without quite revealing it. The point of such enigmatic formulations then was not to edify but to unsettle—to draw the reader into the troubling awareness of his or her own as yet limited experience and understanding. At this point, Thoreau's rhetoric intersects neatly with the negative theological style to which, as we saw in Chapter Four, he deliberately adhered.

The representation of a necessarily obscured encounter that occurs in "The Ponds" serves also to illustrate a second type of rhetorical construction often deployed at strategic points in Thoreau's writing—what I would refer to as confrontational style. Throughout *Walden,* as in the rest of Thoreau's work, there is a good deal of attention to the importance of confrontation, whether it be with the Pond, one's reflection on it, a fact, one's neighbor, or oneself. In Thoreau, as in Paul, the challenge of standing face to face represents a test of who are. Much depends on whether, and how, we face up to our situation. "To be awake is to be alive," he writes famously in "Where I Lived and What I Lived For." "I have never yet met a man who was quite awake. How could I have looked him in the face?" (Walden, 90). In *Walden,* the face often serves as the reflector of the self, just as the Pond serves as the reflector of nature. Success in life requires that we face forward, that we confront the work required of us; the reason Thoreau offers for going to the woods was that he wished to live "deliberately, to front only the essential facts of life" (90). His first book, however, provides one of the most extended explications of the confrontational theme: "The frontiers are not east or west; north or south, but wherever a man *fronts* a fact, though that fact be his neighbor, there is an unsettled wilderness between him and Canada, between him and the setting sun, or, further still, between him and *it.* Let him build himself a log-house with the bark on where he is, *fronting* IT, and wage there an Old French war for seven or seventy years, with Indians and Rangers, or whatever else may come between him and the reality, and save his scalp if he can" (Week, 304). In this pun on "frontier," Thoreau provides sanction for his wider interest in transposing heroism from an outer to an inner quest. The real frontier lies within us, he suggests, and the willingness to confront ourselves serves as the mark of character.

He sometimes draws on this same pattern of figuration to convey moments of ecstasy. Shortly after the introduction of the passage on the ecstatic fisher noted previously, he takes up this confrontational figuration once again: "If you stand right fronting and face to face to a fact, you will see the sun glimmer on both its surfaces, as if it were a cimeter, and feel its sweet edge dividing you through the heart and marrow, and so you will happily conclude your mortal career" (Walden, 98). This evocation of delicious death at the hand of a sword-wielding fact must surely be one of the strangest and most unsettling constructions in *Walden,* but its shock value should not blind us to how characteristic it is of Thoreau's imagination, a tour de force actually of his disjunctive way of looking at things. "Face to face" confrontation between self and other, reminiscent of the reflections on the Pond, leads to a recognition of the two-sided nature of reality itself, sun glinting on both its surfaces. This in turn forces a release from narrow self-consciousness that culminates in a kind of mystical, perhaps even earthly, consummation. As we have seen, Thoreau's use of the intellect as an instrument of redemption appears to owe something to his reading of the Sāṃkhya and Yoga texts, and here is perhaps its most dramatic manifestation: outer discrimination of fact leads to inner discrimination, which in turn leads to transcendence.

Related to this confrontational style is a third type of construction that similarly helps to convey the representation of ecstatic vision, and this is what I would refer to as the deliberative construction. The formulation noted before in the spectatorship passage of "Solitude" provides us with perhaps the best example of this: "I may be either the drift-wood in the stream, or Indra looking down on it" (135). At one level, this construction is simply an attempt to represent in words the dual perception that results from gazing on and into a tranquil stream. But, as in the case of similar passages, Thoreau construes it as a natural emblem and even starting point for the ecstatic vision that follows. As it is represented rhetorically, the experience of self-spectatorship is essentially one of paradox and ambiguity: the "self"—a term made suddenly more problematic by its displacement—is neither this nor that. Actually, where or what the self is cannot so easily be specified. The rhetorical form in which this observation is cast neatly reproduces the ambiguity of the perception itself and helps to convey the sense of psychological displacement it is designed to inaugurate. In context, the alternative "either . . . or" construction is even more indeterminate than its grammatical form would suggest: is it disjunctive, conjunctive, both, or—given such doubts— neither? It is worth remarking that Thoreau's purpose in these representations seems less to provide us with some specific reorientation than to leave us doubtful of our present standing. But this sort of deliberative construction occurs elsewhere in Thoreau's writing also. Here, for example, is how he presents the central epiphany of "The Bean-Field": "When my hoe tinkled against the stones, that music echoed to the woods and the sky, and was an accompaniment to my labor which yielded an instant and immeasurable crop. It was no longer beans that I hoed, nor I that hoed beans; and I remembered with as much pity as pride, if I remembered at all, my acquaintances who had gone to the city to attend the oratorios" (Walden, 159).

As in *Walden,* the narrator of *A Week* describes the ambiguous reflections in a stream this way: "We were uncertain whether the water floated the land, or the land held the water in its bosom" (45). The water once again prompts a reflective reversal, foreground becoming background and background coming to the fore. It is important that we have these reflections, Thoreau wants to insist, otherwise we may be in danger of misconstruing our world. In the journal he remarks: "Nature has her russet hues as well as green—Indeed our eye splits on every object, and we can as well take one path as the other—" (PJ.1.381). This conviction that there are two ways of seeing a thing leads him away from certainty and toward an expectation that at some point "reality" may require a total make-over. This incipient consciousness of alternate realities is what lies behind Thoreau's frequent use of the term "deliberation." In *Walden,* the narrator employs this term with suggestive frequency: he counsels us variously "to live deliberately, to front only the essential facts of life" (90); to "spend one day as deliberately as Nature" (97); to choose our pursuits "with a little more deliberation" (99). As usual, Thoreau plays on etymology in his usage here: to deliberate (Latin *de-liberare*) is, strictly speaking, to weigh or "balance" the alternatives. But we cannot weigh them of course, until we become aware of them. That we, as readers, should take these at times apparently fanciful reflections and alternatives seriously is suggested in Thoreau's advice as regards "reading": "Books must be read as deliberately and reservedly as they were written" (101). The text's "deliberations" must be succeeded by the reader's. It is worth noting that Thoreau introduces this clutch of references to deliberate experience with the familiar parable of the king's son who grows up thinking he is a destitute forester only to recognize when he comes of age that he is a prince after all. Thoreau takes the moral of this story from a Hindu commentator: " 'So soul . . . from the circumstances in which it is placed, mistakes its own character, until the truth is revealed to it by some holy teacher, and then it knows itself to be *Brahme*' " (96). To contextualize his counsel in this way obviously raises the stakes involved in living deliberately; to see things one way as opposed to another can mean the difference between heaven and earth, life and death.

While the reflective alternative may appear fanciful or spurious, there are times in life, as in nature, when it appears to be realer than the real. As the reflective heart of the book, the chapter entitled "The Ponds" serves, not surprisingly, as a kind of central showcase for the narrator's ecstatic meditations. Here his various observations on the Pond repeatedly lead to recognitions of the two-sided dimensions of experience that *Walden*'s narrator attempts to figure in various antithetical conceits and formulations. Fishing in the Pond on dark nights, he is surprised by the faint jerk on his line that returns him to an awareness of his present time and place: "It seemed as if I might next cast my line upward into the air, as well as downward into this element which was scarcely more dense. Thus I caught two fishes as it were with one hook" (175). At other times, deliberative vision serves as a mode of uncovering unsuspected realities, as when, "looking with divided vision" at the surface of the Pond, the narrator is able to discern "a matchless and indescribable light blue . . . more cerulean than the sky itself" (177). At their most developed, these perceptions lead to experiential reversals that prompt the narrator, and by extension his readers, to question the claims of conventional views of reality: "As you look over the pond westward you are obliged to employ both your hands to defend your eyes against the reflected as well as the true sun, for they are equally bright" (186). If they are equally bright, the narrator seems to suggest, how after all can we really distinguish the real from the reflected? And when even the long-settled conviction of the domination of our planet by a single ascendent sun admits of an alternative point of view, what about all the rest of the facts of our lives that are in some sense predicated upon it? Even to entertain the idea of a double sun throws every other fixed idea in our solar system into radical uncertainty. This passage, in other words, like others related to it, serves as a kind of figurative lever to force open as yet unconsidered alternatives. Suddenly, recognition of the relativity of the objects we observe cascades back onto our position as observers. Inoculating us from the dangers of single-minded vision, such deliberative reflection thus apprises us of a fact that, in Thoreau's view, may be requisite to our sanity.

Paradox is the last type of construction that I will consider here, and it epitomizes, perhaps better than anything else does, the dual nature of Thoreau's existential vision. It occurs in acute forms in his texts, and in more relaxed ones, as, for example, in the kind of rhetorical reversals of which he was so fond: "The greater part of what my neighbors call good I believe in my soul to be bad, and if I repent of anything, it is very likely to be my good behavior." Commonly, as in this case, Thoreau's formulation first extends the reversal, then flexes it: "What demon possessed me that I behaved so well?" (Walden, 10). Implicit in such developed passages is the kind of succinct paradox to which he was also characteristically drawn. In the summer of 1840, for example, he reserved a whole page of his journal for a catalog of some of his favorite paradoxes: "The highest condition of art is artlessness." "He will get to the goal first who stands stillest." "By sufferance you may escape suffering." "He who resists not at all will never surrender." The sanction for such apparently contradictory sayings he epitomizes in a paradox around a paradox—"The truth is always paradoxical" (PJ.1.143). In such formulations as these, what appears to be an insoluble contradiction within a single frame of reference becomes resolvable when the first frame is juxtaposed with and supplanted by a more esoteric second.[26]

Thoreau's penchant for paradox was by no means unique among the writers of his day, particularly religious writers. Richard Whately had championed the use of paradox in polemical religious discourse, and Thoreau's own writing teacher, E. T. Channing, emphasized the value of the judicious use of paradox in all forms of written argumentation. The Congregational theologian Horace Bushnell also advocated the use of paradox in theological writing, as several recent writers have pointed out. "We never come so near to a truly well rounded view," Bushnell wrote, "as when it is offered paradoxically."[27] Notwithstanding such encouragements, the habit of vision that gave rise to such paradox—whether of the condensed or extended forms—came naturally to Thoreau; it was a natural expression of his bifurcating eye, the disassociative vision of which we have seen so many manifestations in this study. The fact that many instances of the use of paradox could be found in the scriptures and classics of the world, in particular the Asian scriptures, no doubt contributed also to his fondness for the form. In later years, he found repeated authorization for his use of paradox from the Indian scriptures in particular. The reversal of conventional "good" and "bad" from the passage cited above finds, for example, suggestive precedent in Ward's collection of passages from the Sāṃkhya system: "A wise man sees so many false things in those which are called true; so many disgusting things in those which are called pleasant; and so much misery in what is called happiness, that he turns away with disgust."[28] And Thoreau's favorite Hindu source, the Bhagavad Gita, contains several provocative instances of this figure, including this arresting verse from Chapter Four: "He who may behold, as it were inaction in action, and action in inaction, is wise amongst mankind. He is a perfect performer of all duty."[29]

That Thoreau would get so much mileage from this trope should come as no surprise when we recognize to what extent it tended to epitomize the reversible mirroring structure of his ecstasy. The counterintuitive adage that Thoreau selected to conclude the catalogue of 1840 appears to reflect not only its implicit relationship to ecstatic experience but also the negative theology he favored: "Stand outside the wall and no harm can reach you—the danger is that you be walled in with it"

(PJ.1.143). This formulation offers an implicit defense of the epistemological power of paradox in general. Whatever its particular force, every such passage serves to usher us to an interpretive position beyond the perimeter of present conception and understanding. Initially, such positions of abrupt alterity may prove disorienting, but this is a guarantee of their effectiveness. As if to bring home to his Yankee readers its fuller spiritual import, Thoreau works up what is perhaps his most memorable expression of such momentary disorientation from words attributed to Jesus himself: "Not till we are lost, in other words, not till we have lost the world, do we begin to find ourselves, and realize where we are and the infinite extent of our relations" (Walden, 171).[30] Paradox was even a figure that could help him express the most inscrutable mystery of all— how to activate silence through the medium of speech. The peroration of *A Week* consists essentially of an extended meditation on the identity of sound and silence:

> As the truest society approaches always nearer to solitude, so the most excellent speech finally falls into Silence. Silence is audible to all men, at all times, and in all places. She is when we hear inwardly, sound when we hear outwardly. Creation has not displaced her, but is her visible frame-work and foil. All sounds are her servants and purveyors, proclaiming not only that their mistress is, but is a rare mistress, and earnestly to be sought after. They are so far akin to Silence, that they are but bubbles on her surface, which straightway burst, an evidence of the strength and prolificness of the under-current; a faint utterance of Silence, and then only agreeable to our auditory nerves when they contrast themselves with and relieve the former. In proportion as they do this, and are heighteners and intensifiers of the silence, they are harmony and purest melody. (391–92)

This appeal to subtler and grosser forms of hearing reminds us of the "wondrous" music that served as the catalyst for Thoreau's ecstasies. To hear music, he had discovered then, was to keep silence. Though sound and silence are perhaps not resolvable in principle, there appears to have been an experiential basis for his belief in their deep interpenetration. The task of the author was to render "his volume a foil whereon the waves of silence may break" (PJ.1.64).[31]

If paradox, like the other dialectical forms described above, has its principal representational basis in Thoreau's own ecstatic experience, it received added impetus and articulation in writings like *Walden* from his pervasive and well-attested prophetic motive. Indeed, paradox and para- doxical reversals often served in some form as the perfect vehicles for the prophetic discourse that so often animates the pages of "Economy," as well as Thoreau's various essays and lectures directed to specific issues of social reform.[32] The prophetic oracles of the Bible turn, after all, on oppositions between—and at times reversals of the oppositions between —sin and righteousness, worldly corruption, and covenantal virtue. What the worldly often called good, the Hebrew prophets condemned as evil. Thoreau drew on such prophetic schema in developing his own fiercely dialectical style. As we have seen, juxtaposition and reversal are a familiar rhetorical strategy in his writing, where to deprive was to bestow, to make war was to produce pleasure, to venture out was to return home, to be still was to progress, to be lost was to be found, or to obey the law was to break it. This kind of rhetorical reversal and the disjunctive sensibility which gives rise to it of course dominate the sharply prophetic assaults of Thoreau's famous essay on "Civil Disobedience": "Under a government which imprisons any unjustly, the true place for a just man is also a prison. The proper place to-day, the only place which Massachu- setts has provided for her freer and less desponding spirits, is in her prisons, to be put out and locked out of the State by her own act, as they have already put themselves out by their principles. It is there that the fugitive slave, and the Mexican prisoner on parole, and the Indian come to plead the wrongs of his race, should find them; on that separate, but more free and honorable ground, where the State places those who are not *with* her but *against* her,—the only house in a slave-state in which a free man can abide with honor" (RP, 76). Precedents for this elevation of the prison over society may certainly be found in the pages of Christian and biblical history, and without some such reference to its prophetic affiliations, Thoreau's rhetorical style can never be fully assessed or appreciated.[33] In analyzing, in particular, the religious dimensions of his life and writing, it is clearly not enough to analyze his ecstatic experience alone, since his public writings and many of his journal entries are also animated by a passionate commitment to justice and social change. To construe Thoreau simply as a kind of New England quietist or Yankee contemplative would be as one-sided as to see him exclusively as a social reformer or scientific naturalist. Thoreau admired what he considered the contemplative traditions of the East, but, like other Westerners, he sometimes mourned what he took to be their apparent lack of a religiously inspired social activism, a fact that underscores his sympathy with and dependence upon the traditions of prophetic criticism and social activism found in the Bible.[34] Yet while the social orientations of prophetic religion and meditative experience may sometimes be seen to differ, these two religious attitudes nonetheless express themselves in comparable rhetorical forms. Both Isaiah and Krishna presuppose a fundamental dichotomy between the world of everyday social life and the position of prophet or seer. Like the contemplative witness, the prophet must by definition take up a religious and moral standpoint independent of and removed from the framework of the political and religious status quo. It should not surprise us, therefore, that the voices issuing from such a place apart would result in formulations that characteristically spring from, allude to, and play upon comparable dialectical visions of reality. It worked to Thoreau's decided advantage as a writer that some of the same rhetorical constructions that he used to exhibit and activate his ecstatic inner life served also to fire and fuel his prophetic concern.

Limits of space make it impossible to undertake a fully comprehensive analysis of Thoreau's essayistic style here. It is enough simply to indicate that at those critical points in his writing when he is most bent on the representation of his ecstatic vision or the prosecution of his prophetic testimony, he appeals above all to the sorts of unsettling dialectical treatment discussed above. These rhetorical strategies cannot be divorced from his distinctive religious imagination, and they were shaped for him by both biblical and Asian sources.

Seven

A Meteorological Journal of the Mind

I f we look back over the previous hundred years of critical writing on Thoreau from the vantage point of the beginning of the twenty-first century, it is hard to deny that the single most decisive event in the modern development of Thoreau studies was the publication in 1906 of the first nearly complete edition of his journal. Stretching to some fourteen volumes, this printing of journal entries made up the bulk of the twenty-volume set of Thoreau's writings known as the Walden Edition. While this first comprehensive printing of the journal was not complete by contemporary standards—missing from it were a considerable portion of the early journal volumes not available to its editors, as well as many proper names, numerous long quotations, and lists he kept there of his natural observations—it nevertheless provided readers with their first real glimpse into the rich and voluminous body of writing that was, we can now recognize, Thoreau's main life's work.[1] Zealously kept from shortly after his college graduation in 1837 till a few months before his death in 1862, this two-million-word journal affords us the best, the most detailed, and in places the most intimate record we have of the inner life of Henry Thoreau.[2]

In recent years, the journal has increasingly taken center stage in much of the best critical writing on Thoreau, and by virtue of this recent work, we now have a much better idea of the character and contributions of this distinctive record.[3] Paging through this massive record, the reader is likely to be struck, first of all, by how variable it is. Not only does one note drastic shifts in the subject matter, style, and density of treatment over the course of time, but even in the ostensible uses to which Thoreau put his journals at different periods of his life. An overview of the journals, early to late, suggests that they reflect three more or less distinct periods. The earliest journals, especially those kept from the fall of 1837 till about the end of 1839, seem to have functioned as a sort of showcase or commonplace book for reading notes, poems, and a series of fairly polished mini-essays, often headed with brief titles, on a wide array of topics. The fact that the surviving journals of this period have all been meticulously transcribed from previous, now lost, materials suggests that these entries were sedulously formulated in this way for their own sake. By the beginning of the next decade, however, and continuing on through most of the next ten years, Thoreau tended increasingly to utilize his journal as a kind of literary workshop for material he later hoped to recast in the form of lectures or published essays. The clearest indication of this changing function of the journals was his practice of scissoring out entire sections of prose that he intended to reconstitute elsewhere. The first drafts of large sections of *A Week* and *Walden,* which Thoreau worked on throughout much of the 1840s, were formulated and recycled in just this fashion.[4]

Beginning, however, around May of 1850, the character of Thoreau's journalizing underwent a more momentous change. From this point forward, the journal no longer functioned primarily as a staging area for other writings but as a principal mode of literary production in and of itself. Although he had long been in the habit of dating many of his entries, in the earliest journals days or even weeks might elapse between one entry and the next. By the early years of the 1850s until just a year before his death, however, he recorded journal entries on almost a daily basis, often devoting several pages or more to each one. As a result of this new attention to the journal for its own sake, the late journals—that is, those he kept from 1850 till 1862—constitute by far the main bulk of the work overall, and along with the change in function came a greater focus. Thoreau's journals had always been filled with observations of natural forms and phenomena, but after 1850, this preoccupation increasingly eclipsed all other concerns. While these later journals still occasionally give way to critical commentary on literature, politics, society, and religion, and are periodically witness to the kind of droll vignettes of local characters we find, for example, in *Walden,* for the most part, these other interests come to be subordinated to Thoreau's overriding interest in natural observation.

By this point, except when it was interrupted by surveying jobs or the occasional excursion outside of Concord, Thoreau's daily regimen had assumed the settled pattern that would characterize much of his mature adult life. Afternoons and sometimes evenings he spent rambling in local woods and meadows; mornings he spent in his attic study amplifying and reflecting at more length on the field notes he had recorded in his pocket journal the day before. His apparent preoccupation with the natural world during this period of his life might lead us to anticipate a certain monotony of treatment, but interestingly, this is rarely the case. While the late journal might be generally characterized as a kind of naturalist's log, it contains a wide range of different sorts of information and responses, and appears to serve somewhat different functions. At points the journal seeks to reconstruct a particular walk or excursion and recount a series of discrete, loosely conjoined observations of the natural world; elsewhere it interrogates a particular natural form—whether of trees, flowers, toads, fish, or birds—or provides a catalogue of various species of flora and fauna; sometimes the journal records an experiment, as with honeybees or ice bubbles, or the results thereof, or documents an analysis or measurement of some natural phenomenon; not infrequently it breaks into enthusiastic praise or an extended eulogy of the beauty or wonder of some natural spectacle, whether of the dawn, the mist, a great pine, or scarlet tanager; and increasingly, the journal seems concerned with keeping track of seasonal change, with implicit or explicit comparison to previous years and seasons. Evidence from his notebooks suggests that in the last couple years of his life, he even planned to assemble and tabulate observations made in his journal over many years in the form of a detailed seasonal record he referred to as his "Kalendar."[5]

At such points, the journal aspires to be a kind of cumulative calendar of Concord's seasons.

Despite the late journal's more or less single-minded preoccupation with details of the natural world and Thoreau's relation to them, the repercussions of his personal, intellectual, and social life are also at times evident in its pages. In the interstices of extended field notes, we encounter the occasional personal aside or response to outer events and people. In April of 1851, for example, he vents his outrage for several pages at the arrest in Boston and return of the runaway slave Thomas Sims and other consequences of the passage earlier that year of the Fugitive Slave Act (PJ.3.203–09). In May of 1854, he lashes out once again at slaveholders and the North's complicity with them in the arrest of the fugitive slave Anthony Burns (J.6.339–40; 352–53; 356–57; 365–66). And late in 1859, he devotes extended sections of his journal to his defense of John Brown and the Harper's Ferry raid that had taken place a few weeks before (J.12.400 ff.). Of other momentous events during these prewar years the journal says oddly little. In February of 1859, it is interrupted by the notice and a brief reflection on the death of Thoreau's father, John, but even this entry seems relatively terse compared to the liberal treatment everywhere accorded his daily walks and natural observations.

Such gaps and reticence notwithstanding, the 1850s were a busy and productive time for Thoreau: he had as much surveying work as he needed during this time, his lectures were in greater demand, and he successfully published a host of articles—mostly on natural history, various excursions, and issues of reform—in addition, of course, to *Walden,* which appeared in 1854. He also took two more trips to Maine and a few more to Cape Cod. Yet for all this activity, there were setbacks and personal misfortunes as well. Though he would survive his brother, John, and sister Helen, by the mid-fifties the robust physical health he had once taken for granted now began to elude him. He was plagued intermittently by bouts of bronchitis and weakness in the legs, early symptoms perhaps of the tuberculosis that would kill him in 1862.[6] Thus, even from the threadbare information of his outer activities provided by the journal of these years, we can well see what a turbulent and difficult time this was for Thoreau, as it was for the country generally.

A Regret So Divine

It is surely no exaggeration to say that the access to Thoreau's journal made possible by the publication of the Walden Edition in 1906, and more recently the Princeton critical edition, has gone a long way to insuring the viability and longevity of Thoreau studies as a field of scholarly inquiry: three generations of scholars have drawn deeply on this resource in their efforts to document Thoreau's life and explicate his various works. But the journal is an ungainly and sprawling complex of documents, and resistant, after all, to easy distillations. One result of the complexity and elusiveness of this mammoth record has been the emergence over the past century or more of several distinct portraits of Henry Thoreau and of his life. Attracting particular critical notice has been the abrupt shift in the character of the journal after May of 1850. The notable alteration in the character of the journal entries at this time—from the cosmopolitan and more open-endedly subjective reflections of earlier years to the detailed, empirical, and at times dry formulations of fact after 1852 or so—has served as the basis for several, sometimes competing, narratives of Thoreau's life. For some of the most influential critics of the past century, this ostensible shift in the character of the journal, together with known facts about Thoreau's declining health and other relevant information, has suggested what I would call a narrative of decline. According to this reading, after the tragedies, professional disappointments, and hard knocks of midlife experience, Thoreau found it increasingly hard to sustain the Transcendentalist enthusiasm of his younger years, and began to entertain a growing sense of bitterness and estrangement instead. His zealous recourse to empirical observation and science in the last decade of his life was a reaction, according to this view, to his midlife disillusionment with the spiritual excesses of youth. Mark Van Doren, who conceived the older Thoreau as a disenchanted and embittered man, presented a particularly stark portrayal of this sort in his pessimistic treatment of 1916, but later critical representations have also championed something like this version of Thoreau's life—from Perry Miller's view of the later journal as a sort of compensation for failure to Sherman Paul's conception of the years subsequent to *Walden* as ones of ever "deepening despair."[7]

Although the decline narrative misrepresents the late journal, as I will presently show, it is by no means a purely circumstantial construct: there *is* after all a suggestive alteration in the character of the journal at the beginning of this period, and Thoreau does sometimes give vent to apparently heartfelt expressions of regret and loss, particularly during the first few years of the 1850s. These facts are crucial, moreover, to an understanding of his mature spiritual life. Advocates of the decline theory customarily cite passages such as this one from October of 1851: "I seem to be more constantly merged in nature—my intellectual life is more obedient to nature than formerly—but perchance less obedient to Spirit—I have less memorable seasons. I exact less of myself. I am getting used to my meanness—getting to accept my low estate—O if I could be discontented with myself! If I could feel anguish at each descent!" (PJ.4.141). In November of the following year, he complains of growing "more coarse and indifferent" in view of his diminishing scruples about the eating of meat or the use of tea and coffee (PJ.5.399). Moreover, Thoreau does at times worry that this sense of spiritual diminution has led to an excessive preoccupation with scientific detail to the relative exclusion of a sense of wholeness—as in this entry from August of 1851: "I fear that the character of my knowledge is from year to year becoming more distinct & scientific—That in exchange for views as wide as heaven's cope I am being narrowed down to the field of the microscope— I see details not wholes nor the shadow of the whole" (PJ.3.380). Taken out of their wider journalistic context, such passages certainly lend support to the decline narrative. But if these passages are viewed in the context of other journal entries from the spring and summer of 1851, we see that this was not a time of personal sterility at all, in either the artistic or the religious sense. On the contrary, this period witnessed a resurgence of the kind of enthusiasm and ecstasy to which he had earlier been prone, though in a somewhat diminished degree. In fact, some of the most poignant examples of these expressions of regret and loss occur in roughly the same period of time, within the same context, and in the midst of the same spiritually charged atmosphere as some of his most dramatic expressions of spiritual renewal.

The passages cited above from the summer and fall of 1851 take us back of course to the watershed period with which I began this study, when regretful expressions such as these are crowded out by numerous lengthy journal entries that document in rich and evocative detail what can only be characterized as a summer of unusual spiritual plenty. During this extraordinary period, the journal dwells at length on Thoreau's exhilarating transactions with the natural world. This was the summer of his euphoric walks in moonlight and the ecstatic transports that I noted earlier. The spring and summer of 1851 also witnessed his rereading of Wordsworth, as we have seen, and a revival of his interest in Indian religion and philosophy. The previous year, he had begun reading Rammohan Roy's translations of the Vedas and Upanishads, and in May he quotes passages from Colebrooke's translation of the *Sāṃkhya-Kārikā* in which he encountered provocative formulations of the ecstatic separation of the soul from matter.[8]

What to make of this apparent mingling of regret and euphoria during the summer of 1851 becomes more evident when we examine such passages in detail. Here, for example, is the way Thoreau conveys one such regretful recollection in late May of that year: "Our most glorious experiences are a kind of regret. Our regret is so sublime that we may mistake it for triumph. It is the painful plaintively sad surprise of our Genius remembering our past lives and contemplating what is possible. . . . It is a regret so divine & inspiring so genuine—based on so true & distinct a contrast—that it surpasses our proudest boasts and the fairest expectations" (PJ.3.233–34). With its own intimations of immortality and delicious recollections of some paradisal past life, this passage prepares the way for the dramatic Wordsworthian passage of July 16 that served as the principal touchstone for my earlier analysis of Thoreau's ecstatic witness. In these, as well as kindred passages, the Romantic sense of paradise lost is quickly construed as a prophetic harbinger, even guarantor, of a more beatific present and future. In this summer of exquisite consolations, such feelings of loss served him more as promissory notes to a more heavenly future than as some immutable decree of the present. Actually, these notes of plaintive regret often pave the way, or immediately succeed, the days of rapture and insight of which they mourn the lack. That some of the most poignant expressions of regret should arise not in states of utter spiritual aridity, but in anticipation of or proximity to feelings of elevation makes more sense when we realize that it was precisely Thoreau's awareness of the nearness of these periods of inspiration, even at times of their immanence and inevitability, that so sharpened his tragic sense of how much he was missing in their absence. It is not surprising, therefore, that the passage of regretful longing of May 24 cited above should be succeeded only a few weeks later by the following testimony, more representative of the fuller transports of that summer:

> My pulse beat with nature After a hard day's work without a thought turning my very brain in to a mere tool, only in the quiet of evening do I so far recover my senses as to hear the cricket which in fact has been chirping all day. In my better hours I am conscious of the influx of a serene & unquestionable wisdom which partly unfits and if I yielded to it more rememberingly would wholly unfit me for what is called the active business of life—for that furnishes nothing on which the eye of reason can rest. What is that other kind of life to which I am thus continually allured?—which I alone love? Is it a life for this world? Can a man feed and clothe himself gloriously who keeps only the truth steadily before him? who calls in no evil to his aid? Are these duties which necessarily interfere with the serene perception of truth? Are our serene moments mere foretastes of heaven joys gratuitously vouchsafed to us as a consolation—or simply a transient realization of what might be the whole tenor of our lives? (PJ.3.274)

It is certainly true that such overt expressions of Thoreau's ecstatic experience become less frequent in the later journal, as, for that matter, do most other strictly subjective reflections, but never do they or their manifestations die out of the record completely. When such sentiments do make themselves felt in the journal, they are typically instigated by the experience of music—as in this fairly characteristic passage from the following summer: "A thrumming of piano strings beyond the gardens & through the elms—at length the melody steals into my being—I know not when it began to occupy me—By some fortunate coincidence of thought or circumstance I am attuned to the universe—I am fitted to hear—my being moves in a sphere of melody—my fancy and imagination are excited to an inconceivable degree—This is no longer the dull earth on which I stood—It is possible to live a grander life here—already the steed is stamping—the knights are prancing—Already our thoughts bid a proud farewell to the so called actual life & its humble glories— Now this is the verdict of a soul in health. But the soul diseased says that its own vision & life a-lone is true & sane" (PJ.5.272). That Thoreau remained susceptible to such moments of exhilaration even in the last years of his life is suggested by this journal entry from the spring of 1857:

> While dropping beans in the garden at Texas just after sundown, I hear from across the fields the note of the bay-wing . . . It reminds me of so many country afternoons and evenings when this bird's strain was heard far over the fields, as I pursued it from field to field. The spirit of its earth-song, of its serene and true philosophy, was breathed into me, and I saw the world as through a glass, as it lies eternally. Some of its aboriginal contentment, even of its domestic felicity, possessed me. What he suggests is permanently true. As the bay-wing sang many a thousand years ago, so sang he to-night. . . . I ordinarily plod along a sort of whitewashed prison entry, subject to some indifferent or even grovelling mood. I do not distinctly realize my destiny. . . . But suddenly, in some fortunate moment, the voice of eternal wisdom reaches me even, in the strain of the sparrow, and liberates me, whets and clarifies my senses, makes me a competent witness. (J.9.363–65)

Those who see in the late journal evidence of spiritual decline base their findings mainly on the growing preponderance there of long and detailed examinations of local flora and fauna, to the exclusion largely of the more subjective reports common before 1851 or so. These apparently unspiritual and untranscendental preoccupations, so the argument goes, are indicative of Thoreau's spiritual disenchantment and serve, by some accounts, as a sort of compensation for his former pursuits. But we must avoid jumping to conclusions. To be sure, the decline narrative has a certain literary and psychological appeal in conceiving Thoreau's life according to some familiar tragic arc. But the journal overall actually provides very little warrant for this sort of sweeping claim. There is certainly nothing univocal about this record, and for every passage suggesting disenchantment, ten more can be cited suggesting excitement and joy. The mere fact of Thoreau's devotion to nature and natural observation does not by itself indicate depression or disillusionment. If anything, it suggests only a redirection, and perhaps intensification, of the energies evident in his early life. After all, dejected individuals do not produce two-million-word journals manifesting a seemingly inexhaustible curiosity about and fervor for the natural world. The late journal entries are certainly less subjective than their earlier counterparts, but this seems programmatic, and when personal feelings do make their way to the surface of his prose, we find much the same buoyancy and sense of wonder characteristic of Thoreau's dealings with nature throughout his life. What the co-presence of inspiration and regret indicated above suggests is that there is another way of reading this record that is more consistent with the general tenor of Thoreau's thought, both before and after his new approach to the journal.

One major dividend of a closer examination of the nature of Thoreau's spiritual life is the important recognition that the late journal represents not so much a break with his earlier Transcendentalist reflections as a development and intensification of them. Nowhere do these later journals repudiate his earlier espousal of a higher spiritual life or his practice of reading nature's forms transcendentally—his efforts, that is, always to track the relationship between the inner and outer world—and never does he lose sight of what we might call the spiritual dimensions of the natural world and his place in it. Science does concern him in his later years, apparently more than ever before, but never to the exclusion of the life of the spirit. Furthermore, as I will now demonstrate, the late journal is hardly the exclusive preserve of empirical fact and scientific investigation it has sometimes been taken to be, nor does it manifest any great regard for the scientific project in and of itself.

"Say's I to My-self"

Sounding the late journal for its religious dimensions has a bearing on another critical position that has received significant support in recent years. From the time of its first appearance, critics have marveled at the massiveness of this journal and the painstaking devotion with which it was kept for twenty-four years. The question of course is why. Why did a writer as ambitious as Thoreau apparently was for a wider readership consign so much of his literary energy and mature reflection to the apparent oblivion of a private journal? Various responses to this question have been proposed. Recently, several critics have championed the at first surprising thesis that the journal was not intended to be "private" at all— or at least that Thoreau had ulterior designs for it, hoping that someday, perhaps after his death, it would in fact be published. There is something to be said for this view, besides even the virtue of its prescience—if this is what Thoreau thought, then he was right after all. Thoreau was clearly desirous of getting into print; he carefully cultivated the art of writing, and he obviously lavished enormous time and energy on his journal. One appeal of the theory of intended publication is that, in the words of one critic, it makes Thoreau seem less "deranged."[9] But such devotion to journal keeping for its own sake need not seem deranged, if we give fairer consideration to other possible motives. One obvious objection to this theory is that it would indicate a rather breathtaking hubris, even for someone as self-confident as Thoreau, given the challenges he had already faced in the publication of *A Week* and *Walden*, not to speak of the obvious practical difficulties associated with printing and marketing a journal of this sort. It is true that there are passages in the early 1850s where Thoreau does seem to air, to himself at least, the advantages accruing from publication of a journal, but even in such cases he seems merely to be praising the literary merits of the journal form.[10] Elsewhere he eschews publication—and particularly the lobbying efforts of various unnamed friends encouraging him to publish—as alien to his truest vocation and interests. "Say's I to my-self should be the motto of my Journal," he famously wrote in November of 1851 (PJ.4.177). The following passage from 1852 epitomizes what appears to be his overall attitude to the question: "How many there are who advise you to print!— How few who advise you to lead a more interior life! In the one case there is all the world to advise you, in the other there is none to advise you but yourself. Nobody ever advised me not to print but myself. The public persuade the author to print—as the meadow invites the brook to fall into it. Only he can be trusted with gifts who can present a face of bronze to expectations" (PJ.4.453).

As this passage makes clear, the option of not publishing did not strike Thoreau as odd in the least. On the contrary, it held out what was apparently for him the more sane and promising alternative. Coming as it did from a self-proclaimed Transcendentalist, this configuration of the option of not publishing as one between the individual and society, the "interior" versus the worldly way of life, was obviously designed to stack the deck in favor of privacy and suggests how freighted the question of publishing was for him. There was obviously more at stake here. Journalizing, or so this passage suggests, he conceived as an essential expression of his interior life, and exposing it to the dubious motives associated with publication—of fame, fortune, or personal aggrandizement—would be to corrupt its higher spiritual function. Most critics have sensed the essential link between the journal and Thoreau's spiritual life. Recently, Daniel Peck characterized it as part of his "life-long epistemological search."[11] This formulation seems quite apt, so long as we recognize that this lifelong search was never purely philosophical or scientific in the modern senses of those terms. As Nina Baym has shown, during the last ten years of his life, when his ostensible scientific pursuits appeared to be increasing, Thoreau's commitment to science was actually neither unqualified nor uncritical.[12] And even in its driest stretches, the late journal always retains something of its earlier, more explicitly Transcendentalist character.

The concern of the following pages then is to demonstrate that the late journal did not represent a repudiation of the past, but rather an extension and even progression of Thoreau's lifelong spiritual quest. To be sure, this work served Thoreau in various, often scientific ways in these later years, but amidst all these uses, it also continued to function as the chief vehicle and exhibit of his spiritual life. In serving such a purpose, the journal of this period is not different in kind from his own earlier journals, or, for that matter, the introspective journals of previous generations of pious New Englanders who kept such records as a medium of ongoing religious reflection. The difference, however, between these and his earlier journals was that by this point in his life, Thoreau had all but completely abandoned conventional forms of religious or theological reflection. As always, he continued to attend closely to the ebb and flow of his own inner experience, but now the journal came to serve less as an overt expression of the thoughts and feelings to which such observations gave rise than as a kind of spiritual discipline, even at times a mode of meditation, in itself. While increasingly given over to the task of tracking Concord's changing seasons, it also served as the primary vehicle for his continued tracking of the waxing and waning of his own ecstatic experience. At once a phenological journal of the seasons, it was also, as he himself aptly put it, "a meteorological journal of the mind" (PJ.3.377).

One obvious place to begin such an investigation of the function of the journal is with his own expressed comments about it—and there is no dearth of these—though we would be well advised to keep in mind the hazards of interpreting even such apparently proleptic remarks as purely descriptive or programmatic. In general, such passages from the journal are hardly less writerly or self-dramatizing than the more famous writing published in his lifetime. Nevertheless, such passages clearly have some bearing on what Thoreau is setting about here, and for this reason they repay close consideration. In culling these passages from the journal, the first thing in evidence is that they are by no means evenly distributed throughout. Rather, they cluster around two more or less distinct periods—from 1837 till 1841, that is, the period of the early journals, and from late 1850 throughout most of 1852. Between these two periods, that is from the beginning of 1842 till the end of 1850, the journal falls silent about its own status or function, a fact not altogether surprising since this is the decade when journal keeping for its own sake was definitely subordinated to Thoreau's other literary pursuits. Similarly, after 1852 such explicit references to journalizing give way for the most part to the overriding scientific and meditative preoccupations of the late journal.[13] During this later period, practice seems to subsume theory. It is as if by this point in time, Thoreau has become so entirely consumed by the discipline of the journal itself that he finds less value or need in further elaborating his reflections about it.

However discontinuous, these journalistic self-reflections, taken together, provide an invaluable genealogy of the record overall. For the first several months, Thoreau appears to have kept his journal in the manner of a dutiful Transcendentalist acolyte, rather than a seasoned practitioner. It opens in October of 1837 with the famous unattributed questions "What are you doing now? . . . Do you keep a journal?"—which have anecdotally but plausibly been assigned to Emerson—in response to which the twenty-year-old journalist vows, "So I make my first entry today" (PJ.1.5). Just a few months later, however, the journal already betrays misgivings about its own value or adequacy. Under the rubric "What to do," Thoreau writes: "But what does all this scribbling amount to?—What is now scribbled in the heat of the moment one can contemplate with somewhat of satisfaction, but alas! to-morrow—aye to-night— it is stale, flat—and unprofitable—in fine, is not, only its shell remains— like some parboiled lobster shell—which kicked aside never so often still stares at you in the path" (PJ.1.33–34). Despite such early doubts, Thoreau soon got his journalistic bearings and increasingly began to exploit his journal in more constructive and distinctive ways. In this first phase, that is from 1837 till 1841, the self-referential passages depict the journal variously as a literary notebook, a record of observations and insights, a repository of reflections on nature, and a medium for introspection.[14]

During the resurgence of such reflections from 1850 till 1852, it is characterized alternately as a record of fugitive thoughts and feelings, a depository of inspired experiences, a transcript of nature, an encyclopedia of common perceptions and observations, a writer's exercise book, and increasingly, a calendar of seasonal change.[15] Eclipsing all of these characterizations, however, are entries that reflect more broadly on Thoreau's religious motives. A careful reading of these and related passages indicates that, at least in such entries as these reflecting directly on his journalistic enterprise, all other motives are finally related to and often subsumed within his ongoing spiritual exercises. This is not to argue for some monolithic view of the journal or some unanimity in its function; on the contrary, it is important to acknowledge that Thoreau's journal at all times served multiple roles and a variety of functions. Generalizing about the journal is at best a hazardous enterprise, and at worst a foolishly constricted one. What we need to recognize, though, and what these self-reflections demonstrate, is that at no time in Thoreau's life was his journal without a central spiritual dimension. To take this a step further: more than any other document in the corpus of Thoreau's writings, the journal served as the principal medium of his spiritual life. How it did so and what it tells us of the unconventional nature of Thoreau's religious experience and sensibility can best be fathomed by considering more carefully three essential ways in which this journal functioned religiously—as a record of spiritual experiences and growth, as a medium in which to read and reflect upon the spiritual meanings of nature, and as a meditative practice in its own right.

Ebbs and Flows of the Soul

As early as the summer of 1840, Thoreau had already begun to conceive his journal along the lines of a spiritual diary. This is the first recognizably religious use to which he makes reference in characterizing the journal, and in doing so, he suggests its basic kinship with the spiritual autobiographies and journals of New England's Puritans. The keeping of journals was a common practice among New Englanders, both in earlier periods and his own day, and these writings served a wide variety of uses. From an early time, some of these journals were kept as a form of religious introspection and theological reflection. As we have seen, Thoreau had little use for the theological terminology and patterns of faith characteristic of anguished Puritan self-examination, opting instead for a vocabulary of natural piety and reverence for nature, but this particular way of utilizing his journal was conventional nonetheless. Here in this first such reference, an older form of disciplined observance characteristic of Puritan spiritual diaries is still partly visible beneath the diction of natural religion.

> Have no mean hours, but be grateful for every hour, and accept what it brings. The reality will make any sincere record respectable. No day will have been wholly misspent, if one sincere thoughtful page has been written.
>
> Let the daily tide leave some deposit on these pages, as it leaves sand and shells on the shore. So much increase of *terra firma*. This may be a calendar of the ebbs and flows of the soul; and on these sheets as a beach, the waves may cast up pearls and seaweed. (PJ.1.151)

Signalled already in this early passage are several of the features characteristic of the later journal: its encyclopedic scope, its preoccupation with natural observation, and its attentiveness to writing as an index of personal experience. Especially suggestive is the fusion, through the metaphorical vehicle of the "daily tide," of spiritual experience and natural observation. By this time already, it seems, the journal is being conceived in a spiritual and natural sense simultaneously. Above all though, it appears to function here as a record of passing experience—"the ebbs and flows of the soul." While Thoreau's subsequent journalizing became more nuanced and resourceful, it never abandoned this basic purpose.[16]

More suggestive of the religious ways in which he tended to conceive the early journal is the following allusion to writing as a sacrificial act, entered in the winter of 1841: "We should offer up our *perfect* thoughts to the gods daily—our writing should be hymns and psalms. Who keeps a journal is a purveyor for the Gods. There are two sides to every sentence; the one is contiguous to me, but the other faces the gods, and no man ever fronted it. When I utter a thought I launch a vessel which never sails in my haven more, but goes sheer off into the deep. Consequently it demands a godlike insight—a fronting view, to read what was greatly written" (PJ.1.220). It is hard to know how seriously to take this some-what fanciful conceit of journalistic writing as an esoteric form of communication with the gods. Its conception of writing as a divine offering appears to owe more to Thoreau's interest in ancient Greek and Vedic sacrificial religion than to anything in his own Protestant heritage. Yet there is certainly precedent in Western religion for conceiving such soulful writing as a form of prayer or praise, and it would not be going too far to see such entries as an extension of this broader tradition of Christian piety.

But this formulation also contains a more recognizably Thoreauvian signature in its sense of the numinous power of the act of literary creation and its conception of the double-sidedness of inspired speech. Here again we see the disjunctiveness characteristic of Thoreau's religious imagination: he conceives his journal as facing in two directions at once, toward heaven and back to earth. That he found something quite meaningful in this explicitly religious conception of his journal is made apparent from the way in which he elaborated upon it several weeks later:

> My Journal is that of me which would else spill over and run to waste.—gleanings from the field which in action I reap. I must not live for it, but in it for the gods—They are my correspondent to whom daily I send off this sheet postpaid. I am clerk in their counting room and at evening transfer the account from day-book to ledger.
>
> It is as a leaf which hangs over my head in the path—I bend the twig and write my prayers on it then letting it go the bough springs up and shows the scrawl to heaven. As if it were not kept shut in my desk—but were as public a leaf as any in nature—it is papyrus

by the river side—it is vellum in the pastures—it is parchment on
the hills—I find it every where as free as the leaves which troop
along the lanes in autumn—The crow—the goose—the eagle—
carry my quill—and the wind blows the leaves—as far as I go—Or
if my imagination does not soar, but gropes in slime and mud—
then I write with a reed. (PJ.1.259)

In figuring the act of writing in such evocatively naturalistic terms—
playing, for example, on the homology between the leaf of paper at his
writing desk and the bending leaf on which he would write his prayers—
this passage once again anticipates the journal's later tendency to fuse
ever more closely the act of writing with the act of natural creation. Yet
the conception of journal writing as a form of at least incipient dialogue
or communion illustrated by both of these passages appears not wholly
adventitious. Another expression of it occurs around the same time,
though in a more credible and perhaps recognizable form: "Good writing," Thoreau wrote in January 1841, "as well as good acting will be
obedience to conscience. There must not be a particle of will or whim
mixed with it.—If we can listen we shall hear. By reverently listening to
the inner voice, we may reinstate ourselves on the pinnacle of humanity"
(PJ.1.233). While the concern of this passage is the nature and mechanics of good writing, not its religious motives or objectives, it also
tends to conceive of such writing as an act of communion, only in this
case not some paganlike communion with the gods above, but a more
Quaker- and Transcendentalist-like communion with the god within.
While it would be overstating the case to see these passages as a form of
worship, they at least dramatize the journal's indispensable function as a
vehicle of self-recollection.

Elsewhere, and with increasing frequency amid the deepening elegiac
mood of later years, such journal passages highlight memory itself as a
cardinal faculty of Thoreau's spiritual life. One early expression of the
growing centrality of memory occurs in the journal of 1842:

My path hitherto has been like a road through a diversified
country, now climbing high mountains then descending into the

lowest vales. From the summits I saw the heavens—from the vales I looked up to the heights again.

In prosperity I remember God—or memory is one with consciousness—in adversity I remember my own elevations, and only hope to see God again. (PJ.1.368)

The starkly visual character of the simile that Thoreau uses to figure his life's experience—"a road through a diversified country"—typifies the spatial character of memory itself. But the emphasis here on seeing also makes it clear that he is construing memory more in the vertical, noetic sense employed by Plato, as a "recollection" *(anamnesis)* or knowledge of the soul's higher station, than as remembering in the more conventional sense of the term. In appropriating the religious sense of remembering as a form of spiritual knowledge—"I remember God"—he is quick to make clear that "memory is one with consciousness." Memory in this sense is not an indirect or retrospective form of knowledge but a direct experience of reality.

It is important to acknowledge the spiritual dimensions of such early treatments of memory because they help us to appreciate the fuller resonance of the more poignantly elegiac formulations of the early 1850s. The following related passage from the summer of 1850 might well serve as an emblem of this dimension of Thoreau's religious thought and his spiritual life as a whole: "The life in us is like the water in the river, it may rise this year higher than ever it was known to before and flood the uplands—even this may be the eventful year—& drown out all our muskrats There are as many strata at different levels of life as there are leaves in a book Most men probably have lived in two or three. When on the higher levels we can remember the lower levels, but when on the lower we cannot remember the higher" (PJ.3.84).

How in the world to "remember" higher consciousness from the vantage point of waking experience is an old problem among poets and mystics; in losing the experience, they apparently lose the means of recalling it also. Thoreau himself often wrestled with this problem and struggled at points to turn his journal into a medium for such recollection. Here, together with the ordinary details of his daily experience, he sought to record the most exceptional experiences of his life. But it was one thing to announce the intention to record such exalted experiences and another to capture them effectively in words. At certain points, the journal exhibits gaps, incongruities, or dislocations, symptomatic apparently of its constant and not always successful efforts to find verbal equivalents for experiences of unusual intensity or transport. In November of 1850, for example, he sets out the following lofty objective: "My Journal should be the record of my love. I would write in it only of the things I love. My affection for any aspect of the world. What I love to think of." Yet when he begins to contemplate the meaning of this term in more detail, he can only concede, "I have no more distinctness or pointedness in my yearnings than an expanding bud—which does indeed point to flower & fruit to summer & autumn—but is aware of the warm sun & spring influence only" (PJ.3.143). The characterization he offered of the journal two years later was even more pointed: "A Journal.—a book that shall contain a record of all your joy—your extacy" (PJ.5.219). The proleptic character of this anouncement would lead us to expect some ostensible expressions of ecstasy in the subsequent entry, but oddly there seem to be none. Instead, we are treated to a detailed and fairly prosaic inventory of natural observations made at a Concord woodlot. Apparently this disjunction in the passage simply represents a break in Thoreau's thought. Yet, as I will suggest further on, closer study of the evolution of his journalistic strategies at this time also suggests that he conceived the detailed inventory itself as the predicate or illustration of the opening declaration—that is, that in such close apprehension of natural life ecstasy everywhere resides.

Whatever the case in this instance, the journals of this period are by no means always so reticent about this aspect of their concern. The following passage, from September 7, 1851, amplifies upon the Wordsworthian strain of the passage from July 16 with which I began this study and offers one of the most revealing glimpses we have into the inner workings of this journal:

Our extatic states which appear to yield so little fruit, have this value at least—though in the seasons when our genius reigns we may be powerless for expression.—Yet in calmer seasons, when our talent is active, the memory of those rarer moods comes to color our picture & is the permanent paint-pot as it were into which we dip our brush.

Thus no life or experience goes unreported at last—but if it be not solid gold it is gold-leaf which gilds the furniture of the mind. It is an experience of infinite beauty—on which we unfailingly draw. Which enables us to exaggerate ever truly. Our moments of inspiration are not lost though we have no particular poem to show for them. For those experiences have left an indelible impression, and we are ever and anon reminded of them. Their truth subsides & in cooler moments we can use them as paint to gild & adorn our prose. When I despair to sing them I will remember that they will furnish me with paint with which to adorn & preserve the works of talent one day. They are like a pot of pure ether.

They lend the writer when the moment comes a certain superfluity of wealth—making his expression to overrun & float itself. It is the difference between our river now parched & dried up, exposing its unsightly & weedy bottom—& the same when in the spring it covers all the meads with a chain of placid lakes, reflecting the forests & the skies. (PJ.4.51–52)

In returning here to a natural metaphor to conceptualize the ebb and flow of his ecstatic experience, Thoreau once again shows how closely associated were for him the tides of inner and outer reality. As this lengthy journal entry proceeds, he leaves no doubt as to how much his natural observations were motivated by an uncompromisingly religious quest. Paraphrasing Paul's letter to the Thessalonians, he compares his meditations in nature to unceasing prayer and religious vigil: "The art of spending a day. If it is possible that we may be addressed—it behoves us to be attentive. If by watching all day & all night—I may detect some trace of the Ineffable—then will it not be worth the while to watch?

Watch & pray without ceasing—but not in sadness—be of good cheer."[17] Further on he makes the point more memorably: "My profession is to be always on the alert to find God in nature—to know his lurking places. To attend all the oratorios—the operas in nature" (PJ.4.53–55).

If the remarkable passage from September above defines the nature of Thoreau's religious "profession," this entry from the following January shows us the indispensable role played in this profession by the journal: "Certainly it is a distinct profession to rescue from oblivion & to fix the sentiments & thoughts which visit all men more or less generally. That the contemplation of the unfinished picture may suggest its harmonious completion. Associate reverently, and as much as you can with your loftiest thoughts. Each thought that is welcomed and recorded is a nest egg—by the side of which more will be laid. Thoughts accidentally thrown together become a frame—in which more may be developed—& exhibited. Perhaps this is the main value of a habit of writing—of keeping a journal. That so we remember our best hours—& stimulate ourselves" (PJ.4.277).

What the passages collected above all share is a conception of the journal as a kind of record or medium of extraordinary experience. This is not its only function, of course, not even in the area of religious expression, but it is the most readily recognizable. The emphasis paid here to preservation points to the primacy of memory in these pages. As we have witnessed, now repeatedly, memory, particularly the sort of recollection in tranquility glorified by Wordsworth, served as one of the mainsprings of Thoreau's spiritual life. In the early years, and especially during the exhilarating months of the summer of 1851, memory by itself conferred a kind of gnosis, to some extent calling up directly the blissful states he treasured from the past. With the passage of years, however, these experiences no longer visited him as often or as memorably as they once did. At this point, the journal takes on new urgency as a memorial, to which he could return for nourishment, of those exalted states from which he felt himself increasingly receding. In late January of 1852, we have the most dramatic expression yet of this growing premonition of spiritual dryness:

If thou art a writer write as if thy time was short—for it is indeed short at the longest. Improve each occasion when thy soul is reached—drain the cup of inspiration to its last dregs—fear no intemperance in that. for the years will come when otherwise thou wilt regret opportunities unimproved. The spring will not last forever. These fertile & expanding seasons of thy life—when the rain reaches thy root—when thy vigor shoots when thy flower is budding—shall be fewer & farther between. Again I say remember thy creator in the days of thy youth. Use & commit to life what you cannot commit to memory. I hear the tones of my sister's piano below. It reminds me of strains which once I heard more frequently—when possessed with the inaudible rhythm I sought my chamber in the cold—& communed with my own thoughts. I feel as if I then received the gifts of the gods with too much indifference—Why did I not cultivate those fields they introduced me to? Does nothing withstand the inevitable march of time? Why did I not use my eyes when I stood on Pisgah? Now I hear those strains but seldom—My rhythmical mood does not endure—I cannot draw from it—& return to it in my thought as to a well—all the evening or the morning—I cannot dip my pen in it. I cannot work the vein it is so fine & volatile—Ah sweet ineffable reminiscences. (PJ.4.281–82)

If by early 1852 Thoreau could no longer draw as directly on the experiences of spontaneous ecstasy enjoyed in his youth, he could still do so indirectly through the medium of the journal. In this way alone, therefore, the journal assumed, if anything, increasing spiritual importance to him in later years. But the main lesson to him of the gradual recession of spontaneous ecstasy, as this entry suggests, was to shake him from his spiritual complacency and force upon him recognition of the need to cultivate more deliberately his finer insights and experience. This preoccupation with the cultivation of ecstatic vision amounted in his later life to a kind of spiritual discipline that he pursued primarily through the medium of the journal.

A Book of the Seasons

The profession "to find God in nature" that Thoreau described so evocatively in 1851 apparently represents no great departure from Transcendentalist thought and practice. Any of several other members of the movement might well have characterized his or her spiritual vocation in just this way. It is particularly reminiscent of some of Emerson's own formulations, particularly from *Nature,* his first book, which had an early and formative influence on Thoreau. According to the hierarchical progression Emerson laid out there, nature benefited human beings in several indispensable ways, but its highest uses were religious, even redemptive. From the standpoint of "Language," it was to serve above all as "the symbol of spirit."[18] Behind Emerson's conception of nature as a symbol stood the Swedenborgian visions of the correspondential relationship between the world of spirit and the world of matter, and even to some extent the older medieval notion of "the book of nature" as a kind of prototype or harbinger to the book of revelation constituted by the Christian Bible. Transcendentalists of Emerson's radical ilk no longer regarded the book of nature as preliminary to anything, including Christian Scripture; it was absolutely sufficient and divinely inspired in its own right. But the implication of all such conceptions of nature as a book, especially as a book of revelation, was that, like any book, it must be properly read to be properly understood. For Transcendentalists, indeed, it demanded the most assiduous of readings. Thoreau's own concern to read nature rightly, even, as he notes in 1851, to "detect some trace of the Ineffable," obviously owes something to these older theological conceptions of nature as a scriptural text. More even than his Transcendentalist friends, he was fascinated by the apparent textuality of natural forms—of cracks in the ice, veins on a leaf, or patterns caused by the erosions of a spring thaw. This was the language he most wished to learn, the text he most wished to decipher. Even as late as 1853, it was still typical for him to conceive of nature in this way: "Better learn this strange character which nature speaks to-day than the Sanscrit," he wrote, "Books in the brooks" (J.5.28).

Yet in the process of assuming Emerson's correspondential view of nature, Thoreau also drastically revised and extended it. "Is not Nature, rightly read, that of which she is commonly taken to be the symbol merely?" he quipped in *A Week* (382). It is a commonplace of criticism that with the passing of time, Thoreau became increasingly disenchanted with the sort of armchair Transcendentalism practiced by his famous neighbor and distrustful of his penchant for conceiving natural phenomena too impetuously according to a priori religious or philosophical categories. Nowhere is such suspicion more evident than in his attitude toward Transcendentalist-inspired correspondential readings of nature. Conceiving nature according to the analogy afforded by the book only served to place it in yet another straitjacket of human devising. Thoreau always believed devoutly in the ulterior meaningfulness of natural forms, but he became increasingly doubtful that he or anyone else had the means to fully understand them. As he, and for that matter Emerson also, increasingly recognized, correspondential readings implied a stability utterly foreign to the natural world itself. In a journal entry from May of 1841, Thoreau reflects on notes of an oven bird heard on the horizon and a chewink across the marsh. The impression conveyed by these experiences is one of eternal newness and transiency, not fixity, arrangement, and order. Books should be modeled on nature, not the other way around, he suggests, implicitly reversing the older theological vision: "There is always a later edition of every book than the printer wots of—no matter how recently it was published.—All nature is a new impression every instant" (PJ.1.310). Such impressions he obviously took very much to heart, not only in his philosophical musings, but also in his literary practice. For the attentive student of nature, lessons drawn from the art of reading must soon carry over to the craft of writing. To be worthy of nature, Thoreau believed, his own writing must in some sense reproduce nature's expressive strategies.

This, after all, was the imperative driving the remarkable preoccupation with organic literary form that I considered in the last chapter. That literary art should be modeled upon the organic forms and phenomena of nature was an article of faith among many Romantic writers, but

Thoreau pursued this conviction to astonishing extremes, particularly in his efforts to trace English words to their archaic etymological roots. Even in its earliest phase, the journal witnesses to Thoreau's efforts to find analogies for his own writing, particularly his journal writing, in terms offered by the natural world. When in the passage cited above from February 1841 he imagines his daily journal entries as "prayers" and a "scrawl to heaven," he conveys them in a sheaf of nature's own stationary, "a leaf as any in nature—it is papyrus by the river side—it is vellum in the pastures—it is parchment on the hills" (PJ.1.259). However fanciful such passages, they suggest that even early in his career, Thoreau played with the organicist conceit that one could in some sense adopt nature's idioms and language as one's own. But for him it was apparently not enough merely to analogize. As he rededicated himself to his journalizing in the early fifties, he looked for ways to pursue this ambition even further. He conceived the journal no longer simply as a record of his own observations and experiences in nature, but increasingly as a kind of literary transcript or verbal facsimile of nature itself—or rather, to be more precise, of the impressions created in consciousness by encounters with natural phenomena. The goal now was not simply to record and comment upon natural facts in the manner of a scientific observer, but also to reflect, without distorting, the *experience* of encountering those facts in their native settings. Before 1851 or so, it is as if the journal subordinated nature to Thoreau's own agendas and desires, whereas after 1851, all this becomes subordinated to nature for its own sake. The journalist now looked to nature as a good in and for itself, without reference to his own speculative designs upon it.

This fundamental reorientation of the journal from personal record to a sort of transcript of nature has obvious scientific advantages in that it helps to ensure a more objective reading of the facts, but it is enforced by a more basic alteration in Thoreau's spiritual relationship to nature. The key to nature in both a scientific and a religious sense, the late journal seems to suggest, is to let nature, so far as possible, "speak" for itself, without the interference of personal interest or gain. Suspicious of the inevitably mediatory and obfuscatory effects of language, particularly as they had been manifest in his journal up till this time, Thoreau now opts for a more direct, less artful, and more minimalist approach to his journalistic style. The passage cited above from January of 1852, in which he speculates on the advantages of publishing such a record, speaks favorably of this new mode of journal writing as more worthy of his object. In this more open-ended form, his thoughts are "allied to life—& are seen by the reader not to be far fetched—It is more simple—less artful— . . . Mere facts & names & dates communicate more than we suspect." As if to sum up the implications of this meditation on the new journal style, he writes in his next day's entry: "Perhaps I can never find so good a setting for my thoughts as I shall thus have taken them out of" (PJ.4.296). In view of such characterizations, the discontinuous structure and style of the late journal may be seen as a deliberate, even perhaps programmatic, effort to let natural phenomena, as it were, represent themselves in a mode more natural to them. Gone are the topical and thematic essays of the early journal, the poetry and the literariness. Instead, the late journal is more unstructured, fragmentary, particularistic, and elliptical. Some entries sheer close to the discursive experience of a walk or a meditation; others consist of a series of discontinuous observations or lists of facts. Everywhere, however, the late journal tends to foreground natural objects, while at the same time bracketing or marginalizing the writer's personal reactions or judgments. As a rule, Thoreau also avoids earlier tendencies to anthropomorphize nature; indeed, the journal of this period has a conspicuously antimetaphysical, antiformalist, and antitheoretic cast.[19] Above all, and increasingly with the passage of years, the journal seems to take upon itself the task of tracking and tabulating Concord's seasonal change in a role reminiscent of the meteorological almanacs of an earlier period.[20] This new role Thoreau anticipates in this suggestive note from his journal of June 11, 1851: "A Book of the seasons—each page of which should be written in its own season & out of doors or in its own locality wherever it may be—" (PJ.3.253). The literary goal in all this was to make himself a faithful copyist of nature so as to reproduce in some sense the open-ended, unbounded, and spontaneous character of nature's actual self-presentation.

"A writer a man writing," he wrote in September of 1851, "is the scribe of all nature—he is the corn & the grass & the atmosphere writing" (PJ.4.28). But to impersonate nature in this way also served the religious motive of closing the gap between the man and the objects of his greatest veneration.

Yet, for all Thoreau's efforts to place nature at the center of his journal, it is crucial to point out that he never wished to highlight facts for their own sake, especially not purely scientific facts. While taking issue with the Transcendental vaporizing to which his friend Ellery Channing sometimes gave vent, he would not wish to deny his own interest in the spiritual implications of his scientific researches. "I too would fain set down something beside facts," he wrote in November of 1851: "Facts should only be as the frame to my pictures—They should be material to the mythology which I am writing. Not facts to assist men to make money—farmers to farm profitably in any common sense. . . . My facts shall all be falsehoods to the common sense. I would so state facts that they shall be significant shall be myths or mythologic. Facts which the mind perceived—thoughts which the body thought with these I deal—I too cherish vague & misty forms—vaguest when the cloud at which I gaze is dissipated quite & nought but the skyey depths are seen" (PJ.4.170–71). As this passage suggests, notwithstanding his distrust of overeager Romantic effusions, he never entirely abandoned the symbolical view of nature he so often entertained as a Transcendentalist neophyte. Witnessing the sunset on Christmas Day 1851, he is reminded once again how impoverishing is a strictly scientific viewpoint: "In a winter day the sun is almost all in all. I witness a beauty in the form or coloring of the clouds which addresses itself to my imagination—for which you account scientifically to my understanding—but do not so account to my imagination. It is what it suggests & is the symbol of that I care for—and if by any trick of science you rob it of its symbolicalness you do me no service & explain nothing" (PJ.4.221–22). It is mistaken to assume, as some proponents of the decline theory have done, that Thoreau's interests in scientific facts and spiritual experience were divergent and in some way necessarily incompatible. On the contrary, it is important to emphasize that in his case, these were mutually enriching preoccupations. Thoreau's spiritual quest fed his interest in natural facts, and his interest in natural facts intensified his spiritual yearning. Actually one of the chief catalysts of the rededication of the journal in the early fifties may well have been the interlude of ecstatic experience from the spring and summer of 1851. The symbiotic character of this relationship is not always apparent from individual journal entries, particularly in the more understated treatment of the late journal, but sometimes the connection is quite obvious. The following passage from the winter of 1852 highlights the interpenetration of contemplative and scientific tendencies characteristic of Thoreau's attitude to nature, early and late: "In proportion as I have celestial thoughts, is the necessity for me to be out and behold the western sky before sunset these winter days. That is the symbol of the unclouded mind that knows neither winter nor summer. What is your thought like? That is the hue—that the purity & transparency and distance from earthly taint of my inmost mind—for whatever we see without is a symbol of something within—& that which is farthest off—is the symbol of what is deepest within. The lover of contemplation accordingly will gaze much into the sky.—Fair thoughts & serene mind make fair days" (PJ.4.263). Thoreau's appeal to the mathematical diction of "proportion" and "necessity" exemplifies the interdependent relationship, in his life more generally, between the contemplative and the scientific: here he highlights the "celestial" motivation for this particular excursion and the meditation to which it gave rise. In fact, even when the record becomes concertedly less expressive of the subjective moods and emotions accompanying natural observations, there is little reason to doubt the mixture of admiration and delight with which such encounters were generally greeted. "How sweet is the perception of a new natural fact!" he exclaims in the spring of 1852, "—suggesting what worlds remain to be unveiled. That phenomenon of the Andromeda seen against the sun cheers me exceedingly When the phenomenon was not observed—It was not—at all. I think that no man ever takes an original or detects a principle without experiencing an inexpressible as quite infinite & sane pleasure which advertises him of the dignity of that truth he has perceived" (PJ.4.471). The rapturous tone of this passage reminds us of the ecstatic elegies of youth from the previous summer, but it plainly arises here in part from what Thoreau clearly perceives as the numinous character—suggesting depths of reality yet unplumbed—of the Andromeda against the sun.

As this passage makes clear, it is not the Andromeda shrubs in themselves he finds so fascinating but their *relationship* to him. He seems fascinated above all by the nature and implications of human perception. Often Thoreau was quite critical of scientific observation, in fact, as yielding so little by way of real human fruit. "The intellect of most men is barren," he wrote the previous summer. "They neither fertilize nor are fertilized. It is the marriage of the soul with nature that makes the intellect fruitful—that gives birth to imagination" (PJ.4.3–4). Thoreau could not let go of the primacy of the natural fact, but neither would he lose sight of its nonmaterial significance. "The sight of a sucker floating on the meadow" in April of 1852 helps him to realize the archetypal "*idea* of a fish," he says, and fills his head with a host of related mythological fishlike images. According to this view, when the imagination itself begins to spawn, the fish seen in a meadow begins to realize its fuller promise: this, he notes, is the "moral" of the observation, a glimpse into its fuller significance. In the commentary subsequent to this curious observation, Thoreau forecasts what was to become the late journal's leading preoccupation—to minutely track and document the seasonal changes associated with each passing year. But as this anticipation makes clear, for him the value of even such an ambitiously empirical project resides finally at the interface between the natural world and human consciousness. In charting the circle of the seasons, such a calendar must also encompass and reflect the questioning mind.

> For the first time I perceive this spring that the year is a circle—I see distinctly the spring arc thus far. It is drawn with a firm line. Every incident is a parable of the great teacher. The cranberries washed up in the meadows & into the road on the causeways now yields a pleasant acid.

Why should just these sights & sounds accompany our life? Why should I hear the chattering of blackbirds—why smell the skunk each year? I would fain explore the mysterious relation between myself & these things. I would at least know what these things unavoidably are—make a chart of our life—know how its shores trend—that butterflies reappear & when—know why just this circle of creatures completes the world. Can I not by expectation affect the revolutions of nature—make a day to bring forth something new? (PJ.4.468)

Clearly fueling the ambition sketched here of keeping track of different aspects of seasonal change is Thoreau's fascination with their "mysterious relation" to him. "Why should just these sights & sounds accompany our life?" is the essential question, after all, driving so much of his exploration of nature.

Such questions also shed light on his preoccupation, especially apparent in the several years prior to the publication of *Walden,* with reflection and the reflecting properties of neighborhood lakes and streams. As we have seen, he characteristically invested such pond- or riverside "reflections" with important religious and philosophical import. In the entry from November 9, 1851, shortly after the jubilee of inspiration of the preceding summer, he is at it once again, this time in response to his observations at a "retired pond" owned by James Brown. Concluding his entry, he notes, "These reflections suggest that the sky underlies the hills as well as overlies them, and in another sense than in appearance." The recognition of the relative and contingent nature of the observed phenomenon represents to him an important philosophical lesson; it constitutes, he notes further, "a permanent piece of idealism" (PJ.4.171). It is clear then, from these and other passages from the journals of the 1850s, that Thoreau's preoccupation with natural observations in his later years was neither a reaction to nor compensation for some presumed spiritual disillusionment that occurred about this time. It is true that the ecstasies of his youth visited him less often and with less intensity after 1850 or so, but his recognition of this gradual diminution, and the pangs of loss that accompanied it, actually served to revitalize his ambition, as he professed it in 1851, "to find God in nature," and to heighten his appreciation of the value and possibilities of spiritual insight.

A True Sauntering of the Eye

To see the journal as a record of ecstatic experience or as a medium through which to revere nature alone suggests the important spiritual role it played in Thoreau's later adult life, but these uses do not by themselves give us the whole story. They have little apparent relationship, first of all, to the curiously disconnected and laconic form that dominates the journal after the watershed period we have been considering. The usual view of this altered form is that it was employed by Thoreau as a fitter vehicle for his scientific investigations—and in part so it was. But a closer inspection of many of even the most empirically oriented entries suggests another interpretation, especially in light of Thoreau's preoccupation elsewhere with refined and altered perception—namely, that the late journal was deliberately conceived and zealously kept as a vehicle of meditation. And here I mean the term not in the conventional literary sense, but in something like the sense it has in certain texts of Wordsworth and the Indian philosophers, where it signifies a form of contemplative practice.

Typifying one characteristic mode of journalistic meditation is the following passage, from the long entry of June 13, 1851, introduced at the start of this study, describing in evocative detail the moonlit walk he had taken to Walden Pond the previous night.

As I approached the pond down hubbard's path (after coming out of the woods into a warmer air) I saw the shimmering of the moon on its surface—and in the near now flooded cove the water-bugs darting circling about made streaks or curves of light. The moon's inverted pyramid of shimmering light commenced about 20 rods off—like so much micaceous sand—But I was startled to see midway in the dark water a bright flame like more than phosphorescent light crowning the crests of the wavelets which at first I

mistook for fire flies & thought even of cucullos—It had the appearance of a pure smokeless flame ½ dozen inches long issuing
from the water & bending flickeringly along its surface—I thought
of St Elmo's lights & the like—but coming near to the shore of the
pond itself—these flames increased & I saw that it was so many
broken reflections of the moon's disk, though one would have said
they were of an intenser light than the moon herself—from contrast with the surrounding water they were—Standing up close to
the shore & nearer the rippled surface I saw the reflections of the
moon sliding down the watery concave like so many lustrous bur-
nished coins poured from a bag—with inexhaustible lavishness—
& the lambent flames on the surface were much multiplied seeming to slide along a few inches with each wave before they were
extinguished—& I saw how farther & farther off they gradually
merged in the general sheen which in fact was made up of a myriad
little mirrors reflecting the disk of the moon—with equal bright-
ness to an eye rightly placed. The pyramid or sheaf of light which
we see springing from near where we stand only—in fact is the
outline of that portion of the shimmering surface which an eye
takes in—to myriad eyes suitably placed, the whole surface of the
pond would be seen to shimmer, or rather it would be seen as the
waves turned up their mirrors to be covered with those bright
flame like reflections of the moon's disk like a myriad candles every
where issuing from the waves—i.e. if there were as many eyes as
angles presented by the waves—and these reflections are dispersed
in all directions into the atmosphere flooding it with light—
(PJ.3.262–63)

The preoccupation with watery reflections illustrated once again here
obviously places this passage among the reflective meditations that were
so central to Thoreau's contemplative experience. But in contrast to
other such passages, particularly those from earlier periods, this one
is much more committedly naturalistic and nonphilosophical. Thoreau
strictly confines himself to a minute description of the lavish play of

moonlight on the broken surface of the pond and provides no explicit information about the effects of this stunning display upon him. Yet his vivid description of the phenomenon, together with the highly charged tone, diction, and figuration of the passage—his use, for example, of such passages as "inexhaustible lavishness," "myriad little mirrors," "shimmering surface," et cetera—leave little doubt that the experience filled him with admiration and delight, and perhaps even induced in him something like the ecstasy that he often recalled over the course of these heady weeks. Our sense of the richness and power of the experience is, if anything, heightened by the author's refusal to say anything directly about how it made him feel. This concern to understate or even bracket subjective feelings increasingly comes to characterize the meditative entries of the late journal. In this regard, however, this particular passage may be seen as somewhat transitional, since although Thoreau never seeks to characterize his subjective experiences directly, he makes it abundantly clear that the light show on the Pond's surface is thoroughly embedded in them. The description, after all, is punctuated by references to the first-person point of view—"I saw," "I was startled," "I mistook," "I thought," et cetera—though for the most part, the subject's action and his mediation is limited to sight. By the end, his eyes, and indeed his imagination, become glutted with light. Thoreau's apparent concern here, therefore, is not so much to provide an objective description of moonlight on water but a phenomenological description of the *experience* of moonlight on water. His decision to dwell on this particular episode from his walk is instructive, since the phenomenon he describes here would be in a strict sense nonexistent were it not for the specific participation and positioning of the contemplative witness. As we ourselves know from similar experiences, such shimmering displays on water appear to depend completely on the position and even existence of the observer. Despite the author's overall commitment in this passage to a subjectively understated style, the implications of the integral role of the seer in the phenomenon are clearly not lost to him. In fact, it is precisely his recognition of the constitutive role played by the eye that serves as the point of entry for the imagined ecstatic vision of the entire surface of the Pond as a flood of light: "to myriad eyes suitably placed, the whole surface of the pond would be seen to shimmer . . . like a myriad candles every where issuing from the waves." Such a total vision of light, which from the lake's glittering surface the naturalist can readily imagine, depends entirely upon the maximization of consciousness, figured here as an infinite proliferation of eyes. Thus, while Thoreau himself takes pains in this passage not to intrude on his account, the meditation follows the logic of his experience and moves speculatively in the direction of greater perception, a more awakened consciousness.

The euphoric moonlight excursions from the summer of 1851, of which the above passage is one of the most dazzling expressions, illustrate a second key feature of the meditative mode of the late journal. These are above all what I would call walking meditations, which characteristically take the form of an excursion in the woods or pastureland surrounding Concord. Of course, Thoreau was drawn to the excursion mode and travel narrative throughout his literary career, as was noted in the discussion of his first book. But he selected this form for several of his other works as well, from *Maine Woods* and *Cape Cod* to such shorter works as "A Walk to Wachusett," "A Winter Walk," "Night and Moonlight," and of course "Walking" (Writings.5). In the late journal, however, the literary expression of Thoreau's by now almost daily or nightly excursions assumes a much less artful, more unprepossessing character. These narratives are typically rich in detail and observations, but thin in subjective self-reflection. The preponderance of this form in the journals of the period suggests this choice was not a matter of mere literary, or even scientific, convenience. The main advantage of the excursion form was that it imposed itself so minimally, and so seemingly innocently, on the experiences and observations recorded. Indeed, it was a form that in a sense mimicked the discursive nature of experience itself, as writers, religious and otherwise, have realized for some time. The following passage from "A Walk to Wachusett" reminds us of nothing so much as *Pilgrim's Progress:* "There is, however, this consolation to the most wayworn traveler, upon the dustiest road, that the path his feet describe is so perfectly symbolical of human life,—now climbing the hills, now descending into the vales. From the summits he beholds the heavens and the horizon, from the vales he looks up to the heights again. He is treading his old lessons still, and though he may be very weary and travel-worn, it is yet sincere experience" (Writings.5.150–51).[21] For its part, the journal makes clear what an essential role his excursions played in his spiritual and artistic life. The walks served both to inspire and to epitomize his life's most fruitful experiences: "How vain it is to sit down to write when you have not stood up to live! Methinks that the moment my legs begin to move my thoughts begin to flow—as if I had given vent to the stream at the lower end & consequently new fountains flowed into it at the upper. A thousand rills which have their rise in the sources of thought—burst forth & fertilise my brain. you need to increase the draught below—as the owners of meadows on C. river say of the Billerica Dam. Only while we are in action is the circulation perfect. The writing which consists with habitual sitting is mechanical wooden dull to read" (PJ.3.378–79). A kind of formless form, the excursion mode serves almost invisibly in the later journal to frame and foreground Thoreau's experience without calling much attention to itself. During this period, the form's intrinsic literary or psychological significance generally passes without comment or reflection, but the following more fanciful, albeit transitional passage, again from the summer of 1851, indicates the allegorical way in which, when so inclined, Thoreau was apt to conceive his walks:

Now I yearn for one of those old meandering dry uninhabited roads which lead away from towns—which lead us away from temptation, which conduct to the outside of earth—over its uppermost crust—where you may forget in what country you are travelling—where no farmer can complain that you are treading down his grass—no gentleman who has recently constructed a seat in the country that you are trespassing—on which you can go off at half cock—and waive adieu to the village—along which you may travel like a pilgrim—going nowither. Where travellers are not too often to be met. Where my spirit is free—where the walls & fences are not cared for—where your head is more in heaven than your feet are on earth—which have long reaches—where you can see the approaching traveller half a mile off and be prepared for him—not so luxuriant a soil as to attract men—some root and stump fences which do not need attention—Where travellers have no occasion to stop—but pass along and leave you to your thoughts—Where it makes no odds which way you face whether you are going or coming—whether it is morning or evening—mid noon or midnight—Where earth is cheap enough by being public. Where you can walk and think with least obstruction—there being nothing to measure progress by. Where you can pace when your breast is full and cherish your moodiness. Where you are not in false relations with men—are not dining nor conversing with them. By which you may go to the uttermost parts of the earth—It is wide enough—wide as the thoughts it allows to visit you. Some-times it is some particular half dozen rods which I wish to find myself pacing over—as where certain airs blow then my life will come to me methinks like a hunter I walk in wait for it. When I am against this bare promontory of a huckleberry hill then forsooth my thoughts will expand. Is it some influence as a vapor which exhales from the ground, or something in the gales which blow there or in all things there brought together agreeably to my spirit? The walls must not be too high imprisoning me—but low with numerous—gaps—The trees must not be too numerous nor the hills too near bounding the view—nor the soil too rich attracting the attention to the earth—It must simply be the way and the life." (PJ.3.317–18)

In several obvious ways, this passage anticipates "Walking," a lecture Thoreau delivered repeatedly during the 1850s, that was published in an expanded form shortly after his death in 1862.[22] The theme is the same, but the texts also share much in the way of perspective and style. In both cases, Thoreau's meditations on the meaning and value of walking take the form of a kind of religious allegory. The value of our excursions in this world depend, both texts suggest, on their fidelity to the path we would follow in a higher, more ideal state of existence. "We would fain take that walk," he writes in "Walking," "never yet taken by us through this actual world, which is perfectly symbolical of the path which we love to travel in the interior and ideal world; and sometimes, no doubt, we find it difficult to choose our direction, because it does not yet exist distinctly in our idea" (Writings.5.216–17). In both texts, moreover, Thoreau imagines his walker ideally as a kind of religious pilgrim or "saunterer," a word that, in the opening of the published essay, he derives somewhat whimsically from *Sainte-Terrer* (one who undertakes a pilgrimage to the Holy Land) or *sans terre*—one who having no home anywhere is therefore at home everywhere (Writings.5.205–06). Thoreau plays on the Christian associations of both etymologies and elsewhere paraphrases the Christian Bible, as if to dramatize the hallowed reality of his seemingly mundane theme. The journal's oblique allusion ("It must simply be the way and the life") to John 14:6 raises the stakes even further in its implicit comparison of the way of true walking with the way of salvation embodied in the person of Christ. While the somewhat parodic character of some of these allusions, especially in the lecture and published essay, is undeniable, they obviously invest Thoreau's treatment of the walking theme with a certain air of religious sanctity and commitment. Walking, these texts insist, should be a religious exercise, not a mere form of personal amusement or scientific inquiry.

There was also broad sanction for such religious valuations of walking outside of the Christian tradition, as Thoreau well knew. The peripatetic philosophers of the ancient world, East and West, were so named for their habit of teaching in the act of walking. Interestingly, Thoreau's most suggestive reference to such walking philosophers of the past was not to any member of Aristotle's school, but to India's legendary sage Viṣṇu Śarma, reputed author of the *Hitopadeśa:* "It seems as if the old philosopher could not talk without moving—and each motion were made the apology or occasion for a sentence—but this being found inconvenient— the fictitious progress of the tale was invented. The story which winds between and around these sentences these barrows in the desert—these oases—is as indistinct as a camel track between Mourzuk to Darfur— between the pyramids and the Nile.—from Gaza to Jaffa" (PJ.1.389).

The wisdom of the old philosopher consists in a series of apparently discrete utterances, momentary declarations connected, for the sake of convenience and somewhat artificially, by a "fictitious" narrative form. This depiction of the relationship between walking and speech, between experience and insight, has an interesting bearing on both the message and the narrative form of the long journal passage cited above. Thoreau unfurls this wishful meditation on the higher calling of walking through a distinctly discontinuous series of parallel adverbial phrases, organized in a loosely paratactic arrangement, commencing throughout with the conjunction "where." The structure of this passage is reminiscent of nothing so much as one of Walt Whitman's catalogues, and the effect is similar. The heavy reliance on the iterative devices of anaphora and parallelism increases the momentum of the passage, and evokes a sense of forgetfulness and transport as phrases or sentences wash like waves over the reader, one after the other. What we as readers lose from such a continual succession of parallel phrases is a sense of their connectedness— their relationship, logical or otherwise, one with another; what we gain is an advancing sense of spontaneity and surprise, since there is no way to predict what, apart from the form, the next member of the catalogue will bring. In fact, there was probably nothing particularly casual or sponta- neous in the actual construction of the passage I cited—the use of such literary catalogues is as deliberate and painstaking as any other—but by using it in such an overt way, Thoreau effectively illustrates, and even to an extent evokes, a mode of meditative experience to which he was increasingly drawn. As the passage unfolds, the reader finds him- or herself wandering along "one of those old meandering dry uninhabited roads" of which all these open-ended, indeterminate adverbial phrases were predicated. The emphasis in such meditations is not after all on the connection between one phrase and the next, one observation and the next, or even one moment and the next—but rather on the alternate crystallization and relaxation of the attending mind.

The fanciful and overtly allegorical character of the meandering-roads passage is unrepresentative of the understated, pared-down style of the late journal, but it signals a crucial change in the nature of Thoreau's spiritual reflections. With the waning of spontaneous moods of transport, he began to pay more attention to the nature and dynamics of such experience—its onset, structure, and phenomenology. Having witnessed its ebb and flow, the circumstances and conditions of its expression and cessation, he now deliberately sought out means to reproduce and cultivate such experience for the sake of the knowledge and sense of communion with nature to which it gave rise. Once the innocent and delighted beneficiary, he now became an active and committed practitioner. The practice of walking meditation dramatized in the passage above was of course one major expression of this new preoccupation with the deliberate cultivation of ecstatic experience. But as we will see in this final set of journal passages, what such walking meditations essentially reflect is Thoreau's growing recognition of the need to silence the claims of the personal self in order to experience nature authentically as it is. He now realized that the mind's incessant conceptualizing constituted an imposition upon the natural world and a direct impediment to his fullest contact with being. His response, consequently, was to find ways to quiet and simplify his awareness so as to exhibit nature in a more pristine and accurate way. In his quest for such states of consciousness, the spectacle of the unperturbed and translucent Pond provided more a model than a mere analogue: "To be calm to be serene—there is the calmness of the lake when there is not a breath of wind—there is the calmness of a stagnant ditch. So is it with us. Sometimes we are clarified & calmed healthily as we never were before in our lives—not by an opiate—but by some unconscious obedience to the all-just laws—so that we become like a still lake of purest crystal and without an effort our depths are revealed to ourselves. All the world goes by us & is reflected in our deeps" (PJ.3.274–75). This passage from June of 1851 reflects the euphoria characteristic of those heady summer months. By the next December, Thoreau is ready to speak with more specificity about his conception of the meditative mind:

> It would be a truer discipline for the writer to take the least film of thought that floats in the twilight sky of his mind for his theme—

about which he has scarcely one idea. . . . We see too soon to ally the perceptions of the mind to the experience of the hand—to prove our gossamer truths practical—to show their connexion with our every day life (better show their distance from our every day life) to relate them to the cider mill and the banking institution. Ah give me pure mind—pure thought. Let me not be in haste to detect the *universal law,* let me see more clearly a particular instance. Much finer themes I aspire to—which will yield no satisfaction to the vulgar mind—not one sentence for them—Perchance it may convince such that there are more things in heaven & earth than are dreamed of in their philosophy. (PJ.4.222–23)

Even before this transitional period, Thoreau was already beginning to recognize the limitations of his own and others' more conventionally speculative and Romantic apprehensions of nature. The following excerpt from the previous year provides another glimpse into the direction his meditations were taking: "I saw Fair Haven pond with its Island & meadow between the island & the shore—and a strip of perfectly still & smooth water in the lee of the island—& two hawks—fish-hawks perhaps—sailing over it I did not see how it could be improved—Yet I do not see what these things can be. I begin to see such an object when I cease to *understand* it—and see that I did not realize or appreciate it before—but I get no further than this" (PJ.3.148). Here, plainly stated, is one of the essential attributes of the contemplative awareness that Thoreau was bent upon cultivating at this time. The passage gives expression to his dawning conviction that the faculty of understanding and even of imagination was not a help, after all, but a handicap for achieving the kind of heightened perception to which he aspired. By projecting its own structures upon the phenomenon in view, the creative and conceptualizing mind inevitably hampered the prospect of pure vision. What the student of nature needed was, as he said, "pure mind—pure thought." Indeed, self-consciousness increasingly became for him an obstacle to spiritual progress. Citing with approval Wordsworth's observation about the value of "relaxed attention" for the meditative life, he notes, "A man can hardly be said to be *there* if he *knows* that he is there—or to go there, if he knows Where he is going. The man who is bent upon his work is frequently in the best attitude to observe what is irrelevant to his work" (PJ.4.192–93).

With further reflection, Thoreau soon realized that such strictures regarding the mediating role of the mind in its transactions with nature should also be applied to perception itself. Just as the conceptualizing mind interfered with pure perception, so too directed perception could undermine the possibility of truly comprehensive sight. The culprit in both cases was intentionality, which arose in turn from the desires and self-interest of the investigator. Looking, Thoreau realized, should give way to seeing, just as efforts to understand should give way to less motivated forms of perception. "I must walk more with free senses—," he wrote in the fall of 1852, "It is as bad to *study* stars & clouds as flowers & stones—I must let my senses wander as my thoughts—my eyes see without looking. Carlyle said that how to observe was to look—but I say that it is rather to see—& the more you look the less you will observe—I have the habit of attention to such excess that my senses get no rest—but suffer from a constant strain. Be not preoccupied with looking. Go not to the object let it come to you. . . . What I need is not to look at all—but a true sauntering of the eye" (PJ.5.343–44). This reference to a kind of observational "sauntering" explicitly relates the mode of perception he enjoins on himself here to the actual ambulatory sauntering of which it was merely a finer expression. Both levels of experiential sauntering, the meditative and the ambulatory, were guided by the conviction that the mind could only enjoy its fullest contact with reality when, like the calm, mirroring lake, it reflected the phenomena of nature without distorting them.

Passages from the journals written during this period and in subsequent months indicate that Thoreau's experiments with and reflections on perception were inspired in part by his reading of the English naturalist William Gilpin and other writers on the picturesque.[23] As I noted in the second chapter, such landscape writers generally upheld the value of a sense of distance in the act of seeing. Yet Thoreau's meditations in nature went beyond merely aesthetic considerations, or rather aesthetic experiences always bordered for him on a deeper set of spiritual concerns. Indeed, by this point in his life, the act of observing natural forms took on the character of a religious discipline. "That aim in life is highest which requires the highest & finest discipline," he wrote in late 1852. "How much—What infinite leisure it requires—as of a lifetime, to appreciate a single phenomenon! You must camp down beside it as for life—having reached your land of promise & give yourself wholly to it" (PJ.5.412). The type of disinterested, nonconceptual, and nonpropositional attention to the object indicated in these passages certainly had implications for Thoreau's scientific work, but he clearly conceived such meditative experience as a way to supersede more conventional ways of knowing. Its nearest analogues of course were to be found not in the Western scientific tradition, but in Wordsworth, the literature on the picturesque, and the meditative disciplines of East and West. To apprehend an object with a mind thus unfettered by impressions from the past and expectations for the future was to entertain a mode of experience familiar mostly only to religious contemplatives and a few poets. As Thoreau put his speculations about such experience into practice over the course of the next ten years, these early musings about the value of unpremeditated experience are replaced by more definitive statements. In 1859, Thoreau offered the following mature declaration with all the confidence of a settled conviction:

It is only when we forget all our learning that we begin to know. I do not get nearer by a hair's breadth to any natural object so long as I presume that I have an introduction to it from some learned man. To conceive of it with a total apprehension I must for the thousandth time approach it as something totally strange. If you would make acquaintance with the ferns you must forget your botany. You must get rid of what is commonly called *knowledge* of them. Not a single scientific term or distinction is the least to the purpose, for you would fain perceive something, and you must approach the object totally unprejudiced You must be aware that *no thing* is what you have taken it to be. In what book is this world and its beauty described? Who has plotted the steps toward the discovery of beauty? You have got to be in a different state from common. Your greatest success will be simply to perceive that such things are, and you will have no communication to make to the Royal Society. (J.12.371)

Formulations such as this lend themselves to the sort of cryptic paradox to which Thoreau was so partial: his advocacy here of a kind of path of unknowing and no-thingness seems more reminiscent of the apophatic theology of the Western mystical tradition or Zen teaching, traditions about which he knew very little, than anything he would have encountered in the New England Protestant tradition or his own reading. What makes such declarations so interesting is that they appear to be unborrowed—the product primarily of his own thinking and experience.

The journal clearly played a principal role in Thoreau's new meditative practices. He used its pages to elaborate terse notes taken during his daily walks, and often to re-create and represent the content and character of his meditative experiences. These efforts to represent his experience journalistically led to a new aesthetic—more concrete, minimalist, and less subjectively reflective. His concern, increasingly, was to depict the phenomenology of his experiences in nature: to convey how each moment of experience represented a distinctive—because it was both unprecedented and unrepeatable—encounter between consciousness and objective reality. Given the evident affinities with some Zen practices of this new commitment to playing down purely speculative tendencies, it is perhaps not so surprising that the form of some of the resulting journal entries is strongly reminiscent of such Zen-inspired poetic practices as haiku, as Daniel Peck has suggestively pointed out.[24] One early instance of this occurs in an entry made in August of 1851:

A new moon visible in the east—how unexpectedly it always appears! You easily lose it in the sky. The whipporwill sings—but not so commonly as in spring. The bats are active. The poet is a man who lives at last by watching his moods. An old poet comes at last to watch his moods as narrowly as a cat does a mouse. (PJ.4.16)

Here, taken almost at random, is another passage, from the journal of the following summer:

> I see & hear the king fisher with his disproportionate black head or crest—The pigeon woodpecker darts across the valley—a cat bird mews in the alders—a great bittern flies sluggishly away from his pine tree perch on Tupelo Cliff—digging his way through the air— (PJ.5.321)

And here, in the somewhat smoothed over and altered form of the Walden edition, is a similar passage from May of 1859:

> I came out expecting to see the redstart or the parti-colored warbler, and as soon as I get within a dozen rods of the Holden wood I hear the screeper note of the tweezer-bird, i.e. parti-colored warbler, which also I see, but not distinctly. Two or three are flitting from tree-top to tree-top about the swamp there, and you have only to sit still on one side and wait for them to come round. The water has what you may call a summer ripple and sparkle on it; i.e. the ripple does not suggest coldness in the breeze that raises it. It is a hazy day; the air is hazed, you might fancy, with a myriad expanding buds." (J.12.177)

What, in their almost studied simplicity, such passages provide is a verbal replica of the pure sequentiality of experience. Yet Thoreau avoids any effort to articulate connections or relationships between the items of each sequence. Apart from the simple punctuation of the dash, he even avoids such connecting or orienting parts of speech as conjunctions, prepositions, and the like. The relationship existing between one member of a sequence and the next is thus one of simple juxtaposition. There is no sense of priority, causality, or hierarchy here; on the contrary, this mode of presentation implies a radical leveling of significance and value. The phenomena of each passage are simply presented as they appear to the apprehending consciousness, not as they are arranged and interpreted by the reflective intellect. The effect is thus to expose the nature of experience in its simplest and least adulterated form. By accentuating the naturally disjointed character of experience, and exposing the gaps that naturally exist between one presentation of experience and the next, Thoreau re-creates the freshness of the object of perception as it presents itself unannounced out of a background of silence.

The first of the three passages cited above makes especially clear how different these journal meditations are from a simple record of natural observations. As in this case, Thoreau typically includes the observer among the phenomena observed. It is the *perception* of the phenomenon that intrigues him, not the natural object for its own sake. By virtue of the apparently artless juxtapositional presentation of this entry, Thoreau makes no distinctions between the phenomena of moon, whippoorwill, bats, and poet; all are raised to the same level of distinct but unprejudiced apprehension. But this passage has the further advantage of commenting upon the mode of meditation that it serves to exemplify. "The poet is a man who lives at last by watching his moods," Thoreau writes, as if to extend the arena of observation to even the finest expressions of subjectivity. This is the second time that month that the journal introduces this notion of witnessing one's moods as a qualification incumbent upon the poet. Ten days previously, he had supplied a fuller commentary:

> The poet must be continually watching the moods of his mind as the astronomer watches the aspects of the heavens. What might we not expect from a long life faithfully spent in this wise—the humblest observer would see some stars shoot.—A faithful description as by a disinterested person of the thoughts which visited a certain mind in 3 score years & 10 as when one reports the number & character of the vehicles which pass a particular point. As travellers go round the world and report natural objects & phenomena—so faithfully let another stay at home & report the phenomena of his own life. Catalogue stars—those thoughts whose orbits are as rarely calculated as comets It matters not whether they visit my mind or yours—whether the meteor falls in my field or in yours—only that it came from heaven. (I am not concerned to express that kind of truth which nature has expressed. Who knows but I may suggest

some things to her. Time was when she was indebted to such suggestions from another quarter—as her present advancement shows. I deal with the truths that recommend themselves to me please me—not those merely which any system has voted to accept.) A meteorological journal of the mind—You shall observe what occurs in your latitude, I in mine. (PJ.3.377)

These references to observing "the moods of the mind" help to clarify the scope of Thoreau's journal, but they also shed important light on the nature and goals of his meditative practice. It is one thing to stand back from the arena of one's thoughts, another to include within the meditator's purview the field of moods and feelings. The intention to include moods and feelings among the objects of Thoreau's attention indicates an interiority of which most of his neighbors might not be generally cognizant. By insisting in such passages that the meditator's field of observation includes feelings as well as thoughts, he effectively locates the ground of observation beyond the range of the personal self. That Thoreau could even speak of such an absolute state of nonattachment suggests a notable fact about his own interior life, which is found richly reflected throughout much of his work. The separation he posits here between moods and the consciousness that witnesses to them reminds us of the sense of inner doubleness and disjunctive vision considered previously. These journal references provide yet another expression of the ecstatic experience showcased in the "Solitude" chapter of *Walden*. Like the contemplative poet depicted in the passages above, the ecstatic spectator envisaged in *Walden* stands apart from the arena "of thoughts and affections," witnessing the movements of his mind but "sharing no experience" (135).

Even as a young man, Thoreau had already begun to suspect that what kept him from a more continuous immersion in nature was nothing but the mediating influence of his own thoughts and desires. This brief entry from 1841, normally construed simply as an adumbration of his sojourn at Walden, anticipates what would become a major theme of his interior life: "I want to go soon and live away by the pond where I shall hear only the wind whispering among the reeds—It will be success if I shall have left myself behind, But my friends ask what I will do when I get there? Will it not be employment enough to watch the progress of the seasons?" (PJ.1.347). The odd remark "It will be success if I shall have left myself behind" may be read simply as another of Thoreau's odd nonsequiturs, but it reflects a central impulse in his spiritual and psychological life. He disliked the humanism of Pope's famous dictum "the proper study of mankind is man" because it smacked of the "egotism of the race" (PJ.4.418). Shakespeare, on the other hand, he extolled for his artistic self-transparency (PJ.4.294). In fact, something like a polemic against the pretensions of the self runs all through his literary and aesthetic commentary. But for him there was more at stake in the question of the self's relationship to activity than purely literary concerns. The passionate character of these opinions stems from his recognition of the debilitating role of the self in his own spiritual experience. His greatest ecstasies occurred in moments of sheerest self-transparency, when nature ran through him like a rushing stream. Much of his practical religious reflection, consequently, was dedicated above all to finding ways to purify or neutralize the mediatory activities of the mind, to render it more pervious to the currents of nature. This, for example, is apparently the burden of the disquieting conceit about swallowing a snake that we encounter in the journal of August 17, 1851:

> How many ova have I swallowed—who knows what will be hatched within me? There were some seeds of thought methinks floating in that water which are expanding in me—The man must not drink of the running streams the living waters—who is not prepared to have all nature reborn in him—to suckle monsters—The snake in my stomack lifts his head to my mouth at the sound of running water. When was it that I swallowed a snake. I have got rid of the snake in my stomack. I drank at stagnant waters once. That accounts for it. I caught him by the throat & drew him out & had a well day after all. Is there not such a thing as getting rid of the snake which you swallowed when young? When thoughtless you

> stooped & drank at stagnant waters—which has worried you in
> your waking hours & in your sleep ever since & appropriated the
> life that was yours. Will he not ascend into your mouth at the
> sound of running water—Then catch him boldly by the head &
> draw him out though you may think his tail be curled about your
> vitals. (PJ.3.369–70)

The ultimately redemptive character of this oddly grotesque passage is
suggested by its journalistic context: it comes hard on the heels of an
extended journal entry from the summer of 1851 expressing exhilarations of an extraordinary sort. Like the snake inadvertently swallowed
with stagnant waters, the natural self, imbibed at birth, inhabits our
body and takes our life as its own. To the self, like the snake, we owe all
that we know; it is coiled about our vitals. But nothing can be known
independently of the mediating activity of the self. Even the snake itself
we cannot know until we draw him from the gut. To expel the snake is to
regain one's health; to transcend the self is to regain wholeness and an
unmediated vision of nature. This is why this strange narrative of serpen-
tine violation serves principally as a commentary on one of the most
exultant expressions of communion with nature to be found in the
journal all that summer. Here is an excerpt: "Ah! if I could so live that
there should be no desultory moment in all my life! that in the trivial
season, when small fruits are ripe, my fruits might be ripe also! that I
could match nature always with my moods! that in each season when
some part of nature especially flourishes, then a corresponding part of
me may not fail to flourish! Ah, I would walk, I would sit and sleep, with
natural piety! What if I could pray aloud or to myself as I went along by
the brooksides a cheerful prayer like the birds!" (J.2.391).[25] The religious
value of such moments of self-transcendence was experienced in the
wave of exhilaration and happiness that Thoreau felt when he innocently
experienced a perfect concordance and sympathy between nature's expressions and his own. At such moments, the inveterate barrier between
himself and nature was for the moment let down, and he was free, if only
briefly, to experience the phenomena of nature without mediation, as if

they were his own thoughts and feelings. "What other impulse do we wait for?" he wrote in 1852. "Let us preserve religiously—secure—protect—the coincidence of our life with the life of nature" (PJ.4.290). This midlife self-admonition might well be said to epitomize the character of Thoreau's mature spiritual life. It also provides a succinct expression of what came to be the primary spiritual function of his journal. While the journal also served at times as a commemoration of ecstatic transport and a medium through which to reflect upon the religious meanings of nature, after the summer of 1851, it functioned increasingly as a record, and even the vehicle itself, of Thoreau's contemplative experiences. Before this transitional period, the journal primarily served the functions of conception, composition, and recollection. When it addressed his experiences of jubilation and euphoria in nature, it did so retrospectively, reflecting the aftershocks and gathering the implications of these momentous experiences. As he recalled repeatedly during the summer of 1851, his early years provided abundant testimony to the spontaneous and unhindered influx of higher consciousness. He was often beside himself, he said, his moods of euphoria triggered merely by the sound of crickets or the singing of a telegraph wire. At such moments, his "pulse beat with nature" (PJ.3.274). By 1850, however, these experiences of spontaneous ecstasy came less often and with less intensity. Yet the late spring and summer of the following year witnessed a notable reprise of his earlier sensitivity, poignantly reminding him how much he had taken for granted when he was young and how much he was now at risk of losing. The journal of this period, from 1851 till the end of his life, represents in considerable part his deliberate response to this sobering recognition. What he experienced spontaneously as a youth—moments of transparency and acute sensory sensitivity—he now sought to restore and cultivate through his attentive meditations in nature. The natural expressions of these moments of heightened lucidity—the sense of self-transparency, separation from his own thoughts and feelings, and freshness of perception—he now conceived as the necessary ingredients of a spiritual discipline. From his recollections of the curious phenomenology of these episodes, he developed a contemplative discipline in which feelings, projections, and mental constructions were methodically put aside for the sake of an enriched and purified perception, and a more innocent apprehension of the object before him. He sought, as he said, not so much an understanding of nature but "a coincidence" of his life with its own. The journal served as the formal medium through which to pursue this discipline of contemplative practice. Its goal was to bracket the inquiring self; to render the mind transparent to the object he was witnessing; to write himself, in effect, deliberately out of the picture.

As we have seen, the altered character of the journal after 1851, its increased preoccupation with specific natural facts and observations, has served as a point of departure for various critical readings of Thoreau's life. But his preoccupation with material facts needs to be read in conjunction with the various entries cited above. Not to recognize the meditative character of these and other such entries leads not only to a misapprehension of the late journal but also to misreadings of Thoreau's life as a whole. His was not a religion of inherited scriptures, collective rites, or theological doctrines, to be sure, but to ignore the intensely religious character of his personal transactions with nature skews our understanding both of the man and his work. On the other hand, when these dimensions of his experience do come into focus, we can better appreciate the importance not only of his contributions to American literature and culture, but also to the history of American religious experience. In this field, as in others, Thoreau was ahead of most of his contemporaries, opening trails some of us now simply take for granted.

Afterword:
One World at a Time

In the biographies of saints and other such charismatic figures, it is customary to point to death, and the circumstances surrounding it, for a final testament to the character and meaning of a subject's life. And so it has been among many of Thoreau's biographers, early and late.[1] The story, reduced to bare essentials, may be summarized as follows. Thoreau began his slow consumptive decline in December of 1860, when he developed a severe cold while working outside one afternoon in freezing weather. In the weeks following, the cold turned into a bronchial condition, accompanied by a chronic, nagging cough. When the warm weather failed to bring the hoped-for improvement, he resolved to take a long trip to Minnesota, whose dry air was recommended as a cure for unhealthy lungs. But the trip West served merely to sap his strength further, and when he returned to Concord in mid-July, he knew the prognosis was not good. By the following December, still wracked by a chronic cough and weakened by extreme weight loss, he was too sick to venture outside. Yet so long as his strength held out, he worked diligently to prepare several of his lectures and essays for publication. His mother, Cynthia, attended him, as did his sister Sophia, who also helped with his correspondence and the task of putting his manuscripts in order. Friends and neighbors, solicitous of his welfare, called on him regularly, and despite his emaciated physical condition, by all accounts he remained lucid, humorous, and characteristically buoyant till the very end. On the morning of May 6, 1862, he passed almost imperceptibly away.

Some of our most reliable information about Thoreau's last days comes, not surprisingly, from Sophia, who was at his side throughout his entire ordeal. A month before her brother's death, she wrote a sobering letter to his doting friend Daniel Ricketson, to bring him up to date on Thoreau's deteriorating condition: "My dear brother has survived the winter, and we should be most thankful if he might linger to welcome the green grass and the flowers once more. Believing as I do in the sincerity of your friendship for Henry, I feel anxious that you should know *how* ill he is. Since the autumn he has been gradually failing, and is now the embodiment of weakness; still, he enjoys seeing his friends, and every bright hour he devotes to his manuscripts which he is preparing for publication. For many weeks he has spoken only in a faint whisper. Henry accepts this dispensation with such childlike trust and is so happy that I feel as if he were being translated, rather than dying in the ordinary way of most mortals."[2] Other visitors marveled also at the patient's buoyancy and seemingly imperturbable sense of evenness, maintained even during the darkest days of his illness. The imminence of death apparently evoked no great sense of anxiety or dread. On the contrary, visitors were impressed by Thoreau's good humor and self-possession. Illustrative of his outward and inward demeanor is this amusing anecdote, reported by Edward Waldo Emerson, who was seventeen when Thoreau died: When Thoreau's Calvinistic aunt felt obliged to ask, "Henry, have you made your peace with God?" the unruffled Thoreau mildly replied, "I did not know we had ever quarrelled, Aunt."[3]

A more telling recollection occurs in a letter addressed to Ricketson from Thoreau's Worcester friend Theo Brown, who visited Thoreau in the last weeks of his life, together with their mutual friend Harrison Blake:

> It may interest you to hear of the last visit which I with Blake made at his (Thoreau's) house a short time before he died. We took our skates, and then the cars as far as Framingham. From some two

miles north of Framingham we took to the river and skated nearly to Thoreau's house. We found him pretty low, but well enough to be up in his chair. He seemed glad to see us. Said we had not come much too soon. We spent some hours with him in his mother's parlor, which overlooks the river that runs all through his life. There was a beautiful snowstorm going on the while which I fancy inspired him, and his talk was up to the best I ever heard from him,—the same depth of earnestness and the same infinite depth of fun going on at the same time. . . . He seemed to be in an exalted state of mind for a long time before his death. He said it was just as good to be sick as to be well,—just as good to have a poor time as a good time.[4]

In letters she sent in the weeks and months following her brother's death, Sophia also marveled at her brother's radiance and equipoise. Responding to Ricketson's request for more information about Thoreau's last weeks, she wrote: "During his long illness I never heard a murmur escape him, or the slightest wish expressed to remain with us; his perfect contentment was truly wonderful. None of his friends seemed to realize how very ill he was, so full of life and good cheer did he seem. One friend, as if by way of consolation, said to him, 'Well, Mr. Thoreau, we must all go.' Henry replied, 'When I was a very little boy I learned that I must die, and I set that down, so of course I am not disappointed now. Death is as near to you as it is to me.' "[5] When asked by another friend how death looked to him from his present vantage point, he responded simply, "One world at a time."[6]

If such anecdotes can be taken as any guide, Thoreau's attitude toward death was very much of a piece with his attitude toward other religious and metaphysical questions. Disinclined as always to speculate about such matters as he could neither confirm nor deny, he was instead zealous to make the most of present circumstances. Even in his final days, he was not in the least prepared to engage in some wishfully speculative thoughts about the hereafter, but to enjoy what was left of his own life to the fullest extent possible. Ellery Channing, despite his own crotchets, recognized the integrity of Thoreau's position and understood better than most the nature of his hidden spiritual resources: "He accepted it [death] heroically," Channing wrote, "but in no wise after the traditional manner. . . . He retired into his inner mind, into that unknown, unconscious, profound world of existence where he excelled; there he held inscrutable converse with just men made perfect, or what else, absorbed in himself. 'The night of time far surpasses day. . . .' An ineffable reserve shrouded this to him unforeseen fatality: he had never reason to believe in what he could not appreciate, nor accepted formulas of mere opinions; the special vitalization of all his beliefs, self-consciously, lying in the marrow of his theology."[7]

This remark of Channing's throws some helpful light on the pervasively empiricist cast of Thoreau's religious thought, but it does little to explain the apparently innocent state of peaceful assurance with which he greeted his imminent death. To many visitors, Thoreau exhibited an unaccountable sense of detachment from his physical debility and the prospect of his approaching death. Sophia's remarks to Ricketson echoed the reactions of Brown cited above: "You asked for some particulars relating to Henry's illness. I feel like saying that Henry was never affected, never reached by it. I never before saw such a manifestation of the power of spirit over matter. Very often I have heard him tell his visitors that he enjoyed existence as well as ever. He remarked to me that there was as much comfort in perfect disease as in perfect health, the mind always conforming to the condition of the body. The thought of death, he said, could not begin to trouble him. His thoughts had entertained him all his life, and did still."[8]

In her efforts to make sense of her brother's remarkable equanimity, Sophia resorts here to the familiar religious dualism of "spirit over matter." Channing, who perhaps knew Henry's peculiar inner life even better, provided a more distinctive formulation. Recounting a curious dream that Thoreau had related to him during his illness, he gave fuller expression to what others had apparently sensed also: "The wasting away of his body, the going forth & exit of his lungs, which, like a steady lamp, give heat to the frame, was to Henry an inexplicably foreign event, the labors of another party in which he had no hand; though he still credited the fact to a lofty inspiration. He would often say that we could look on ourselves as a third person, and that he could perceive at times that he was out of his mind. Words could no longer express these inexplicable conditions of his existence, this sickness which reminded him of nothing that went before: such as that dream he had of being a railroad cut, where they were digging through and laying down the rail,—the place being in his lungs."[9]

To Thoreau, the sense of detachment he experienced in these last days, even the disquieting dream, must have seemed familiar. This was not the first time he had felt a stranger to his physical form, standing back as it were from the arena of his thoughts and physical existence. The paradox of Thoreau's inner life was that while he exulted in the joy and knowledge conferred by his bodily senses, he sometimes felt unaccountably removed from them, as if he were a witness observing the experience without participating in it directly. Indeed, it is just this sense of disjunction—perceptual, imaginative, and spiritual—that distinguishes so much of his art. Whether in the delicate conceit of witnessing himself in the transparent surface of Walden Pond, the unsettling construction of himself in *Walden* as the "spectator" of his life's dramatic scenes, or his preoccupation with self-transparency in the late journal, this awareness of self as in some sense separate from thought and activity governs his overall religious and artistic outlook. That it did not desert him, even in the shutting down of his physical life, suggests how deeply founded it was in the structure of his mind and heart.

Notes

Preface

1. Lawrence Buell, "The Thoreauvian Pilgrimage: The Structure of an American Cult," *American Literature* 61 (May 1989): 175–199; revised as "The Thoreauvian Pilgrimage" in Lawrence Buell, *The Environmental Imagination: Thoreau, Nature Writing, and the Formation of American Culture* (Cambridge: Harvard University Press, 1995), 311–338.

Introduction: A Simple and Hidden Life

1. One notable consequence of the recent turn in Thoreau studies from literary to cultural criticism has been to complicate facile notions about the imputedly conservative status and function of American literary canons. Recent treatments of the history of Thoreau's changing critical reputation have, if anything, highlighted the protean, rather than establishmentarian, character of his position in American culture. However literary canonization occurs in any given instance, whether through the advocacy of influential critics, popular appeal, or aggressive marketing campaigns launched by publishers and booksellers—and Thoreau's case involved elements of each of these—once it is achieved, the values associated with a figure such as Thoreau are as much a reflection as a determinant of changing cultural configurations. For an overview of the current status of Thoreau scholarship, see Elizabeth Hall Witherell, "Henry David Thoreau," in *Prospects for the Study of American Literature: A Guide for Scholars and Students,* ed. Richard Kopley (New York: New York University Press, 1997). Also helpful are several review essays that chart the major contributions to Thoreau studies between 1977 and 1995: Richard Schneider, "Humanizing Henry David Thoreau," *ESQ* 27 (1981):

57–71; Robert Sattelmeyer, "Study Nature and Know Thyself: Recent Thoreau Criticism," *ESQ* 31 (1985): 190–208; Philip Gura, "Traveling Much in Concord: A Sampling of Recent Thoreau Scholarship," *ESQ* 38 (1992): 71–86; and William Rossi, "Education in the Field: Recent Thoreau Criticism and Environment," *ESQ* 42 (1996): 125–151.

2. I am aware of other important exceptions to this generalization, even so qualified, posed by the occasional philosopher or psychologist, but I believe a survey of the critical literature on Thoreau will in a general way bear me out.

3. See, for example, David D. Hall, ed., *Lived Religion in America: Toward a History of Practice* (Princeton: Princeton University Press, 1997).

4. On the history of the Transcendentalist movement, see especially Barbara Packer, "The Transcendentalists," in *The Cambridge History of American Literature,* vol. 2: *Prose Writing 1820–1865,* gen. ed. Sacvan Bercovitch (Cambridge: Cambridge University Press, 1995), 331–604; and Lawrence Buell, "The Transcendentalists," in *Columbia Literary History of the United States,* ed. Emory Elliott (New York: Columbia University Press, 1988), 364–378. Additionally, Charles Capper provides a helpful review of the historiography of the movement in " 'A Little Beyond': The Problem of the Transcendentalist Movement in American History," in *Transient and Permanent: The Transcendentalist Movement and Its Contexts,* ed. Charles Capper and Conrad Edick Wright (Boston: Massachusetts Historical Society, 1999), 3–45.

5. For the following sketch, I have relied especially upon the following studies: Fritz Oehlschlaeger and George Hendrick, eds., *Toward the Making of Thoreau's Modern Reputation* (Urbana: University of Illinois Press, 1979); Walter Harding and Michael Meyer, eds., *The New Thoreau Handbook* (New York: New York University Press, 1980), 202–224; Lawrence Buell, "Henry Thoreau Enters the American Canon," *New Essays on* Walden, ed. Robert F. Sayre (Cambridge: Cambridge University Press, 1992), revised as "The Canonization and Recanonization of the Green Thoreau" in Buell, *The Environmental Imagination: Thoreau, Nature Writing, and the Formation of American Culture* (Cambridge: Harvard University Press, 1995), 339–369; Gary Scharnhorst, *Henry David Thoreau: A Case Study of Canonization* (Columbia, S.C.: Camden House, 1993); Walter Harding, "Thoreau's Reputation," in *The Cambridge Companion to Henry David Thoreau,* ed. Joel Myerson (Cambridge: Cambridge University Press, 1995), 1–11.

6. See Gary Scharnhorst, *Henry David Thoreau: An Annotated Bibliography of Comment and Criticism Before 1900* (New York: Garland, 1992); and Joel

Myerson, ed., *Emerson and Thoreau: The Contemporary Reviews* (Cambridge: Cambridge University Press, 1992).

7. See Buell, "American Canon," 23-52.

8. Henry David Thoreau, *Early Spring in Massachusetts,* ed. H. G. O. Blake (Boston: Houghton Mifflin, 1881). *Early Spring* was followed by *Summer* (1884), *Winter* (1887), and *Autumn* (1892). See Scharnhorst, *Case Study,* 29-33.

9. Scharnhorst, *Annotated Bibliography,* 169. For the fullest treatment of Thoreau's political reputation, see Michael Meyer, *Several More Lives to Live: Thoreau's Political Reputation in America* (Westport, Conn.: Greenwood Press, 1977).

10. No one did as much as Henry Salt to pave the way for this eager reception among British Fabians. Between 1890 and 1891, Salt published several pieces designed to recommend Thoreau to a wider reading public, including a reliable and still respected biography, *The Life of Henry David Thoreau,* and the first British edition of *Anti-Slavery and Reform Papers.* In his introductory note to the latter, Salt praised Thoreau's "anarchist principles," which he essentialized as "the claim for the individual man of the right of free growth and natural development from within." See Henry David Thoreau, *Anti-Slavery and Reform Papers,* ed. Henry S. Salt (London: Swan Sonnenschein and Co., 1890), 7-9.

11. Macy rejected the exclusive attention paid by what he called the "cult of the open air" to Thoreau's nature writing and praised him instead as "the one anarchist of great literary power in a nation of slavish conformity to legalism." See John Macy, *The Spirit of American Literature* (New York: Doubleday, Page, and Co., 1913), 171-172. See also Buell, "American Canon," 42 ff.

12. Vernon Louis Parrington, *Main Currents in American Thought: An Interpretation of American Literature from the Beginnings to 1920* (New York: Harcourt, Brace and Co., 1927), 400, 406.

13. For a more fine-grained reconstruction of the rise and institutionalization of the political Thoreau, see Scharnhorst, *Case Study,* 43-65, and Buell, "American Canon," 42-45.

14. F. O. Matthiessen, *American Renaissance: Art and Expression in the Age of Emerson and Whitman* (London: Oxford University Press, 1941), 78.

15. The three approaches outlined here do not do justice of course to the plethora of criticism published on Thoreau over the last 120 years, and neither is the history of Thoreau's critical reception as neatly chronological as

might appear from this sketch. As the palimpsest metaphor invoked above suggests, earlier appropriations of Thoreau continued to exert influence even when they were somewhat pushed aside by newer critical trends. Especially noteworthy in the criticism of the past decade or two has been the vigorous revival of interest in Thoreau as a nature writer and ecologist, a fact obviously reflecting the growing popularity of the genre of American nature writing outside the Academy and its formal academic authorization by the newly emergent field of ecocriticism. For the best treatment to date of the tradition of American nature writing and Thoreau's place in it, see Buell, *The Environmental Imagination.* An accurate gauge of the revival of interest in this area are the bibliographical essays on Thoreau and Transcendentalism supplied in recent years in *American Literary Scholarship.* See, for example, David M. Robinson, "Emerson, Thoreau, Fuller, and Transcendentalism," *American Literary Scholarship* (1997), 16–19. For a critical review of some of this recent work, see Leo Marx, "The Struggle Over Thoreau," *The New York Review of Books* 46 (11): 60–65, and 46 (12): 44–45; see also Buell's response to Marx and Marx's response to Buell in *The New York Review of Books* 46 (19): 63–64.

16. It must be acknowledged, however, that even while popularizing Thoreau as a nature writer, in more rarefied forums such as the Concord School of Philosophy, Blake did not hesitate also to raise him to the status of a kind of "prophet" and "witness in our own times." See reviews of Blake's readings of Thoreau's journals in Scharnhorst, *Annotated Bibliography,* 212 ff.

17. Edward Waldo Emerson, *Henry Thoreau as Remembered by a Young Friend* (Boston: Houghton Mifflin, 1917), 80.

18. See Anna and Walton Ricketson, eds. *Daniel Ricketson and His Friends* (Boston: Houghton Mifflin, 1902), 155.

19. Ibid., 153.

20. Emerson's eulogy was included in the volume entitled *Excursions.* See R. W. Emerson, "Biographical Sketch," in Henry D. Thoreau, *Excursions* (Boston: Ticknor and Fields, 1863), 17–28. For a corrected edition, see Joel Myerson, "Emerson's 'Thoreau': A New Edition from Manuscript," in *Studies in the American Renaissance,* ed. Joel Myerson (Boston: Hall, 1979), 35–55; reprinted in William Rossi, ed., *Walden and Resistance to Civil Government,* 2nd ed. (New York: W. W. Norton, 1992), 320–333.

21. Bronson Alcott, "The Forester," *Atlantic Monthly* 9 (April 1862): 445.

22. William Ellery Channing, *Thoreau: The Poet-Naturalist* (Boston: Roberts Brothers, 1973), 341.

23. John Weiss, *The Christian Examiner* (July 1965). Reprinted in Samuel A. Jones, ed., *Pertaining to Thoreau* (Detroit: Edwin B. Hill, 1901), 144, 147.

24. H. A. Page, *Thoreau: His Life and Aims* (London: Chatto & Windus, 1878), ix, 259–260, 271.

25. Equally reverent, if not at times zealous, was the New Bedford Quaker Daniel Ricketson, who began corresponding with Thoreau soon after reading *Walden* in 1854. For some of Ricketson's most expressive correspondence, see Ricketson, eds., *Ricketson and Friends*, 29, 51, 54, 61, 97. On Blake, see Joseph J. Moldenhauer, s.v. *Biographical Dictionary of Transcendentalism*, ed. Wesley T. Mott (Westport, Conn.: Greenwood Press, 1996).

26. See Austin Warren, "The Concord School of Philosophy," *New England Quarterly* 2 (April 1929): 199–233; Kenneth Walter Cameron, *Concord Harvest*, 2 vols. (Hartford: Transcendental Books, 1970).

27. Warren, "Concord School," 205.

28. Julia R. Anagnos, *Philosophiae Quaestor; or, Days in Concord* (Boston: D. Lothrop and Company, 1885). Reprinted in Cameron, *Concord Harvest*, vol. 2, 401–416.

29. See Kenneth Walter Cameron, *Transcendentalists in Transition* (Hartford: Transcendental Books, 1980).

30. In 1929, *American Literature,* the bellwether of the critical study of American literature, began publication, and the next year the American Literature section of the Modern Language Association was formed. In time these scholarly venues became the main vehicles for the propagation of Thoreau's reputation. In 1941 the Thoreau Society was founded in part to foster and promote the growing scholarly interest in Thoreau. From this point forward, most of what was written about Thoreau took the form of academic books, articles, and doctoral dissertations.

31. Even Perry Miller, who famously reminded us that the Transcendentalist movement was most accurately characterized as "a religious demonstration," scarcely conceived Thoreau in religious terms at all, tending rather to see him as an offspring of Wordsworth and "a child of the Romantic era." See Perry Miller, *The Transcendentalists* (Cambridge: Harvard University Press, 1950), 8; and Perry Miller, "Transcendentalism in the Context of International Romanticism," *New England Quarterly* 34, no. 2 (June 1961), 149.

32. I do not wish to exaggerate this neglect. I am speaking here of a general tendency in the modern critical tradition as a whole and recognize several important individual exceptions. Among the modern critical treatments that have contributed insightfully to understanding this dimension of Thoreau's

life, and upon which I have especially relied, I would particularly single out the following: Sherman Paul, *The Shores of America: Thoreau's Inward Exploration* (Urbana: University of Illinois Press, 1958); Joel Porte, *Emerson and Thoreau: Transcendentalists in Conflict* (Middletown, Conn.: Wesleyan University Press, 1965); Lawrence Buell, *Literary Transcendentalism: Style and Vision in the American Renaissance* (Ithaca: Cornell University Press, 1973); Stanley Cavell, *The Senses of* Walden: *An Expanded Edition* (San Francisco: North Point Press, 1981); and H. Daniel Peck, *Thoreau's Morning Work: Memory and Perception in* A Week on the Concord and Merrimack Rivers, *the* Journal, *and* Walden (New Haven: Yale University Press, 1990). For a general discussion of the problem I am addressing, see Kevin Van Anglen, "Emerson, Thoreau, and the Myth of Secularization," in *Seeing into the Life of Things: Essays in Religion and Literature,* ed. John L. Mahoney (New York: Fordham University Press, 1998), 152–170.

33. It is interesting that on the few occasions when Thoreau's name has appeared in the histories of North American religion, it has been in the context mostly of some of the recent work on the history of Asian religions and religious groups in North America. Note, for example, Rick Fields, *How the Swans Came to the Lake: A Narrative History of Buddhism in America,* rev. ed. (Boston: Shambhala, 1986); Thomas Tweed, *The American Encounter with Buddhism, 1844–1912: Victorian Culture and the Limits of Dissent* (Bloomington: Indiana University Press, 1992); and Richard Hughes Seager, *Buddhism in America* (New York: Columbia University Press, 1999). For their part, when recent literary critics have considered this area of Transcendentalist interest, they have done so for the most part solely in the historicist terms set forth by Edward Said. See Edward Said, *Orientalism* (New York: Random House, 1979).

34. Porte, *Transcendentalists in Conflict,* 163.

35. Critics have responded to this somewhat esoteric dimension of Thoreau's life in several distinct ways. Some have simply ignored Thoreau's representations of his ecstasy or dismissed them as the excesses of youth or the products of poetic license. Others bracket such passages as inaccessible to the critic and therefore outside the purview of literary critical treatments. This response is understandable in its judicious recognition of the investigative limits of the critical enterprise, but it is also somewhat fainthearted, given the centrality of this dimension of Thoreau's experience for understanding the character of his literary contributions. Among literary psychologists we find yet a third response. Such critics would have little hesitation assigning specific meanings to such confessional passages from the journal in keeping with one or an-

other clinical or psychological paradigm. Here the issue is not one of faint-heartedness, and most critics would probably agree that we understand Thoreau better as a man in considerable part because of the attention paid in recent decades to his psychological profile. No religious psychologist today would dismiss the facts of a child's early development as irrelevant to his or her later spiritual growth, and few would deny the role of sexuality and unconscious forces in religious experience of all kinds. Richard Lebeaux, in particular, has offered two sensitive and balanced analyses of Thoreau's personal growth in the terms provided by an Eriksonian developmental paradigm. See Richard Lebeaux, *Young Man Thoreau* (Amherst: University of Massachusetts Press, 1977), and *Thoreau's Seasons* (Amherst: University of Massachusetts Press, 1984). For a less sanguine view of literary psychoanalysis, see Robert Sattelmeyer, "Study Nature and Know Thyself: Recent Thoreau Criticism," *ESQ* 31 (1985): 199–200.

Another, not uncommon response to Thoreau's confessional passages has been to frankly acknowledge the existence of these ecstatic episodes and then to somewhat hastily dispose of them under the problematic rubric of "mysticism." Such critics have often found authorization for their designation of Thoreau as a "mystic," or certain features of his writing as "mystical," from the famous self-declaration he made in response to a letter from Harvard College soliciting information from its alumni: "The fact is I am a mystic—a transcendentalist—& a natural philosopher to boot" (PJ.5.469). Yet notwithstanding such specific authorial sanction, the problem here is that the related terms "mystic," "mystical," and "mysticism" have all lost whatever descriptive value they formerly enjoyed and become so vague or derogatory as to be almost wholly useless. For this reason, I have generally avoided their use in respect to Thoreau, except in specifically qualified instances; other terms are more illuminating and representative of his own usage.

In his generally judicious appraisal, Edward Wagenknecht warns of the pitfalls associated with any indiscriminate use of the term mystic in reference to Thoreau, but then goes on to exemplify the general problem by characterizing mysticism rather narrowly in reference to nineteenth-century spiritualism. See Edward Wagenknecht, *Henry David Thoreau: What Manner of Man?* (Amherst: University of Massachusetts Press, 1981), 168–172. For his part, the theologian William J. Wolf introduced the term mystic in the subtitle of his 1974 study. Wolf's analysis of Thoreau's religious outlook contributes some useful theological discriminations, but his discussion of Thoreau's religious experience now seems somewhat rote. Cf. William J. Wolf, *Thoreau: Mystic, Prophet, Ecologist* (Philadelphia: Pilgrim Press, 1974). More searching is a 1977 article by Michael Keller in which he explicates Thoreau's religious experience in terms of the wider literature of mysticism and the critical work available to him at that time on nonordinary states of consciousness. In doing so, he plumbs Thoreau's journal for a number of suggestive citations and offers some fresh insights on this dimension of his life. See Michael Keller, "Henry David Thoreau: A Transpersonal View," *Journal of Transpersonal Psychology* 9 (December 1977): 39–82. On the origins and historical uses of the term mysticism, see Louis Bouyer, "Mysticism: An Essay on the History of the Word," in Bouyer, *Mystery and Mysticism* (London: Blackfriars, 1956); reprinted in *Understanding Mysticism*, ed. Richard Woods (Garden City, N.J.: Doubleday, 1980), 42–55.

36. William James, *The Varieties of Religious Experience* (Cambridge: Harvard University Press, 1985), 34.

37. The fact that this single citation exhausts James's references to Thoreau, whereas Emerson and Whitman, for example, receive far more attention, suggests that even James was not inclined to conceive Thoreau mainly in religious terms. See William James, *The Varieties of Religious Experience* (Cambridge: Harvard University Press, 1985), 221–222.

38. Cf. Robert R. Magliola, *Phenomenology and Literature: An Introduction* (West Lafayette, Ind.: Purdue University Press, 1977); Georges Poulet, "Phenomenology of Reading," *New Literary History* 1 (1969–70): 53–68.

39. Determinedly psychoanalytic readings raise particular methodological objections, especially from an approach of this kind focusing on religious experience. As historians of religion often point out, Freud and his disciples never accepted "religious experience" as a valid category in itself, insisting rather on explaining "religion" by reducing it to some psychological mechanism, usually an unconscious one. It necessarily followed, therefore, that a subject's own account of his or her religious experience could not be taken at face value: rather, it must be analyzed and interpreted by the analyst at levels outside the client's own experience and evaluation. To anthropologists and historians of religion concerned to affirm, at least in part, the meaningfulness of their subjects' reports, such totalizing psychological approaches have opened themselves to ethical and methodological doubts. Concertedly psychoanalytic readings of Thoreau are, in any case, formally inconsistent with the phenomenological and pragmatist methodology adopted for this study. Long ago James convincingly argued that the real meaning of religious experience resided not in its origin, whatever that may be, but in its implications for present and future experience. See James, *Religious Experience*, 11–29.

40. For the contributions of the Dutch School, see William Brede Kristensen, *The Meaning of Religion: Lectures in the Phenomenology of Religion,* trans. John B. Carmen (The Hague: Martinus Nijhoff, 1960, 1968); Gerardus van der Leeuw, *Religion in Essence and Manifestation,* 2nd ed., 2 vols., trans. J. E. Turner (London: Allen & Unwin, 1938). Among Eliade's numerous books, see especially Mircea Eliade, *Patterns in Comparative Religion* (London: Sheed and Ward, 1958). See also Jacques Waardenburg, *Classical Approaches to the Study of Religion,* 2 vols. (Berlin: Walter de Gruyter, 1999), 381–523; 639–666. For an overview of the phenomenology of religion and its relationship to philosophical phenomenology, see Douglas Allen, s.v. "Phenomenology of Religion," *The Encyclopedia of Religion,* ed. Mircea Eliade et al. (New York: Macmillan, 1987).

Chapter 1: My Life Was Ecstasy

1. In this and all subsequent citations to the critical edition of the journal, no effort is made to correct redundancies or typographical errors, or to alter Thoreau's own punctuation.

2. For the best full-dress narrative of Thoreau's life, see Walter Harding, *The Days of Henry Thoreau* (Princeton: Princeton University Press, 1962). On Thoreau's intellectual life, see Robert D. Richardson, Jr., *Henry Thoreau: A Life of the Mind* (Berkeley: University of California Press, 1986).

3. See also JMN.10.344, 343; JMN.11.404.

4. See Joel Porte, *Emerson and Thoreau: Transcendentalists in Conflict* (Middletown, Conn.: Wesleyan University Press, 1965); and Robert Sattelmeyer, " 'When He Became My Enemy': Emerson and Thoreau, 1848–49," *New England Quarterly* 62, no. 2 (1989): 187–204.

5. Harding, *Days of Henry Thoreau,* 274–277.

6. Cf. PJ.5.205–206; J.6.382–383.

7. Cf. Harding, *Days of Henry Thoreau,* 77–79.

8. Cf. Writings.5.143; see also Harding, *Days of Henry Thoreau,* 26, 34.

9. A list of items Thoreau borrowed from the Harvard Library is provided in Kenneth W. Cameron, *Emerson the Essayist* (Raleigh, N.C.: Thistle Press, 1945), ii, 191–208. For the closest reading of Thoreau's lifelong interest in Milton, see K. P. Van Anglen, *The New England Milton: Literary Reception and Cultural Authority in the Early Republic* (University Park, Penn.: Pennsylvania State University Press, 1993), 189–227.

10. Harding, *Days of Henry Thoreau,* 77–78.

11. On the origins and evolution of *A Week*'s essay on friendship, see Linck C.

Johnson, *Thoreau's Complex Weave: The Writing of* A Week on the Concord and Merrimack Rivers (Charlottesville: University Press of Virginia, 1986), 66–69.

12. PJ.1.98–100; PJ.3.18–19.

13. Cf. CW.2.113–127.

14. Cf. Joel Porte, "Thoreau on Love: Lexicon of Hate," *The University Review* 31 (December 1964): 111–116.

15. Johnson, *Thoreau's Complex Weave*, xvii.

16. H. Daniel Peck, *Thoreau's Morning Work: Memory and Perception in* A Week on the Concord and Merrimack Rivers, *the Journal, and* Walden (New Haven: Yale University Press, 1990), 134–158.

17. See Walter Harding, "Appendix: A Hound, a Bay Horse, and a Turtle-Dove," Walden: *An Annotated Edition* (Boston: Houghton Mifflin, 1995), 327–329.

18. Barbara Johnson, *A World of Difference* (Baltimore: Johns Hopkins University Press, 1987), 50–54.

19. On Thoreau's source for this and other such Confucian passages, see Hongbo Tan, "Confucius at Walden Pond: Thoreau's Unpublished Confucian Translations," *Studies in the American Renaissance* (1993): 275–303.

20. Cf. PJ.2.380.

21. See "Tintern Abbey," ll. 73–75. Cf. Laraigne Fergenson, "Was Thoreau Rereading Wordsworth in 1851?" *Thoreau Journal Quarterly* 5, no. 3 (July 1973): 21.

22. By insisting, as I do in the following pages, on the indispensable role of Wordsworth in so shaping Thoreau's elegiac sense, I do not mean to ignore entirely its wider provenance. To some extent, such elegiac feeling is a legacy of Romanticism itself. Before Wordsworth, it may be traced to the sensibility poets: Thomas Gray, William Collins, William Lisle Bowles, and Charlotte Smith. It may also be found, of course, in Coleridge and Shelley, as well as their heirs. While Thoreau was certainly aware of some of these other precedents, Wordsworth clearly provided the principal conduit. See Mary Jacobus, *Tradition and Experiment in Wordsworth's Lyrical Ballads* (London: Oxford University Press, 1976). More recently, see Laura Quinney, *The Poetics of Disappointment: Wordsworth to Ashbery* (Charlottesville: University Press of Virginia, 1999).

23. One of the earliest treatments of Thoreau's reliance on Wordsworth was James G. Southworth's rejoinder to an article by William Templeman on Thoreau's use of the picturesque. See James G. Southworth, Comment and Criticism on William Templeman's "Thoreau, Moralist of the Picturesque,"

PMLA 49, no. 3 (Sept. 1934): 971–974. Fuller treatments have been provided in Perry Miller, "Thoreau in the Context of International Romanticism, *New England Quarterly* 34 (June 1961): 147–159; Fergenson, "Rereading Wordsworth"; Laraigne Fergenson, "Wordsworth and Thoreau: The Relationship Between Man and Nature," *Thoreau Journal Quarterly* 11, no. 2 (April 1979): 3–10; Neill R. Joy, "Two Possible Analogues for 'The Ponds' in *Walden:* Jonathan Carver and Wordsworth," *ESQ* 24, no. 4 (1978): 197–205; Joseph Moldenhauer, "*Walden* and Wordsworth's Guide to the English Lake District," *Studies in the American Renaissance* (1990): 261–292; and Frederick Garber, "Thoreau and Anglo-European Romanticism," in *Approaches to Teaching Thoreau's* Walden *and Other Works,* ed. Richard J. Schneider (New York: Modern Language Association, 1996), 39–47.

24. On his handling of Goethe, cf. Week, 326; on Wordsworth, see PJ.1.321: "The best poets, after all, exhibit only a tame and civil side of nature. . . . Day and night—mountain and wood are visible from the wilderness as well as the village—They have their primeval aspects—sterner savager—than any poet has sung. It is only white man's poetry—we want the Indian's report. Wordsworth is too tame for the Chippeway." To us such criticism may seem a little like hair-splitting, especially considering the enormous distinction bestowed by the implied though understated acknowledgment of Wordsworth as chief among our best poets, but it does of course leave room for Thoreau to take his own place as representative poet of the North American wilderness.

25. See Moldenhauer, "*Walden,*" 261. For a full accounting of Thoreau's wide reading, see Robert Sattelmeyer, *Thoreau's Reading: A Study in Intellectual History with Bibliographical Catalogue* (Princeton: Princeton University Press, 1988).

26. Garber, "Thoreau and Anglo-European Romanticism," 44.

27. Writings.5.151.

28. Other precedents might include Irving's *Sketchbook* and Longfellow's *Outre-Mer: A Pilgrimage Beyond the Sea.*

29. Cf. PJ.2.200–201: "To live to a good old age such as the ancients reached— serene and contented—dignifying the life of man—Leading a simple epic country life—in these days of confusion and turmoil—That is what Wordsworth has done—Retaining the tastes and the innocence of his youth—There is more wonderful talent—but nothing so cheering and world famous as this."

30. Moldenhauer, "*Walden,*" 277–279.

31. PJ.4.193; Moldenhauer, "*Walden,*" 278.

32. Cf. Wordsworth's "The Recluse," ll. 52–53.
33. See in particular the cycle of Lucy poems in Wordsworth, *Poems and Prefaces,* ed. Jack Stillinger (Boston: Houghton Mifflin, 1965), 113–117, but other examples abound.
34. Cf. PJ.1.242. For a superb reading of the Immortality Ode as a vehicle of Wordsworthian ecstasy, see "The 'Immortality Ode' and the Problem of Connection," in Frances Ferguson, *Wordsworth: Language as Counter-Spirit* (New Haven: Yale University Press, 1977), 96–125.
35. Wordsworth, "Excursion," ll. 220–243.
36. Harding, *Days of Henry Thoreau,* 31.
37. EEM, 93–99, 370–371.
38. Neither of the first two volumes of journals that Thoreau kept—the first from October 1837 till June 1840, the second from June 1840 till January 1841— has survived in its original form. What we have instead is a series of volumes into which Thoreau transcribed the material from the original journals. These transcribed entries read almost as a series of mini-essays, complete with dates and headings, documenting Thoreau's current thoughts, readings, and experiences. The title Thoreau appended to the first of these transcript volumes, "Gleanings—Or What Time Has Not Reaped Of My Journals," suggests that the entries in the transcribed volume had been subjected to a process of selection and editing. Indexes that have survived from the original volumes suggest that this transcribed material is not appreciably different than what was contained in the original volumes, but it is hard to say for sure. This information indicates the need for some caution in how we go about interpreting the journals' contents: on the one hand, it is clear that these entries have gone through a significant process of formalization in their transcription; on the other hand, they were apparently important enough for Thoreau to save. In any case, they provide the best record we have of the changing currents of Thoreau's intellectual and spiritual life. See "Historical Introduction," PJ.1.596–597.
39. See Elizabeth Hall Witherell, "Thoreau as Poet," in *The Cambridge Companion to Henry David Thoreau,* ed. Joel Myerson (Cambridge: Cambridge University Press, 1995), 57–70.
40. Emerson, "Thoreau," in *Walden and Resistance to Civil Government,* 2nd ed., ed. William Rossi (New York: W. W. Norton, 1992), 330.
41. PJ.1.42–44, 47–49, 65–68, 100–103.
42. On Unitarian religious culture at Harvard see Daniel Walker Howe, *The Unitarian Conscience: Harvard Moral Philosophy, 1805–1861* (Middletown, Conn.: Wesleyan University Press, 1970), esp. 151–173.

Chapter 2: A Clear and Ancient Harmony

1. Cf. PJ.1.469: "The least sensual life is that experienced through pure senses."
2. Samuel Taylor Coleridge, *Biographia Literaria,* ed. James Engell and W. Jackson Bate (Princeton: Princeton University Press, 1983), 295–306.
3. JMN.5.76.
4. PJ.2.15; PJ.1.171, 469; Walden, 123.
5. Cf. Week, 41–42.
6. "Walking" is reprinted in Wendell Glick, ed., *The Great Short Works of Henry David Thoreau* (New York: Harper and Row, 1982), 294–326.
7. Cf. PJ.4.143; Week, 50.
8. Cf. Correspondence, 252.
9. Cited in John Hollander, "Wordsworth and the Music of Sound," in *New Perspectives on Coleridge and Wordsworth,* ed. Geoffrey H. Hartman (New York: Columbia University Press, 1972), 49.
10. Hollander, "Wordsworth," 49.
11. Correspondence, 74. PJ.1.361–362.
12. Sherman Paul, "The Wise Silence: Sound as the Agency of Correspondence in Thoreau," *New England Quarterly* 22, no. 4 (December 1949): 511–527; also see his *The Shores of America: Thoreau's Inward Exploration* (Urbana: University of Illinois Press, 1958), 64–70. Cf. Kenneth W. Rhoads, "Thoreau: The Ear and Music," *American Literature* 46, no. 3 (November 1974): 313–328.
13. Cf. PJ.1.320; PJ.2.167.
14. Cf. Week, 176–177.
15. On the motif of the Aeolian harp in Romantic poetry, see Hollander, "Wordsworth," 61–64.
16. PJ.1.50, 54, 249, etc.
17. Iamblichus, *Life of Pythagoras,* trans. Thomas Taylor (London: 1818). Thoreau first mentions his reading of Iamblichus on March 28, 1842. See PJ.1.395.
18. Iamblichus, *Life of Pythagoras,* 72. See Wordsworth's note to Isabella Fenwick cited in William Wordsworth, *Poems, in Two Volumes, and Other Poems, 1800–1807,* ed. Jared Curtis (Ithaca: Cornell University Press, 1983), 428.
19. Iamblichus, *Life of Pythagoras,* 33.
20. See also Sherman Paul, *Shores of America,* 64 ff.
21. For the source of the *Walden* passage, see PJ.3.313.
22. Cf. PJ.1.23, 68, 87, 91 ff., 165, 179, 298–299, et al.
23. PJ.1.91–98, 604. Rejected for publication in 1840 by Margaret Fuller, the

Dial's first editor, "The Service" was never published in Thoreau's lifetime. See RP, 3–17.

24. See M. H. Abrams, *Natural Supernaturalism: Tradition and Revolution in Romantic Literature* (New York: Norton, 1971).

25. See Alan D. Hodder, *Emerson's Rhetoric of Revelation:* Nature, *the Reader, and the Apocalypse Within* (University Park: The Pennsylvania State University Press, 1989).

26. Thomas Carlyle, *Sartor Resartus: The Life and Opinions of Herr Teufelsdröckh,* vol. 1 of *The Works of Thomas Carlyle,* ed. H. D. Traill (New York: AMC Press, 1969).

27. See Paul, *The Shores of America.*

28. Mason Lowance, Jr., "From Edwards to Emerson to Thoreau: A Revaluation," *American Transcendental Quarterly* 17 (Winter 1973): 3–12.

29. Very described his own dramatic conversion experience in a letter to Henry W. Bellows in December of 1838. For a reprinting of this remarkable letter and a helpful introduction to Very's religious experiences and their relation to his ecstatic poetry, see Helen R. Deese, ed. *Jones Very: The Complete Poems* (Athens: University of Georgia Press, 1993): xi–lviii.

30. Cited in *The Essential Margaret Fuller,* ed. Jeffrey Steele (New Brunswick, N.J.: Rutgers University Press, 1992), 10–11.

31. Preface to *Lyrical Ballads,* in Wordsworth, *Selected Poems and Prefaces,* ed. Jack Stillinger (Boston: Houghton Mifflin, 1965), 460.

32. In this, Wordsworth's poems may be said to exemplify a key function of all artistic representation. See Rudolph Arnheim, "Space as an Image of Time," in *Images of Romanticism,* ed. Karl Kroeber and William Walling (New Haven: Yale University Press, 1978), 1–12.

33. The phrase is Emerson's. See Ralph Waldo Emerson, "The Transcendentalist," in CW.1.213. Cf. Joel Porte, "Emerson, Thoreau, and the Double Consciousness," *New England Quarterly* 41 (March 1968).

Chapter 3: To Redeem This Wasted Time

1. Sherman Paul, *The Shores of America: Thoreau's Inward Exploration* (Urbana: University of Illinois Press, 1958), 193–195; 220.

2. Linck Johnson adapts this term from Thoreau. See Linck C. Johnson, *Thoreau's Complex Weave: The Writing of* A Week on the Concord and Merrimack Rivers (Charlottesville: University Press of Virginia, 1986), xii.

3. See also PJ.1.124–126, 134–138.

4. See "Historical Introduction," Week, 605.

5. PJ.2.449–454.
6. On the origins and development of Thoreau's first book, see Johnson, *Thoreau's Complex Weave*, 202–247.
7. John Aldrich Christie, *Thoreau as World Traveler* (New York: Columbia University Press, 1965), 44. See also Robert Sattelmeyer, *Thoreau's Reading* (Princeton: Princeton University Press, 1988).
8. Johnson, *Thoreau's Complex Weave*, 7.
9. PJ.1.11–12, 30.
10. Christie, *Thoreau as World Traveler*, 62–70.
11. Joseph Moldenhauer, " *Walden* and Wordsworth's Guide to the English Lake District," *Studies in the American Renaissance* (1990): 275.
12. Lawrence Buell, *Literary Transcendentalism* (Ithaca: Cornell University Press, 1973), 191.
13. Johnson, *Thoreau's Complex Weave*, 52–53, 66–69.
14. For a classic study of the development of the pastoral tradition leading up to *Lycidas,* see James Holly Hanford, "The Pastoral Elegy and Milton's *Lycidas,*" *PMLA* 25 (1910): 403–447.
15. Walter Hesford, " 'Incessant Tragedies': A Reading of *A Week on the Concord and Merrimack Rivers,*" *ELH* 44, no. 3 (Fall 1977): 515–525.
16. See H. Daniel Peck, *Thoreau's Morning Work: Memory and Perception in* A Week on the Concord and Merrimack Rivers, *the Journal, and* Walden (New Haven: Yale University Press, 1990), chaps. 2–3.
17. On the interests of classic American writers in myth and myth theory, see Robert D. Richardson, Jr., *Myth and Literature in the American Renaissance* (Bloomington: Indiana University Press, 1978).
18. For helpful treatments of the Thoreauvian quest, see Paul, *Shores of America,* esp. 173–233; Jonathan Bishop, "The Experience of the Sacred in Thoreau's *Week,*" *ELH* 33 (1966); Paul David Johnson, "Thoreau's Redemptive *Week,*" *American Literature* 49 (March 1977); Jamie Hutchinson, " 'The Lapse of the Current': Thoreau's Historical Vision in *A Week,*" *ESQ* 25 (1979): 211–223.
19. Cf. Johnson, *Thoreau's Complex Weave*, 22 ff.
20. Cf. Mircea Eliade, *The Myth of the Eternal Return, or Cosmos and History,* trans. Willard R. Trask (Princeton: Princeton University Press, 1954); and Joseph Campbell, *The Hero With a Thousand Faces* (Princeton: Princeton University Press, 1949).
21. R. W. B. Lewis, *The American Adam: Innocence, Tragedy, and Tradition in the Nineteenth Century* (Chicago: University of Chicago Press, 1955). On Thoreau's thorough indebtedness to Milton in his conception of *A Week,* see K. P.

Van Anglen, *The New England Milton: Literary Reception and Cultural Authority in the Early Republic* (University Park: The Pennsylvania State University Press, 1993), 196.

22. Cf. PJ.3.187: "I believe that adam in paradise was not so favorably situated on the whole as is the backwoodsman in America—You all know how miserably the former turned out—or was turned out—but there is some consolation at least in the fact that it yet remains to be seen how the western Adam Adam in the wilderness will turn out—."

23. See also Hesford, " 'Incessant Tragedies,' " 518; Hutchinson, " 'Lapse of the Current,' " 215.

24. Week, 290–291; 314–315. See Van Anglen, *New England Milton*, 202.

25. Buell, *Literary Transcendentalism*, 237–238.

26. See also Week, 89.

27. Week, 122–124, 158.

28. Johnson, *Thoreau's Complex Weave*, 45.

29. Buell, *Literary Transcendentalism*, 208–209.

30. Among the various analyses of this episode, see in particular Hutchinson, " 'Lapse of the Current,' " 217; Buell, *Literary Transcendentalism*, 230; Peck, *Thoreau's Morning Work*, 27–30.

31. Johnson, *Thoreau's Complex Weave*, 24–25.

32. John 20: 24–29.

Chapter 4: Born to Be a Pantheist

1. Horace Greeley, "H. D. Thoreau's Book," New York *Daily Tribune* (13 June 1849). Reprinted in Joel Myerson, ed., *Emerson and Thoreau: The Contemporary Reviews* (Cambridge: Cambridge University Press, 1992), 342; James Russell Lowell, "A Week on The Concord and Merrimack Rivers," *Massachusetts Quarterly Review* 3 (December 1849), 40–51; also reprinted in Myerson, ed., *Contemporary Reviews*, 357.

2. See especially "Wendell Phillips Before the Concord Lyceum," RP, 59 ff.; "Slavery in Massachusetts," RP, 99, 104; "A Plea for Captain John Brown," RP, 120–121. Also PJ.3.203. On Thoreau's abolitionism, see Wendell Glick, "Thoreau and Radical Abolitionism" (Ph.D. diss., Northwestern University, 1950).

3. See also PJ.2.381–382.

4. Cf. C. G. Jung and C. Kerenyi, *Essays on a Science of Mythology* (Princeton: Princeton University Press, 1949).

5. See Robert D. Richardson Jr., *Myth and Literature in the American Renaissance* (Bloomington: Indiana University Press, 1978).

6. See James Engell, *The Creative Imagination: Enlightenment to Romanticism* (Cambridge: Harvard University Press, 1981).

7. On the Higher Criticism, see Hans W. Frei, *The Eclipse of Biblical Narrative: A Study of Eighteenth and Nineteenth Century Hermeneutics* (New Haven: Yale University Press, 1974).

8. See Jerry Wayne Brown, *The Rise of Biblical Criticism in America, 1800–1870: The New England Scholars* (Middletown, Conn.: Wesleyan University Press, 1969). Also relevant is Barbara Packer, "Origin and Authority: Emerson and the Higher Criticism," *Reconstructing American Literary History,* ed. Sacvan Bercovitch (Cambridge: Harvard University Press, 1986). See also Barbara Packer, "The Transcendentalists," in *The Cambridge History of American Literature,* vol. 2: *Prose Writing 1820–1865,* gen. ed. Sacvan Bercovitch (Cambridge: Cambridge University Press, 1995), 343–349, 403–423.

9. Cf. Raymond Schwab, *The Oriental Renaissance: Europe's Rediscovery of India and the East, 1680–1880,* trans. Gene Patterson-Black and Victor Reinking (New York: Columbia University Press, 1984).

10. See, for example, PJ.2.183, 260.

11. Ludwig Feuerbach, *The Essence of Christianity,* trans. Marian Evans (George Eliot) (London: John Chapman, 1854); Émile Durkheim, *The Elementary Forms of Religious Life,* trans. Joseph Ward Swain (London: Macmillan, 1915).

12. Cf. PJ.1.428.

13. Cf. Revelation 22:16, where Christ is symbolized by the morning star. One of the most fervent expressions of Thoreau's Christian sensibility may be found in the concluding paragraphs of a review essay from 1843, "Paradise (To Be) Regained," RP, 45–47.

14. See also Week, 223, 311.

15. This citation Thoreau derives from his reading of Taylor's translation of "The Life of Pythagoras." See Iamblichus, *Life of Pythagoras,* trans. Thomas Taylor (Rochester, Vt.: Inner Traditions International, 1986), 196.

16. Cf. Alan D. Hodder, "'After a High Negative Way': Emerson's 'Self-Reliance' and the Rhetoric of Conversion," *Harvard Theological Review* 84, no. 4 (1991): 423–446.

17. Cf. PJ.1.55.

18. Cf. PJ.3.185, 198.

19. Catherine L. Albanese, *Nature Religion in America: From the Algonkian Indians to the New Age* (Chicago: University of Chicago Press, 1990).

20. Walden, 311; cf. Luke 15:32.

21. The modern theological use of the term "process" derives from A. N. White-

head's classic treatment *Process and Reality; An Essay in Cosmology* (New York: Macmillan, 1929). See also his earlier *Religion in the Making* (Cambridge: Cambridge University Press, 1927). For a seminal source in the pragmatist tradition, see William James, *Pragmatism* (Cambridge: Harvard University Press, 1975), esp. lectures 2, 6, 8. On the foundational position of Transcendentalism in the tradition of pragmatist philosophy, see especially Cornel West, *The American Evasion of Philosophy: A Genealogy of Pragmatism* (Madison: University of Wisconsin Press, 1989); Olaf Hansen, *Aesthetic Individualism and Practical Intellect: American Allegory in Emerson, Thoreau, Adams, and James* (Princeton: Princeton University Press, 1990); Richard Poirier, *Poetry and Pragmatism* (Cambridge: Harvard University Press, 1992); and Richard Poirier *The Renewal of Literature: Emersonian Reflections* (New York: Random House, 1987).

22. For a full elaboration of his notion of experience, see William James, *The Varieties of Religious Experience* (Cambridge: Harvard University Press, 1985), esp. Lectures 1–3, Conclusion, and Postscript.

Chapter 5: The Artist of Kouroo

1. Reprinted in Joel Myerson, ed., *Emerson and Thoreau: The Contemporary Reviews* (Cambridge: Cambridge University Press, 1992), 341–343; 352–359. For more on the critical reception of *A Week,* see Linck C. Johnson, "Historical Introduction," in Week, 470–477.

2. On Thoreau's career as a professional writer, see Steven Fink, *Prophet in the Marketplace* (Princeton: Princeton University Press, 1992).

3. See Raymond Schwab, *The Oriental Renaissance: Europe's Discovery of India and the East, 1680–1880,* trans. Gene Patterson-Black and Victor Reinking (New York: Columbia University Press, 1984).

4. In 1814 the sinologist Abel Remusat was granted a chair at the College de France. See Schwab, *Oriental Renaissance,* 6 ff.

5. Established to promote the study of Indian civilization, the society sponsored the research of several notable British scholars and magistrates who would make lasting contributions to the study of India in the West. Preeminent among these was Sir William Jones (1746–1794), the society's first president and a polyglot linguist and scholar of extraordinary erudition, appointed to the Supreme Court of Bengal in 1783. Next to Jones should be mentioned the name of Charles Wilkins (1749–1836), also a magistrate in the colonial government and Jones's chief tutor in his early study of Sanskrit. Wilkins has the distinction of being the first European to translate classical Hindu texts

directly from Sanskrit into English. His momentous translation of the Bhagavad Gita in 1785 in particular constitutes a milestone in the history of modern Indology. To the early efforts of Jones and Wilkins were soon added the contributions of two other key scholars: Henry Thomas Colebrooke (1765–1837), a mathematician and linguist by training, and Horace Hayman Wilson (1786–1860), who though arriving in Bengal only in 1808, soon became one of the most accomplished Sanskritists and prolific translators of his generation. In the English-speaking world of the nineteenth century, Wilson's reputation as an Indologist was surpassed only by that of F. Max Müller (1823–1900), Wilson's German-born successor at Oxford and a leading architect of the field of comparative mythology.

In 1788 the Asiatic Society began publishing *Asiatic Researches,* a learned journal that went through twenty volumes before its final edition in 1839 and became the leading vehicle for the transmission of information about India to the West. During the next fifty years, these early British Orientalists issued a series of translations of Hindu scriptures and classics, as well as learned monographs, that shed much light on Indian civilization. Of special note are Wilkins's translations of the *Bhagavadgita* (1785) and *Hitopadeśa* (1787), a traditional collection of morality tales known to Emerson and Thoreau by 1841; Jones's translations of Kālidāsa's *Śakuntalā* (1789), Jāyadeva's *Gītāgovinda* (1792), and, importantly for Emerson and Thoreau, *The Institutes of Hindu Law* ("The Laws of Manu," 1794); Colebrooke's *Essays on the Religion and Philosophy of the Hindus* (1815) and his translation of the *Sāṃkhya-kārikā* (1837), a commentary on the Sāṃkhya system of Indian philosophy, which Thoreau studied carefully in 1851; and Wilson's translations of Kālidāsa's *Megha-dūta* (1813) and the *Viṣṇu Purāṇa* (1840), a work that was being perused in Concord by 1845.

6. Friedrich Schlegel's remark in 1800 was programmatic: "Im Orient müssen wir das höchste Romantische suchen" (We must seek the supreme romanticism in the Orient). Cited in Schwab, *Oriental Renaissance,* 13.

7. For full discussions of Transcendentalist interest in Asian thought, see Carl T. Jackson, *The Oriental Religions and American Thought: Nineteenth-Century Explorations* (Westport, Conn.: Greenwood Press, 1981); and Arthur Versluis, *American Transcendentalism and Asian Religions* (New York: Oxford University Press, 1993).

8. Emerson's designation, in a letter to family friend and townswoman Elizabeth Hoar, of the Bhagavad Gita as "the much renowned book of Buddhism" reflects the confusion. Letters.3.290.

9. *Dial* 4 (January 1844): 391–401. See Jackson, *Oriental Religions*, 140–156; and Rick Fields, *How the Swans Came to the Lake: A Narrative History of Buddhism in America*, rev. ed. (Boston: Shambhala, 1986).

10. Although his focus is more on the Levant than on India, Said provides the now classic treatment of Orientalism as a European projection; see Edward Said, *Orientalism* (New York: Random House, 1979). Of direct interest is Wilhelm Halbfass, *India and Europe: An Essay in Understanding* (Albany: State University of New York, 1988); A. Leslie Willson, *A Mythical Image: The Ideal of India in German Romanticism* (Durham: Duke University Press, 1964); and Ronald Inden, *Imagining India* (Oxford: Basil Blackwell, 1990). The relative neglect evident in all of these works of forms of Orientalism found in the United States is now being more effectively redressed: see Malini Johar Schueller, *U.S. Orientalisms: Race, Nation, and Gender in Literature, 1790–1890* (Ann Arbor: The University of Michigan Press, 1998).

11. JMN.2.195; PJ.1.428; Week, 148.

12. PJ.1.168–169, 177; 2.371; Week, 142–143.

13. Or "Menu," as it was commonly transliterated. See Sir William Jones, trans., *Institutes of Hindu Law; or, the ordinances of Menu, according to the gloss of Culluca*, 2 vols. (London: Rivington and Cochran, 1825). Besides Manu, Thoreau found other Oriental texts in Emerson's personal library worthy of note, in particular Wilkins's translation of the *Hitopadésa* and the *Gulistan* of Sa'di. See Robert Sattelmeyer, *Thoreau's Reading: A Study in Intellectual History with Bibliographical Catalogue* (Princeton: Princeton University Press, 1988), 231, 202, 264.

14. Kenneth Walter Cameron, "Books Thoreau Borrowed from Harvard College Library," in *Emerson the Essayist*, 2 vols. (Raleigh: Thistle Press, 1945) 2:191–208; also Sattelmeyer, *Thoreau's Reading*, 3–24.

15. Cf. PJ.1.51, 142, 144, 169.

16. The *Dial*, 4 vols. (Boston: James Munroe, 1840–1844). Joshua Marshman, *The Works of Confucius* (Serampore, India, 1809) and *The Phenix; A Collection of Old and Rare Fragments* (New York: William Gowan, 1835). See EEM, 382–383. On Thoreau's contributions to the *Dial*, see Joel Myerson, ed., *The New England Transcendentalists and the* Dial (London: Associated University Presses, 1980). "The Preaching of the Buddha," appearing in the issue of January 1844 and conventionally attributed to Thoreau, appears not to have been his contribution. See K. P. Van Anglen, "Introduction" to Translations, 160, note 1.

17. See Hongbo Tan, "Confucius at Walden Pond: Thoreau's Unpublished Confucian Translations," *Studies in the American Renaissance* (1993), 275–303.

18. See Sattelmeyer, *Thoreau's Reading,* 29.
19. Cf. Week, 78–79, 388.
20. Letters.6.245–247; 1.322; 3.303. Charles Wilkins, trans., *Bhagvat-geeta, or Dialogues of Kreeshna and Arjoon* (London [n.p.], 1785).
21. Week, 135–143; see also PJ.2.253 ff.
22. On Thoreau's first reactions to the Gita, see PJ.2.253 ff. William Ward, *A View of the history, literature, and religion of the Hindoos* (Hartford, Conn.: H. Huntington, Jr., 1824); Rammohan Roy, raja, *Translation of several principal books, passages, and texts of the Veds, and of some controversial works on Brahmunical theology,* 2nd ed. (London: Parbury, Allen & Co., 1832); Iswara Krishna, *The Sankhya Karika,* trans. Henry Thomas Colebrooke (London: H. J. Valpy, 1837).
23. M. A. Langlois, trans., *Harivansa,* 2 vols. (Paris, 1834–35). Henry David Thoreau, "The Transmigration of the Seven Brahmans," ed. Arthur Christy (New York: William Edwin Rudge, 1932). This translation is also included in Translations, 135–144.
24. Cf. Miriam Jeswine, "Henry David Thoreau: Apprentice to the Hindu Sages" (Ph.D. diss., University of Oregon, 1971), 28–29. Cited in Walter Harding and Michael Meyer, eds., *The New Thoreau Handbook* (New York: New York University Press, 1980), 94.
25. Franklin Sanborn discusses Thoreau's friendship with Cholmondeley in "Thoreau and his English Friend Thomas Cholmondeley," *Atlantic Monthly* 72 (December 1893): 741–756.
26. See Schwab, *Oriental Renaissance,* 33–38, 52; Said, *Orientalism,* 78–79.
27. See Arthur Christy, *The Orient in American Transcendentalism* (New York: Columbia University Press, 1932), 221. Here it seems helpful to note that while in the West the term "yoga" has come to be construed narrowly as referring only to the physical postures taught in the discipline of *haṭha-yoga,* in fact, it refers to a whole range of spiritual practices—involving body, breath, meditation, devotion, etc.—whose purpose is union with the personal deity or transcendent being.
28. Mark Van Doren set the temper for such readings long ago in observing that "the total influence of Oriental philosophy upon Thoreau was neither broad nor profound." Mark Van Doren, *Henry David Thoreau* (Boston: Houghton Mifflin, 1916), 95. More recently Robert Sattelmeyer epitomizes this reading when he asserts that in the end Thoreau's interest in this literature "was relatively short-lived and led to no discernible literary results." See Sattelmeyer, *Thoreau's Reading,* 67–68. For a more balanced though still somewhat skeptical appraisal, see Harding and Meyer, eds., *New Thoreau Hand-*

book, 91–94. For the most balanced full-length treatments, see Jackson, *Oriental Religions,* and Versluis, *American Transcendentalism and Asian Religions.* Also see my "Concord Orientalism, Thoreauvian Autobiography, and the Artist of Kouroo," in *Transient and Permanent: The Transcendentalist Movement and Its Contexts,* ed. Charles Capper and Conrad Edick Wright (Boston: Massachusetts Historical Society, 1999).

29. See also my earlier treatment, " 'Ex oriente lux': Thoreau's Ecstasies and the Hindu Texts," *Harvard Theological Review* 86, no. 4 (1993): 403–438.

30. *Manu* 1:3; 1:21; 1:52; in Sir William Jones, trans., *Institutes of Hindu Law: or, The Ordinances of Manu, according to the Gloss of Culluca,* vol. 7 of *The Works of William Jones* (London, 1807), 100 ff. Hereafter cited as *Manu.* See also Week, 152.

31. *Manu* 2:6–8, 76 ff.

32. *Manu* 1:23.

33. Cf. Stephen Nissbaum, *Sex, Diet, and Debility in Jacksonian America: Sylvester Graham and Health Reform* (Westport, Conn.: Greenwood Press, 1980); also Taylor Stoehr, *Nay-Saying in Concord: Emerson, Alcott, and Thoreau* (Hamden, Conn.: Archon, 1979). For a useful review of the range of attitudes represented by the body reformers of the antebellum period, see David S. Reynolds, *Walt Whitman's America: A Cultural Biography* (New York: Knopf, 1995), 207–213.

34. Eccles. 12:13. Cf. *Westminster Shorter Catechism,* Q.1, 39.

35. Cf. Week, 45–46.

36. J. Lyndon Shanley, *The Making of* Walden (Chicago: University of Chicago Press, 1957), 30–31, 72–73.

37. Cf. Plato, *The Republic,* Book 10. For the role of the mirror metaphor in Western literary theory, see M. H. Abrams, *The Mirror and the Lamp: Romantic Theory and the Critical Tradition* (New York: Oxford University Press, 1953), 30–46.

38. *The Cloud of Unknowing,* trans. Clifton Wolters (London: Penguin, 1978), 102. See also Thomas Shepard, "Ineffectual Hearing of the Word," in *The Works of Thomas Shepard,* vol. 3 (Boston: Doctrinal Tract and Book Society, 1853), 370; and Thomas Hooker, *The Soul's Preparation for Christ* (London, 1638), 58.

39. Cf. Emerson: "The troubled water reflects no image. When it is calm it shows within it the whole face of heaven." JMN.3.244. Also JMN.5.103: "Man stands on the point betwixt the inward spirit & the outward matter. He sees that the one explains, translates the other: that the world is the mirror of the soul." See also the Swedenborgian Sampson Reed: "This world

is the mirror of him who made it," *Observations on the Growth of the Mind* (Boston: Cummings and Hilliard, 1826), 41.

40. *Buddhacarita,* canto 12:2, in *Buddhist Scriptures,* trans. Edward Conze (London: Penguin, 1959), 50.

41. On Zen, see Dōgen, *Moon in a Dew Drop: Writings of Zen Master Dōgen,* ed. Kazuaki Tanahashi (San Francisco: North Point Press, 1985), 71; on Kabbalah, see *Zohar: The Book of Enlightenment,* trans. Daniel Chanan Matt (New York: Paulist Press, 1983), 61, 75, 80; on Sufism, see Fakhruddin 'Iraqi, *Divine Flashes,* in *Classics of Western Spirituality,* trans. William C. Chittick and Peter Lamborn Wilson (New York: Paulist Press, 1982), 70, 73, 77; on Taoist and Confucian instances, see Julie Ching, "The Mirror Symbol Revisited: Confucian and Taoist Mysticism," in *Mysticism and Religious Traditions* ed. Steven Katz (New York: Oxford University Press, 1983), 226–246. For an exploration, with a particularly suggestive bearing on *Walden,* of the relation between the mirror and Aztec ritual and sacred geography, see Lawrence Sullivan, "Reflections in the Miraculous Waters of Tenochtitlan," in *To Change Place: Aztec Ceremonial Landscapes,* ed. David Carrasco (Nuwot, Co.: University Press of Colorado, 1991), 205–211.

42. Wilkins, trans., *Bhagvat-geeta,* 49.

43. Ward, *Hindoos,* 204; also 149, 166, 221, 171. For a more contemporary analysis of such yogic "witnessing," see Maharishi Mahesh Yogi, *Maharishi Mahesh Yogi On the Bhagavad-Gita: A New Translation and Commentary* (Harmondsworth: Penguin, 1969), 98, 291, 350, 354.

44. Wilkins, trans., Bhagvat-geeta, 59.

45. Colebrooke, trans., *Sankhya Karika,* 35.

46. Rammohan Roy, trans., *Translation of Several Principal Books, Passages, and Texts of the Veds,* 2nd ed. (London: Parbury, Allen, and Co., 1832). Reprinted in *Two Brahman Sources of Emerson and Thoreau,* ed. William Bysshe Stein (Gainesville, Fla.: Scholars Facsimiles and Reprints, 1967), 14–15.

47. A glance at the context of the "Solitude" passage as a whole and its evolution out of the journals accentuates these Hindu affiliations. This paragraph did not appear at all in the *Walden* manuscript until Thoreau introduced it in his fourth version sometime in 1852 or 1853. (See Shanley, *Making of* Walden, 72–73). Its principal source appears to be an entry that he drafted into his journal on August 8, 1852 (J.4.289–291). In *Walden,* a reworked version of this entry is introduced with a series of some of Confucius's more metaphysical musings. In the original entry, however, the Persian mystical poet Sa'di has this honor. Early on in *Walden,* Thoreau quotes a story from Sa'di's *Gulistan* (Walden, 79), but in the journal passage, Sa'di merely appears to

serve the function of an emblematic other in Thoreau's concern to argue for a perennialist view of religion.

48. For example: Week, 61, 68, 114, 380; Walden, 112; J.1.38, 118, 135, 257, 312, 473; PJ.2.201.

49. Augustine, *Expositions on the Book of Psalms,* vol. 6 (Oxford: John Henry Parker, 1857, 46–47.

50. Cf. Lynda G. Christian, *Theatrum Mundi: The History of an Idea* (New York: Garland, 1987).

51. One of the books that Thoreau received in the Cholmondeley collection in 1855, too late of course to influence his composition of *Walden,* was Wilson's translation of six classic Hindu dramas. See H. H. Wilson, trans., *Select specimens of the theater of the Hindus,* 2 vols. (London: Parbury, Allen, and Co., 1835).

52. See also Kenneth Walter Cameron, *Transcendental Apprenticeship* (Hartford, Conn.: Transcendental Books, 1976), 234.

53. Colebrooke, trans., *Sankhya Karika,* 97.

54. Ward, *Hindoas,* 222.

55. Colebrooke, trans., *Sankhya Karika,* 258–259.

56. There is still no consensus about the exact origin of this story or its proper interpretation. Arthur Christy construed it as essentially an allegory of Thoreau's own life and his pursuit of personal perfection (*The Orient in American Transcendentalism,* 193–194). In Sherman Paul, *The Shores of America: Thoreau's Inward Exploration* (Urbana: University of Illinois Press, 1958), 352–53, Paul provides a helpful but partially inaccurate gloss on the name Kouroo and supposes Thoreau may have run across it in his reading of *Manu;* more recently, Kenneth Cameron has located a possible source in Chuang-tzu's story of the Woodcarver of Lu ("An Archetype for Thoreau's Fable of the Artist of Kouroo," *American Renaissance Literary Report* 5 [1991]: 4–6). See also Walter Harding, ed., Walden: *An Annotated Edition* (Boston: Houghton Mifflin, 1995), 317–318. All of these assessments contribute something to our appreciation of Thoreau's story. Cameron comes closer than most to identifying a specific source, but even here the parallels between the stories of Chuang-tzu and Thoreau are only approximate, since several of the key details of Thoreau's story clearly have a Hindu, not Chinese, provenance. The story of the artist of Kouroo exhibits what might be termed a family resemblance to the Taoist story, just as it does to other related parables of transformation in the Hindu and Buddhist traditions.

57. Shanley, *Making of* Walden, 68–73. But see also Ronald Clapper, who

concludes that the Kouroo story was a product of the fourth through sixth recensions, and was therefore composed as early as 1852: Clapper, "The Development of *Walden:* A Genetic Text" (Ph.D. diss., University of California at Los Angeles, 1967), 30–31, 863–865.

58. See Arvind Sharma, *The Hindu Gītā: Ancient and Classical Interpretations of the Bhagavadgītā* (La Salle, Ill.: Open Court, 1986).

59. Wilkins, trans., *Bhagvat-geeta,* 40.

60. It is interesting to note that Thoreau extracted a similar teaching from his reading of the Confucian *Chung-yung.* See Tan, "Thoreau's Confucian Translations," 289, paragraph 61.6.

61. Walden, 134–135.

62. Cf. PJ.1.414, 424, 473; J.13.77.

63. On the rise and fall of the American ice trade, see Philip Chadwick Foster Smith, "Crystal Blocks of Yankee Coldness: The Development of the Massachusetts Ice Trade from Frederick Tudor to Wenham Lake, 1806–1886," *Essex Institute Historical Collection* 97 (July 1961): 197–232.

64. The earliest drafts of both these works did not contain anything like the wealth of Asian material included in the published versions. See Shanley, *Making of* Walden, 30; on *A Week,* see Johnson, *Thoreau's Complex Weave,* 263–393.

65. Cf. PJ.1.387, 409; PJ.2.252; PJ.3.21; Week, 126.

66. See also, PJ.1.177, 386; PJ.3.200.

Chapter 6: To Speak Somewhere Without Bounds

1. See J. Lyndon Shanley, *The Making of* Walden (Chicago: Chicago University Press, 1957); and Ronald Clapper, "The Development of *Walden:* A Genetic Text" (Ph.D. diss., University of California at Los Angeles, 1967).

2. See Joseph J. Moldenhauer, "Paradox in *Walden,*" in *Twentieth-Century Interpretations of* Walden: *A Collection of Critical Essays,* ed. Richard Ruland (Englewood Cliffs, N.J.: Prentice-Hall, Inc., 1968), 76–80; and Stanley Cavell, *The Senses of* Walden: *An Expanded Edition* (San Francisco: North Point Press, 1981), 5 ff.

3. "Thomas Carlyle and His Works," EEM, 232.

4. F. O. Matthiessen, *American Renaissance: Art and Expression in the Age of Emerson and Whitman* (Oxford: Oxford University Press, 1941), 153–175.

5. Cf. William Bysshe Stein, "The Yoga of *Walden,*" *Literature East and West* 13 (June 1969): 1–4.

6. As in, for example, Bhagavad Gita 2:18.

7. Walter Harding, *The Days of Henry Thoreau* (Princeton: Princeton University Press, 1962), 34–35.

8. George Campbell, *The Philosophy of Rhetoric,* ed. Lloyd Bitzer (Carbondale: Southern Illinois University Press, 1963); Richard Whately, *Elements of Rhetoric,* ed. Douglas Ehninger (Carbondale: Southern Illinois University Press, 1963). See Richard Dillman, *Essays on Henry David Thoreau: Rhetoric, Style, and Audience* (West Cornwall, Conn.: Locust Hill Press, 1993).

9. Edward T. Channing, *Lectures Read to the Seniors in Harvard College,* ed. Dorothy Anderson and Waldo Braden (Carbondale: Southern Illinois University Press, 1968). See Dillman, *Essays on Thoreau,* 17–21, 90.

10. On Thoreau's style, see Walter Harding and Michael Meyer, eds., *The New Thoreau Handbook* (New York: New York University Press, 1980), 160–201. For his reliance on precepts found in Whately, see Dillman, *Essays on Thoreau,* 72–73; and Annette Woodlief, "The Influence of Theories of Rhetoric on Thoreau," *Thoreau Journal Quarterly* (1975): 13–20.

11. William Ellery Channing, Jr., *Thoreau the Poet-Naturalist,* ed. F. B. Sanborn (1902; rpt. New York: Biblo and Tannen, 1966), 77 n, quoted in Michael West, "Thoreau and the Language Theories of the French Enlightenment," *ELH* 51, no. 4 (Winter 1984): 747.

12. Channing, *Lectures,* 234, quoted in Philip F. Gura, *The Wisdom of Words: Language, Theology, and Literature in the New England Renaissance* (Middletown, Conn.: Wesleyan University Press, 1981), 112.

13. Thomas Reid, *Essays on the Intellectual Powers of Man,* ed. James Walker (Cambridge: Harvard University Press, 1850), 1–9. See Gura, *Wisdom of Words,* 19–24.

14. See Michael West, "Thoreau and the Language Theories of the French Enlightenment," *ELH* 51, no. 4 (Winter 1984): 760 ff. Evidence of Thoreau's interest in Gebelin is preserved in a manuscript reprinted by Wendell Glick in "Three New Early Manuscripts by Thoreau," *Huntington Library Quarterly* 12 (1951): 68–70.

15. See Robert Sattelmeyer, *Thoreau's Reading: A Study in Intellectual History with Bibliographical Catalogue* (Princeton: Princeton University Press, 1988), 134.

16. For a useful history of Western language theory, see Hans Aarsleff, *From Locke to Saussure: Essays on the Study of Language and Intellectual History* (Minneapolis: University of Minnesota Press, 1982).

17. Cf. Philip Gura, "Language and Meaning: An American Tradition," *American Literature* 53 (March 1981): 1–21.

18. Charles Kraitsir, *The Significance of the Alphabet* (Boston: Peabody, 1846),

and *Glossology: Being a Treatise on the Nature of Language and on the Language of Nature* (New York: G. P. Putnam, 1852). See Michael West, "Charles Kraitsir's Influence on Thoreau's Theory of Language," *ESQ* 20, no. 4 (1973): 262–274. Cf. also Gura, *Wisdom of Words,* 124–141.

19. Cf. also J.4.466, 482.

20. See especially the essays entitled "Chesuncook" and "The Allegash and East Branch" in MW. On Thoreau's interest in Native American culture, see Robert F. Sayre, *Thoreau and the American Indian* (Princeton: Princeton University Press, 1977).

21. Cf. Week, 326.

22. CW.3.22.

23. On the comic dimensions of *Walden* and its relation to Thoreau's divided vision, see Edward Galligan, "The Comedian at Walden Pond," *South Atlantic Quarterly* 69 (1970): 20–37.

24. For more exhaustive catalogues of Thoreau's wordplay, see David Skwire, "A Check List of Word-play in *Walden,*" *American Literature* 31 (1959), and Donald Ross, Jr., "Verbal Wit and *Walden,*" *American Transcendental Quarterly* 11 (1971): 38–44. See also Michael West, "Scatology and Eschatology: The Heroic Dimensions of Thoreau's Wordplay," *PMLA* 89, no. 5 (Oct. 1974): 1043–1064.

25. Week, 151; cf. PJ.1.375; see also PJ.1.219.

26. For a superb discussion of the central rhetorical role of paradox in Thoreau's work, see Moldenhauer, "Paradox in *Walden.*" See also Richard H. Dillman, "The Psychological Rhetoric of *Walden,*" *ESQ* 25 (1979), 81.

27. Quoted in Moldenhauer, "Paradox in *Walden,*" 74–75.

28. William Ward, *A View of the history, literature, and religion of the Hindoos* (Hartford, Conn.: H. Huntington, Jr., 1824), 162.

29. Cited in Week, 138–139; Bhagavad Gita 4:18.

30. Cf. Matthew 10:39: "He that findeth his life shall lose it; and he that loseth his life for my sake shall find it." (Cf. Mark 8:35; Luke 9:24).

31. Also Week, 393.

32. See in particular "Resistance to Civil Government" ("Civil Disobedience"), "Slavery in Massachusetts," "A Plea for Captain John Brown," and "Life Without Principle," in RP.

33. See, for example, the several prison type-scenes found in Acts, e.g. Acts 5:12, 16, 17 ff.

34. The fullest analysis of Thoreau's reliance on the English Bible is John R. Burns, "Thoreau's Use of the Bible" (Ph.D. diss., University of Notre Dame,

1966). For its impact on *Walden* specifically, see Larry R. Long, "The Bible and the Composition of *Walden,*" *Studies in the American Renaissance,* ed. Joel Myerson (Boston, 1979): 309–353.

Chapter 7: A Meteorological Journal of the Mind

1. Cf. Elizabeth Hall Witherell, "Henry David Thoreau," *Prospects for the Study of American Literature,* ed. Richard Kopley (New York: New York University Press, 1997), 23–24.

2. The decision by the Boston publishing house Houghton Mifflin to bring out this first edition of the journal signaled, on the one hand, Thoreau's somewhat belated admittance into the rarefied company of newly canonized nineteenth-century American writers and, at the same time, helped to ensure his continued presence among them. Efforts to find a wider audience for Thoreau's journals had actually been underway for some time, however. As early as 1853, Emerson had proposed that Ellery Channing make up a volume of selected journals of Emerson, Channing, and Thoreau, but this project was never realized. More productive were the efforts of Thoreau's friend and protégé, Harrison Blake, who upon inheriting his friend's manuscripts after the death of Sophia Thoreau in 1876, published a total of four volumes of journal entries from 1881 to 1892, showcasing the passage of seasons. See Walter Harding and Michael Meyer, *The New Thoreau Handbook* (New York: New York University Press, 1980), 72–73; Lawrence Buell, "The Canonization and Recanonization of the Green Thoreau," in *The Environmental Imagination: Thoreau, Nature Writing, and the Formation of American Culture* (Cambridge: Harvard University Press, 1995), 26; and Walter Harding, "Thoreau's Reputation," *The Cambridge Companion to Henry David Thoreau,* ed. Joel Myerson (Cambridge: Cambridge University Press, 1955), 6–7.

3. The impetus for much of this recent work has been the ongoing publication of a critical edition of the journal under the auspices of Princeton University Press. See William Howarth, *The Book of Concord* (New York: Viking, 1982); Sharon Cameron, *Writing Nature: Henry Thoreau's Journal* (New York: Oxford University Press, 1985); H. Daniel Peck, *Thoreau's Morning Work* (New Haven: Yale University Press, 1990); Leonard N. Neufeldt, "*Praetextus* as Text: Editor-Critic Responses to Thoreau's Journal," *Arizona Quarterly* 46 (1990): 27–72; Leonard N. Neufeldt, "Thoreau in his Journal," *The Cambridge Companion to Henry David Thoreau,* ed. Joel Myerson (Cambridge: Cambridge University Press, 1995).

4. For one of Thoreau's own characterizations of his method at this time, see PJ.2.205–206.

5. See William Howarth, *The Book of Concord: Thoreau's Life as a Writer* (New York: Viking Press, 1982), 161–189; Peck, *Thoreau's Morning Work*, 90–114, 163–166.

6. See Walter Harding, *The Days of Henry Thoreau* (Princeton: Princeton University Press, 1962), 357.

7. Mark Van Doren, *Henry David Thoreau: A Critical Study* (Boston: Houghton Mifflin, 1916); Perry Miller, *Consciousness in Concord: The Text of Thoreau's Hitherto "lost journal," 1840–41* (Boston: Houghton Mifflin, 1958), 31, and "Thoreau in the Context of International Romanticism," *The New England Quarterly* 34, no. 2 (June 1961): 158; Sherman Paul, *The Shores of America: Thoreau's Inward Exploration* (Urbana: University of Illinois Press, 1958), 193. While many contemporary critics appear to subscribe to some (usually more tempered) version of this decline narrative, it should be pointed out that the theory has by no means carried the day among all scholars. Walter Harding, for example, sees no evidence in the journal for such theories of late-life declension but only the continuance of joy and spiritual assurance up to and even through the suffering of his last days. See Harding and Meyer, eds., *New Thoreau Handbook*, 24, 125; and Harding, *Days of Henry Thoreau*, 295.

8. PJ.3.61; PJ.3.215–216.

9. Cameron, *Writing Nature*, 23, see also 16.

10. Cf. PJ.4.296–297.

11. Peck, *Thoreau's Morning Work*, 64.

12. Nina Baym, "Thoreau's View of Science," *Journal of the History of Ideas* 26 (April–June 1965): 221–234.

13. For several notable exceptions, however, see J.8.64, 134; J.10.115.

14. Cf. PJ.1.35, 151, 158, 180, 233, 237, 253, 310, 351.

15. Cf. PJ.3.143, 178; PJ.4.17, 28, 170, 177–178, 277–278, 281–282, 296–297.

16. Cf. PJ.3.178.

17. 1 Thessalonians 5:17.

18. CW.1.17.

19. See Cameron, *Writing Nature*, especially chaps. 1 and 5.

20. See Peck, *Thoreau's Morning Work*, 39–114.

21. Cf. PJ.4.297: "Our life should be so active and progressive as to be a journey—Our meals should all be of journey-cake & hasty pudding. We should be more alert—see the sun rise—not keep fashionable hours."

22. *Atlantic Monthly* (May 1862). "Walking" was then republished in *Excursions*. See Writings.5.205–248.

23. For example: PJ.4.406 ff.; PJ.5.276, 283–284, 330–334, 378, 380. Among the books Thoreau perused were Gilpin's *Remarks on Forest Scenery,* 3rd ed. (London, 1808); *Observations on Several Parts of England,* 3rd ed. (London, 1788); *Observations on Several Parts of Great Britain,* 3rd ed. (London, 1808); and *Observations on the Western Parts of England,* 2nd ed. (London, 1808). See Robert Sattelmeyer, *Thoreau's Reading: A Study in Intellectual History with Bibliographical Catalogue* (Princeton: Princeton University Press, 1988), 185–186.

24. Cf. Peck, *Thoreau's Morning Work,* 69–73.

25. The Princeton critical edition, which as of this writing includes the year 1851, reads the word "match" in this entry as "watch." See PJ.3.368. This rendering makes no sense in the context of this and related passages, and having consulted a microfilm of the holograph, I must agree with the editors of the Walden edition in construing this word as "match." In this instance, therefore, I have broken with my usual practice of citing wherever possible the Princeton edition and invoked the earlier edition instead.

Afterword: One World at a Time

1. Cf. Daniel Ricketson: "But it was in the closing scenes of his life, and when confined to his room and bed, that this truly good and brave man showed the depth and power of divine wisdom in his soul, giving him strength in his weakness, and making the sick-room and the chamber of death resplendent in beauty and hopefulness." Anna and Walton Ricketson, eds., *Daniel Ricketson and His Friends* (Boston: Houghton Mifflin, 1902), 17. See also Walter Harding, *The Days of Henry Thoreau* (Princeton: Princeton University Press, 1962), 442–468.

2. Ricketson and Ricketson, eds., *Ricketson and Friends,* 136–137.

3. Edward Waldo Emerson, *Thoreau As Remembered by a Young Friend* (Boston: Houghton Mifflin, 1917), 117–118.

4. Ricketson and Ricketson, eds., *Ricketson and Friends,* 213–214.

5. Ricketson and Ricketson, eds., *Ricketson and Friends,* 155, 142.

6. Franklin Sanborn, *The Personality of Thoreau* (Boston: C. E. Goodspeed, 1901), 68–69.

7. William Ellery Channing, *Thoreau: The Poet-Naturalist* (Boston: Roberts Brothers, 1873), 337.

8. Ricketson and Ricketson, eds., *Ricketson and Friends,* 141.

9. Channing, *Thoreau: The Poet-Naturalist,* 339.

Index